# Hayek's Modern Family

# Hayek's Modern Family

## Classical Liberalism and the Evolution of Social Institutions

*Steven Horwitz*

palgrave
macmillan

HAYEK'S MODERN FAMILY


Chapter 6 was originally published as "Heterogeneous Human Capital, Uncertainty, and the Structure of Plans: A Market Process Approach to Marriage and Divorce" (with Peter Lewin), *Review of Austrian Economics*, 21 (1), March 2008, pp. 1–21. Republished with the kind permission of Springer Science+Business Media

First published in 2015 by
PALGRAVE MACMILLAN®
in the United States—a division of St. Martin's Press LLC,
175 Fifth Avenue, New York, NY 10010.

Where this book is distributed in the UK, Europe and the rest of the world, this is by Palgrave Macmillan, a division of Macmillan Publishers Limited, registered in England, company number 785998, of Houndmills, Basingstoke, Hampshire RG21 6XS.

Palgrave Macmillan is the global academic imprint of the above companies and has companies and representatives throughout the world.



ISBN: 978–1–137–44822–4

Library of Congress Cataloging-in-Publication Data

Horwitz, Steven.
Hayek's modern family : classical liberalism and the evolution of social institutions / Steven Horwitz.
pages cm
Includes bibliographical references and index.
ISBN 978–1–137–44822–4 (hardback : alk. paper)
1. Families—Economic aspects. 2. Liberalism.
3. Economics—Sociological aspects. I. Title.

HQ515.H68 2015
306.85—dc23 2015009755

A catalogue record of the book is available from the British Library.

Design by Newgen Knowledge Works (P) Ltd., Chennai, India.

First edition: September 2015

10 9 8 7 6 5 4 3 2 1

*For Andrew and Rachel.*

*May your children bring to you the joy and pride you have brought to me*

# Contents

# Figures and Tables

## Figures



## Tables

# Acknowledgments

Bringing this book to publication has been an unexpectedly long process. Before I wrote on the economics of the family, I wrote on money and macroeconomics. When I started this book in 2007, I anticipated finishing it within a couple of years, but the financial crisis in 2008 and the subsequent recession stimulated the demand for my earlier expertise and diverted me from working on this book as I had planned. The past couple of years have allowed me to return to it and finally bring the project to fruition. With almost ten years of being a work in progress, there are many people and institutions deserving of thanks for their contributions to the final product. I offer my apologies in advance to those I may have forgotten in the mists of time.

The first round of research and writing on this book benefitted greatly from ten weeks spent in the summer of 2007 as a visiting scholar at the Social Philosophy and Policy Center at Bowling Green State University. The faculty and staff there were excellent hosts, and James Stacey Taylor and Brad Smith provided stimulating company in our overlapping time together. I wish this book had seen the light of day before the center ended its days at Bowling Green. I also thank my family for putting up with my extended absence during that period and for understanding the irony of leaving my family to write a book about the family. The Earhart Foundation provided funding for the summer of 2008, and I thank them for that support and for all that they have done to advance my work over the past 25 years.

Portions of the book were presented at a number of workshops and conferences. The Fund for the Study of Spontaneous Orders ran conferences in 2007, 2008, and 2011 at which various chapters were presented. I benefitted greatly from the feedback of a number of participants there, and I thank Lenore Ealy and Gus DiZerega for organizing those events. Workshop participants at George Mason University gave me helpful suggestions for chapters presented there in 2007 and 2009. As always, my good friend Pete Boettke was a gracious host and gave me particularly valuable ideas for revision. In 2011, seminar participants at Kings College London were generous with their comments on material presented there, and I thank Paul Lewis and his colleagues for inviting me. My friends at Liberty Fund gave me the opportunity to present chapter 9 in August of 2014, and I am most grateful for the fruitful discussion that followed. I thank Amy Willis and Sarah Skwire for arranging that visit. Finally, a Liberty Fund conference on "Liberty and the Family" in 2009 was an enormously productive opportunity to talk through these issues with a room full of very smart people. I thank Sarah Skwire and Liberty Fund for making that weekend possible and the participants for their time and talents.

I have also been giving a public lecture on "Capitalism and the Family" at a variety of venues since 2007, ranging from college campuses, to libertarian student organizations, to a crowd of 400 in Bratislava, Slovakia. Each time I give that talk, questions from the audience and the postlecture discussion give me some new idea, or raise some new issue, or just make me think more carefully about how to frame and present much of the material that is in this book. I thank all of the people who have sponsored and attended those talks over the years. I would also like to thank the Institute for Humane Studies and the Foundation for Economic Education for the opportunities they have provided me to explore issues of classical liberalism and the family with students from around the world, both in person and via the Internet.

My departmental colleagues at St. Lawrence continue to make this an extraordinarily productive environment for my teaching and research. My friends on the faculty and staff here constantly remind me what it means to have a community of intellectual and personal support. I must also thank the SLU Board of Trustees for their sustained commitment to recognizing the value of faculty research, as two full years of sabbaticals/leaves in 2007–8 and 2009–10 enabled me to get much of the early research and writing completed. I also thank Grant Cornwell and Valerie Lehr for the funds that the Dean's office provided me to travel to present portions of this book. St. Lawrence as an institution has been remarkably supportive of letting Horwitz be Horwitz, and for that I will be forever grateful.

Much of the content of this book took shape in a number of classrooms at St. Lawrence. I have been teaching some kind of course on the family since 1996, and there are a large number of students from my First-Year Program and First-Year Seminar courses, as well as my Economics of Gender and Family class, who put up with a professor who was trying to figure this stuff out on the fly. I thank them for their patience and for the questions they raised that improved this work. I also thank my former colleagues P. J. McGann and John Hunter who got me started on this topic when we team-taught the first iteration of the First-Year Program course in 1996 and thereby contributed to my thinking in ways that I never have had the opportunity to thank them for until now.

My greatest intellectual and personal debt at SLU is to my dear friend and colleague Cathy Crosby-Currie for her role not just with respect to this book, but to so much of how I think about, and teach, the family as a social institution. Our work as a teaching team is what prompted me to take the idea of being a scholar of the family seriously. Her contributions to the many conversations and moments of classroom serendipity that we have shared in the past 17 years are so infused into the DNA of this book that it is impossible to identify even a fraction of them. This book would not exist were it not for her intellectual partnership and close friendship.

A number of other people have offered me comments and feedback over the years, and I apologize again for any omissions. Commenters on blog posts at Coordination Problem and Bleeding Heart Libertarians forced me to hone a number of my arguments, and my ferocious and fearless Facebook followers did the same, even as they occasionally drove me to the edge of madness. I thank Nicole Youngman, Lenore Skenazy, Roger Koppl, Bruce Caldwell, Deirdre McCloskey, Chris Sciabarra, Julie Novak, Jon Gottschall, Kevin Currie-Knight, Lauren Hall, and Pete Boettke for various conversations and suggestions. Stephen Davies read earlier drafts of the historical material and Aeon Skoble read parts of chapter 10 at the last minute, and both provided me with very helpful suggestions. My good friend and coauthor Peter Lewin has been a constant conversation partner on the subject of the family for a very long time, and his implicit contributions to this project are too numerous to detail. I also thank Springer for permission to use a revised and extended version of our 2008 *Review of Austrian Economics* paper as chapter 6. Sarah Lawrence and the rest of the crew at Palgrave Macmillan made it very easy to transform my manuscript into a finished product. Harry David not only produced an excellent index, he also saved me from a serious copyediting oversight at the last minute.

Finally, I thank Sarah Skwire for pushing me to get this book done when I needed the motivation, as well as for reading over several chapters and providing a number of very helpful suggestions and historical references. Her black pen, and sometimes just the threat thereof, also improved the prose significantly. While doing all of those things, she has brought unexpected and enormous delight to all facets of my life. I will always be her biggest fan, and I look forward to continuing to delight in her wisdom, laughter, and love (and even her black pen) for a very long time.

As they have for the past 20 years, my buddies at alt.music.rush made me laugh when I needed it and continue to demonstrate that distance and technology are not barriers to having long-lasting and meaningful friendships. My parents and the rest of my family of birth, and my children Andrew and Rachel, are models of what it means to be functional and supportive in the world of the twentieth and twenty-first centuries. Lastly, deep thanks go to my iTunes library for providing the soundtrack, because writing without music is simply not possible.

# PART I

## *Classical Liberalism and the Evolution of Social Institutions*

# CHAPTER 1

# Introduction: The Family and Classical Liberalism

## Introduction

The past 40 years or so have seen a remarkable rebirth of scholarship in the classical liberal or libertarian tradition. A series of events that began in the late 1960s and early 1970s became the catalyst for this rebirth, most notably the failures of the Keynesian consensus in economics manifested in the stagflation of the period, as well as the increasingly hard-to-ignore evidence about the economic failures and mass murder that resulted from nominally socialist regimes across the world. Along with an expansion of civil liberties for minorities, the increase in rights and roles available to women, the cultural openness that emerged out of events such as Woodstock and the Stonewall riots of the late 1960s, and the obvious failure of adventurous American foreign policy in Vietnam, the time seemed ripe to revisit the older liberal tradition that envisioned a world in which adults were free to pursue their own choices in *both* their social and economic lives, as long as they were not harming others. That older tradition, perhaps best encapsulated by John Stuart Mill's (1985 [1859]) "harm principle," saw free markets, respect for diverse, consensual lifestyles, and a military narrowly restricted to defense as deeply intertwined in a liberal, cosmopolitan commitment to tolerance and peace. Free markets and free minds or, in Thomas Jefferson's words, "peace, commerce and honest friendship with all nations; entangling alliances with none"[1] were the hallmark of the classical liberal tradition.

The scholarly revival of that tradition can date its origins to two books and one event that took place in 1973 and 1974, each of which has relevance for the argument that follows. In 1973, the economist Israel Kirzner published *Competition and Entrepreneurship*, which began a revival of interest in the long-dormant Austrian school of economics. Kirzner's book engaged and challenged the then-dominant theoretical mainstream in economics as well as opening the door for a whole new set of arguments about the effectiveness of free markets and explanations of the failures of both Keynesianism and the various attempts at socialist planning that characterized so much of the world of the time. The following year saw the publication of Robert Nozick's (1974) *Anarchy, State, and Utopia*, whose argument for a libertarian political order rekindled philosophical thinking about libertarianism, and whose clever and powerful responses to John Rawls's (1971) *A Theory of Justice* immediately put libertarian ideas on the radar of serious thinking people in philosophy and political theory. Later that year, the economist and social theorist Friedrich A. Hayek was awarded the Nobel Prize in Economics (along with Gunnar Myrdal). Not only did Hayek's Nobel enhance the interest in Austrian economics begun with Kirzner's book, it led to a reexamination of his work in political philosophy, social theory, and the history of ideas. After 40 years, the ideas addressed by all three of these thinkers have blossomed into a full-fledged intellectual and political community, and that community has had a significant impact on the course of world events as classical liberal ideas have influenced political change toward markets and individual liberty.[2]

Contemporary classical liberalism often goes by the name "libertarianism." I have chosen very deliberately to use the term "classical liberalism" in my title. My reason for doing so is that I wish to be as broad as possible in who and what positions fit under that umbrella. Most within the tradition consider "libertarian" to be a somewhat more radical subset of "classical liberal." Making a precise list of what sorts of positions would distinguish one from the other is both difficult and largely unnecessary. It suffices to say that, for my purposes, "classical liberal" encompasses those who believe that the path to peace, prosperity, and social cooperation means that governments, at all levels, need to exercise very little involvement in the economic and personal lives of citizens and should, generally, do the same with respect to the governments and citizens of other countries. For libertarians, more narrowly, "very little involvement" may well be very little indeed, while for classical liberals it might mean somewhat more. I will try to be as broad as possible in referring to this tradition, even as I sometimes use the terms interchangeably.

I also want to distinguish "classical liberal" from conservative from the outset. Because both groups favor a high degree of economic freedom and thus are often aligned in their opposition to contemporary American liberalism on those issues, they are often treated as "the Right." As I hope to show in this book, that is a grave error. The underdevelopment of classical liberal approaches to noneconomic issues is likely responsible for this error. Generally, conservatives are willing to use government to support or discourage particular kinds of personal behavior (e.g., the "war on drugs," antipornography laws, antisodomy laws, and tax credits for having children) in ways that classical liberals generally are not.[3] In the context of exploring the modern family, these differences will become stark.

## The Contemporary Politics of the Family

One of the purposes of this study is to distinguish the way classical liberalism might look at the family from the ways it is seen by both the contemporary Right and Left. For many conservatives, defending the "traditional family" or "family values" has become a central concern. They believe that the family is an institution under attack by the culture and by public policy and often bring out the various statistics on divorce, single-parenthood, and low marriage rates as evidence. However, the issue that brings this perspective out the most viscerally is the debate over same-sex marriage. The increased cultural acceptance of homosexuality, culminating in the ongoing process of granting the legal right to marry, seems to have been the last straw for many of these conservatives. From their perspective, the past few decades have seen a crumbling of the "traditional" two-parent, heterosexual marriage with children and its pretty clear division of labor between men and women. It was problematic enough when divorce and single-parenthood became rampant and when cohabitation and childlessness became more frequent, but to treat same-sex relationships as the legal and moral equivalent of male-female ones seemed to many on the Right to strike at the last piece of the "traditional" family that had been left unscathed.

There are at least two problems with this line of argument that I hope to address. First, conservatives often fail to distinguish between the *form* families take and their ability to *function*. More accurately, they often assume that only one particular form (the "traditional" family) is able to function sufficiently well. This is also frequently combined with an unwillingness to recognize that the functions that families perform have evolved over time, thereby necessitating, or at least allowing for, a similar evolution in form. As I will argue in more detail later, what we should ultimately care about is the ability of families to perform their various functions and that those functions have indeed changed over time. Of those functions, rearing children to competent adulthood is among the most important but is hardly the only one that matters. Too often, conservative critics of the contemporary family seem to believe that the *only* function of families is to procreate and then raise those children to some very high standard of adulthood. As we shall see, families do many other things, and any realistic consideration of the functionality of the modern family will have to recognize those multiple functions and the possibility of tradeoffs among them.

Second, as my use of quotation marks around "traditional family" suggests, this favorite term of conservatives has its own problems. If that phrase is meant to refer to the married, heterosexual family with children where dad is the primary earner and mom the primary caretaker of the household that was the central image of television in the postwar years, then it is hardly "traditional." As later chapters will develop more thoroughly, the predominance of that family form from the end of World War II until sometime in the 1960s was largely the product of a variety of historical contingencies. The decades and centuries prior reveal a whole variety of family forms, many of which were quite functional. Those forms changed as the functions families needed to perform changed, and those changes in function were driven by changes in the economic and political landscape. Even marriage more narrowly has evolved over the long run of human history, making it questionable to point to the structure of marriage at any particular point in time as traditional. That point includes the claim that marriage has "always" been one man-one woman. The use of traditional as an adjective for either marriage or the family more generally is, as we shall see, ahistorical. It also serves as a convenient rhetorical marker for conservative objections to these more recent changes in the family, particularly the call for legalization of same-sex marriage.

Beyond this unwillingness to distinguish function and form, many conservatives do not see the causal relationship between the dynamism and growth generated by the market economy, which they claim to love, and the changes in the family that they generally dislike. One of the running themes of this book is the role that the advent of capitalism, and the over 200 years of increasing wealth it created, has played in driving the evolution of the modern family. It was capitalism that created the conditions for marriage to transform from being a partnership for economic production into a relationship based on love. The increase in wealth that the market economy produced has made it possible for women to work outside the home in large numbers, for people to survive economically outside of heterosexual marriage, and for single parents to raise children. All of these together made it easier for women to exit marriages, thus leading to higher divorce rates. The ability to survive outside of heterosexual marriage also made it possible for those with homosexual orientations to identify as gay or lesbian and to live their lives as such. The very dynamism of the market economy has been reflected in the dynamism of cultural change, including the family. For conservatives who claim to love capitalism but who decry the speed of cultural change, this presents a dilemma. I will argue that there is no way to put the cultural toothpaste back in the tube and that as long as we have a market economy that continues to create wealth, and does so across the world, marriage and family will continue to evolve apace.

All of that being said, the conservatives are right about one thing: we cannot do without the institution of family. For some progressives, the family is seen as outdated or unnecessary, or an institution that continues to promote patriarchy over the needs of women.[4] Other left-liberals blame capitalism for family dysfunction, arguing that the ways in which capitalism has supposedly led to mass poverty, or caused a steady decline in middle-class incomes, are responsible for many of the problems faced by contemporary families. The Left's celebration of the diversity of family forms can sometimes, like the Right, cause them to overlook questions of functionality or choose to ignore social scientific evidence that runs counter to the claim that "all family forms are equally functional." The evidence, for example, that children do better on average in two-parent homes than in single-parent homes is very well established in the social scientific literature. That is not to say that other family forms cannot function sufficiently well, but it is to say that we should not ignore the differences.

The dislike of capitalism that runs through so much progressive writing about the family presents the mirror image of the problem facing conservatives. Where conservatives will have to reconcile their supposed love of capitalism to the reality of the dynamic cultural change it produces that they dislike, progressives may have to recognize that the diversity of family forms that they rightly celebrate is significantly due to capitalism and the wealth it has created. Alongside that wealth, the market economy has brought with it access to new and diverse ideas, cultures, and practices that have helped lead to that flowering of family forms. Societies that have tried to restrict the market in significant ways have almost always also seen the family as the enemy of the powerful states or communities they created, and such societies have sought to restrict the options available to couples, and especially to women.[5] One need only think of China's one-child policy, or the ways in which the Soviet Union banned abortions and made divorce very difficult in the 1940s. The low levels of wealth in such societies also limited the options facing women and families in ways that were in stark contrast to Western capitalist economies. If one wants to maximize the opportunities to form families of choice, then one should be more openly supportive of capitalism and policies that enable market economies to produce wealth.

Beyond this, I will argue that the family is a necessary institution in any society. There is simply no way that it can be abolished. The advantages that parents have in socializing children, for example, cannot be replicated sufficiently by schools, "the village," or the state. Only a family with one or more adults having ongoing responsibility for particular children has the requisite incentives and knowledge to get this job done. Further, even if parents are imperfect at doing so, that is not an ipso facto argument for someone else to step in, as those other institutions may be even worse at the task than imperfect parents. Given the earlier discussion, it should be clear that "parents" here need not mean the people who provided the genetic material that makes up the child. Adoptive or step-parents also have better knowledge and incentives with respect to their children than do nonparents. Finally, the gender of parents is also not the key issue, nor is the number of parents. Even if a two-parent family is best all other things equal, this does not mean that single parents are incapable of getting the job done sufficiently well, especially when we recognize that rarely are all other things equal. We can acknowledge and celebrate the diversity of family forms, but we cannot ignore the fact that the family as an institution performs functions that only it can do sufficiently well.

A running theme of this study is that classical liberalism offers a third way to think about family that gets around the dilemmas faced by both conservatives and progressives. One way of viewing this project is that it offers a nonconservative defense of the family. That argument starts with the recognition that the economy and the culture are deeply interconnected. I will argue that the historical evolution of the family is in many ways an off-shoot of the enormous economic growth that capitalism has produced and that those changes in the family have liberated first men then women and children from the drudgery and physical exhaustion of preindustrial labor. Capitalism has enabled the family to move up Maslow's (1943) hierarchy of needs to where we now see our familial relationships and the family's functions as being more often about the self-actualization that occupies the top of that list rather than the basics of survival that are at the bottom. The self-actualization at the top of Maslow's hierarchy is often a major goal of progressives across the world, yet they remain reluctant to give capitalism the proper credit for enabling the family to better achieve that goal for an increasing number of people. Conservatives wring their hands about the expansion of freedom in the cultural realm while they continue to praise, for the most part, the freedom in the economic realm that made it possible and drives its ongoing evolution.

A classical liberal perspective on the family can see through the tensions and contradictions of both Left and Right by providing a rigorous analysis of the inter-relationship between economic and social freedom. In understanding, and appreciating, why both kinds of freedom are necessary for human social cooperation, classical liberalism can offer an alternative perspective that both acknowledges the irreplaceability of the family and values the diversity in family forms, while also understanding the ways in which each is rooted in economic freedom. Classical liberalism also has an optimism in the face of social change that distances it from the economic pessimism of the left and the cultural pessimism of the right. A classical liberal perspective on the family as a social institution will bring fresh insights to this long-standing conversation.

## Can Classical Liberals Have a Meaningful Theory of the Family?

All of these political distinctions run the risk of obscuring what I hope is a more important contribution of this book. Too often classical liberalism is defined in terms of its policy conclusions rather than its analytic tools, by both its proponents and opponents.[6] One of my goals is to argue that there are a set of questions and analytic tools that are part of the classical liberal tradition, emerging both from past thinkers and contemporary ones, that can dramatically enhance our ability to understand social phenomena, including the family. These questions and analytic tools generate propositions about the social world that are not, in and of themselves, normative. Those propositions require the addition of normative statements in order to generate the political conclusions that are normally associated with classical liberalism. I raise all of these issues here as a way of explaining why the policy chapters have a section of their own because they are distinct from, though derived from, the analysis that precedes them. Moreover, as the policy chapters will make clear, I do not believe that classical liberalism offers easy and obvious policy conclusions for every issue involving the family.

For understandable reasons given the context of a century of socialism, the vast majority of scholarship in the classical liberal revival has focused on the question of "the market versus the state." The revival of Austrian economics as well as the rise to prominence and power of the Chicago school and the evolution of Keynesian thought to more market-friendly forms put economic concerns at the forefront of the classical liberal agenda. The first task was to show that economic planning and intervention would fail to achieve the very goals that the planners put forward. The mounting evidence from the West as well as the Third World provided a treasure trove of scholarly opportunities to apply the theoretical frameworks emerging from the Austrians and the Chicagoans. Much less attention was paid, however, to the other strands of the tradition: civil liberties and trade-based international relations.

Even less attention has been devoted to those institutions that do not fit into the categories of "market" or "state."[7] The past few years has seen the emergence of a distinct classical liberal literature on the institutions of civil society. Of that relatively small literature, there are very few articles or books that address the object of this book's concern: the family.[8] For example, in the thousands of pages of Hayek's work, there are only a small handful of references to "family" and each of those no more than a couple of sentences. Other major figures in the classical liberal revival (Milton Friedman, Ludwig von Mises, and Nozick to name a few) also had relatively little to say about the family as a social institution. Among those working in the classical liberal tradition, the only sustained attention to the family has been from economists, particularly the late Gary Becker and others working in the Chicago tradition from which he wrote. As I will argue later, the economics of the family is an important part of a classical liberal analysis, but it is far from complete, and the Chicago approach, in particular, has shortcomings.

In fact, outside of the literature on the economics of the family, there have really been only two major works in the classical liberal social scientific tradition that have addressed family issues in any depth.[9] The first of those is a 1986 edited collection (Peden and Glahe 1986) entitled *The American Family and the State*, which is a mix of theory, history, and policy by a variety of authors, covering a whole range of ground. There is much of value there, but there has been precious little scholarship on many of those issues in the almost 30 years since its publication. The second major work is Jennifer Roback Morse's (2001) *Love and Economics: Why the Laissez-Faire Family Doesn't Work*. Morse's book also has much of value in it, especially in the earlier chapters covering how families function. However, it has two major shortcomings that make it less than satisfactory. First, Morse assumes from the start that the consistent "libertarian" position is to favor "laissez-faire" in both the economy and the family. As a result, in criticizing, often rightly in my view, what she calls the "laissez-faire family," she suggests that she is demonstrating some sort of serious inconsistency in libertarianism. Unfortunately, she overlooks Hayek's notion that families and economies are structurally different in a way that makes it neither surprising nor inconsistent that the family should not be "laissez-faire." Second, the second half of Morse's book takes on a much more conservative tone than I think is justified by a more historically informed and theoretically sophisticated analysis of the family. In particular, she is much too quick to condemn family forms that differ from the two-parent, heterosexual model. I will argue that a classical liberal approach should be more focused on function and less focused on form than Morse's is.

The relative paucity of work on the family by classical liberals raises the question of whether classical liberalism can even have a coherent theory of the family. Critics suggest that the classical liberal focus on ownership rights and its apparent denigration of the "social" and veneration of the "individual" make it difficult to use the framework to understand the family as a social institution. A representative example of each criticism can be found in Okin (1989) and Hodgson (1999), respectively.

In her overview of the role of gender and the family in late-twentieth-century theories of justice, Okin (1989) devotes a full chapter to a critique of Nozick's libertarianism. Her argument amounts to a long reductio ad absurdum that attempts to trace out the consequences of taking a Lockean theory of ownership seriously when it comes to the creation of children. If libertarians believe that people are entitled to ownership rights over what they create with their own labor, then should not children, who are created by the labor of their parents, and their mothers specifically, be the complete and utter property of those parents, if not just the mother? Okin then suggests that this leads to a world where people cannot own themselves unless their mothers either "gave or sold them their freedom" (pp. 84–86). When confronted with the reality of children, the expansive notion of individual rights associated with libertarianism, she argues, must devolve into a bizarre sort of matriarchal slave society where women own their children, even as adults, until and unless the mothers enable them to become free beings. She further argues that any attempt to get out of this reductio puts the rest of Nozick's theory of just acquisition in peril. If the production of children is mixing one's labor with nature just like the creation of any piece of property, then how can her conclusions be resisted from a Nozickean perspective and, by implication, how can classical liberalism offer a coherent theory of the family?

There are at least three problems with Okin's argument that I wish to address briefly here. First, libertarianism need not be based only on Lockean or on natural rights arguments. There are other ways to argue for the primacy of private property that do not leave themselves open to Okin's reductio. These will be explored later. Second, Okin is focused on theories of justice and is examining gender and family issues through those lenses, asking what a just family would look like. Non-Nozickean classical liberal approaches, such as Hayek's, might view justice in a different way and one that is immune to Okin's argument. In addition, Hayek's view implies that different notions of justice might be appropriate for the family versus the broader political order, undermining Okin's attempt to argue from the latter to the former as if they were sufficiently the same. Finally, as Narveson (2002, p. 274) argues, even within Nozick's own framework, Okin fails to distinguish between the "human organism" that parents create and the "person" that organism becomes. The facts of human development are such that a "person" is what the "organism" becomes, partially due to the role of the parents of course but certainly due to biology and influences from other humans, such as peers and teachers. What it means to be an adult is that an organism has become a person, and this in turn suggests that human organisms are different from other "products of nature" in that they grow into an entity that we think should have rights. Combined, these three responses suggest that Okin's reductio does not demonstrate the incoherence of a classical liberal theory of the family.

Hodgson's (1999) criticism emerges from his understanding of libertarian defenses of the market economy. He argues that the market individualism associated with libertarianism leaves no room for institutions that operate outside the realm of market behavior. As he sees it:

> Generally, if contract and trade are always the best way of organising matters, then many functions that are traditionally organised in a different manner should become commercialized... Pushed to the limit, market individualism implies the commercialisation of sex and the abolition of the family. A consistent market individualist cannot be a devotee of "family values"... They cannot in one breath argue that the market is the best way of ordering all socio-economic activities, and then deny it in another. If they cherish family values then they have to recognise the practical and moral limits of the market imperatives and pecuniary exchange. (p. 84)

The fundamental flaw in Hodgson's argument is the claim that classical liberals believe that "the market is the best way of ordering all socio-economic activities." As noted earlier, it is certainly understandable, given classical liberalism's disproportionate focus on economic issues in the past several decades, that critics might make this sort of argument. However, it is not clear that there is any classical liberal who has argued that every single human activity should be run on market principles. Even the majority among those who would describe themselves as believing there is no need at all for government would still say that *markets* cannot do everything and that the nongovernmental institutions of civil society (including families) have important roles to play in any advanced social order. More tellingly though is that some classical liberals, including Hayek in particular, have argued *explicitly* that markets are not the appropriate way of organizing some subset of human social activities. Markets work in some contexts but not in others, and one of those others is the family. Classical liberalism, at least in Hayek's hands, has a set of conceptual tools for making these distinctions, which provides a response to Hodgson's criticism.

Another argument against the possibility of a classical liberal theory of the family comes from within classical liberalism itself. To some classical liberals, classical liberalism is just a theory of justice and therefore can only speak to the relationship between the individual and the state. It can say nothing qua classical liberalism about how other social institutions should operate, or even what role they might or might not play in a classical liberal social order. In this account, a classical liberal theory of the family would be not significantly different from a classical liberal theory of music, which is to say that neither one would be meaningful. Conceived this way, classical liberalism could certainly say something about what the *state* might or might not legitimately do with respect to families, but that remains a theory of the limits of the state rather than a theory of the family per se.

This view of classical liberalism was more common at the onset of its recent revival when, again, the key issue was delimiting the proper sphere of the state, especially with respect to the market. More recently, classical liberals have paid more attention to the history and roles of the institutions of civil society. Much of that literature has focused on the ways in which institutions such as religious organizations, mutual aid societies, and social networks based on ethnicity, race, or kin can provide the sorts of social services that we have come to expect from the welfare state.[10] This work focuses on the importance of such institutions in the overall functioning of a classical liberal society and the fact that the knowledge of their history and functions has often been lost as the state has taken on so many of their roles. In providing a theoretical conception of the importance of civil society institutions, this work suggests that classical liberalism is more than just a theory of the limits of the state, rather it is a set of questions and tools that enable us to understand how human beings might organize themselves in the absence of central direction. This notion of unplanned or spontaneous order will be central as we explore the evolution of the modern family in the chapters to follow.

## Hayekian Classical Liberalism and the Framework of this Study

The previous section's discussion suggests that an approach to classical liberalism that is based on the work of F. A. Hayek might prove to be the most fruitful for understanding the evolution of the modern family, as my title suggests. That is, in fact, the approach to be taken in this study.

In general terms, modern classical liberals ground their arguments in one of three ways: natural rights, contractarianism, or consequentialism/utilitarianism. Natural rights theorists begin with some accepted view of human nature or some fundamental premise about human behavior and then attempt to articulate what sorts of rights would be necessary for humans to live according to that nature or to engage in that behavior.[11] These theorists believe that such an approach will lead to a set of rights that matches those of classical liberalism. Contractarians use a variety of methods, including thought experiments involving tools such as veils of ignorance or uncertainty, to hypothesize about what sorts of arrangements all humans would agree to as the basis for a social order.[12] Their work has argued that agreement behind a veil would produce a social contract that created and protected rights of a classical liberal sort. Both natural rights theorists and contractarians are certainly concerned with the consequences that alternative specifications of rights might produce, but for neither group do those consequences serve as a *justification* for such rights.

The consequentialists, by contrast, ultimately do take the consequences of alternative sets of rights as justifications for those rights.[13] The difficulty facing consequentialists is determining what precisely defines the "good consequences" that an appropriate set of rights will produce. For some, it might be the Pareto-optimality associated with economics (e.g., Richard Epstein), for others it would be some notion of coordination (e.g., Hayek, Kirzner, and many Austrian school economists), and for others it will be a somewhat broader notion of social cooperation (e.g., Mises and Leland Yeager). All three subgroups would argue that their particular description of "good consequences" is one that would be broadly agreed upon by most people. All would also agree that to the extent that particular rights, or groups of rights, generate "good consequences" they are justified.[14]

The Hayekian approach I outline later is a broadly consequentialist one. It is composed of four major theoretical elements. First, it is grounded in what might best be described as "Hayekian social theory." Over the course of his work after World War II, Hayek offered a number of insights, some more systematically developed than others, that add up to a framework for understanding the historical evolution and ongoing development of modern human societies. The core insights are those involving the concept of spontaneous order, the distinction between order and organization, and briefer observations about how humans have to learn to function in a social world radically different from the prehistoric environment in which our brains and our corresponding moral instincts developed.

Hayek's social theory itself emerges out of his work in the Austrian school of economics, and this study will make liberal use of that tradition as well, especially work since the aforementioned revival. Hayek's work in economics stands on the shoulders of the earlier Austrian work of Ludwig von Mises, and Mises had a number of things to say about the implications of his approach to economics for broader social issues, with a focus on the way in which society has moved from hegemony to contract as the basis for social order. I will make use of that work as well. Of particular interest to this study will be the Austrian focus on the role of knowledge in the generation of social order. Austrians see the economy and the larger society as epistemic ecologies where knowledge is created, discovered, and made available to others through traditions and social institutions, especially market prices. Fundamental to their approach are three claims about knowledge: it is dispersed, contextual, and often tacit. We all know different things, what we know is dependent on the context in which we are deploying knowledge, and we cannot always articulate everything that we know. Knowledge is, therefore, much more than what can be communicated in words or numbers.

Two other sets of theoretical insights I will make use of are public choice economics and evolutionary approaches to social institutions. Public choice economics applies the logic of economic choice to political processes by assuming that political actors use self-interested exchange to acquire resources and to satisfy wants in the same way that actors do in the economy.[15] The change in venue does not lead to a change in what motivates behavior. As I analyze economic history and contemporary policies, these insights will be relevant. Finally, recent work on the evolution of social institutions, some of it by people working in the three aforementioned areas but some not, will be central to understanding both the functions of the modern family and the ways in which those functions came to be.

The central Hayekian question is how in a world of divided knowledge humans find ways to make use of the knowledge of others to engage in activities that promote social coordination and cooperation. This question forces us to explore how institutions evolve to address problems of knowledge, under what sorts of circumstances such institutions are more likely to evolve to do that job most effectively, what role politics might play in assisting or retarding such processes, and how the complex epistemic ecology that emerges creates challenges for human beings whose mental systems were forged in a very different environment.

This last point about the difference between our evolutionary past and our modern present was articulated somewhat differently by Hayek in *The Fatal Conceit* (1989). There he distinguished between the "micro-orders" of the various face-to-face institutions and organizations in which we move from day to day (e.g., the family, the firm, and community groups) and the "macro-order" of the complex, anonymous Great Society. Ultimately, he argued, the rules and procedures of one cannot be applied to the other without doing great damage to it; the principles by which intimate, face-to-face groups operate are fundamentally different from those by which complex anonymous ones do. This is one way of viewing the arguments he made in the debate over the possibility of rational economic calculation under socialism in the interwar years. Socialists have long argued that the world would be more fair and just if the broader society were run more like a family, where each of us treated others as brothers or sisters. The desire to plan an economy along socialist lines is ultimately a desire to turn the spontaneous order of the market into an organization.[16] Hayek and others argued in the interwar years that it was impossible to plan an economy in that way because the planners could not have access to the knowledge they would need in order to allocate resources consciously and intentionally in a complex economic system. One cannot transfer structural features of the small, simple organization to the larger, complex order without doing grave damage. But the same applies to attempting to remake intimate organizations along the lines of a spontaneous order. In the passage that provides one of this book's major themes, Hayek argued:

> If we were to apply the unmodified, uncurbed, rules of the micro-cosmos (i.e., of the small band or troop, or of, say, our families) to the macro-cosmos (our wider civilization), as our instincts and sentimental yearnings often make us wish to do, *we would destroy it.* Yet if we were always to apply the rules of the extended order to our more intimate groupings, *we would crush them.* So we must learn to live in two sorts of worlds at once. (p. 18, emphasis in original)

This notion of living in "two sorts of worlds at once" refers to the fact that our daily existence involves moving back and forth between organizations and spontaneous orders and therefore requires that we differentiate between them and understand the processes by which each operates.

The conclusion that Hayek draws from the notion of living in "two sorts of worlds at once" is that we face an ongoing problem of recognizing that the appropriate norms of behavior in the various intimate settings that we inhabit are different from those of the broader Great Society. Though humans have been, and continue to be, more likely to assume wrongly that the rules of intimate organizations can and should be extended to the anonymous Great Society, the reverse is a challenge we must face as well. For Hayek, the conflict is between our "evolved moral instincts" and the requirements of rule-following in the Great Society. Having spent most of our species-history in small intimate groups, we have evolved responses that are appropriate to such groups. For example, what seems to be a cross-cultural automatic concern about great inequalities of wealth might be an evolved moral response to the zero-sum nature of hunter-gatherer societies where one person's gain had to come at the expense of another and where sharing within the small group was essential to survival. Such instincts may continue to serve us well within various small groups, such as the family, but are not as functional in the context of the positive-sum game of the market.

Hayek (1989, p. 18) argues that the general idea that our instincts clash with the demands of civilization is similar to Freudian theory but with different conclusions. Both involve the idea that civilization involves repression of some natural instincts, but for Hayek, it is less "repression" than "supercession." That is, civilization demands that we "supercede" our evolved moral instincts, which are geared toward intentional and collective achievement of agreed upon ends, with the learned rules of the Great Society, which are geared toward the unintentional generation of order through the pursuit of multiple ends coordinated by abstract rules. The use of "supercession" suggests, intentionally, a value judgment: superseding our moral instincts and adopting the learned rules of the Great Society provides a better life for all than would attempting to allow those moral instincts to rule our behavior.

All of this ties nicely to the field of evolutionary psychology.[17] I will address these arguments in more detail later, but the link to Hayek's work is that the core premise the field works from is that the human brain developed over many millennia in a social environment very different from the world humans inhabit today. In attempting to understand human behavior, we have to remember that we are living in a technologically advanced world with a mind that evolved to survive in the most primitive of conditions, what is referred to as the "Environment of Evolutionary Adaptiveness" or EEA.

The challenge posed by living in two sorts of worlds at once is that it implies that our ethical systems must be contextual. What counts as appropriate moral behavior within the confines of intimate made orders might not be appropriate in the larger world and vice versa. Understanding where the lines are between the two sorts of worlds and what sort of behavior is functional in each should be part of the development of moral behavior in human beings, yet it is clearly a tricky business. It is made even trickier because during the years in which we do the most learning, we do so in two organizations that operate very differently than the Great Society as a whole: families and schools. This poses a large challenge for families, which operate as wonderful examples of face-to-face organizations, yet have as one of their key functions preparing human beings to live an adult life in which they must participate in a Great Society that operates by very different principles. In a later chapter, I will suggest that this particular function of the family is a classical liberal take on the socialization role that families have long been recognized as having. With an understanding of the "two sorts of worlds at once" problem, the socialization process becomes somewhat more complicated and subtle, and even more important.

## A First Look at Family Policy

At the level of public policy, children and the family pose challenges for classical liberals, as they do for adherents of almost any intellectual or political worldview. For classical liberals, the challenge is that the main conclusion of their social theory is that people left to their own devices to make use of their own knowledge will evolve social institutions that are better at generating social cooperation than those imposed from the top down. For consequentialist classical liberals, the benefits of that social cooperation in turn justify giving people the maximum freedom of action compatible with an equal freedom for others. This conclusion rests on an assumption, usually explicit, that the actors in question are adults, at least in the functional sense of people able to make their own decisions, exercise consent, and plan with some degree of foresight. The theory has rightly recognized that, for example, humans with developmental disorders that make them incapable of having meaningful knowledge, or exercising consent and foresight, will not be entitled to the same freedoms that fully competent adults are. The same is true of children.

Most classical liberals have not believed that children have been deserving of the full range of adult rights and freedoms.[18] Given that they are not deserving, we entrust parents with a set of rights that includes the right to direct the upbringing of said children. As I shall discuss in more detail, this is also the view of the US Supreme Court. Fundamental to any classical liberal view of family policy will be some statement of the rights that parents have with respect to their children. The problem, of course, is where such parental rights end and the child's own rights as a human being begin. This is complicated even further by the age of the child. It seems intuitively plausible that there is a difference between the average "adult competency" of a 5-year-old and a 15-year-old. Should the law and public policy treat them the same? If so, why? If not, how do we make such distinctions? And will such distinctions be relevant for all the sorts of issues that might arise in family law and policy? For example, we might think a 15-year-old girl is "adult enough" to have a significant say in which parent she lives with during a contested custody battle in a divorce, but would we also say she is "adult enough" to decide to have an abortion without parental notification or consent? Current law allows a 15-year-old access to an abortion without parental consent (for the most part) but not a tattoo. My point here is not to make the case for one view or the other, but only to point out that it is at least possible that our view of adulthood might vary from case to case. If so, this suggests that parental rights look a little different than other forms of rights in the contextuality of their application.

It is tempting, from a classical liberal perspective, to view children as property of their parents. After all, it does seem like the decision-making rights that parents have over them look an awful lot like property rights. Unlike physical property, however, there are real limits to those rights that derive from the fact that children *are* human beings and will eventually become the full adults who will have complete classical liberal rights. Here too, determining whether a decision that a parent makes for a child is a legitimate exercise of parental rights or a violation of the child's rights as a human being can be tricky. For example, should deeply religious parents be allowed to use faith-healing rather than standard medical treatment for their severely ill children? Ignoring the religious freedom question for a moment, do parents have the right to deny standard medicine in the name of their right to direct the upbringing of their children? From a classical liberal or almost any other perspective, these issues pose challenges in balancing parental rights against the best interest of the child.

Classical liberalism cannot provide easy, pat answers to questions such as these, but it can perhaps provide a framework for analyzing family policy issues that would at least offer a set of questions to ask when faced with such cases. One of the toughest things about family-related public policy is that particular cases are often highly idiosyncratic, making it difficult to come up with hard and fast a priori rules. Guiding questions and principles are necessary, but their application is almost never mechanical given the complexity of actual cases. Readers looking for "the" classical liberal policy on any number of particular family policy issues may therefore be disappointed by the discussions of policy in the last two chapters.

The theoretical and historical analysis to be presented will, however, offer some guidelines for policy. These will be developed in more length later, but in summary form they are as follows. First, policy should focus on the functioning of families not their form. The historical evolution of family form, and the variety of forms that can possibly be functional, suggests that policies focused on particular family forms are likely to make both Type I and Type II errors. Form-based policies may conclude that nonfavored forms are necessarily dysfunctional when they are actually quite functional and also overlook the ways in which favored forms might be dysfunctional. Second, the burden of proof for intervening in the family lies with the state and that burden must be high. The argument, in short, is that there are strong reasons to believe that parents have both the knowledge and incentives to act in the best interest of their children. If the state wishes to intervene in that decision-making process, it must show both reason why that presumption does not hold *and* that its alternative solution will better further the child's best interest than whatever the parents are doing. These two burdens are standard fare for classical liberal analyses of other public policies and I will refer to that literature in developing an approach to family policy. The general conclusion will be that the state should give a relatively high degree of latitude for parents to make decisions for and about their children but to also recognize that such latitude is not absolute.

## Outline of the Book

This introduction and the next chapter's deeper exploration of the intellectual framework for my analysis comprise the first section of the book. The second section explores the historical evolution of the modern family. Chapter 3 looks at the history of the family before industrialization, examining how the family served economic and political functions as well as enabling an expansion of social networks and social cooperation. Chapter 4 discusses the profound impact of the industrial revolution and the advent of capitalism on the family, emphasizing the ways in which it shifted families from being about economic cooperation to emotional satisfaction. In chapter 5 the historical story is extended through the past 50–100 years as I examine the effects of the unparalleled economic abundance of the twentieth century, and especially the era since World War II, on the evolution of the form and functions of the family. There I will argue that ongoing economic growth is a key factor in the increase in female labor force participation, the continuing intensification of the role of affection within the family, and the changes brought on by advances in birth control.

The third section explores the economic, sociological, and psychological functions of the modern family. The focus in chapters 6 through 8 is on the modern family and how it engages the various functions it is now understood to perform. Chapter 6 explores the economics of marriage and divorce from the perspective of modern Austrian economics, while chapter 7 discusses the ways in which the relative economic comfort of Western market economies has affected the functions of the family, particularly with respect to Maslow's hierarchy of needs. In chapter 8, I look at the ongoing debate over parenting in the United States, asking whether we are raising a nation of wimps rather than free-range kids.

The fourth and final section applies the prior material to public policy. In chapter 9 the classical liberal tools of public policy analysis get applied to family policy to develop a framework of analysis for looking at particular cases, with an emphasis on the importance of parental rights. The last chapter, chapter 10, looks at the issue of same-sex marriage through Hayekian eyes. There is much debate among libertarians as to whether it is a good idea for the state to issue marriage licenses to same-sex couples. This chapter will explore that debate, ultimately concluding that in a world where the state does have control over marriages, both justice and social science should lead us to legalize same-sex marriages.

Absent from the discussion of policy is any extended look at the effects of the welfare state on the family. There are two reasons for this absence, other than the limits of space. First, that subject has been explored in depth in the literature by a variety of scholars from different disciplines, and I do not have much to add to it. Second, my goal is to develop a unique classical liberal perspective on the family and particularly the long-run factors that have affected its evolution. Welfare and tax policies, not to mention the War on Drugs and a whole host of other public policies, matter for the short run, but my concern here is with the longer-run bigger picture. One of my hopes is that other scholars will find ways to apply the framework of this book to some of those questions in ways the current literature has not.

That hope is reflective of the spirit this book takes to its subject matter, which is to see it as very much of a "first step." In all of the scholarship that has been produced in the revival of classical liberal thinking in the past 40 or more years, there has been very little devoted to the family. In the growing literature applying Hayekian thought to almost every social scientific topic conceivable (not to mention some in the natural sciences), nothing has been done in sketching a Hayekian perspective on the family. This book aims to fill these gaps, and it aims to do so in a way very cognizant of the new ground it is treading. I hope that what follows is the beginning of a very fruitful and productive conversation among classical liberals and between classical liberals and other scholars of the family.

# CHAPTER 2

# Two Sorts of Worlds at Once

## Introduction

Before turning to the history of the family, I need to develop in more detail the theoretical framework with which I will approach that history. Inasmuch as history-free theory is often a problem in economics, and particularly with respect to the economics of the family, so can theory-free history lead us astray. Ultimately, all historical studies make use of some theoretical framework, as there must be some organizational principle by which historians select and report on their findings. However, the theories deployed can be implicit or explicit, and they can certainly be better or worse. The best history is written when historians make clear the frameworks they bring to their narratives and when those theories are ones solidly rooted in scholarship outside of history. Laying out such a theoretical framework is the task of this chapter.

In looking at the family in its role as a social institution, I will make use of theoretical approaches that have shown themselves effective in understanding the evolution and operation of social institutions in general. The family, however, poses a more complex challenge than most other social institutions in that it is so deeply intertwined with biological processes. Although the exact relationships have varied throughout time, the historical connections among family, sexual behavior, and procreation require taking into account the ways in which these elements of the family are affected by nature. Such considerations might be far less necessary in analogous histories of other institutions where the natural world plays a far less central role (e.g., a history of money as a social institution would seem to require little use of biology though perhaps some chemistry), but biology and psychology cannot be ignored in any attempt to tell a historical narrative about the institution of the family.

The approach this chapter takes is an evolutionary one. The advantage of taking an evolutionary approach to social institutions is that many of the intellectual strategies used to explain how social evolutionary processes operate are very similar to those used in explaining evolution in the natural world. This should not be a surprise, given that Darwin was very familiar with the evolutionary social theory of the Scottish writers of the late eighteenth century such as Adam Smith and David Hume (Schweber 1977). The intertwined intellectual history of theories of biological and social evolution is an advantage in using evolutionary approaches to explain an institution such as the family that involves elements from both areas.

After outlining the basics of what it might mean to offer an evolutionary account of social institutions in general, the chapter will turn its focus more specifically to the family in two ways. First, I apply the general theoretical approach to the family in some very broad ways. Second, I turn to evolutionary psychology to see how the natural history of humanity might help us to understand issues of gender and procreation in the context of the family. As much as the family is, ultimately, a social institution, there are biological explanations for why humans have engaged in the social patterns of mating and reproduction that we observe. In addition, understanding something of the way in which early evolutionary environments have shaped our brains and, therefore, how we perceive and react in the world, will be of importance in later discussions of the socialization functions that families must perform.

The varied material covered in this chapter is all intended to help unpack the observation of Hayek's quotation in chapter 1 that we have to learn to live in "two sorts of worlds at once," thanks to the ways in which our evolutionary past has hardwired us with certain moral and ethical instincts that are in tension with what is required for peace and prosperity in the extended order of a modern commercial society. Those instincts may well work just fine in the intimate worlds of the family or other institutions of civil society (and perhaps the firm too) but fail us in the more anonymous world of the Great Society. Understanding the modern family requires engaging with this set of issues, and this chapter provides a set of tools for doing just that.

## The Knowledge Problem

The starting point of all social scientific explanations is the observation that human knowledge is dispersed, contextual, and often tacit. Each of us knows different things, and what it is that we know often depends on the particular context in which we act. Our knowledge is often tacit, or inarticulate, in that the things that we know are not amenable to explicit expression in language or numbers. For example, many people can ride a bicycle but cannot explain how it is that they keep their balance while doing so. A good deal of our knowledge is of this sort: things that we have learned so deeply, usually through "learning by doing," that we do them almost automatically and cannot explain precisely what it is we are doing.[1] Knowledge is, in this way, often fundamentally "private" in that it cannot be easily transmitted in language or numbers. If knowledge is both dispersed and often difficult to articulate, the challenge facing any social order is how to make that knowledge available for others to make use of. Society requires that human beings cooperate, and such cooperation is fundamentally about the sharing of knowledge.

In his famous essay "The Use of Knowledge in Society" in 1945, Hayek formulated the problem very clearly. Though expressed in the context of economics, the point can be extended to all of society: "[The construction of a rational economic order] is a problem of the utilization of knowledge which is not given to anyone in its totality" (p. 78). More specifically, the "essential part of the phenomena" relevant to understanding how social order emerges is "the unavoidable imperfection of man's knowledge and the consequent need for a process by which knowledge is constantly communicated and acquired" (p. 91). In the context of economics, Hayek argued in that paper that the price system of the market could be understood as just such a communication process. Exploring briefly the more narrow economic argument will allow it to be generalized to other sorts of social phenomena.

As Hayek suggested, the economic problem is one of the use of knowledge. With millions of individuals all possessing their own bits of knowledge, many of which cannot be put into words or data, the economic problem is how to coordinate what is being produced and how it is being produced with what people wish to have. More specifically, these are questions of the creation of value. Producers need to know how people value resources so that they produce the things that others want and produce them in ways that use the least valuable resources possible in the process.[2] The problem of economic coordination and efficiency is a problem of turning individually held knowledge into a form that is socially accessible by others. Somehow, value must be communicated outside of language.

Economic value is a paradigmatic case of the problem of social communication. Economists, and especially those of the Austrian school such as Hayek, argue that value is subjective in that things have economic value because people believe that they are useful for whatever purposes they might have in mind. The value of a good or service derives from the belief by some person that it can help achieve some end they desire. Whether, *in fact*, the good or service can do so is not relevant to its having economic value. Even if tarot card readings have no basis in science, the fact that people *believe* they are useful gives them economic value and enables tarot readers to command a price. The same could be said of many other products on the market. Economic value is a matter of privately held beliefs that must somehow be made accessible to those who produce goods and services.

Hayek's argument in 1945 was that making knowledge usable to others is precisely what the market price system does. When individuals make decisions to buy and sell (and refrain from buying and selling), they are making their private knowledge accessible to others via the prices they choose to pay or offer in the market. When I buy a good, I am communicating that my private valuation of that good exceeds the value to me of the money I give up to acquire it. When I sell a good, I communicate in a similar way the higher value of the money I receive than whatever I might do with the good in question. Individual actors and organizations in the market engage in these sorts of calculations on an ongoing basis, and market-level outcomes, such as prices and profits and losses, reflect a kind of social consensus about the value of the goods and services being produced. For producers, profit and loss signals give them a measure of whether their transformation of inputs into outputs has increased the value of those inputs (accounting for the passage of time in the form of interest). For consumers, the use of the goods and services they acquire will determine if they, in fact, got more than they gave up. Both sides of the market examine the results and adjust accordingly: producers might try new inputs or change their output and consumers might choose to buy a different set of goods and services.

All of this mutual adjustment reflects the multiple roles that prices play as nodes of communication. Consumers have income and wealth constraints that limit the total that they can buy, and prices serve as guideposts in deciding how to allocate those funds. Although they do not have the bottom-line profit and loss signals of producers, the degree of their own subjective satisfaction with their purchases plays an analogous role. They adjust their behavior after realizing after the fact that they made a bad decision. Ultimately, consumers/households do face the bottom line of their wealth constraints and may face cash flow constraints from period to period, which will penalize continued poor decision-making. All of the interaction between producers and consumers leads to the emergent phenomena of market prices, which serve as surrogates for the knowledge that went into the consumption and production decisions.

As unintended consequences of choices on both sides of the markets, prices are, in many ways, the quintessential example of the ways in which undesigned social institutions emerge to help humans overcome the problems of dispersed, contextual, and tacit knowledge that define the human condition. As such, they serve as a model for how we might understand the emergence and operation of all kinds of undesigned social institutions.

## Rules, Ideal Types, and the Emergence of Institutions

I have already asserted that the family is a necessary component of any social order because it performs functions that no other social institution can match sufficiently. All social institutions perform certain functions. Some functions are particular to specific institutions, while others are functions that are part of any institution. The most important general function of social institutions is to facilitate the coordination of expectations among actors with fragmented knowledge operating in a social world of uncertainty. By coordinating our expectations, social institutions contribute to an orderly social world.

The idea that social order is about the coordination of expectations is the crucial element of Hayek's (1973, 1989) theory of social evolution. For social relationships to be "orderly," actors must (1) be able to form expectations about the actions of others that have some probability of being correct, (2) have some way of learning of the accuracy of their expectations, and (3) have some guidance as to how to correct them if they are mistaken. Ideally, social institutions can be the vehicles by which high degrees of social order are achieved. They can both communicate the information needed to form expectations and provide feedback to actors to help them adjust their expectations over time. Social institutions are part of the process of social communication and learning that enables actors to orient their behavior toward the expected behavior of others.

Ludwig Lachmann offered a clear statement of this sort of approach to institutions in his 1971 book *The Legacy of Max Weber*. After focusing on the plan as his central conception of individual human action, Lachmann asked about "the interrelationship between the actions of various actors" (p. 49). When the success of each individual's plan depends on the success or failure of the plans of millions of others, how are we able to acquire information about those plans of others? In the face of this apparent ignorance of others' plans, how does social coordination ever come about? The answer, according to Lachmann (as taken from Weber), is through social institutions. In Lachmann's conception, institutions

> enable each of us to rely on the actions of thousands of anonymous others about whose individual purposes and plans we can know nothing. They are nodal points of society, coordinating the actions of millions whom they relieve of the need to acquire and digest detailed knowledge about others and form detailed expectations about their future action. (p. 50)

Lachmann ties the role of institutions into Austrian conceptions of divided and contextualized knowledge. It is in this sense that this theory of social institutions is a generalized version of the explanation of the epistemic function of prices discussed earlier. Lachmann suggests that Weber's theory of institutions points us toward seeing all economic and social institutions as communication processes that make our diverse and often tacit knowledge socially usable.

Institutions perform this communicative function by constraining the actions of those who utilize them. Participants in social institutions are agreeing to abide by the procedures that are part of the institutions in question. As a result, actors are able to form expectations about each other by observing each one's use (or nonuse) of an institution. The way in which institutional processes are sets of rules that constrain behavior, and allow for more accurate expectation formation processes, can be seen by sketching out a general explanation of the evolution of social institutions.

Social institutions find their origins in the need to solve some sort of problem. Given the human desire to "remove felt uneasiness," humans are always on the lookout for ways to satisfy their wants (Mises 1966 [1949]). Faced with an ongoing problem, humans are likely to develop multiple ways of potentially solving it. These practices need not be developed with the conscious intention of solving the problem in question; they may be stumbled upon by accident. Whatever the origin of the potential solutions, some are likely to work better than others. Those actions that are more successful become adopted as rules of thumb by the acting individuals. The success of these actions will be noticed and imitated by others. As more imitation occurs, these rules of thumb will likely be increasingly successful because many such rules involve economies of scale in rule following. In other words, certain rules are more successful when there are more people using them. These so-called network externalities can be seen in the use of a language or something like a telephone. The use of either is more effective when larger numbers of other people are doing the same.

As more actors follow a given rule, the expectation formation processes of those who interact with them will become more accurate. As long as the act of following the rule is knowable by others, actors can utilize the information conveyed by the rule-following behavior in forming their expectations. What is happening is that participants in these institutions and institutional practices are causing the emergence of an "ideal type." Ideal types refer to the abstract "ideal" conception of a particular social role or institution. For example, the ideal type "police officer" would describe the various sorts of things that a police officer does, allowing us to construct a stylized description of a police officer without reference to any specific officer. Thus when someone says "my daughter is a police officer," we know what that means by reference to the ideal type we have of a police officer. The same sort of process can apply to institutions. The phrase "they are married" communicates a whole set of functions and roles associated with the concept of "being married" as it is practiced in that particular culture. This allows us to have the ideal typical representation of "a married person."

Early on in the evolution of institutions, or when such institutions are undergoing a significant change during their maturity, ideal typical behavior may not be as well-defined, and thus expectations may not be as easily coordinated. For example, early in the evolution of money, there were more commodities that were all being used as media of exchange, but no one of them had yet to become "generally accepted" to the degree that it was "the" medium of exchange. In such a situation, social coordination is harder as the ideal type "money user" may well be insufficiently specific to know what to offer that person in exchange. However, this process of competition and imitation continues until at some point, a large enough number of people follow particular rules of action so that quite reliable expectations can be formed and feedback to incorrect expectations can be disseminated. Then we might say that such rules of action have become "generally accepted" and thus transformed into social institutions.

Once social institutions emerge, they ease the difficulties involved with executing our particular purposes and plans. Those who participate in social institutions are putting limits on the kind of possible actions they might take. Institutions are thus a form of collective, though not necessarily consciously so, self-constraining behavior. These constraints make our behavior more predictable to others and increase our chances of mutually coordinating our actions.[3] In other words, social institutions and their constituent rules are forms of communication. Importantly, social institutions are repositories of knowledge that we might otherwise find difficult, or impossible, to articulate. Frequently we are not even aware of the knowledge that such institutions impart to us, and only when someone acts in ways that grossly violate our sense of propriety do we realize that institutions involve these tacit expectations of the limits to action.[4] The fact that the range of permissible actions is frequently tacit makes it no less binding in that we expect that range to be respected.

It might also be the case that the range of actions expected from participation in an institution has little to do with the intentions of the first actors who began the process of emergence. Institutions take on a kind of "life of their own," which is dependent upon the various purposes of those who currently use institutionalized practices. As a result, institutions must be flexible enough to change with these differing purposes, yet still maintain enough coherence to serve as guideposts.[5] Insufficiently flexible institutions will be unable to adapt to new purposes for which they might be useful, while overly flexible institutions will be unable to provide the stability necessary to allow the formation of reasonably accurate expectations. Successful social institutions strike a balance between too little and too much flexibility.

## Function, Form, and the Family as a Social Institution

Several aspects of this all-too-brief account of the emergence of social institutions will be of importance in looking at the actual history of the family as a social institution. First and foremost is the idea that the family solves a "problem." In the case of human beings, certainly one problem is the physical care of helpless infants, and another is the continued physical care and then socialization of children as they mature. The family might also perform crucial economic and political functions, such as providing resources through production activities, insurance for adults as they become elderly, or a structure of rules or hierarchy for resolving conflict. As noted at the outset, families cross the lines of biology and society in the kinds of functions they perform. In looking at the history of the family, it becomes clear that these functions have changed over time as the social, economic, and political problems that constituted the context within which families operate changed. Like other social institutions, the family has continued to evolve, shedding old functions and picking up new ones as the environment changes. In ways parallel to biological evolutionary processes, families that found ways to address the new problems thrown up by the environment thrived and were imitated, spreading the new practices society-wide.

The other element of this story that will be center stage is the idea that social institutions have to be sufficiently flexible in not just their functions but their forms. As the social environment changes and families potentially have to change the functions they perform, the forms or structures that families take may change as well. As new functions emerge, new family forms might be better able to fulfill them than current or past ones. This is just the story I will tell in exploring the evolution of the modern family.

This crucial distinction between function and form is one that often gets overlooked or elided in popular discussions of the family in ways that cause intellectual and political confusion. Nowhere is this clearer than in the use of the term "a normal family." Both families and policymakers are concerned with whether or not their family, or families in general, are normal. The problem with the word "normal" in this context is that it has two possible meanings, one descriptive and the other normative. People concerned about normality could be concerned about whether or not their family is "typical" or "average." This is the descriptive notion of normal. Is it normal to have a married couple living with two of their own biological children? Is it normal to own a house? Is it normal to have a household income of $75,000 per year? All of these questions can be answered by reference to demographic and other data, and all refer to the *form* or structure or organization of the family. They are, in some sense, what the family looks like.

Contrast this with the other sense of normal that might be in play, which refers to what the family *does*. In this context, normal might be synonymous with "healthy" or "functional," and abnormal would be "unhealthy" or the more common "dysfunctional." Consider these questions: is it normal to have a father who refuses to help with childcare? Is it normal to use physical discipline against children? Or is it normal to use market-purchased childcare? If we interpret this use of normal as being about function, then the challenge for answering these questions is first coming to an understanding of what the functions of the family might include, then determining, perhaps through empirical evidence in psychology or sociology or other social sciences, whether or not particular behaviors work to enhance those functions or to detract from them. These are questions to be explored in what follows. But the problem is that questions about function can also be understood as questions about form. The normal in all of these might refer to how healthy such behaviors are *or* how typical they are. That ambiguity is at the heart of many misunderstandings and cross-talk when it comes to issues around the family.

For now, however, the point is simply to clarify that form and function are distinct and that people who ask about the normality of families need to clarify which notion of normal they are invoking. It is also worth noting that both notions of normal admit of a positive answer to the question "is there any such thing as a normal family?" In the case of form, we can answer "yes" by pointing to demographic data, especially modal forms. In the case of function, we can answer "yes" by determining whether or not a given family is functional, as best we can tell.

Although form and function are analytically distinct, there is no doubt that they are interrelated when we turn to look at the history of the family and its current state. As the chapters to follow will argue, both the forms and functions of the human family have changed over the course of known human history. The speed of those changes has largely paralleled the speed of social evolution more generally, with most of human history being relatively stable and then much more rapid change in the past several hundred years, especially since the Industrial Revolution. In particular, the emergence of the spontaneous order of the Great Society has been central to those changes in form and function, as the wealth produced by capitalism, and the organization of production that has been at its center, have been major factors in changes in the family. Although biology, at least until recently, has required a male-female proximal bond to create children, how that sexual act was located within the social organization of child-raising and other functions we associate today with families has varied immensely across human history. Who has comprised families and what those families did, and how they came to be, show a remarkable diversity both at any given time and over centuries of social evolution.

In general, changes in form have followed changes in function, as might be expected. Those changes in function have most often resulted from changes in the institutions that surround the family, such as the economic, political, and legal orders. The focus in this study will be on the economic factors, but the others have mattered as well. In some cases, those economic changes have led to changes in the political and legal rules that have in turn led to changes in the functions of families (e.g., the ending of coverture laws as women's economic status improved enough to create pressure to end them). In other cases, political and legal changes have had a direct impact on form (e.g., *Loving v. Virginia* [1967] overturning laws in US states that prohibited interracial marriage). But over the long run, the general direction of change has been from surrounding institutions to family function to family form. As with other evolutionary processes, faced with new environmental challenges, those families that altered their forms in adaptive ways were better able to prosper, leading to imitation by others. To the extent that these changes in the family have largely been adaptive, the evolution of the family as a social institution can be seen as an example of unplanned or "spontaneous" social order, a key concept in classical liberal social theory.[6]

## Order without Design

The idea that social institutions and social order more generally can arise without a plan or conscious human design is one of the key contributions that classical liberalism has made to the study of society. Contrary to the common belief that whatever is orderly must have been designed, classical liberal thinkers have sought to explain that the social world is an orderly product of undesigned evolution in much the same way that Darwinian theory explains the orderly unfolding of the natural world. As noted at the outset, the line of influence runs more from the social to the natural, as Darwin was inspired to some degree by the social thought of the Scots and early economists such as David Ricardo. Among classical liberals, the works of Adam Smith in the eighteenth century, of Carl Menger in the nineteenth, and of F. A. Hayek in the twentieth all had the notion of unintended order at their center.[7] For Smith, of course, the "invisible hand" was his contribution to this line of thinking, and the idea of unplanned order was evident in his contemporaries Bernard Mandeville, Adam Ferguson, and David Hume. It was Ferguson who provided Hayek with his working definition of spontaneous order: "the products of human action but not human design." Smith's invisible hand concept was an attempt to explain how self-interested actions could produce beneficial results that were no part of the actor's intention. The idea of beneficial unintended consequences is the core insight of spontaneous order theory. Without the tools available to later thinkers, Smith could not quite get at the underlying social processes that produced unintended order, but he did correctly recognize it for what it was.

For Menger, explaining the emergence of social institutions, with the recognition that some significant number of them were unplanned orders, was the major task of the social sciences. In his 1883 book on the methodology of the social sciences, Menger (1985 [1883], p. 146) put the central question this way: "How can it be that institutions which serve the common welfare and are extremely significant for its development come into being without a common will directed toward establishing them?" What is now sometimes called "the Mengerian question" was but an extension of the invisible hand concept found in Adam Smith and developed through much of classical economics and the broader classical liberal tradition of the nineteenth century. Menger did have the advantage of writing the methodology book after the development of the marginalist and subjective theory of value, to which his own earlier book was a key contribution. This advantage enabled him to begin to identify the issues of knowledge, imitation, and competition that are crucial to understanding spontaneous orders.

Hayek's thought in the twentieth century took this classical liberal line of inquiry to a new level as an approach to understanding social institutions. Borrowing from his friend Michael Polanyi and others, Hayek used and popularized the term "spontaneous order" to describe the unintended but orderly products of human action. Furthermore, he made his indebtedness to the earlier classical liberal tradition clear by explicitly linking the idea back to the Scots and Menger. In much of his work from the 1950s on, the concept of spontaneous order was central to his attempts to understand economic and social interaction. In Hayek's hands, spontaneous order became a way to show how complex social phenomena could emerge in a world of divided knowledge and diverse ends.

In the 1970s, Hayek (1973, chapter 2) expanded on the basic notion of spontaneous order by contrasting such orders with what he termed "organizations," or "made orders" (as opposed to "grown" or spontaneous orders). Organizations were planned institutions, what Menger (1985 [1883]) in his work termed "pragmatic institutions." At various points, Hayek uses other terminology to describe the same essential distinction. He introduces the Greek terms "taxis" and "kosmos" to refer to "made" and "grown" orders, respectively. In his later discussion of economic order more specifically (Hayek 1977, chapter 10), he uses "economy" to describe the made orders of the firm or household and "catallaxy" to describe the grown order of the broader market that emerges from exchange (the word "catallaxy" derives from the Greek word for exchange). At other points, and especially in *The Fatal Conceit*, Hayek (1989) uses the phrase "The Great Society" to describe the overarching spontaneous order of the social world at its most expansive. All of these various bits of terminology are driving at a consistent distinction that matters greatly for this study. For consistency's sake, I will use the terms "spontaneous order" and "organization" to distinguish between those institutions that emerge unplanned and those that are intentional human creations.

Organizations and spontaneous orders are distinguished by the way in which they come into being, designed or undesigned, respectively. What they share is that both are "orders" in the broadest sense of the term. As Hayek (1973, p. 36) defines it, order is

> a state of affairs in which a multiplicity of elements of various kinds are so related to each other than we may learn from our acquaintance with some spatial or temporal part of the whole to form correct expectations concerning the rest, or at least expectations which have a good chance of proving correct.

The elements of an order are integrated or coordinated by processes that are discoverable by human reason and whose relationships, at least at the level of "principles" or "patterns," can be understood by extrapolating from the relationships of some part of the whole. The ways in which those elements are coordinated will differ across different kinds of orders, and those differences will matter for the tasks each kind of order can accomplish and the complexity each one can coordinate. Organizations, or made orders, are limited in these ways, while spontaneous orders are capable of coordinating a much broader range of activities and attaining a much greater degree of complexity.

For our purposes, it is important to make clear some distinctions between the ways in which spontaneous orders and organizations operate and under what conditions one or the other will be more appropriate.[8] Although the distinction between spontaneous orders and organizations is better conceived of as along a continuum than as a pure dichotomy, nonetheless one major criterion for distinguishing between the two is the degree of simplicity or complexity involved. Organizations are structures that are simple enough so that those at the top are capable of comprehending them. Hayek (1973, p. 38) also argues that organizations are usually directly perceivable by inspection and are able to serve the specific purpose(s) of those who constructed them. This contrasts with spontaneous orders, such as the market or the Great Society more generally, which can be of any degree of complexity, are rule-based, have structures that may not be obvious, and serve no particular purpose. Instead, they serve the various purposes of those who participate in them. For example, a firm has a very specific overriding purpose, which is to maximize profits, whereas something like a language or a market has no specific purpose. Rather, they exist to serve a multitude of purposes determined by those who make use of them.

One of the key differences between organizations and spontaneous orders is that the former tend to be structured by hierarchy and command, while the latter are based on rule-following behavior. The relative simplicity of organizations combined with an agreed upon goal or goals enables them to be structured hierarchically and to make use of command as the primary way of allocating resources within the organization. Those at the top of the hierarchy can sufficiently survey the organization to understand the link between means and ends directly. For example, managers can direct employees to one or the other part of the factory, or a military commander can direct troops toward one location or another, or a baseball manager can ask a player to sacrifice bunt in a particular situation. At some level, the employees, soldiers, and players are all agreeable to this arrangement because they can understand their place in the organizational structure and how it contributes to the agreed-upon ends.[9] Organizations can also lend themselves to forms of participatory decision-making where the group as a whole decides what commands will order their activities. What is distinctive is that the sphere of action of individuals is circumscribed by commands intended to serve the unified end of the organization.

Spontaneous orders operate on the basis of abstract rules that guide the behavior of individuals and organizations within them. Importantly, those rules are, as Hayek terms them, "ends-independent" in the sense that the rules enable individuals to pursue a multiplicity of ends, rather than being geared toward a specific, agreed-upon end as in organizations. These rules are most often framed negatively, as in "do not steal" or "do not coerce others." Where framed positively, they are sufficiently abstract to permit them to serve a variety of purposes, for example, "respect property and live up to contracts." In neither of those cases does the rule specify what is to be done with the property or what is being contracted for. Such rules simply indicate that *whatever ends one has, these are the rules one must follow to pursue them*. When the relevant rules are followed by the component parts, orders emerge spontaneously from the actions of those parts. The parts will behave in ways that are generally predictable to each other and that enable such orders to evolve in increasingly complex ways. Understanding spontaneous orders requires discerning how the rules serve to coordinate the activities of a number of constituent parts all pursuing different ends. In circumstances where there are a large number of people all pursuing different ends, it would make sense to try to find some way to engage the forces of spontaneous order to coordinate their activities.

Perhaps the two best examples of these features of spontaneous orders are money and language. Both are social institutions that are ends-independent in that they can be used for a variety of particular purposes by individuals and groups. Both involve sets of rules that need to be followed in order to participate in the institution. To be understood as a user of a language, one must be able to construct grammatical sentences in which the words being used are intended to have the commonly accepted meaning. If one uses the wrong words or puts words together randomly in a sequence, one will not be understood.[10] Notice that this argument holds regardless of the particular thing that one is attempting to communicate. Language is a rules-driven, ends-independent spontaneous order. Note too that language changes and evolves not by hierarchical commands (hence, the failure of the French Academy) but by usage changes that come from those who actually speak the language. New words get adopted, old words get discarded, and rules of usage and grammar evolve in unplanned ways as new practices seem more functional or efficient than old ones.[11] Many of the same things can be said of money, as it too operates by a set of rules that enable people to participate in using it, and its form and function, though influenced by the significant role played by government in its production and regulation, have largely evolved in response to changes in the economic and technological environment. Most important, neither language nor money were invented; both emerged and continue to evolve as unplanned, undesigned, social institutions.

In contrast to these spontaneous or undesigned orders, which work best when the group using them are large and heterogeneous, small and homogenous groups with an agreed-upon specific purpose would more appropriately be "made orders." Hayek (1973, p. 46) argues:

> In any group of men of more than the smallest size, collaboration will always rest on both spontaneous order as well as on deliberate organization. There is no doubt that for many limited tasks organization is the most powerful method of effective coordination because it enables us to adapt the resulting order much more fully to our wishes.

For the numerous limited and specific tasks that occupy most of our days, deliberate organizations work better than spontaneous orders because we are able to consciously construct them to achieve the agreed-upon goals. It is when coordination *among* these organizations, each having different purposes, is necessary that we must rely on spontaneous ordering processes. The Great Society, in Hayek's view, is the spontaneous order that emerges from the mutual interaction of these deliberate organizations, as each pursues its plans within the rules of the legal order. Hayek describes the process as follows:

> The family, the farm, the plant, the firm, the corporation and the various associations, and all the public institutions including government, are organizations which in turn are integrated into a more comprehensive spontaneous order. (p. 46)

Family occupies the first place on his list of organizations, and that whole discussion is also an effective response to Hodgson's claim, noted in chapter 1, that "market individualists" think the market is the appropriate way to order all human activity. For Hayek, tasks of limited complexity where the people involved agree upon the goal are the appropriate domain of intentional organizations that will operate in a manner unlike the spontaneous order of the market. A theory of the family can fit comfortably into Hayek's framework, as it is one of the key organizations that make up the broader spontaneous order of the Great Society.

One key implication of this distinction between spontaneous orders and organizations is that the broader spontaneous order of the Great Society is comprised of many organizations. It is those organizations, especially households and firms, whose interactions produce the emergent and undesigned order we call the Great Society. The two categories of human institutions are therefore inextricably linked. Organizations contribute to the emergent order and, importantly, that emergent order serves as the necessary backdrop for the functioning of the organizations. For example, as Lewin (1999) argues, although it is the interaction of firms engaged in very intentional planning that constitutes the unplanned order of the catallaxy, those firms can only engage in their intentional planning because they can construct budgets and balance sheets that make use of the spontaneously emergent prices of the marketplace. More generally, organizations draw from the broader order in the very actions that make them part of the unplanned order that then emerges from those actions.

In terms of the family, this interconnectedness between the component organizations and the overall order has two implications. First, in examining the functions of the family, we need to understand what things families do that contribute to the overall order of the Great Society. To the extent that families are also households, we will see that they have had a major role as a component economic institution, as their supplies of labor and consumption activities contribute to the overall spontaneous order of the catallaxy. Beyond those economic functions, families also contribute to the Great Society by functioning as a socializing institution with respect to the raising of children. To the extent that families help children understand and obey social norms and legal rules, they contribute to the rule-following behavior that is part of the spontaneous order of the Great Society. In understanding the functions of the family, we will situate those functions in terms of how families are a central component institution of the Great Society.

At the same time, many of the things that families do are a consequence of existing in the broader context of the Great Society. That is, the Great Society makes it possible for families to do some things and not others. Specifically, in exploring the ways in which the forms and functions of the family have changed over time, I will argue that these changes have been responses to changes in the broader legal and social rules as well as the wealth and technology that the market made possible. What families "do" is not just a matter of how they contribute to the broader order, but also a result of the functions that the broader order makes possible or renders unnecessary. As those functions change in response to the broader environment, we also see changes in the forms the family is most likely to take. There is a dialectic relationship between the institution of the family and the broader Great Society: we cannot understand the emergent order of the social world without understanding the contributions made by the family to that order, but we also cannot understand how the family functions as an institution without paying attention to the rules and outcomes that characterize the social orders in which it operates.

## The Human Mind and the Social Order

Any discussion of the family as a social institution must take account of the fact that family both emerged from, and is still intertwined with, the biological make-up of human beings. The most obvious of the biological bases of the family are the necessity of male and female gametes for reproduction and the helplessness of human infants. I will address those in the following section, as well as in the discussion of the functions of the family in later chapters. Before doing so, it is worth exploring one other biological connection that is often neglected in discussions of the family. The human mind itself is a product of the biological features of the human brain. As all human social institutions are products (intended or unintended) of human action and intentionality, it seems appropriate to discuss, at least briefly, the operation of the brain/mind and note how it might matter for understanding the family. This topic is even more relevant when one is approaching the social role of the family from a Hayekian perspective, as Hayek has written on cognitive theory in his 1952 book *The Sensory Order*, as well as several follow-up papers in the decades after it was published.[12] In this section, we will look at Hayek's theory of mind and then in the next section connect that up with insights from evolutionary psychology about the biological and psychological roots of key elements of family behavior.

The goal of *The Sensory Order* is to explain how it can be that the world we understand to exist through the methods of science presents itself to us in the mind as a different sort of world.[13] Science may tell us, and we might agree, that what we see is but a jumble of waves, particles, and the like, but we also know that our minds take those raw physical inputs and provide us with an orderly picture of the world. This is what we mean by having a "mind" and being "conscious." Hayek (1952, p. 7) wants "to know the kind of process by which a given physical situation is transformed into a certain phenomenal picture." Hayek also wants to understand the relationship between the "physical" and "mental" orders and how mind renders the world orderly in a way that is different from the order we know exists in the physical world:

> There exists, therefore, no one-to-one correspondence between the kinds (or the physical properties) of the different physical stimuli and the dimensions in which they can vary, on the one hand, and the different kinds of sensory qualities which they produce and their various dimensions on the other. The manner in which the different physical stimuli can vary and the different physical dimensions in which they can be arranged have no exact counterpart in the manner in which the sensory qualities caused by them will differ from each other, or in the dimensions in which these sensory qualities can be arranged. This is the central fact to which we have referred when we insisted that the two orders, the physical order of the stimuli and the phenomenal or mental order of the sensory qualities, are different. (p. 14)

Mind is "thus a particular order of a set of events taking place in some organism and in some manner related to but not identical with, the physical order of events in the environment" (p. 16). Though it is not a theme I will develop in this study, it is worth mentioning that, for Hayek, the mind is yet another example of a spontaneous, or emergent, order, but this time one rooted in the natural world rather than the social world.

More specifically, Hayek (1952) argues that mind is a "relational" order. What makes any given situation orderly is not just that there is a certain set of events occurring together, but, as we have seen with his more general definition of order earlier, that there are "certain relations between them" (p. 47). It is in this sense that the whole (the order) is greater than the sum of its parts. One has to understand the relationships among the various elements in order to understand how their arrangement in particular ways can lead to an order that is something distinct from the sum of the elements. It is not just the presence of certain elements that generates an order, but how those elements are arranged, that is, the rules by which they operate. In the case of the mind, it is certain relationships among physical stimuli that produce the orderliness in the world that we associate with consciousness.

These relationships and the order they facilitate are made possible because mind is ultimately a classification system. The mental order is the result of the mind classifying physical stimuli as they arrive through the senses. Hayek is careful to argue that the mind does not just take "pre-sorted" stimuli and then "put" them in the right place. Rather, the mind is the way in which stimuli are classified in the first place. The world presents itself to us as orderly because the mind "pre-classifies" stimuli based on networks of neural connections that have been built up through our history of interaction with the external world. We can only recognize something as an instance of "x" because the mind so classifies it in the very act of perceiving it through the senses. The complex part of this process is that what is normally happening is a process of "multiple classification." The category to which particular inputs get assigned may differ depending on the other inputs that accompany it.

As organisms learn through time, these connections and systems of multiple classification become progressively more sophisticated. Hayek (1952, p. 109) uses the metaphors of "map" and "model" to explore the way in which the mental order is structured. The map and the model generally reflect the more static and more dynamic aspects of cognition. The map refers to the relationship between the "network of connections" among stimuli acting upon the organism and the "structure of external events which it can be said to reproduce" (p. 109). These are the established connections that have been built up in the mind over the lifetime of learning. They reflect the "lay of the land" in terms of the learned associations that the mind has made through time. They are neural and physical phenomena. As we will see in the next section, the physical elements of these connections are the result of evolutionary processes that have their origins deep in prehuman history. Hayek is careful to say that this is a "very imperfect map, but also a map which is subject to continuous although very gradual change" (p. 110). It is a record of past relationships. He continues:

> The model, by contrast, refers to the pattern of impulses which is traced at any moment within the given network of semi-permanent channels [and] may be regarded as a kind of model of the particular environment in which the organism finds itself at the moment and which will enable it to take account of that environment in all its movements. (pp. 114–15)

The map is a reflection of the past, but the model is what the organism uses to "represent" the present.

The semi-permanent nature of the map restricts the kinds of things that the organism can model at any point in time. We understand our present environment on the basis of the experiences we have accumulated through time, both as individuals and as humans with a brain structured in a particular way. However, the model is dynamic in the sense that it guides behavior in the particular context the organism finds itself. It reflects the set of current impulses that are taking place in the brain, as opposed to the channels for directing those impulses that are captured by the map. How the behavior resulting from that set of current impulses plays out in that particular instance may feed back over time to gradually adjust the map by restructuring the underlying physical relationships (either through new neural connections over the lifetime of the individual or as part of the evolutionary development of the species), but in the short run, the model is bounded by the map.

More interestingly, Hayek (1952, p. 120) argues that the model "will thus continually tend to run ahead of the actual situation." Because the model frames the current situation in which the organism finds itself, based on the historical relationships embedded in the map, the model is essentially predictive in that it can be used to anticipate the result of various actions the organism might take.[14] The classification process that is the mind is largely one that classifies by function, in the sense that it classifies by the likely consequences that any set of stimuli will jointly produce. As a result, mental processes are very much processes of expectation:

> The representation of the existing situation in fact cannot be separated from, and has no significance apart from, the representation of the consequences to which it is likely to lead. Even on a pre-conscious level the organism must live as much in a world of expectation as in a world of "fact," and most responses to a given stimulus are probably determined only via fairly complex processes of "trying out" on the model the effects to be expected from alternative courses of action. The reaction to a stimulus thus frequently implies an anticipation of the consequences to be expected from it. (p. 121)

Central to Hayek's theory of mind is that the brain as an organ is the product of a long evolutionary process and that the mental order it produces is also rooted in the history of both the human race and individual humans. We are not born with a tabula rasa. Rather we come into the world with a brain already structured in ways that are likely to produce certain kinds of understandings of the world, often because what the mind does is to form expectations based on that history.

If Hayek is right, and contemporary neuroscience is largely consistent with the broad contours of his argument, it suggests that a good deal of how we perceive the world and the psychological dispositions that underlie our actions in the modern social world are the products of a mind-producing brain that is itself the product of a long evolutionary process. We should not be surprised, therefore, to find that it will be helpful in understanding those perceptions and dispositions to think about the prehistoric natural and social environment in which the human mind evolved. It will also not be a surprise if we should discover that some of the ways in which our minds work evolved in a very different environment than the modern world and that this fact might explain some of the tensions we see in the ways in which we behave in that world today. The family is likely to be a particularly rich example of these tensions, given that mate selection, reproduction, and child-raising have been core elements of human behavior for millennia. Such an approach to these questions is taken up by evolutionary psychology, to which I now turn.

## Evolutionary Psychology and the Family

As noted earlier, one cannot talk about the family without recognizing that the social institution we call the family has been intimately related with the biological process of reproduction. Furthermore, if the argument of the last section is correct in arguing that our brains, and therefore our minds and our ability to navigate the world, are themselves products of that biological evolutionary process, then explanations of social phenomena, emerging as they do as the consequences of human action, will have to grapple with the biological basis of human perception and action. The burgeoning field of evolutionary psychology claims to offer just such a perspective on human social phenomena, seeing them as emerging from human actions that must be understood by reference to the evolutionary history of the human mind. A look at evolutionary psychology and a brief discussion of its relevance to the family will occupy us in this section. In later chapters, we will apply some of these insights to more specific issues.

Evolutionary psychology begins by rejecting the views that the mind is either a "blank slate" on which the human's lived life imprints itself or "all-purpose" information processor. Instead, evolutionary psychologists, as Hayek did, argue that the mind, emerging from the biological processes of the brain, has to be understood as an evolved biological phenomenon. The minds of individual humans already have, as it were, software installed, thanks to evolution. Thus, we are not blank slates on which our external experiences press themselves, generating our minds and their interpretations of the world. But neither are our minds one giant program for information processing. Rather, to continue the software analogy, we have distinct "programs" for solving particular kinds of problems. The mind is better seen as a distributed network of problem-solving routines. As we try to understand human behavior and the social institutions it produces, evolutionary psychology argues that we must start by understanding what those programs might be and what their functions are and how those functions emerged.

These problem-solving modules of the mind have the apparent disadvantage of limiting the kinds of things the mind can do. However, as we noted earlier in our discussion of social institutions, sometimes limiting options is for the better. In the case of social institutions, limiting the realistic options actors have enhances social coordination by better facilitating the formation of accurate expectations across actors. Having specialized modules enables the mind to attend selectively to certain sorts of sensory inputs and not others. Bjorklund and Pellegrini (2000, pp. 1688–89, emphasis in original) capture the enabling aspect of limits:

> Stated differently, [the idea that the mind has domain-specific problem-solving mechanisms] proposes that there are *constraints* on learning. Constraints imply restrictions, and restrictions are usually thought of negatively. The human mind is noted for its flexibility. We, more than any other species, live by our wits and have been able to adapt to the most varied range of environments of any large animal. But constraints, from this perspective, *enable* learning rather than hamper it... [I]nfants and young children are constrained to process certain information in "core domains"... in certain ways. They come into the world with some idea of how the world is structured, and this leads to faster and more efficient processing of information within specific domains.

The constraints of having domain-specific mental processes certainly have clear drawbacks, but the selective focus enables the mind to be very good at certain sorts of tasks, and the long-term survival of these mental modules suggests that the benefits of the limitations clearly outweigh the opportunity costs.[15] Social practices, norms, and institutions that have similarly survived also suggest that the advantages of limiting options outweigh the costs.

The key to understanding the way the mind operates in the modern world is the recognition that the bulk of humanity's biological evolution took place in an environment radically different from modernity. Termed the "Environment of Evolutionary Adaptiveness" or "EEA," it refers to the conditions under which specific adaptations took place. As Tooby and Cosmides (2005, p. 23) point out:

> the EEA is not a particular place or time. The EEA for a given adaptation is the statistical composite of the enduring selection pressures or cause-and-effect relationship that pushed the alleles underlying an adaptation systematically upward in frequency until they became species-typical or reached a frequency-dependent equilibrium... Because the coordinated fixation of alleles at different loci takes time, complex adaptations reflect enduring features of the ancestral world. The adaptation is the consequence of the EEA, and so the structure of the adaptation reflects the structure of the EEA.

They also note that because different adaptations occurred at different times in response to different environmental phenomena, the "EEA for one adaptation may be somewhat different from the EEA for another." As most of humanity's biological evolution took place where the environmental problems were those of a hunter-gatherer society, explaining particular features of the mind involves remembering that they were adaptations to solve problems such as "finding a mate, cooperating with others, hunting, gathering, protecting children, navigating, avoiding predators, avoiding exploitation, and so on" (p. 16).

As an example, experimental research shows that humans are better at detecting changes in the state and location of animals than we are at the same task for vehicles.[16] At first, that result might seem strange, as for most humans their day-to-day need to detect such changes would be much more focused on vehicles than animals. However, the result is not surprising from an evolutionary perspective: for most of human history, tracking animal movement was a matter of life and death. Concern with animal movement is the EEA in which our mental programs for judging changes in state and location emerged and evolved. The evolutionary effects of the century or so during which vehicles such as cars have been relevant pale in comparison to the millennia during which animal movement was a matter of major concern. One important implication is that when trying to understand human psychology, we have to ask what function a particular behavior might have served in the EEA. In other words, psychology is a matter of reverse engineering: we know how humans behave, now how do we reconstruct the processes by which this behavior might have emerged as a solution to a particular problem in the EEA and then design experiments to refute or confirm them? Answering that question can also help to understand whether a particular property of humans is "a design feature, a functionless by-product, or noise" (Tooby and Cosmides 2005, p. 25).[17] Our ability to track animals better than cars is indeed a "design feature" and if we were trying to help new drivers judge distance, understanding how our evolution-produced "pre-installed" program for judgments about state and location works could be very important.

An implication of this line of inquiry is that our decision-making heuristics have to be judged contextually. The social sciences, and especially economics, have made much use of the terms "rationality" or "rational choice." For most of their history, the accepted notion of rationality has been an a priori, universalistic one, for example, the characteristics associated with "rational economic man." Only in the past few decades, with the rise of experimental and behavioral economics, have economists really begun to explore what empirical psychology might have to say about human decision-making. One of the results of that work is a reconceptualization of "rationality" as a series of decision-making rules to guide us through a world of uncertainty rather than a perfectly informed, precise calculation machine.[18] It is of interest that both evolutionary psychologists and economists working in the experimental subdiscipline are using the term "ecological rationality" to describe the claim that what is rational will depend upon the environment being examined.[19]

In particular, Vernon Smith's (2003) research agenda, well summarized in his Nobel Prize lecture, captures the issues in play.[20] He distinguishes "constructivist" from "ecological" rationality, where the former refers to the sort of full-informed Cartesian rationalism that characterizes the "standard social science model" and neoclassical economics in particular. Smith argues that both the "autonomic, neuropsychological systems" of the brain and the fact that we cannot say all that we know (i.e., Hayekian tacit knowledge) suggest that much of what we do, and do successfully, moment to moment has little to do with the "conscious and deliberate use of reason" (p. 468). For Smith, rationality is better understood as "ecological" in the sense that what we know "emerges out of cultural and biological evolutionary processes: homegrown principles of action, norms, traditions, and morality" (pp. 469–70). In this conception of rationality, we use "reason" to "discover the possible intelligence embodied in the rules, norms, and institutions of our cultural and biological heritage that are created from human interactions but not by deliberate human design" (p. 470). Smith ties this conception of rationality to the Scottish Enlightenment tradition and Hayek as its modern representative.

Experimental economics, in Smith's vision, demonstrates the ways in which humans who possess only ecological rationality can still produce the systemic unintended beneficial consequences long associated with the stronger, and false, constructive rationality assumption of the standard model. In addition, experimental economics offers empirical evidence for the "two sorts of worlds at once" perspective by indicating that people will deploy different behavioral strategies in intimate situations than they will in more anonymous ones. Smith terms this distinction "personal" versus "impersonal" exchange. In both cases, reciprocity is at the core of our propensity to exchange, but the development of property rights, money, and exchange enables us to not have to "keep track of who owes who what" (Smith 1998, p. 6).[21] That transition enables us to be self-regarding in the anonymous world of impersonal exchange in a way that we are not in more intimate personal exchanges. The evidence summarized in Smith's Nobel lecture backs up this point.

Smith explicitly cites the work of evolutionary psychology as providing the argument that many of the underlying mental rules that can be discovered as part of ecological rationality were formed in the EEA. Behavior that appears to be irrational may be the result of deploying evolved programs in environments far different than those in which they emerged as adaptive. Context is a key part of ecological conceptions of rationality, and both culture and biology can provide explanations of the relevant context in which behavioral rules emerge. One result might be reclassifying behavior that seems dysfunctional or irrational as functional or rational once we understand the evolutionary source from which it sprang.[22]

Smith's co-Nobelist Daniel Kahneman has developed this argument in a somewhat different direction, best summarized in Kahneman (2011). He distinguishes between what he calls "System 1" and "System 2." System 1 refers to the evolved, nearly automatic responses that we have when processing information, and especially when we are asked to engage in rational decision-making. It is very efficient and makes use of heuristics and shortcuts to get quick answers, much in the way one might imagine our ancient ancestors having to do in order to survive. These advantages of System 1 are also their weakness, as they are subject to all kinds of biases that were functional in the EEA but less so in the modern world, as calling them "biases" would suggest. For example, there is abundant laboratory evidence of humans suffering from "loss aversion." Faced with a bet where one has an equal chance of winning $150 or losing $100, many people will not take the bet because the fear of the loss looms larger than the prospect of the gain, even though the expected value is a gain of $25. This bias is understandable from an evolutionary perspective because if one is living on the margin of survival, avoiding losses would be more important than obtaining gains.

Kahneman's System 2 is our constructivist rational side that checks on System 1 to try to correct or anticipate those built-in biases. As useful as System 1 is because it is fast, it also constrains our choices because it overlooks options that thinking slower might recognize as being superior. Engaging System 2 takes conscious effort and practice and might well be too slow for many decisions that require quick responses. These tradeoffs between the two systems are the core of human cognitive processing. For my purposes, Kahneman's work is a further example of the ways in which much of how we understand the world on a daily basis is driven by our evolutionary past.

As the family is perhaps the oldest of human institutions and because its basic underlying behaviors of searching for a mate, reproducing, and raising children have been part of humanity as long as there has been humanity, it is unsurprising that evolutionary psychologists have found in gender, sex, and family issues a fertile set of applications for their work. A quick summary of the work of Geary and Flinn (2001) on parental behavior and the emergence of the family and Bjorklund and Pellegrini (2000) on child development can provide an introduction.

Geary and Flinn (2001, p. 7) argue that the family and its associated parenting behavior emerged as a way for humans to create "competition-related social networks, including families" that "facilitate competition with other coalitions... to gain access to and control over essential resources." More specifically, parental behavior is designed to "provide a social context that enables the acquisition of sociocompetitive competencies" including the "social skills that enable the cooperative formation of coalitions" (p. 7). They identify a "suite" of observed human characteristics that can be "reverse engineered" as adaptations to the context described earlier. The dynamic might work as follows: the children whose parents' investment in them was such that it enabled them to form coalitions that were more likely to promote survival were likely to pass on that disposition toward providing the beneficial parental investment. As coalition size increased, the complexity of social relationships would have favored humans with larger brains to process the information, parenting strategies that provided good social skills, and longer developmental periods in which offspring could develop the needed skills. Moreover, social structures in which males and females were pair-bonded and thereby likely to stay together, with the male providing parental investment in the offspring, were also likely to be selected as the ability to navigate the increasingly complex social world required the learning environment of the family (pp. 24–25). This short summary hardly does justice to the richness of their analysis but does suggest the ways in which we can see features of human families and parenting that are still with us as evolutionary responses to survival pressures.

Bjorklund and Pellegrini's (2000) overarching goal is to explain elements of the child development process in terms of their adaptiveness for particular environmental challenges at specific times in the developmental process. For example, they argue that the ability of newborns to, under the right circumstances, imitate facial gestures is a way to "facilitate mother-infant interaction" to ensure that the child is sufficiently nursed and cared for (p. 1693). Their analysis of play offers several possible explanations for its evolutionary adaptiveness, from being a source of creativity to a way to master social skills and roles that are functional for adult survival (p. 1694).[23] This perspective might also explain the fairly universal gender differences in play, with boys tending to prefer rough-and-tumble kinds of play, while girls tending to prefer to play at parenting and other forms where "physically based dominance relationships" are less central (p. 1701). The higher propensity for adolescent males to engage in risk-taking can also be understood as an evolved response along similar lines. The source of these differences is that for most of human history, male and female roles were strongly differentiated, with women primarily responsible for parenting and males primarily responsible for finding food and protection. It is in that environment that gender differentiated evolved dispositions toward particular kinds of play during childhood emerged.

In all of these cases, the argument is not that we must bow before the evolved dispositions. Instead, the point is that understanding the ways in which such behavior was adaptive for most of human history can help to explain observed behavior in the modern world. Noting that there are gendered differences in play does not mean we cannot encourage girls to play more competitively or encourage boys to play at parenting. To the contrary: in the world we inhabit, where gender roles are not nearly as well defined, having each gender learn each set of skills will likely be *more* adaptive than keeping them to gender differentiated forms of play. This is analogous to how Kahneman talks about the role of System 2 with respect to System 1.

What this analysis *does* suggest, however, is that arguments like "gender differences in play are completely socially constructed" are probably wrong. It may well be that these differences are not solely the product of socialization, but rather the results of the social environment interacting with underlying evolved dispositions. Because any learned behavior must be learned by a mind that has evolved particular dispositions, the behavior "cannot be solely attributed to the action of the environment on the organism" (Tooby and Cosmides 2005, p. 31). They continue: "Thus, *innate* cannot be the opposite of *learned*. It is just as mistaken to think of *evolved* as the opposite of *learned* because our evolved learning programs were organized by evolution to learn some things and not others" (p. 31, emphasis in original). Understanding human behavior requires that we understand how the current environment interacts with the evolved "learning programs" that constitute the mind, and attempts to change that behavior therefore cannot ignore the underlying learning programs that facilitate human action.

It is this interaction between the current environment and evolved learning programs and the dispositions they create that brings us back to how we might understand the role of the family in the modern world. The fundamental problem is well-framed by Tooby and Cosmides (2005, p. 17):

> Although the behavior our evolved programs generate would, on average, have been adaptive (reproduction promoting) in ancestral environments, there is no guarantee that it will be so now. Modern environments differ importantly from ancestral ones, particularly when it comes to social behavior. We no longer live in small face-to-face societies, in seminomadic bands of 20 to 100 people, many of whom were close relatives. Yet our cognitive programs were designed for that social world.

Evolutionary psychologists use this insight to understand why human behavior is sometimes dysfunctional. For our purposes in looking at the family, it has two important implications. First, although human societies in general are no longer small and face-to-face, *the family itself remains such a social group*. Thus certain of our evolved programs might serve us quite well *within the confines of the family but not in the larger, more anonymous social order*. We are raised in an environment that more closely matches our evolutionary past, yet we simultaneously move in and out of that environment from the wider society in which our evolved programs are less likely to be adaptive. This is the problem of living in "two sorts of worlds at once" identified in the introduction and explored in the next section.

The second implication has to do with what it is that families must do. If the family evolved the function of providing socialization that was adaptive for the EEA, how certain can we be that it is providing the socialization that is now necessary for life in the larger, anonymous order of the Great Society? As with our example of gendered differences in play, we need not accept the parenting dispositions provided by evolution as an unquestioned given. Rather by identifying the predispositions that evolution has provided us with, we can help parents and families understand them and recognize the potentially different sorts of socialization they need to provide for children to survive and flourish in a social world very different from that of the EEA. In exploring the functions of the family in the modern world, this challenge will be of central concern. Although I am not interested in developing a full-fledged theory of parenting, I am interested in understanding the *goals* that parents should be striving for in preparing their children for adulthood in the world of modernity.[24] Evolutionary psychology provides us with a context for understanding the challenges of achieving those goals when our evolved dispositions emerged from a very different social context.

## Living in Two Sorts of Worlds at Once

The last two sections provide the backdrop for an observation that Hayek made late in his career that serves as the organizing principle for our explorations of the modern family. This chapter's opening discussion of orders and organizations can now be wedded to the excursion into cognitive theory and evolutionary psychology by drawing a distinction between what Hayek called the "micro-orders" of intimate organizations and the "macro-order" of the anonymous Great Society. As noted in the introduction, Hayek argues that the differences between the structures and appropriate behavior within each are stark enough that we must learn to "live in two sorts of worlds at once" as we constantly navigate back and forth between these two different kinds of social institutions.[25] With the material from the current chapter in hand, I want to re-examine this point, which was only touched on in the introduction.

Evolutionary psychology suggests that much of our behavior in the modern world can be explained by reference to the fact that our minds evolved in an environment where most of our interactions were face-to-face with other humans. In *The Fatal Conceit* (as well as the epilogue to *Law, Legislation, and Liberty*), Hayek suggests that a similar explanation accounts for the ways in which our "moral instincts" are at odds with the moral rules that are necessary to sustain the extended order of the Great Society. The behavioral rules, and the moral judgments that accompany them, that were appropriate in the intimate, face-to-face world that humans have operated in for most of our biological history, and in which our minds took evolutionary shape, define those moral instincts. The problem is that the world of the Great Society is one characterized by anonymity and abstract relations, rather than the intimacy of the small group—a point stressed by the evolutionary psychologists. We can bring Hayek's cognitive theory together with evolutionary psychology and argue that the portion of our mental map that is the result of biologically evolved elements of the brain and mind can produce expectational models of the world that are not as viable in the very different context of the modern extended order. However, they may well still be highly adaptive to the variety of more intimate individual organizations of which we are also members. The intimate organizations such as families and firms in which we spend much of our days remain close enough to the environment in which our minds developed that our moral instincts are reasonably trustworthy there. Their trustworthiness declines rapidly as we are called to act and make moral judgments within the broader spontaneous order of the Great Society. Hayek's sociological observation that we live in "two sorts of worlds at once" therefore finds support from both evolutionary psychology and his own cognitive theory. These two worlds are the institutional analogues of Kahneman's System 1 and System 2, and the tensions that the two worlds create for us sit at the intersection of the biological and the social.

To understand the challenges of living in two sorts of worlds at once, some additional discussion of the differences between organizations and orders is necessary. As I have already suggested, it is much easier to make use of made orders in contexts where individuals have a significant degree of face-to-face contact and are aware of what each other might know or might prefer. Finding agreement upon the ends and employing the command or intentionally cooperative (as opposed to rule-based) structures that often characterize Hayekian organizations are much more possible if individuals have a high degree of familiarity with each other. As a result, organizations are often built around belief systems or aspects of one's identity that make the common goals of the organization more obvious and easier to agree on, for example, a church or an ethnicity-based service organization. In such organizations, our moral instincts of altruism and our belief that the consequences of our actions will be what we intend, both of which were honed in the simple face-to-face environment of the EEA, are likely to be more accurate guides to behavior. The relevance for the study of the family should be obvious as families have all of these characteristics.

The market, by contrast, is a process of anonymous interaction. We do not know the "others" with whom we are interacting in sufficient depth to be able to appeal to their love for us or their knowledge of us when trying to get them to act in the ways we desire. We must rely on, as Adam Smith (1976 [1776], p. 18) put it, their "self-love" and get them to cooperate through exchange. The rules of the market, and the other institutions that constitute it, enable people to interact and cooperate without needing to know very much detail about others. In its anonymity the market is unforgiving, as it judges all by profit and loss, rather than by personal connections or emotional dispositions. Unlike the family or many other social institutions (including to some extent the firm), the market cannot reward on merit in any meaningful sense, and this makes it an institution that generates results that, although they tend to improve society as a whole, can pay no concern to their effects on particular individuals. Understanding that good intentions are not enough, and recognizing that self-interested behavior can lead to benefits for all, requires resisting the moral instincts and mental programs that developed over millennia of living in intimate groups.

In the more intimate setting of the family, for example, we are able to focus our concern on individuals because our interactions are intimate and are not based on the unintended social cooperation that emerges from ends-independent rules and self-interested exchange, but at least ideally on intentionally cooperative behavior that is made possible by that very intimacy. Our intentions often translate quite easily into results. This intimacy makes the family an ideal site for focusing on the development of particular individual skills and habits of thought. The family can pay attention to the nuanced differences between individuals in a way that the abstract calculations of the market and the broader Great Society cannot. The chapters to follow will provide additional support for this contention. The anonymity of the market precludes such arrangements for society as a whole, and as I shall argue in later chapters, other nonmarket social institutions will never be able to replicate the unique abilities of the family along these lines.

In some ways, Hayek's two worlds are an extension of Tonnies' classic sociological distinction between *Gemeinschaft* and *Gesellschaft*, or the natural community and the unnatural society. Gemeinschaft is the world of the face-to-face and known, where we are linked by direct, concrete interpersonal relationships. Gessellschaft is the anonymous world of the market, where we are linked by indirect, abstract relationships such as contract and exchange. In fact,

McCloskey (2006, p. 130) recasts that distinction as the "loving family and associational firm." Many who make use of Tonnies' distinction are tempted to treat the two forms of society as being historically sequential, with Gesellschaft following Gemeinschaft, but as the historian Thomas Bender (p. 131) remarks, the distinction is "to be understood, not as designating strictly discrete and sequential phases in the evolution of human social relations, but as signifying two kinds of relations that, particularly in a modern society, coexist and contend with each other." Recognizing that these two kinds of social relations "coexist and contend" with each other is central to understanding the functions of the family in the contemporary era.[26]

Understanding the notion of having to live in two sorts of worlds at once provides us with a number of questions that will guide the argument in the chapters to follow. In looking at the evolution of the modern family in the next three chapters, the focus will be on the ways in which the family's form and functions changed in response to the expansion of the social order, in particular due the spread of market capitalism and the increased anonymity and abstractness of the relationships it brought in its wake. How did the family change as the scale and scope of the social order expanded from small communities to the anonymous Great Society? And in the last 100 years, how has the wealth and well-being produced by the market changed the functioning of the family? Is it possible that families are becoming somewhat more like the Great Society in which they are embedded and less like intimate organizations?

In looking at the functions of the family in chapters 6–8, the "two sorts of worlds at once" problem will direct our attention to the ways that the sociological and psychological functions of the family are or are not attentive to the issues Hayek raises and in what ways they *could* be more attentive. If the family is the key site in which children are taught the rules of the social world, should not one key function of families in this regard be to help children not just understand those rules but to further understand that the appropriate rules of intimate associations and the Great Society may well be different? Just because sharing with your sibling is the right thing to do within the context of a family does not necessarily mean one can apply that logic to the question of how the social world writ large should be organized. In the same way it might make sense to recognize but push back against children's evolved disposition to engage in gendered forms of play, it might be socially beneficial to resist what Hayek termed the atavistic callings of our moral instincts. After all, explaining where behavior comes from is not the same thing as justifying it. The family could play a key role in that process of resistance. The discussion of the economic functions of the family will focus on the ways in which the growth and extension of the market-based Great Society have changed and shrunk those economic functions. Nonetheless, economic considerations, and understanding the inter-relationship between household production and market production, provides a useful lens for exploring some of the structural changes in the family we have seen in the past generation.

The discussion of policy in the final chapters will rest on issues of knowledge and complexity, and how they feed a comparative institutional analysis of the ability of the family and the state to perform those functions necessary for the survival and flourishing of children, both biologically and sociologically. Here too, the advantages of the intimacy of the family combined with what we know about the evolved disposition of parents to care for their young, in contrast to the more anonymous processes involved in political intervention, will guide us.

The notion of living in two sorts of worlds at once sits at the intersection of biological and social evolution that is the concern of evolutionary psychology, Hayek's cognitive theory, and the distinction between spontaneous order and intentional organization (and the epistemological issues that lie behind it). As this chapter has argued, the social institution of the family sits in roughly that same intersection. Understanding the role of the family in the modern world therefore requires situating our discussion in that context. Unpacking how we manage to live in two sorts of worlds at once is the theme of the rest of this study.

# PART II

# *Capitalism and the Creation of the Modern Family*

# CHAPTER 3

# The Family in a World of Poverty

## Introduction

The next five chapters constitute the core of the argument I wish to make. The first three of those five provide a history of the family from a classical liberal perspective, focusing on the ways in which capitalism and the market economy produced what we call the modern family. In chapters 6 and 7, I apply the insights of the earlier chapters to take a closer look at marriage, divorce, and family in the early twenty-first century. Specifically, chapter 6 offers an economic analysis of marriage and divorce that draws heavily upon the Austrian school of economics and more general classical liberal insights. In chapter 7, I turn back to broader issues of the form and function of the family in what Brink Lindsey (2007) has termed the "The Age of Abundance," referring to the historically unparalleled levels of wealth and social freedom that characterize the contemporary world. That discussion extends the themes of the longer-term historical story told in this chapter and the next two.

In offering a classical liberal history of the family, I will not be making use of anything new in the way of primary sources or historical documents. Historians and other scholars of the family have provided us with a rich array of material to work with over the past several decades and more. Instead, I hope to reinterpret that material from the framework of the ideas put forward in chapter 2 and argue that the changes in the family over the past several centuries are a beneficial result of the emergence of the market economy, capitalism, wage labor, and industrialization. I also want to argue that many, but not all, of the changes in the family that took place during the twentieth century were good ones, as they opened up more choices and more freedom to more people. Not only did the family slowly separate itself from the state in many ways, but a greater variety of family forms and behavior became acceptable in the eyes of the community, both of which expanded the range of relationships that people could pursue. The overarching theme is that the family, thanks to capitalism, slowly became much more humanized as love and affection became more prominent as the primary ways in which family members related to one another.

In her book *The Bourgeois Virtues*, Deirdre McCloskey (2006) argues that, contrary to the views of most of its critics and many of its defenders, capitalism is not a matter of what she calls "Prudence Only." That is, capitalism neither requires nor encourages that humans make use of only the one virtue of Prudence, which is best understood as the sort of broadly calculative, instrumental rationality associated with mainstream economics. McCloskey argues to the contrary that "[b]ourgeois life has not in practice, I claim, excluded the other virtues. In fact, it often has nourished them" (p. 8). In her account, capitalism has produced a society in which we are better able to act in ways that demonstrate Love, Faith, Hope, Courage, Temperance, Justice, as well as Prudence. The story I hope to tell in the chapters to follow can be understood as an application of McCloskey's argument, specifically tracking the relationship between Prudence and Love within the Western family. No doubt, as McCloskey points out, Love has always been present in the family (pp. 93–94). However, the political and economic circumstances of the preindustrial era frequently put a premium on Prudence over Love in how the family functioned from day to day. Love came to the forefront when it could, but Prudence often demanded that Love take a back seat. What capitalism did was to invert the relative importance of Prudence and Love in the context of the family. Capitalism made it possible for families to be first and foremost about Love and has led us to think that family decisions made by Prudence alone are not very virtuous. To the extent capitalism's success requires functional families, McCloskey is quite right to say that capitalism both promotes and requires the virtue of Love.

An important corollary to this broad historical story is that it is nearly impossible to create some kind of firewall between economic change and cultural change. The unpredictable change produced by market economies will often lead to changes in the culture that are equally difficult to predict and nearly impossible to control. As I will argue in this chapter and the next, the industrialization produced by capitalism led to profound changes in the way that families were structured and the functions they performed. In chapter 5, I will show how the economic growth that twentieth-century capitalism produced opened up opportunities for women that had enormous effects on both the functions and forms of the family. In both cases, there was no way that the social changes could have been stopped and certainly no way that we can "turn back the clock" on those cultural changes while doing nothing about the underlying economic processes that are largely responsible for them. This observation is where classical liberals can make a real contribution to our understanding of the family. Many on the left celebrate the cultural changes but are also highly critical of the economic system that produced them, and many on the right pay lip service to the importance of capitalism and unhampered economic change but also often wish to stop or reverse the cultural changes that system has produced. Classical liberals understand that both forms of change are deeply intertwined and that both advance human freedom and human flourishing.

In the next three chapters, I will argue that the features we associate with the modern family are largely, though not solely, the result of the progressive advance of market capitalism that has characterized the past several hundred years. What we shall see is that market capitalism did two things that changed the family forever. First, it separated, through the advent of wage labor, home and work to a degree never before seen in human history. This fundamentally moved the family away from having economic survival as its primary function. Second, it produced a degree of wealth also previously unseen in human history. This also enabled the family to shed many of its other economic functions, in this case those associated with household production. It also made possible first the withdrawal of women from the labor force but then their massive reentrance and all of the changes that has brought in its wake. Market capitalism took the West from hardscrabble scarcity and poverty to relative abundance in the course of just over 200 years. In this chapter, I look at the premodern family in that world of precapitalist poverty. In chapter 4, I explore the process by which the advent of capitalism produced, over the course of the nineteenth century, the core features of the modern family as we now know it. Chapter 5 looks at the twentieth-century family through the changes in women's roles that capitalism and the wealth it produced made possible.

After a discussion of the economics of divorce in chapter 6, the way these changes due to market capitalism have transformed the contemporary family comprises the argument of chapter 7. One way of understanding the changes that have produced the modern family is that as the institution of the family shed the economic (and political) functions that were once central to its existence, it was able to pick up new functions to replace them. The new functions that families acquired might best be described as emotional or psychological ones; families became the central institution for the fulfillment of a variety of psychological and emotional needs. The term "needs" is used intentionally here, as one can understand this transformation as the family climbing the famed "hierarchy of needs" associated with the twentieth-century psychologist Abraham Maslow. Maslow (1943) argued that people generally address their lower order needs first (e.g., those associated with basic survival) and then move up a hierarchy of needs that has "self-actualization" and "self-realization" at the very top. The evolution of the modern family is the story of its central functions being transformed from those associated with needs at the bottom of the hierarchy to those at the top as a result of the opportunities and wealth created by market capitalism. As economic growth has produced increasing abundance, making basic survival easier, more and more families in the Western world can also focus on the needs at the very top of the hierarchy, leading us to see marriage and the family as a site of self-actualization rather than serving solely social functions. Seeing marriage and the family as first and foremost institutions in which adults invest their deepest and richest emotional and psychological needs is a peculiarly modern phenomenon, trailing in the wake of the modernization that market capitalism brought elsewhere. I argue in chapter 7 that the transformation of the family from being seen as nearly only about fulfilling a function for society to a place where adults satisfy their psychological and emotional needs has not come without its dangers. But before we get to our own time, we need to understand the family structures and functions that existed for the centuries before capitalism.

## Defining the Modern Family

For most of human history, marriage and family were not arenas open to individual choice or realms of privacy in the ways that we would understand those now. Even the concept of marriage as a structured social institution emerged relatively recently. In the earliest stages of marriage, the creation of a new family via marriage was fraught with a range of economic, political, and social implications that overrode any desires of the couple at the center of the process. Both parents and the community at large had a stake in the success of individual marriages, whether primarily economic or political, and that stake justified what we would now call interference in both the choice of marital partner and the day-to-day operation of the family. Largely absent from this premodern world are four features that are characteristic of the modern family:

1. Marital partners chosen by individuals, and on the basis of affection, with the expectation that the marital relationship will be companionate and broadly equal and where sex plays a central role in that relationship.
2. The family thus created is nuclear, in that it generally includes the married couple and children by themselves and that it is generally private and insulated from the forces of the community or other family members.
3. Children are sentimentally seen as uniquely valued, rather than as one more household asset subject to calculation, and childhood becomes a time to shelter children from the outside world rather than immediately placing them into the productive activities of the household as had long been the case.
4. The legal equality of men and women and a substantial number of women able to survive economically on their own, and the corresponding commonality of divorce.

This list is not meant to be exhaustive, but rather to capture the core elements of the modern family.

The nature of modern marriages is something we often take for granted in the Western world. It is often only when presented with other cultural or historical models of marriage that we are able to realize the distinctiveness of modern practice. Item one illustrates this with each of its four components.

The first of those components is that marital partners are chosen rather than arranged by parents, the community, or even political figures. In both the history of the West and as we look across cultures today, we can see that the demise of arranged marriages generally parallels rising levels of wealth and the spread of democracy and markets. The spread of democracy and markets generally has the effect of making the political stakes of marriages that much smaller in comparison to a monarchical or feudal society, where a distinct aristocracy had every reason to make sure their children married others with political and economic power. For different reasons, similar incentives are at work in poorer societies, where marriage can be seen as a path toward increased well-being. When economic security is hard to come by, marrying right is essential. In addition, to the degree that parents rely on their children for resources and care in their old age, making sure that children married right so that they would have the ability to provide such care becomes a high priority. In societies with greater wealth overall and little to no ruling elite, the risk of marrying wrong is much lower and the overall ethos of individual choice in economics and politics pushes back against arranged marriages. As wealth and democracy have become more widespread, so has this element of the modern family.

The idea of being able to choose one's spouse is distinct from the notion that the marital choice is primarily based on love and affection. Marriages of choice predate marriages of love. Even when people could choose their marital partners, it was not necessarily the case that they chose primarily on the basis of what we would now call romantic love. To the extent that the family/household was first and foremost a unit of economic production for most of human history, love was secondary to other considerations. Only in the past few hundred years, as market capitalism transformed the relationship between home and work and therefore the functions of the family, has the love match increasingly became the criterion by which marital choices are made, thus making it an element of the modern family.

The companionate and equal nature of the marital relationship is an outgrowth of marriage historically being first a matter of choice then later about love. The long history of male domination both in the household and the public sphere need not be rehashed here. Only within the past 100 years or so could Western marriages be described as anything that was close to equal and where the relationship between the spouses could rightly be seen as truly companionate. As we will see later, for most of human history women's inferior legal status in the public world was mirrored by their inferior social status within the household and in the very nature of marriage itself. Market capitalism brought in its wake a shift from status to contract as primary basis for human relationships, and this shift eventually changed the very nature of marriage and gender relationships by spreading the ethos of contract and rights into the marital dyad.[1] Finally, the centrality of sexual compatibility and activity to the marriage is equally modern and linked up with the increasing role played by the love match, as well as improvements in birth control technology, that came in the wake of capitalism and industrialization.

The second item in the list is that the modern family is distinct in that it is nuclear and private and thereby insulated from the interference of the state and the community. The question of the relative frequency of extended families throughout history is much debated among historians, but there is pretty clear evidence that the nuclear family was not the expected norm until after industrialization, hence its inclusion in our list of elements of the modern family. The whole idea that the family is a kind of private enclave shielded from the state, the market, and the rest of the community is peculiarly modern as well. This too was an outgrowth of the same economic processes that produced the companionate marriage discussed earlier. Prior to the advent of capitalism and industrialization, families were very porous to surrounding institutions.

The third element of the modern family is the idea that children are uniquely sentimentalized and sheltered from the adult world. For most of human history, families could not afford to ignore the fact that children were an important economic resource. Capitalism and industrialization and the wealth they brought made it possible for families to see children the way we see them today and to keep them out of the adult world until at least adolescence. The whole concept of childhood and adolescence as being a time distinctly different from adulthood is unique to the modern family.

Finally, the modern family is one in which women have a significant degree of financial independence as well as equal rights both inside the home and in the public worlds of the market and civil society. One of the questions I will explore is the degree to which the advancement of women's rights was both a cause and effect of their increasing economic status. Surely women needed the basic rights of contract, including to the terms of work, in order to gain a financial foothold, but it is equally the case that women's increased presence in the public sphere of the market created pressure for further legal changes to provide them with greater equality. The best example of this, to be explored in chapter 6, is the advent of no-fault divorce. No-fault is better understood as a consequence of ongoing economic and cultural changes than a cause of such changes. Women's financial independence has been, in the long run, a product of the advent of market capitalism, both in terms of the nature of the labor market and the wealth it has produced. In turn, the increased leverage that women's wealth has provided has made divorce easier and more frequent. Putting aside to later whether this is a good or bad development, there is no question that single-parenthood and step-parenthood resulting from divorce are features of the modern family that were not part of the longer run of human history.[2]

What these four items have in common is that they reflect an increase in respect for the individual in the realm of marriage and family. The choices of adult individuals are increasingly respected, the individuality of children becomes valued in and of itself, the family is seen as a distinct entity worthy of privacy, and men and women are increasingly treated as individuals of equal standing before the law, if not in the marketplace. As such, these changes in the family parallel to one degree or another, and arguably are the result of, similar trends happening in economics (capitalism liberated the individual from feudal bonds), politics (democracy and constitutionalism liberated the individual from monarchy and oppressive states), and religion (where the Reformation similarly challenged the power of larger, centralized institutions over the individual). In this way, we will see that the evolution of the modern family is part of a larger trend of liberalization and respect for the individual that was at the core of what classical liberalism has been arguing for, and was produced in society, over the past few centuries.

## The Family and the Law of Association

To understand the evolution of the family, we need to understand how it is situated in the broader story of economic evolution that has characterized recorded human history. Presenting any sort of detailed economic history of the West is beyond my scope here, but a stylized overview that highlights elements of the story that are relevant to the role played by the family will be helpful. One way of characterizing the long-run story of human economic evolution is to see it as an evolution from social orders structured by direct, face-to-face interaction based largely on hierarchy to anonymous social orders based on abstract, ends-independent rules. This transition is from the simple societies of our past to what Hayek and Popper called "The Great Society" of modernity. This move from hierarchy to rules can also be seen in a variety of major social institutions all around the same time (the fifteenth, sixteenth, and seventeenth century), reflecting the earliest emergence of the Great Society. Science breaks free of the church, and knowledge acquisition is seen to work better when coordinated by rules than by hierarchy. Politics begins the shift from hierarchy to rules with the Magna Carta and other steps away from monarchy toward democracy. And the Catholic Church itself is challenged by the Reformation's critique of hierarchy.

The evolution of the family parallels this process, though with something of a lag. The distinction I will make is between the premodern and modern family. The rise of capitalism and democracy slowly eliminated the economic and political functions of the family, opening up space for it to acquire new functions and new forms as a result. The key event in the transformation of the family was industrialization, which really has its effect by the early or mid-nineteenth century, or a few hundred years after the other processes of transformation began. To some degree this lag is because the changes in those other institutions were causal contributors to the changes in the family. The modern family, for our purposes, will be the one we see emerge with and after industrialization.

Another advantage of using premodern and modern in the way we have is that it makes clear two important historical points. One is that there has, in fact, been change in the way that families are structured and the things that they do. Too much contemporary conversation about the family often invokes the phrase "traditional family" to describe the nuclear family as depicted in 1950s' television and often does so with the implication that it has been around for generations, hence it is traditional. However, as I will discuss in some detail in chapter 5, the idealized family of the 1950s was the product of a unique set of historical circumstances and, at that, not as overwhelmingly common as many have come to believe. If by traditional we mean "the kind of family that has been most common over centuries of human experience," then it is the premodern family, and not the one associated with the post–World War II era, that deserves the title. The second historical point is simply that using the modern family to describe the family that we are generally more familiar with allows us to identify other features of the modern (e.g., industrial and postindustrial) world that helped to bring that family into existence and continue to frame its ongoing evolution.

The key to the emergence of the Great Society is this increased dependence upon relationships with strangers for the vast majority of our cooperative economic and political enterprises. The emergence of markets and their associated institutions of contract, exchange, and money prices as the central process of social coordination extends and expands the division of labor both within productive organizations and society-wide. Mises (1966 [1949], p. 160) explained this phenomenon by generalizing David Ricardo's "law of comparative advantage" into what Mises called the "Law of Association." Mises used that phrase to describe the ways in which the differences among humans can be turned to their advantage by recognizing that cooperation under the division of labor leads to both higher productivity and a more peaceful, interdependent society than do attempts at autarky. In the same way that Ricardo argued that nations that specialize in what they produce at lowest cost (their comparative advantage) and then exchange with other nations will be better off than those who try to do everything themselves, the benefits of specializing by comparative advantage and exchanging the surplus also makes individuals better off. Specialization and exchange promote prosperity and peace by creating cooperative relationships among strangers: "The greater productivity of work under the division of labour is a unifying influence. It leads men to regard each other as comrades in a joint struggle for welfare, rather than as competitors in a struggle for existence. It makes friends out of enemies, peace out of war, and society out of individuals" (Mises 1981 [1922], p. 261). For Mises, our ability to understand the improvements brought about by this process is the driving force of social evolution.

In order for this social evolutionary process to work, humans had to develop ways to cooperate with strangers. Applying the Law of Association only to those we know face-to-face would limit the gains that could be reaped from extending the division of labor. The Great Society is defined by the fact that instead of only interacting face-to-face with the people whose cooperation is required for us to procure the resources we need for survival, we are able to cooperate with anonymous others through the institutions of the market and the legal order: prices, contracts, and property, among others.[3] Those institutions enable us to extend our range of contact beyond our kin or physical location to persons far away, both genealogically and geographically. The phenomenon we call globalization is, in many ways, the full fruition of the Law of Association as the networks of economic and social interaction have moved well beyond the nation-state to a more truly global economy and society. The development of the Internet is a cause of this economic globalization process, by reducing the costs of communication and transportation as more products appear in digital form, but it is also a prime example of the sort of cooperation in anonymity that the Law of Association describes.[4] We are able to engage in all kinds of economic, political, and social activities without any direct sensory contact with our cooperators.

One frequently underappreciated aspect of this process is the necessity of finding ways to trust people we do not know. This is most obvious on the Internet, as we cannot be sure who we are dealing with or even if it is a real person or some piece of artificial intelligence technology. Extending the Law of Association to strangers requires ways to discern whether we can trust them.[5] Paul Seabright (2004) puts it this way: "[T]he unplanned but sophisticated coordination of modern industrial societies . . . needs an explanation." He points out that there is nothing in our biological evolution to suggest that we have any aptitude for dealing well with strangers, as modernity requires. Instead, he continues, the "explanation is to be found in the presence of institutions that make human beings willing to treat strangers as *honorary friends*" (p. 8, emphasis mine).[6] Seabright could equally have said that the challenge we face in the Great Society is finding ways to treat strangers as *honorary kin*. The core process underlying the evolution of the modern family has been the transference of the family's economic and political functions to the institutions of the Great Society. Whereas in the past, families and kin were the central ways in which economic and political processes were constituted, the ascent of capitalism and democracy moved those functions to institutions that enabled cooperation in anonymity to replace face-to-face solidarity as the primary process by which resources get allocated and political decisions get made. The trust-promoting institutions of the modern world enabled us to expand the trust and cooperation of family and kin to anonymous strangers through the Law of Association. The Great Society is well-described as one where market and legal institutions turn strangers into honorary kin.

## Prehistoric Marriage as the Earliest Form of Social Cooperation

The advent of capitalism and democracy dethroned the family's long-standing role as the major economic and political organization in the Western world. Until about the 1700s, marriages in the Western world were not the love-based, companionate, chosen partnerships we value today. They were largely the product of parental or communal arrangements in which the consent of the spouses was a secondary consideration at best. The reasons for this were straightforward: for the poor, and this was most of humanity for most of its history, the centrality of family formation through marriage as an economic and political institution meant that the risks to the community as a whole of a bad marriage were very high. When marriage is a way of forming crucial political alliances or gaining access to resources or opportunities for trade, such decisions could not be left in the hands of the young and certainly not made on the basis of something as ephemeral as emotional attachment. Family and kin were all-encompassing institutions, the perpetuation and improvement of which were the most important political and economic tasks for each generation.

For the earliest of humans living in extended family-based tribes, marriage was a way of creating alliances with other similarly structured groups. In his overview of evolutionary social theory, Michael Shermer (2008) discusses the laboratory evidence that suggests that humans have an evolved propensity to cooperate and collaborate, as doing so registers in areas of the brain that we share with related primates. Such cooperation, however, requires that we develop relationships of trust with our collaborators. Within family and kin groups, trust could largely be taken for granted if for no other reason than the evolutionary drive to pass on our genetic material through kin. However, as Shermer also points out, the same evolutionary processes that lead us to this sort of "within-group amity" also lead us to engage in "between-group enmity" (p. 206). In protecting our genetic assets, we are inherently suspicious of strangers. *The challenge of building a society is learning to trust strangers.*

In its earliest form, marriage can be understood as a way to build these bonds of trust. Given that marriage was very tightly linked with reproduction, social groups that discovered the genetic perils of marriages that were too tightly in-group and encouraged marriages to humans in other social groups were more likely to survive than those that did not. Evolution provides a reason to expect attempts at exogamy of some sort. Marriages outside the extended kin group had another advantage, as they, in Coontz's (2005, p. 45) words, "turned strangers into relatives and enemies into allies." Thus marriage did (and still does) more than just turn strangers into honorary friends or kin, it turns them into literal kin, both through the marital bond itself and through the shared relationships to any children the marriage produces. This is the beginning of the social cooperation generated by the Law of Association. Family creation via marriage became a way to extend the effective range of cooperation and the division of labor, although still in an intimate rather than an anonymous social order. In a Paleolithic world where all lived at the margins of survival, the "ability to forge networks of cooperation beyond the immediate family group or local band" was a necessity, and one of the most important functions of marriage was to do so (p. 40).

Marriage was not the only way of gaining the cooperation of others of course, and Coontz as well as various anthropologists have discussed several others, including gift-giving, sharing, and similar opportunities for face-to-face interaction, either informally or at more formal rituals. However, as Coontz (2005, p. 41) notes, the major advantage of marriage over all of these other options was that "it produced children who had relatives in both camps." Where members of different bands had children who married each other and then shared grandchildren, tensions were likely to be lower and levels of cooperation higher, as these interdependencies harmonized their self-interest with that of the other group.[7] Marriage was a microlevel application of the famous quote (often misattributed to Frederic Bastiat), "When goods don't cross borders, soldiers will," or what Shermer (2008, p. 252) calls the corollary thereof "where goods do cross frontiers, armies will not." The marital version is "where marriages cross biological borders, conflict will not and cooperation will." Like all aphorisms, this one was not true 100 percent of the time, but it was a reliable description of a key social function of marriage and a precursor to modern arguments (such as Mises's Law of Association) about the conflict-reducing and cooperation-inducing effects of exchanges of goods, services, and ideas across political borders.

More broadly, marriage was one among several ways in which reciprocal arrangements between groups could be created. Given the biological evidence for an evolved human disposition toward reciprocity, the most successful early human groups were those who had reputations for reciprocity and who could skillfully use reciprocity to create new relationships and get greater access to resources. For nomadic groups, carrying physical forms of wealth was normally prohibitively costly, so acquiring wealth in the form of favors owed was the more manageable method. Coontz (2005, p. 39) observes that "[s]haring beyond the immediate family or local group was a rudimentary form of banking. It allowed people to accumulate personal credit or goodwill that could be drawn upon later." Offering one's children up for marriage was one way to do this, especially if the child would take up residence with the other group. The reciprocal interdependencies created by marriage enabled those groups that practiced it to be more likely to survive and thrive than those that did not. Children can be conceived and raised without the social custom of marriage (especially in the smaller face-to-face bands of antiquity), so marriage's advantages as a social custom must be found elsewhere, and the desire to create extended cross-group networks of social cooperation through reciprocal behavior offers one such very powerful explanation for marriage's origin and long history. Coontz summarizes this well:

> Marriage is not the only way to impose an incest taboo, organize child rearing, pool resources, care for elders, coordinate household production, or pass on property to the next generation. It is, however, the only way to get in-laws. And since the dawn of civilization, getting in-laws has been one of marriage's most important functions. (p. 33)

It is through in-laws that cooperative networks are forged, despite our disposition to distrust strangers.

A key element of prehistoric marriage was that the social benefits of marriage were mainly at the group level. Clearly, there were benefits to humans who engaged in long-term pair-bonding, as it offered assured and perhaps exclusive sexual access for the male and resources from the male (what evolutionary biologists call "parental investment") to the female and to their children. In this way, humans are not fundamentally different from a number of other related species. Long-term pair bonding makes life better for both the adults and the children with respect to their ability to bear and raise children but in the narrowest of biological terms. However, all of this pair-bonding, and even the earliest ritualized forms of marriage, took place in a social context where the tribal band was the foundational political and economic unit, not the individual marital dyads within it. Our modern notion of a married couple existing as a distinct and fundamental social unit that, along with other such couples, produced the emergent outcome of social order is just that: modern. The reverse was nearer the truth, as the marital dyads of prehistory were the *product* of the larger social group, not the constituent parts thereof.[8]

It was also true that there was a general sexual division of labor in the Paleolithic world, based largely on the superior physical ability of males to engage in some hunting activities, but the relevant unit of analysis was not the individual couple rather the group as a whole. That is, individual females were not dependent on their individual male mates for the products of the hunt, rather females as a whole were dependent on males as a whole for them. In turn, males were dependent on females for the things they specialized in, which included the production of clothing and other food-related tasks. This specialization by gender, as does all specialization and exchange, led to interdependence between males and females (again, as a whole). It also provided an incentive for individual couples to stay together for extended periods of time as, in a process like the pin factory described by Adam Smith, this specialization led to increased productivity and greater complexity of technique, requiring more time for parents to teach them to their offspring (Coontz 2005, p. 38). Marriage can fruitfully be understood as one of the first methods of generating social cooperation through the division of labor and exchange in human history. Not only did it lead to greater cooperation across groups, it allowed for the division of labor and the resulting social cooperation within groups as well. As an early form of exchange between groups, marriage is arguably the start of the process of the evolution of social cooperation that Mises identifies in his discussion of the Law of Association.

## The Premodern Family as an Economic Organization

The development of sedentary agriculture profoundly transformed humanity in a number of ways, including the institution of the family. The opening discussion of this chapter noted the way in which agriculture led to the division of labor and exchange via specialization as increasingly central elements of human society. Agricultural specialization and exchange required the complementary development of early forms of private property and basic legal institutions to ensure the successful use of exchange as an economic allocation process. The extension of the division of labor, and the rising level of wealth that accompanied it, made it possible for the marital dyad to separate itself geographically and economically from the community and to establish itself as the constituent institution of the social order. Though this is not the nuclear family of modernity, it does represent an important shift from the community to the family as the basic economic and, in many ways, political unit of the social world. Another way to see this is that individual families began to take on functions that were previously those of the band/tribe/community as a whole. Importantly, taking on those functions did not mean the family was immune from the community's intervention and oversight. Quite the contrary: the very importance to the community of the functions that had now devolved to the family meant that its stake in the family's activities was as great as ever. Although families were beginning to live separately and function as units with their own standing, what marked most of them off from the rest of the community was more like a line in the sand than a castle wall.

With family-based agriculture and exchange came the distinction between production activities done for the market and those done for the household, which together comprise the economic functions of the family. The line between these two forms of production was not as clear as it often is today, but analytically the distinction was relevant. As families began to specialize, each one had to make use of market exchanges to acquire the goods and services they could not provide for themselves. The labor time families devoted to producing goods and services that they would sell to others can be understood as market production, while the labor time spent on providing goods and services for the members of the family and the rest of the household is what we now call household production. Families who earned market incomes by selling crops surely used some of what they grew for their own consumption, which makes it difficult to determine precisely whether any specific investment of labor time was intended for one purpose or the other. Nonetheless, it was clear that both tasks had to get done, whether the household was growing crops or engaging in small crafts. Although the particular tasks and balance between them have undergone constant change since then, the family today must still organize itself in a way such that it can engage in both forms of production.

Economically, families in the preindustrial era can be fruitfully understood in terms close to how we might analyze firms today. Members of the household, which likely included not just mom, dad, and children, but extended family members and possibly servants or others, were seen as assets for the household's productive activities. Those assets were in the control of the male head of the household, as women, and somewhat later only married women, were often prohibited from owning land or being a party to a contract. Wives and children were expected to contribute to production activities, with children working the fields as soon as they were able to do so in a meaningful way. Within the household, wives split their time between the activities associated with child care and general household management activities such as food and cleanliness. Edward Shorter (1975, p. 68) offers a list of the different productive activities men and women typically engaged in in preindustrial France. As he comments, "Farm women were active in the fields as well as within the home." His list contains an equal number of outside the home tasks for men and women (though the tasks typically did not overlap) but far fewer for men inside the home.[9] As we saw in Paleolithic families, there was a gendered division of labor in preindustrial times, but that division was not one between market and household production. Rather, it was a division by task, with both genders contributing at least something to both forms of production.

Marriage created a new unit of production as well as the context in which new producers (children) could be created. In hunter/gatherer and agricultural societies, labor to collect or grow food was the basic necessity and the family as a structure for the inheritance of the land to grow food on was equally important. Children filled several important functions within the economic unit of the family. First, having children was the most convenient way to augment the labor force and increase the family's ability to generate income, though hardly without serious risks to women. Obviously, this came at a cost, both in terms of the direct resources required to feed, clothe, and house children and in terms of the opportunity cost in terms of market production of the labor devoted to the marginal quantity of household production time required to care for children.

This trade-off was especially steep while children were very young and less so as children aged, with economies of scale implying declining marginal and average costs of caring for additional children as they aged.

The second important economic function of children was as a form of old-age insurance. The physical nature of work in the centuries before industrialization meant that most humans, especially men doing the most taxing work, had a limited number of productive years (assuming they were able to avoid death by disease or accident). Provisioning for old age was an important consideration in a time long before institutionalized forms of savings or redistribution. Having a large number of children was one way to try to ensure a flow of resources when one's productive years were done. Though there remains much debate on how much the net flow of resources was from children to parents as opposed to parents to children, it was assumed that one or more of one's children would take in their parents when necessary. Having a large number of male children was even more desirable, as they would be more likely to own property and have control over the household, both of which would increase their ability to provide for elderly parents. In return, elderly parents who were taken in were still expected to contribute at least to household production in one form or another, with child care being the most important, given the lower opportunity cost of an older grandparent caring for children versus a younger and healthier mother or older siblings.

Finally, it should be noted that in a time of very high rates of infant and child mortality, having an acceptably large number of children live long enough to be productive likely required a very large number of pregnancies. Many women, especially peasant women, found themselves constantly either pregnant or nursing, both of which would come at the cost of their being able to work the fields. Moreover, the rate of maternal mortality during pregnancy and childbirth was fairly high, which was an additional cost to be considered in weighing the decision to have additional children. Unfortunately, women's preferences did not usually matter that much in these decisions.

The centrality of the family's economic functions meant that even parent-child relationships were often seen in crudely economic terms. As Shorter (1975, p. 5) describes it: "While a residual affection between mother and child . . . has always existed . . . in traditional society the mother had [to be] prepared to place many considerations—most of them related to the desperate struggle for existence—above the infant's welfare." This is but another way of noting the high opportunity cost of maternal time. Having extended family members present helped free up the mother's time especially in poorer, rural families. Shorter documents another strategy that poorer mothers sometimes used, which was to simply leave their children alone for very long stretches of time, not only leaving them "to stew in their own excrement for hours on end," but also making them vulnerable to death by fire or being attacked by wild animals (pp. 170–71). In some cases, parents simply abandoned children altogether when the costs of caring for them exceeded their expected (and discounted) future contributions to household output.[10] In a world of extreme scarcity, Prudence must go where Love would fear to tread.

Another way that many of these poorer women juggled the challenge of the need for survival and caring for their own children was by serving as wet-nurses for the children of more urbanized small craftsmen and service providers. As Flandrin (1979, p. 204) notes, the wives of the townsmen of preindustrial France were also needed to help run the family's shop no less so than the rural wives were needed in the fields. But their somewhat better economic circumstances enabled them to pay other women to nurse their children, roles gladly filled by poorer rural women who saw it as a way to earn income and take advantage of economies of scale in child care and potentially reduce their own fertility and risk of maternal death through the contraceptive effects of lactation.[11] Unfortunately, the conditions under which wet-nursing took place were abhorrent by modern standards. Children were left alone for long periods there as well, and fairly mercenary wet-nurses were often trying to provide nutrition for more children than their bodies could handle, especially given the diets of most poorer households. To the degree they could produce a decent supply of milk, they invariably fed their own children first. Bedding was infrequently changed, and children were rushed to solid food so that new ones could be taken in. Both Shorter (1975) and Flandrin (1979) offer data on the high rates of mortality associated with infants put out to wet-nurse, which in many areas of France was well above 50 percent in the eighteenth century and between 25 and 50 percent in the early nineteenth.

If conditions were so awful, why do it then? Little labor could be spared for the care of infants when sheer survival required all available hands to work the land to feed the rest of the family. What appears as indifference to the plight of their own children was simply a calculated risk-lowering strategy for maximizing the potential for survival for the family as a whole.[12] Flandrin (1979, p. 205) argues:

> Generally speaking, the women . . . all had, in former times, an important role to play in the economy of the household; if they were unable to fulfill it, the entire family business ran the risk of collapsing . . . Nor could the economic function of households, which impeded the development of the affective function . . . be put aside, even temporarily, as a result of the needs of the reproductive function.

There has been a long-standing debate over the question of whether preindustrial parents loved their children the way modern parents do. There is clear evidence that children were treated in ways that modern parents would never engage in, yet there is also substantial evidence from historical documents, as well as art and literature, that demonstrates both parental and spousal love.[13] Earlier work, such as Shorter's, made a strong case for the greater indifference of parents, while Stone (1977) and Ozment (1983), as well as more recent research, suggest that this parental detachment was not as clear-cut as Shorter argues. All agree that childhood, including the death of children, was dealt with very differently from the postindustrial era.

A better explanation is that the point is not that parents did not *feel* love for their children, but that the very real resource constraints they faced made it difficult for them to *express* that love in the way modern families, at least in the developed world, can. In the language of economics, it is not that modern parents have different preferences with respect to loving their children but that they operate under far less binding constraints in how they might be able to satisfy those preferences. In other words, parents have always loved their children, but in the marginal subsistence world predating modernity, expressing that love more frequently came at a cost higher than they were able to bear. To indulge their desire to love would have risked their sheer survival, as Flandrin noted. Again, Prudence took precedence over Love. As we will see later, when the wealth produced by the advent of capitalism and industrialization raised living standards and reduced family sizes, it lowered the cost of expressing those parental sentiments, and the sentiments poured forth both between parents and children and in the marital dyad itself.

It was not only children whose lives were subject to narrowly economic considerations. Similar calculative decisions characterized the husband-wife relationship as well. Husbands remained both the de jure and de facto ruler of the household, putting wives in a situation not all that different from other household assets that contributed to both market and household production, and whose allocation was largely at the whim of the husband. To a significant degree, wives were not necessarily as valuable as other household assets as they were cheaper to replace. Shorter (1975, p. 57) notes that peasant husbands were much more likely to call for medical help when their cattle got ill than when their wives did, as one could always find a new wife cheaply, but a good cow or bull would be very expensive to replace. Coontz (2005) nicely summarizes the way in which marriage was intertwined with work by referring to married couples as "yoke-mates" rather than "soul-mates." The use of the word "mates" should not imply any sort of equality. Rather their relationship was driven by the fact that their partnership, however unequal, was first and foremost based on their ability to engage in economic production together. Love would come later, as the struggle for survival did not allow for sentiment to dominate the economic and the Prudential: "But in most cases, marriage was still a matter of practical calculation rather than an arrangement entered into for individual fulfillment and the pursuit of happiness" (p. 65). As Ozment (1983, p. 59) puts it: "the love that drew husband and wife together was a mutual willingness to make sacrifices for one another, hence a duty that developed within marriage." In more modern terms, married couples learned to love each other after having married for other reasons.[14]

The economics of the decision to marry were largely a matter of creating a complementary combination of human and physical capital (usually land) with respect to the dual tasks of market and household production. At the most general level, a marriage can be understood as formulating a production plan for household and market production that involves two sets of human and physical capital that the couple imagines will be complementary toward that end. It is to that extent parallel to what the entrepreneur does in assembling the various financial, physical, and human inputs she imagines necessary to produce a good for sale on the market. Courtship can be understood as a process of determining both what the outputs of any joint production process might be and whether the spouses are good complementary fits toward those ends. In our own time, these complementarities are much more a matter of consumption preferences rather than human capital strictly speaking, mostly because marriage is not as central for the earning of income as it was in the past. And in a much wealthier world, physical capital plays a relatively smaller role than in times past. Of course differences in skills and preferences still do exist, but even where more production-oriented complementarities are relevant, complementary preferences about consumption activities are vastly more important than centuries ago.[15]

The complementarity involved in the premodern marriage, especially among the much more numerous peasantry, was not the strict sexual division of labor that would characterize marriages in the period after industrialization (i.e., women specializing in the household and men in the market). With both spouses doing at least some of both sorts of work, finding a good match required different criteria. Given the thin margin of survival on which most of the population has rested throughout human history until the last couple of centuries, and given that the families based on the marital dyad were the site of market production for the thousands of years between the advent of agriculture and the flowering of industrialization, it should come as no surprise that the decision to marry was of necessity a calculation about the ability of the partnership to engage in economic production rather than forge an emotional connection.

In the more simple economy of the premodern world, these calculations were fairly simple as well. The range of economically productive skills that any individual might have was very narrow, thus making prospective marriage partners fairly undifferentiated and therefore close substitutes for one another. All else equal, this lowered the costs of marriage by reducing the search costs for a good match, even where productive ability was the key. By contrast, in our own world where matches are about the complementarity of consumption preferences more than production-related human capital, and where such preferences are much more complex in a developed economy, the costs of finding a good match are much higher. This might help to explain why the secular rise in the average age of marriage parallels the increasing wealth and complexity of the economy. It also explains the popularity in our own time of web-based matchmakers such as eharmony.com or match.com, as they dramatically reduce the much higher costs of meeting the much higher threshold of an acceptable match. As Georg Simmel (1978 [1907], p. 381) observed a century ago: "The declining frequency of marriage which is to be found everywhere in highly civilized cultural circumstances is undoubtedly due, in part, to the fact that highly differentiated people in general have difficulty in finding a completely sympathetic complement to themselves."[16] Simmel's concept of differentiation corresponds to the idea that modern individuals are more different from one another than were premoderns. Those differences exist in both productive human capital and consumption preferences, with the latter being much more important to marriage in our own time.[17]

The role of sex in premodern marriage, not to mention sexual behavior more generally, remains a matter of much controversy, given the challenges of finding accurate data. What we do know with some confidence is that fertility rates and population rise as modernity approaches. Abelove (1989) infers from demographic data that this is because vaginal intercourse became increasingly popular over the course of the "long eighteenth century." If so, this suggests two further possibilities: either people simply engaged in less sexual activity in general prior to this period, or they engaged in a variety of nonprocreative activity that gradually shifted to vaginal intercourse as modernity approached. Abelove argues for the latter interpretation, and historical sources of the time, from literature to Pepys's diary, certainly indicate that people were engaging in a wide range of sexual activity. What does seem more certain is that as families began to have more resources, the costs of procreation would fall, which might explain an increase in vaginal intercourse.[18] Once again, premodern families were trying to indulge their preferences as best they could in a world of much more binding constraints than we face today. As those constraints shifted, it is no surprise that sexual behavior changed as well.[19]

## The Political Dimensions of the Premodern Family

The premodern family's functions were not only economic. At least among the better-off, the family had important political functions as well. And for almost all families for most of human history, there was no wall of separation between the family and the local community and the combination of church and state that made up the political institutions of premodernity. In this section, I take a brief look at both the direct political functions of premodern families and the ways in which such families were under the watchful eyes and coercive controls of the community, church, and state.

Among the wealthy, marriages were mostly about politics and increasing the family's control over economic resources, especially land, through what amounted to mergers of powerful families. The discussion of the Paleolithic past pointed out the ways in which marriage served to create alliances out of strangers as far back as marriage has existed. This was both economic, as it provided access to new resources via trade, and political, as it reduced intergroup tensions and provided for networks of common defense against other outside groups. As marital dyad-based families separated from early tribal bands and struck out on their own, and as early forms of market production changed the economy, and the various forms of monarchy and oligarchy dominated the polity, important differences arose between the marital practices of those in the middle and lower classes and those with more resources and political power. Coontz (2005, p. 69) summarizes this difference: "For thousands of years, beginning in the earliest civilizations, the economic functions of marriage were far more important to the middle and lower classes than were its personal satisfactions, while among the upper classes, the political functions of marriage took first place." For the few that were well off, Prudence was about power; for everyone else, it was about ensuring economic survival.

Parents of the well-off exercised a great deal of control over marriage decisions, perhaps even more so than among the poorer classes, as both the political and economic stakes were high. Those with wealth and power used marriage as a strategy to enhance large land holdings or to create military alliances with neighboring rulers: "In all [of the ancient world], kings, pharaohs, emperors, and nobles relied on personal and family ties to recruit and reward followers, make alliances, and establish their legitimacy. Marriage was one of the key mechanisms through with such ties were forged" (Coontz 2005, p. 53). In line with the view that marriage turned strangers into kin and thus enhanced trust, rulers of the ancient world saw marriage, of both their sons and daughters, as key ways to attempt to extend their political power or to check that of an enemy. So many of our most ancient stories involve the intrigues of the intersection of marriage and power, from the Hebrew Bible to Ancient Egypt to Greece and Rome to the Middle Ages and the Shakespearean plays, not to mention fairy tales and children's stories such as *Cinderella*. Many of these are also stories of the tension between marriages arranged for the power and economic interests of the parents and the affection, or lack thereof, between the betrothed. Stories of sons or daughters of nobility or royalty "needing" to be married by a certain date reflect these themes as well.[20]

One of the things that both the wealthy and poor had in common with respect to marriage was that their marital choices and the success of marriages mattered greatly for many others around them. Later, we will see what this meant for the peasantry. For the wealthy, extended family members clearly cared greatly about the who and how of marriages, as marital success affected the family's continued access to wealth and power and, potentially, the ability to pass that wealth down to future generations. To say that marriages were arranged is not to say that only parents made such choices for their children. There were numerous other stakeholders, from extended family to rival political actors to potential other spouses to the Church. The high stakes of marriage also explains why so many rulers asserted the right to control the marriage of their nonkin subjects. Many ancient rulers used their ability to veto marriages of their subjects as a political tool to keep themselves in power in the face of potential marriage-generated alliances against them. Overdoing this, however, put them at risk of being overthrown for it, so many walked a very careful line in exercising this power.

One institution in the West that exercised a great deal of power over marriage and family was the Catholic Church. Over the course of the Middle Ages, the Church slowly built up a set of rules governing marriage and family that put significant limits on the freedom of individuals to marry and organize families in ways they wished. Given the state-like role of canon law, violating these rules and prohibitions was a serious matter. The four major areas the Church regulated were: marriage to kin, marriage to widows of close kin, adoption, and the taking of concubines as a secondary marriage. In all four cases, the Church set very strict limits or outright prohibited these practices and these provided a context for the family choices of persons in that era. All of these regulations can be understood to be means toward a particular end. As

Jack Goody (1983) argues, the Church used these rules as a way to regulate the inheritance and distribution of property such that it would be harder to keep property in families and more likely that property would be transferred to the Church. In Goody's words: "If they [the Church] inhibited the possibilities of a family retaining its property, then they would also facilitate its alienation" (p. 45). He then goes on to document the increase in the Church's landholdings during the era of its enforcement of those limitations on family choices. In contemporary terms, these political regulations on family were "rent-seeking" devices by Church leaders to transfer wealth and control over property from the populace to the Church.

The Church created elaborate rules involving the degree of kinship that marked the point within which marriage was not acceptable. In our own time, first or second cousins tends to be the legal boundary beyond which marriage is acceptable. But under the Church's authority, that boundary was set at a much farther degree of kinship. By 800 CE, the Church had prohibited marriages "up to the seventh degree of separation," meaning that one could not marry "a descendant of one's great-great-great-great-great-grandfather" (Coontz 2005, p. 98; see also the discussion in Goody [1983, p. 134] where he also notes the differences in how degrees of kinship were calculated in different parts of Europe). It was also illegal to marry step-relatives and god-relatives of a close degree. As Coontz and others note, none of these rules have a basis in the Hebrew Bible or New Testament. Instead, they served as a way to prevent families from accumulating wealth and power by forcing people to marry both outside any vague notion of kin and to search for marital partners in other geographic locations. In reality, however, these rules were largely unenforceable as providing evidence of degrees of kinship was difficult, and the Church cared a lot less about the peasantry's choices so largely let them be.

In addition, the Church itself allowed people to get around the prohibitions through the sale of dispensations or by simply granting exemptions for marriages that served the Church's own interest. The Church thereby benefitted both from enforcing the law when convenient (by keeping land and power divided) and earning income when it decided to allow a violation. Both Goody and Coontz note that these laws "appear to have been made only to be broken" (Goody 1983, p. 145). The complex set of incest rules also gave the Church potential arguments for invalidating any marriage, which in turn effectively gave it the power to decide the validity of any marriage it wished to pass judgment on. This was a significant degree of power to have, given the economic and political stakes involved in premodern marriages. Rules that are unenforceable and therefore applied arbitrarily normally result from their being intended to benefit the ruler in the first place.[21]

The limits on marriage to widows of close kin grew out of objections to the Judaic practice of levirate marriages, whereby a childless widow would be required to marry the brother of her deceased husband. The Church eventually banned this practice as a form of incest, even though it was not relevantly different from the original marriage. What was the gain from this ban? For one, levirate marriage was a strategy for keeping property in a family. By the brother marrying the childless widow, the dead husband's lands remain in the control of his family. In prohibiting levirate marriages, the Church was banking on either creating more long-term widows by reducing the likelihood of remarriage or ensuring that any remarriage led to a wider distribution of land. The result was often more the first than the second. The advantage to the Church of widowhood was that it could care for these women and then, when they died, take possession of their land. In other cases, these women set up religious houses, often nunneries, which became part of the Church's holdings as well. More generally, anything that increased the number of childless widows, such as the prohibition on levirate marriages, was in the Church's economic self-interest.

The Church generally objected to practices that involved shifting children between households. It long opposed wet-nursing, though ineffectively, and it tolerated the practice of "fostering," whereby children were raised in the houses of kin, often temporarily and on a reciprocal basis,[22] but it strongly prohibited adoption for nearly 1,500 years (Goody 1983, p. 68). Adoption differed from the other two practices by virtue of it being a legal procedure rather than a social custom. By creating a child through the law rather than blood, parents created an heir for themselves that they would not have otherwise. This explains the Church's concern with the practice: like levirate marriage, adoption was a strategy for creating an heir when a property owner had no biological children.[23] If the Church could effectively prohibit adoption, it would increase the chances that the married couple's land might end up in its hands, as other charitable options were few.

The taking of concubines, a form of informal marriage with a second or even third wife and her children living with the legal husband and wife, had a long history in the societies of the Hebrew Bible as well as others. The children of concubines did have the right to inherit from the father even given the lower status of the concubine compared to the legal wife. In fact, Goody (1983, p. 76) argues that one of the rationales for concubinage was the lack of an heir for the legally married couple. Again, the ability to keep property within the family was connected with a particular family practice that the Church went to great lengths to outlaw. The Church ruled that the concubine was a mistress and the children were bastards, thus cutting off any legal claim they had to inheritance. The result was that the Church again made it more likely that it would acquire the lands of childless couples.[24] All of these Church-imposed restrictions on marriage and family choices can be understood, at least to a significant degree, as an attempt to redistribute wealth in its favor. Under such constraints, marital and family choices were hardly free. It would take the economic and political changes associated with classical liberalism (and its immediate precursors) to start to wrest control of such choices away from the Church and the state.

Outside of the ways in which the Church used the power of the law to limit the choices available for organizing families, local communities, including parents, also did so using both formal and informal methods. For much of the premodern era, marriages, even among the peasantry, frequently involved a high degree of parental involvement, though in later times this began to vary more as the Catholic Church gave children more freedom of choice than did the Anglicans or various Protestant denominations (Flandrin 1979, pp. 131–32). Although marriages might not necessarily be "arranged" in a strict sense, parents, especially fathers, had a large role in deciding who was or was not acceptable as a marital partner for their children. The rationale for parental involvement was simply that the political and economic implications of marriage were both large and not confined to the married couple. Who a child married had spillover effects on the parents and extended family. Flandrin captures this nicely:

> [I]n a society in which marriage had the effective and avowed function of perpetuating the "house" and of ensuring honorable matrimonial alliances for it, it was normal that the master of the house should assume the responsibility for the marriages. Besides, each marriage implied financial agreements which concerned not only the two spouses but all the members of their families of origin. (p. 132)

Parental power here was not unlimited, but it was very strong. As so many works of literature attest, the struggle between parental wishes and the marital desires of their children was a major drama through much of human history.

One historical change that did give individuals somewhat more choice before the arrival of the modern family was that, eventually, mutual consent slowly began to replace parental preference as the necessary condition for a marriage. Because the Church eventually recognized marriage by the consent of the partners, it was possible for a couple to be married in the eyes of the Church if they successfully escaped their parents' watchful eyes and were willing to risk the wrath of the community for violating the norm of parentally approved marriage. However, as Coontz (2005, p. 117–18) points out, given the economic and political functions of marriage for all social classes and the implications they had for extended family, "people generally believed it would be foolish to make such a momentous decision entirely on their own... Marriage usually grew out of a collaboration among parents, friends, and the two individuals involved, and it was often based on very practical considerations." Even as the consent of the betrothed became a relevant consideration, it hardly ended the community's interest in the marriage. In addition, it is important to distinguish consent from affection. Couples could agree to marry of their own volition because they recognized the value of the economic partnership that they would create.

Because the economic and political stakes of marriage were so high for peasant families, the community had a significant interest in both the formation of families and their continuance. In perhaps the most extreme recognition of the community's interest in family formation, the Massachusetts colony "even had laws prohibiting unmarried adults from living outside family units" (D'Emilio 1993, p. 470). The community had certain "expectations" for the family and along with those expectations came monitoring from the community. More generally, the notion of the private, self-contained nuclear family that we associate with modern times was not to be found, especially among the common folks. Members of the community would monitor couples for adultery or for either one abandoning their responsibilities in the household and/or farm. The rationale for that interference was not a kind of paternalism toward the married couple, but rather a (correct) understanding that the success of any individual family could not be isolated from the success of the community as a whole. At the edge of survival, the community was in some sense only as strong as its weakest link. Shorter (1975, pp. 63–64) summarizes this well:

> What counted... was not the quality of the couple's intimate life... but how well the couple performed the tasks that life imposed on them. What was important was doing the essential work of the society: grinding the grain, transmitting the property from generation to generation in an orderly way, clothing and feeding the members of the family sufficiently so that they wouldn't become a burden to the rest of the community.

The major economic and political functions of the premodern family, not to mention the centrality of ensuring children were raised to adulthood, were all in service of ensuring the survival and growth of the community as a whole. Marriages and families were not primarily about meeting the needs of parents or children in and of themselves, rather they were first and foremost instruments for the needs of the broader community, which in turn gave the community the right to impose various expectations on those families.

When families, or individual members, failed to live up to those community expectations, the community intervened, through both legal and extralegal means. Premodern societies were full of legal penalties for all kinds of behavior that today are largely or increasingly beyond the reach of the law. Prohibitions on adultery, especially female adultery, were strong as were laws against fornication, and punishment for adultery was severe, including, at least on the books in some parts of the world, death. In fact, Massachusetts law in the 1630s defined adultery as "sexual relations between a man and a married woman." Any other combination of sexual activity outside of marriage, either between a married man and a single woman or two singles, was viewed as the somewhat lesser crime of "fornication" (D'Emilio and Freedman 1988, p. 28). The focus on married women had to do with ensuring that children were conceived within marriage so that the father could be clearly identified for the purposes of property distribution. This important political function explains the more severe punishment of female adultery. An adulterous wife who became pregnant now carried a child whose father was uncertain. This created complications for a legal system that was based on male property ownership passed down to their biological sons.

It also meant that the husband would potentially have to raise and expend resources on a child not his own. Posner (1992, p. 184) argues that the desire to avoid the imposition of external costs on a cuckolded husband explains the higher punishments for female adultery through most of human history. From an evolutionary perspective, human social groups that did not punish female adultery in this way risked serious confusion about paternity that, in the extreme, might lead to a withdrawal of necessary parental investment by males. Where paternity cannot be reliably established, child-raising can quickly become a kind of tragedy of the commons where no male has any incentive to invest in the children his wife bears. Marriage and a social norm of monogamy, especially for women, can be seen as attempts to privatize the commons and create incentives for male parental investment. This analysis would be particularly true at a time when overall levels of wealth were low and opportunities for women to acquire the resources necessary to raise children without a male present were limited. The relaxation of this norm and the lack of legal penalties for adultery in our own time reflect the near-disappearance of these wealth and gender role constraints.

Prohibitions on nonprocreative sex (sodomy laws) even among heterosexuals were another form of communal legal intervention, in this case designed to channel sexual activity into producing children as they were the labor necessary to maintain the community politically and economically. Colonial America provides an excellent example of this point, as sodomy was defined in terms of the nonprocreativity of the acts rather than the participants, with the exception in most places of sexual relations between two women, which were punished less severely with different terminology (e.g., "lewd behavior"). Oral or anal sex between a married couple was an act of sodomy, as was any sexual activity between two males. Although the death penalty was available under stringent conditions, it was rarely applied. Nonetheless, the severity of the lesser punishments, which could include "whipping, burning with a hot iron, or banishment," might discourage the behavior, at least on the margin (D'Emilio and Freedman 1988, p. 30). What the adultery and sodomy laws together did was to send the message that those in power thought that all sexual activity was to take place within marriage and to be about procreation and not pleasure for its own sake. Given the centrality of the economic and political functions of the family (as opposed to the more modern emphasis on the happiness of the couple) and the degree to which the community relied on individual families to fulfill those functions, these set of regulations, onerous as they were, could be understood as a rational response to the circumstances.

There is, of course, a difference between the intent of the law and its actual effectiveness. As noted earlier, the historical evidence suggests that the premodern era was full of a variety of sexual activity, even if the types of activity being engaged were of a different mix than today. All these attempts by the community to intervene met with limited success as people simply found ways around the laws, as they often have with other attempts to punish victimless crimes.

Of course divorce was difficult to impossible as well, except among the most privileged or wealthy, and even if it were available, it was difficult for women to survive on their own. Even as consent of the spouses became more of a consideration, the constraints on leaving a marriage freely consented to became tighter, thanks mostly to the Church on one hand and the continued lack of opportunities for unmarried women on the other. Coontz (2005, p. 108) notes that by the twelfth century, the Church made no "provision for divorce at all," although it did allow "judicial separation" for adultery, a partner's heresy, or (very) extreme cruelty. Even here, however, neither of the separated parties could remarry (Stone 1977, p. 37). As with other laws that attempt to stop a practice that seems unlikely to disappear, the public found ways around the legal prohibitions on divorce. The most common was to request an annulment on the grounds that one or the other of the married parties had already consented to a marriage with another partner. This was easy enough to fake if a separation was really desired, and annulment had the advantage of making it possible to remarry. Of course the death of a spouse allowed for remarriage and step-parents and step-children were all too common in the centuries before industrialization, as disease and childbirth were much more frequent causes of death at a young age.[25]

Enforcement of both the formal legal restrictions and informal norms of marital behavior fell upon members of the community: "The regulation of adultery, like all forms of nonmarital sexuality, depended on extensive involvement of community members in each other's lives" (D'Emilio and Freedman 1988, p. 29). In the case of the laws against adultery, fornication, and sodomy, often witnesses were required, at least for the worst of the crimes and to get the maximum punishment. Recognizing the reasons for such laws, community members were all too ready to provide the requisite testimony if the circumstances arose. D'Emilio and Freedman offer some examples from Puritan America of the sorts of testimony and intrusiveness that were seen as the responsibility of the community, both to religious purity and the enforcement of the law (the difference between which was not always clear) (pp. 28–29).[26] For the legal restrictions on people's marital, sexual, and familial choices to have any effectiveness, this degree of communal involvement was a necessity. What it illustrates vividly is the degree to which the law offered no defense of what we would now call the privacy of the family. Given the family's economic and political importance to the broader community, the family had to be seen not as a private unit out of which societies were built, but an entity created by, and constantly under the watchful eye of, the community as a whole.

The most common extralegal form of community monitoring was the charivaris of peasant Europe. A charivari was "a noisy public demonstration to subject wayward individuals to humiliation in the eyes of the community" (Shorter 1975, pp. 218–27; see also Flandrin 1979, pp. 124–26; and Coontz 2005, pp. 111–12). A variety of violations of community expectations were subject to the charivari treatment, including married men who impregnated single women, men whose wives had committed adultery but not the wives (on the grounds that he had lost control over her and the household), marital matches that did not meet the community's notion of appropriateness (e.g., wide divergence of ages), and couples who did not follow any number of customary wedding-related practices. The husbands of adulterers or men who took on female roles were especially vulnerable targets for the charivari treatment as keeping control over the household was central in a world where the male head of household was the key political actor and where the thin margin of survival required a well-ordered household. One common practice was to parade such men around facing backward on a donkey. The charivari had no legal status, rather it was simply a very strong informal mechanism for enforcing community standards. The nearest analogy in modern times might be the way in which community groups put up posters when a sex offender moves into a neighborhood.[27]

## Conclusion

What all of these various ways in which the Church, the law, and the community restricted people's choices about marriage, sexuality, and family, and intervened in their lives to enforce those restrictions, amounted to was a very different relationship between the family and the political world than that of the twenty-first-century West. The central importance of the family as an economic and political unit made these sorts of political and community interventions into its operation to be both unsurprising to us upon reflection and accepted by most of those who they affected. Until the late eighteenth or early nineteenth century, the family, like the economy and the polity more generally, was not an arena in which individuals had much scope for independent action through which they could carve emotionally meaningful lives of their own. All of the psychological and emotional importance that the family carries with it today is peculiar to the last one or two hundred years of human history. The family could only become a site to satisfy those needs when it shed its economic and political functions. Prudence had to be displaced for Love to come to center stage more consistently. The advent of capitalism (and to a lesser extent democracy) began that process of transformation.

One of the great benefits of history is that it is often a very effective cure for our nostalgia by deromanticizing the supposed golden ages of years gone by. This is especially true with respect to the worlds before and after capitalism. As McCloskey (2006, p. 141) writes about life in premodern villages, with their high murder rates and other problems of the precapitalist era:

> The century-and-a-half-old premise among anticapitalists is that we have through capitalism lost a good world worth keeping. But evidence . . . assembled by generations of social historians . . . is overwhelming. The historians have found that the *Gemeinschaft* of olden times was defective . . . Love, in short, is arguably thicker on the ground in the modern, Western capitalist world.

There is very little if any evidence for the romantic view of precapitalist times, especially with respect to the family. The stifling environment created by the church, community, and state in the premodern era should make us skeptical of claims that "it takes a village" to raise children, especially when those are connected to calls to reinvigorate the state and community's intervention into families. The world where "the village" saw monitoring the functionality of families as a collective responsibility was hardly a vision of sweetness and light. The precapitalist village was no less well-intentioned than modern child advocates, and there's not much reason to think that family privacy and individual freedom, not to mention the well-being of children, would survive the reinvigoration of a collectivist view of child-raising. As we will see, capitalism and the freedom from state and community control it brought with it made the modern family and its privacy and scope for individual choice possible. Attempting to undo those advances, even in the name of protecting "the children," is bound to recreate the worst aspects of the premodern family environment, no matter how good are the intentions of those exercising such power.

CHAPTER 4

# Capitalism and the Emergence of the Modern Family

## Introduction

As I argued in the last chapter, the preindustrial family was first and foremost an economic and political institution and only secondarily a place for humans to realize emotional and psychological aspirations. Yes, such families had a place for Love, but Prudence remained the overriding concern thanks to the constraints that poverty put on the expression of love. As such, there was no major distinction for our ancient ancestors between the two worlds of the micro-orders and the Great Society, as the latter had not yet fully emerged. With politics and economics so intertwined with the functions of the family and household, it was not surprising to find that the community, in the formal laws and rules of both the state and the Church, as well as through informal institutions such as the charivari, was very much involved with the day-to-day life of the family. The community's survival depended very heavily on families and their members living up to the social obligations of tradition. Deviating from those obligations could not be, and was not, a private choice when the consequences for third parties were so salient.

For the family to break away from the control of the community and the state and begin to form what we would now call the nuclear, private family, the degree to which the community as a whole depended on the family as an economic organization would have to be dramatically reduced. If the overall level of wealth were to rise to such an extent that fewer people and communities were living on the margin of survival, decisions about marriage and family would have much lower stakes for the community as a whole, making it possible for individuals to increasingly indulge their own choices. If this increase in wealth were to occur as a result of the family/household losing its central role as the fundamental unit of market production, it would reinforce that process of separation from the community and also enable the family to acquire new functions to replace those lost in the shift in economic organization. Prudence would recede, leaving more space for Love. In fact, this is more or less what happened as capitalism and the industrialization process, and the increase in wealth that came with them, transformed the nature of economic production in ways that had profound implications for the family, unmooring it from its deep ties to the fate of the community as a whole and making possible the modern, nuclear family unit.

## The Industrial Revolution and the Demise of the Economic Functions of the Family

Because agriculture and small craft work both involved the household as the site of production with family members serving as the labor, economic survival in the preindustrial age meant, for the overwhelming majority of the population, that one had to be part of a family-based household. For the great many who did not or could not own land, families survived by working lands owned by others with their labor still structured by the household. By the mid- to late eighteenth century, this began to change. A number of factors coalesced around this time to constitute what is normally referred to as the Industrial Revolution. This term is something of a misnomer on both counts: it was not a revolution if by that one means a very quick change in the nature of economic activity. And it was also not primarily industrial, in that industrialization in and of itself was not the only, and perhaps not the primary, causal factor in what Julian Simon (2000) called "The Great Breakthrough" in the expansion of productivity, economic growth, and human well-being.[1]

The fundamental transformation of work that began to take place was that wage labor slowly supplanted agriculture and household-based small crafts as the dominant way income was earned through market production. Though it was hardly the only form wage labor took, the factory system was an important part of this process. As some producers managed to acquire larger profits and as technological advances made mechanized, larger-scale production possible, factories arose as new, more efficient, ways to organize market production. In contrast to the structure of the household-based economy, where those who produced for the market applied means of production that they owned along with their labor and that of their household, factory work separated the ownership of the means of production from those who did the actual work with the means of production. Rather than the farmer or small crafts manufacturer who owned his ox and plow or his blacksmith tools, factories put the ownership of the means of production in the hands of those who built the factory and provided the equipment for production. And rather than labor in one's own home or shop or lands, factories required that people leave the physical household in order to work. Instead of controlling the production process from beginning to end themselves and reaping the profits or losses thereof, factory workers, in contrast to farmers or small craftsmen, were paid either a fixed wage or a piecework rate for the time spent and for output produced using *someone else's* physical capital.

In some cases factory work developed out of the earlier method called "putting out." Putting out involved firms providing households with raw materials for them to turn into finished products, which were then collected by the firms and sold in the market. This work took place in the household and normally involved the entire family in the production process. It was often done alongside agricultural work at times when the lands needed somewhat less attention.[2] What the factory did was to provide even more productive machinery that required more capital than individual families could afford and that could provide employment for more than one household. By moving the machinery out of the household, the factory system was crucial to ending the family's role as a unit of economic production. Some early factories also provided housing on-site for workers, but this practice also faded as factories grew in size and complexity, leading to factory workers having households of their own.

The factory was not the only cause of this change. In many ways, the factory system was an effect of larger explanations for the fundamental changes that took place starting in the later eighteenth century, all of which contributed to other forms of wage labor. Underlying the move to wage labor were the conditions that made its development possible and profitable. Simon (2000) argues that the sine qua non of the Great Breakthrough was population growth. Population had to grow significantly for two conditions to come to pass. First, a larger population made it more likely that new and better ideas would be generated, including those related to technology that made industrial production possible. Second, a larger population created a larger market for the output of new production processes and forms of organization. The insight that the division of labor is limited by the extent of the market is as old as Adam Smith, and the same truth can be put as "an expansion of the extent of the market enables a finer division of labor." The growth in population over the century or two that preceded the Industrial Revolution made possible new forms of organization, from the factory to the joint-stock company, as well as new, more specialized jobs, many of which could not be performed in the home.

More recently, Deirdre McCloskey (2010) has argued that the key factor driving the transition to the modern world of trade and industrialization was a change in how we valued economic activity. Rather than institutional change or population growth per se, McCloskey argues that the way people began to talk and think about the middle class changed, with "ordinary conversation about innovation and markets [becoming] more approving" (p. 7). She claims that "the modern world was made by a new, faithful dignity accorded to the bourgeois," the result of which was the increased willingness of people to innovate and trade, leading to a greater division of labor, industrialization, and humanity finally escaping the centuries of poverty that had been its lot. Whether McCloskey is correct in arguing that these "habits of the lip" were far more important than the institutional factors in driving the transition to the modern world will be the subject of much further debate, but the increased dignity accorded to the bourgeoisie was surely relevant.

A key part of this process was the growth of towns and cities. This growth came from at least two sources. First, the combination of rising population and increased agricultural productivity meant that there were more and more people who needed to find employment somewhere other than on the farm. Although the adjustment process was often difficult, "it is quite clear that the new factories and towns were a large part of the solution to Europe's problem of employing a rising population outside of agriculture" (Rosenberg and Birdzell 1986, p. 147). Second, better means of transportation enabled a larger amount of trade to take place, and towns and cities grew as central sites for such trade, as is clear from most of the early, larger cities being located on the water. As the towns and cities grew, serving the needs of the new urban class created additional opportunities for employment, both due to the wealth that the urban class brought with them and the fact that without the land, equipment, and extended family of the farm household, much that the generation before would do for itself within the household now had to be purchased on the market (e.g., clothing, food, and perhaps renting an apartment). Manufacturing and selling these goods and providing these services involved an increase in the number of people earning a living through wage labor for another who owned the capital, or setting up their own shops in the towns, disconnected from their household. The rising wealth also created new jobs in areas such as education, the arts, and the civil service, which also contributed to the separation of market production from the household.

The increased role of wage labor and the rise of the towns shifted the nature of exchange from the personal to the impersonal. The economy became monetized as more and more transactions took place via money or credit among more anonymous traders than through face-to-face exchanges that did not necessarily make use of the formal monetary institutions of the economy. With economic well-being increasingly dependent on the efforts and reputation of individuals rather than connections based on family, face-to-face personal relationships became less central to economic activity. So too did inheritable property become less important, which weakened any individual's "allegiance to the ancestors of the past and to the inheritors of the future" (Shorter 1975, p. 264). The rise of monetary exchange, the declining role played by family connections in economic production, and the resulting ability of workers to separate work from home "was an enormous leap toward greater personal independence and a less servile status" (Rosenberg and Birdzell 1986, p. 153). The changes in the economic structure and the loss of the market production function of the household had significant effects on the family.

The economic and demographic effects of the advent of capitalism remain nothing short of astounding. McCloskey (2006, Chapter 1) offers a useful condensation of the changes that took place in the nineteenth and twentieth century combined: population increased by a factor of about 6, the amount of goods and services produced and consumed rose by a factor of about 8.5, the adult years that a 16-year-old could expect to live increased by a factor of 2 and for a newborn by a factor of 5. She further argues that if you create a measure of "world adult maturity supplied years" to gauge how many more lives are being lived longer and well, and thus multiply 2 by 8.5 by 6, you get human life improving by a factor of 102, or 9,000 percent. Whatever one thinks of that particular measure, the general point remains that the changes that began in the late eighteenth century kick-started an astounding increase in economic growth and human well-being.

Changes in the political process taking place at the same time ultimately led to the disappearance of most of the political functions of the family. Democracy, by broadening the base of political sovereignty and eliminating the monarchies and oligarchies that ruled much of the world, undermined the linkages between family connections and political power. Modern governments, by providing for the common defense and the protection of rights at various levels of administration, eliminated the political value of the networks of cooperation that marriage had been instrumental in forging for most of human history. In ending the political functions of marriage and family, democracy, at least as practiced early on, also enhanced the political importance of the household by making it the unit out of which larger political processes were built. Given that males were heads of households, restricting the vote to white, male, property owners effectively made them the voice for their entire household. In some sense their votes were the household's voice in the new democracies. Only as the franchise was extended to all adult citizens did the individual become the foundational unit of democratic processes rather than the household. This process paralleled the one taking place in the economy, as capitalism-driven growth started by providing independence for (white) males as the representative of the household but slowly spread that independence to more and more of the nonwhite and nonmale population, making individuals increasingly able to survive without a household or family to support them.

## The Emergence of the Modern Family

In his discussion of the effects of the Industrial Revolution, Julian Simon (2000) notes that the effects major economic changes have on cultural practices and norms tend to happen with something of a lag. It takes a generation or two for newer practices, and ones that are more finely tuned to the changed economic circumstances, to become adopted and imitated. As capitalism, wage labor, and industrialization began to spread in the late eighteenth century, the effects they would have on the form and function of families slowly began to unfold over the century that followed. The nineteenth century is really the time during which the core features of the modern family emerged and increasingly became the aspirational norm for middle-class families in the Western world. The twentieth century brought significant changes of its own, but it was during the nineteenth century that the shift from the traditional to the modern family really took place.

One of the first and most fundamental of those transitions was the rise of the love match as the basis for marriage. The transition is the theme of Coontz's (2005) history of marriage as she traces out the revolutionary implications it had for marriage, family, and the social order more generally. In summary, she argues:

> By the end of the 1700s personal choice of partners had replaced arranged marriage as a social ideal, and individuals were encouraged to marry for love. For the first time in five thousand years, marriage came to be seen as a private

> relationship between two individuals rather than one link in a larger system of political and economic alliances. The measure of a successful marriage was no longer how big a financial settlement was involved, how many useful in-laws were acquired, or how many children were produced, but how well a family met the emotional needs of its individual members. Where once marriage had been seen as the fundamental unit of work and politics, it was now viewed as a place of refuge from work, politics, and community obligations. (pp. 145–46)

As wage labor ended the family's role in the generation of income from the market, and as democracy and the rise of classical liberalism's emphasis on the individual and individual rights made consent central to human interaction, especially in the political realm, the historic need for marriage to be a vehicle of economic or political advantage disappeared as well. When income could be earned outside the context of the family and when political power became increasingly, if imperfectly, vested in individuals rather than families per se, the decision to marry could be based on other elements of human behavior.

As Flandrin (1979) argues, love had a long history as a human emotion, including in the context of male-female relationships. However, as the basis for *marriage*, it came with a certain sort of shame, as love was seen as a distraction from the various duties and obligations that marriage brought with it when it served crucial economic and political functions. The Church also generally looked down on this sort of romantic love in the context of marriage, not just because of the distractions noted earlier, but because it also turned people's heads from the love of God and Church.[3] So for hundreds of years, love could only be lived "outside marriage or at the risk of upsetting the social order... [and] illicit love-affairs has been severely harassed both by the public authorities and the Church" (p. 171). Love was what one had as part of a sexual or romantic relationship outside of a marriage, as marriage required much more prudential considerations as well as the various duties and obligations imposed on it by the community. It was not until the power of the Church and those duties and obligations were broken by the increased presence of wage labor, capitalism, and democracy that the love match could become more widespread as the basis for marriage. Flandrin observes that:

> [t]he new aspirations were expressed for a long time before economic changes made possible their realization. However, the revolution of the conjugal system did not take place until after that of the economic system, for only then could the marriage founded on love be instituted without challenging the hierarchical structure of society. (p. 173)

As love became accepted as a socially legitimate basis for marriage, the legal codes of Europe and North America also slowly began to change in the early nineteenth century to recognize the importance of freely chosen consent as the foundation of marriage.

One way of understanding the effects of wage labor and capitalism in particular is that prior to the eighteenth century, the marital decision had what economists would call "external effects," and significant ones at that, on both potential spouses's families and the surrounding community. The costs and benefits of the marital decision were not isolated to the couple; they affected numerous others as well. Those external effects, as documented in the prior chapter, provided the explanation for the involvement of parties outside the couple in the marital decision and in the couple's married life. By relocating political power and the ability to earn an income in the individual (i.e., by privatizing the commons), the advent of democracy and capitalism effectively internalized most of the costs and benefits of the marital decision to the couple themselves. Who one married became of decreasing importance to the political and economic fortunes of the extended families and community. With the demise of those external effects, potential spouses no longer needed to consider to nearly the same extent the effects of their choice on others, and those others became less interested in the choice as well. The result was that couples could now afford to indulge their romantic sentiments in a way previous generations could not have done. This is the insight behind Flandrin's comment that it took economic changes to make possible the realization of the love-related aspirations of couples in the seventeenth and early eighteenth century.

The combination of the loss of the family's economic and political functions and the rise of the love match marriage paved the way for the nuclear family. The various combinations of extended family forms that were more common prior to the advent of capitalism can be understood as ways of finding the optimum organizational size to engage in the combination of household and market production required of that household. In addition, the ways in which marriages served the needs of the community rather than those of the spouses meant there was little concern with what we would now call marital privacy. For much of recorded human history, including the early stages of the Industrial Revolution, it was very common for multiple family/household members to sleep in the same room, if not the same bed. Flandrin (1979, p. 98) discusses the various communal sleeping arrangements of preindustrial French peasants, noting in most houses, the most valuable furnishing in the home was the overly large bed designed for communal sleeping. He also points out that this practice continued despite the Church's concern with the opportunities for illicit sexual behavior the situation created. As he rightly observes, all the moralizing in the world could not change the material reality facing poor peasants: "Yet how many beds could a poor peasant, if he was the father of a large family, both afford to buy and find room for in his house?" (p. 99). Such communal sleeping arrangements also posed a challenge for the sexual activity of married couples, as stories abound of children seeing or hearing their parents in the act.[4] While couples continued to engage in sexual activity, and perhaps even more frequently over the course of the long eighteenth century (Abelove 1989), modern notions of marital privacy would have to await the spread of rising wealth through the entire class structure.

The general architecture of typical peasant or even middle-class houses was an important factor in making marital privacy challenging. One-story homes with a very small number of larger rooms were the norm through the late Middle

Ages, and these rooms were normally not divided by function with the possible exception of an area dedicated to food preparation.[5] It was only over the course of the eighteenth century that the hallway with separate rooms increasingly became a standard feature of middle-class and then peasant homes. Of course such homes were more expensive to build and their increased commonality reflects rising wealth among the middle and lower classes. During the nineteenth century, even more specialization by room became common, as houses contained not only distinct rooms for the couple and children for sleeping, but separate kitchens, dining rooms, and living rooms, not to mention indoor bathrooms by the end of the century. All of these innovations also reflected rising wealth across the income group.

As the need for a large household labor force declined and the incomes of families rose during the nineteenth century, the privacy of the married couple, their children, and the family as a whole became a more central concern. The need to have extended family members, or even boarders, to be part of the economic functions of the household quickly diminished with the rise of factory work and other wage labor opportunities in the towns and cities. At the same time, the love match was internalizing the external effects of the marital decision. Combined, these two changes made it increasingly possible for families to stake a claim to privacy against the demands of extended family, Church, community, and the state, especially at a time when the rights of individuals were being expanded in the political and economic arenas more generally. The change in the institutional environment in which marriages took place and families functioned, along with the shift in cultural beliefs about the role and rights of the individual, made it possible for families, and parents specifically, to create within the home a kind of private space distinct from both the market and politics.[6]

Of course in a world where political rights and economic opportunities were disproportionately the province of men, the increasing privacy of the family provided husbands/fathers with a large degree of power within the household, mostly unchecked by the same kinds of external forces that had previously exercised unwanted interference with family decisions. The idea that "a man's home is his castle" captures the classical liberal notion of the right to privacy embedded in the private property of the home. Unfortunately, for much of recent history it also meant leaving women's and children's rights to the tender mercies of the men in their lives. To the degree that claims of family privacy were an excuse for tolerating domestic violence or child abuse, they ran against the grain of the classical liberal movement toward increased respect for the rights of individuals. It would take until the twentieth century, as it did with so many other extensions of classical liberal principles, for the privacy of the family to refer to a unit created by male and females who were legal equals and in which adults and children were protected from violence by each other. Even though completely fulfilling that vision of equality took much time, it began with the classical liberal economic and political changes of the late eighteenth century. The nuclear family of our own time, with mom/dad and children living in a house of their own, finds its origins in the institutional changes and wealth brought on by the advent of capitalism, wage labor, and democracy.

Aside from the changes brought on by the increased presence of wage labor, the wealth that capitalism brought with it had profound implications for the transition to the modern family. The enormous gains in material well-being that have characterized the over 200 years since the Industrial Revolution and the first spread of capitalism hardly need a detailed rehashing. Even the poorest of Westerners today have consumption possibilities, not to mention a life span, that would be the envy of kings and queens of the rest of human history. Those increases in material well-being are the product of the competitive market process that classical liberalism made possible. Goods and services (with very few exceptions) cost less now than ever before in human history when calculated in terms of the amount of time the average industrial worker would have to labor in order to buy them.[7] Market competition has pushed producers to continue to innovate by finding more cost-effective methods of production, developing new products, and improving the quality of existing ones. As economies broke away in the late eighteenth century from the system of monopolistic guilds and protectionism, they unleashed the forces of free trade and competition, leading to the innovation, improvements, and reductions in cost that have characterized the past 200 plus years.

These same competitive forces are responsible for the increases in real wages that have also been a theme of the past 200 years. At the most basic level, wages are a reflection of the value of the products that workers help to produce. That value is a combination of the price the output fetches on the market and the contribution via his or her productivity that the worker makes to creating it. That productivity, or more precisely the worker's *marginal productivity*, is itself the result of two factors: the productivity of the worker's own labor and the productivity of the capital that labor is applied to. The higher the price of the output, the higher the worker's own productivity and/or the higher the productivity of the capital being used, the higher will be the value the worker produces and therefore the higher will be the wage the employer is able and willing to pay. Should the employer pay less than the value of the worker's marginal product, another potential employer could bid that worker away by offering to pay him or her slightly more and still reap the differential between the value of the output and the wage being paid.[8]

The secular increase in wages was a result of all of these factors coming together. The expansion of the population and resulting growth of the market increased the demand for goods and services, adding to the value of the productivity of the workers producing them. As firms profited from one set of production technology, they often reinvested those profits in more and better capital equipment, which in turn increased the productivity of the workers using that capital. Even where such capital replaced workers, the corresponding reduction in the cost to consumers of the goods being produced left those consumers with money to spend on other items, including new products, increasing the demand for labor, and wages, in those markets. With more valuable output and better capital to work with, thanks to competition, wages began to climb.

Finally, workers themselves became more productive as rising levels of wealth permitted individuals to invest in education and training either before entering the labor market or on the job. The financial returns to a college education in the modern West, even given its rising cost, are evidence of the ways in which investing in human capital contributes to higher wages. Beginning in the late eighteenth century, wages began to climb for all of these reasons.

Rising wages were responsible for several aspects of the transition to the modern family. In the early stages of the Industrial Revolution, it was common for husbands, wives, and children to all work for wages, with the wives and children often in the factories. The relatively low wages of the earlier years required multiple incomes to exceed the opportunities left behind on the farm. However, as the forces outlined earlier quickly took hold, wages rose sufficiently such that an increasing number of men could support families on their own and women and children left the labor force. The often universalized family where dad works, mom stays at home, and the children go to school did not exist as any sort of norm until late in the nineteenth century and then did not last for all that long. It could hardly be called traditional in the way it often is in conversations about the family today. I will have much more to say about this process in the next section.

Of related importance is the reduction in family size that followed this increase in wealth with the same sort of lag that Julian Simon observed. As wage labor expanded, the need for children to contribute to the household's market production diminished and the direct economic benefits of a large number of children therefore fell as well. The result was the beginning of the decline in the average number of children per family that has continued into our own time. Early on in the Industrial Revolution, children were contributing to household income by working in the factories, though with the better opportunities there than on the farm, fewer children were needed to produce income. With women also working the factories, child care was a greater challenge if families continued to have children after the older ones began to work. Eventually, as wages rose, the contributions of children were less necessary, prompting a further decline in family size. Finally, as the withdrawal of children from the labor force became complete and their time could be spent in school, the costs of raising children began to climb. Between the reduction in children's value as an economic asset and the increase in the cost of bringing them to adulthood, the net economic contribution of children fell significantly.[9] With the very general assumption that parents respond to the costliness of children, this increase in their net costs prompted families to reduce the number of children they produced.[10] The historical evidence suggests that at least early on in this process, the reductions in family size were not accomplished through birth control, other than perhaps coitus interruptus. Rather, couples either substituted nonprocreative forms of sexual activity for intercourse, or resorted to forms of abortion or infanticide (see the discussion and sources in Posner [1992, p. 268]).[11]

In general, the rising wealth produced by capitalism transformed the family from primarily, if not nearly exclusively, a site of economic production to one of economic consumption. Although in our own time families and households in the West still engage, though less so than ever before, in various forms of household production, very few engage in meaningful forms of market production in the household.[12] The rising living standards made it possible for families to afford consumption items that were previously unattainable: everything from the very size and structure of houses, to the kind and number of furnishings, to the investments that could be made in children, to the everyday items of comfort and convenience that we today take for granted.[13] The same increase in wages also allowed families to purchase leisure time that they could not have had before. Although work days and weeks were long, especially in factories, they were somewhat less so than farm work had been and families over the course of the nineteenth century slowly became able, as they climbed the income ladder, to afford to indulge in various leisure time activities that required both time and resources, a trend that has continued to grow since then.[14] These longer-term trends also get their start with the wealth creation processes opened up by classical liberalism and the capitalism that came with it.

With the family quickly losing its economic and political functions and also becoming increasingly organized with the man as the only member responsible for market production, the roles of women and children were about to undergo a transition of their own. The love-based marriage had, perhaps for the first time, created a promise of equality between husbands and wives, as their relationship was predicated on emotional attachment and mutual commitment rather than economic or political necessities, or the preferences of their parents or the community. The combination of consent and love changed the ground rules for marital relationships, but it would take some time before that promise of equality was brought anywhere near fruition. The process by which that transition began to take place will be covered in the next section, followed by a discussion of the changing nature of childhood. The same economic dynamics led to childhood becoming sentimentalized as it was seen as a unique phase of human development. With new wealth at the disposal of parents, childhood became a time for education and play and a sheltering from the world of adult responsibilities and concerns. These changes to the roles of women and children, and the ways in which they created new functions for the family to replace the economic and political ones lost in the classical liberal revolution, require more detailed discussion.

## The Doctrine of the "Separate Spheres"

The middle-class family of the nineteenth century faced a series of tensions brought on by the changes in the economic and political structure resulting from the advent of capitalism and democracy. Over the course of the century, the loss of the household's role in market production and the increasing remuneration for wage labor that was making it more possible for families to live with reasonable comfort on the income of the male alone, had left women and children in the home but without clearly defined roles to play in the context of the family. At the same time, the love-match and the slow expansion of rights to women had for the first time brought significantly greater equality between the genders into the realm of possibility. So just as women were beginning to see the promise of equality in marriage, thanks to consent and mutual emotional commitment, a distinct division of labor emerged that posed a threat to this promise of equality. In addition, the demands of the emerging market economy had created conflict between the quickly spreading morality of commerce and the long-standing moral codes connected to kin and community. For many, the world of the market was perceived to require a baser existence than the traditional ties of kin and community. Resolving the tension between the heightened promise of equality and the reality of the deep and unequal differences that were growing between men's experiences and women's would require some tricky rhetorical dancing, as would dealing with the emerging conflict of moral codes. The resolution of these tensions also had implications for children's lives as well.

The solution that the English-speaking world developed to the tension between love and the increasingly gendered division of labor was the doctrine of the "separate spheres." Simply put, the argument was that men and women differed in fundamental ways such that each gender should seek to excel in one sphere of activity. Men's reason and competitiveness enabled them to excel in the public spheres of the market and politics, while women's capacity for empathy and care suited them to private sphere of the household. An important element of this doctrine was that the differing aptitudes of men and women did not make them unequal, just different.[15] The claim was that the public sphere was not intrinsically more valuable or important than the private sphere—diligent work in both was necessary for a good society. Since neither sphere was more valuable, the argument continued, the person responsible for either sphere was no more or less valuable or important than the other.

The idea of separate spheres became a social myth that performed the function of reconciling the promise of equality inherent in marriages based on consent and love with the objective differences in each gender's access to resources and power. These differences in resources and power arose as markets became more heavily the province of men and as democracy had extended the vote to more men but often not at all to women. The reality of the nineteenth century was that men and women really were not thought of as equal nor did society really value equally the work done in the public and private spheres. Control over economic resources and political power was clearly in the hands of men, symbolized most vividly in the economic sphere by the legal doctrine of coverture under which the legal identity of a married woman was subsumed into her husband's, and in the political sphere by the denial of the vote to women. It is also worth noting the way in which this differed from preindustrial families in which women had a role as family coproviders when the household was the site of income-earning economic activity. As Coontz (2005, p. 156) observes, the shift from women as coproviders to being responsible for household production "freed them from the strict hierarchy that had governed the old household workplace, where the husband had been the 'boss' of his family's economic activities." But women's control over the household came at a price: the ideology of the separate spheres ended up making women perhaps more dependent upon marriage than ever before, as not only objective circumstances but social expectations shut them out from earning income in the marketplace. The result was that most women had to marry to avoid poverty or a life of very unpleasant work, including prostitution.

The economics of the separate spheres doctrine were interesting as well. As many economic historians have noted, ideology aside, *given* the substantially lower wages available in the few occupations open to married women, and *given* the labor-intensivity of household production in an age before modern conveniences, it was a reasonably rational economic decision for women to devote themselves fully to household production. It was nearly impossible to maintain a household with children with both parents in the workforce full time. The one exception to this was among working class wives, where they were most likely to work while their children were young (as surviving on one very low income was a challenge) and then return to the household when the children became old enough to contribute to the family income.[16] The doctrine of the separate spheres also can be understood as the ideological force behind the late-nineteenth-century demands that working men be paid an above-market family wage and the call for legal restrictions on female employment.[17]

What the combination of the love match and the doctrine of the separate spheres also did was shift "the basis of marriage from sharing tasks to sharing feelings" (Coontz 2005, p. 156). Or in Coontz's more evocative phrase, couples changed from "yoke mates to soul mates." Both of these phrases capture the ongoing shift in the functions of marriage and family from being primarily economic to primarily emotional. Beyond marriage specifically, the ideas of female purity and the sacredness of the home became symbols of this shift through their connection to the separate spheres concept.

The purity of women was a central part of this ideological structure. Much has been written about Victorian Era purity movements and the belief that women both were and should be above the baser things in life. With the expansion of capitalism and the morality of commerce, men were increasingly seen as motivated by the more animal instincts, such as competition, status, and self-interest. Both in the market and in politics (and war as well), men were seen as engaged in one or another form of battle from which the home was a respite. By giving women responsibility for the home, they were given the task of being a counterweight to the pressures and morality of the public sphere. Women could only discharge this task if they really were isolated from the worlds of the market and politics, to the point where even reading the newspapers was seen as "improper." Any entrance into those worlds ran the risk of sullying their purity and connection to the older and higher values. Men bought into this dichotomy as well, as many saw the morality of the private sphere as superior and accepted the more self-interested competitive behavior of the public sphere as a kind of necessary evil. Men's devaluation of the morality of their own activity gave them every reason to continue to promulgate the separate spheres and female purity. This can also be seen as the start of the rejection of the bourgeois virtues that concerns McCloskey (2006).

One of the interesting consequences of the view that women held to a higher morality was that it empowered women with respect to their sexual relationships with their husbands. The view of women as pure certainly translated to the marital bed, where women were supposed to be above base, animal sexual needs. Here too, men accepted the moral dichotomy and often tried their best to live up to a similar standard of purity, even to the point of trying not to think about the women they loved as sexual beings (Coontz 2005, p. 189). Aside from the way in which this diminished or even destroyed the sexual component of many Victorian marriages, it did at least give women a way to say no to unwanted sex that might be persuasive to their husbands. And given that the emotional bonds between husbands and wives were stronger than in earlier periods of history, men were less likely to attempt to coerce sex from their wives and less likely to use physical violence against them. Where once men who could not or did not control their wives, often with violence, were shunned by the community, the reverse was nearer the truth by the end of the nineteenth century, as domestic violence, while surely still common, was on the decline and less socially acceptable. With women viewed as morally higher than men, hitting one's wife opened a man to public condemnation more so than in the past.[18] However, women were dependent upon their husbands' good will as the law was still far from recognizing spousal abuse and marital rape as criminal.

The middle and upper classes during the nineteenth century provided the blueprint for the nostalgic version of home that continues to serve as a cultural ideal even into our own time. The home was the physical representation of the refuge from the competitive and amoral, if not immoral, world of the public sphere, whether that be the market or politics. Being the sphere controlled by women, it became the symbol of purity that women were supposed to represent. The ongoing nuclearization of the family threw off many of the ties to extended kin that in prior generations opened the home to concerns beyond the marital dyad and their children. With separate spheres having made the house women's space, where the domestic virtues set the rules of the game, even men began to value the space of the home as a desirable change from their lives in the public sphere. As the century progressed, increasing numbers of men began to spend more of their time away from work with their wives and children. Moreover, they did so to the exclusion of other members of the household. Whereas wealthier families in earlier times would have eaten with servants or boarders, it became increasingly common for the immediate family to eat by themselves with the servants or boarders eating separately (Coontz 2005, p. 166). Holiday celebrations also moved from the broader community into the home, involving only the immediate family. Marriage, children, and home were increasingly supposed to be the sources of emotional satisfaction and both genders largely accepted the idea that each needed to contribute their own specialty to the creation of a rich domestic life.

## Child Labor and the Ideal of the Sheltered Childhood

Also central to the Victorian cult of domesticity was the changing role of children. At the start of the nineteenth century, children were likely to be employed either on the family farm or in the early factories. In both cases, the household required the child's contribution to its income generation in order to get by. Historian of childhood Steven Mintz (2004, p. 136) notes that wages of children between the ages of 10 and 15 "often amounted to 20 percent of a family's income and spelled the difference between economic well-being and destitution." As Mintz also points out, "key decisions... were based on family needs rather than individual choice... [in] the cooperative family economy." Surely if parents of that era could have survived without their children working, they would have, as is demonstrated by the relative absence of child labor among the very wealthy of the time. But economic constraints meant that Prudence still held sway over Love early in the industrial era.

When adult wages did begin to rise over the course of the century, children (and eventually women) were withdrawn from the labor force. Contrary to popular myth, laws against child labor were not the primary reason for its disappearance. Rather it was the rising wages produced by nineteenth-century capitalism that ended the need for children to be employed. Nardinelli (1990, pp. 109–12) offers evidence of declining child labor rates in the British cotton and flax factories for two decades before the first Factory Act in 1833, as well as ongoing declines in child labor in the silk factories up until 1890 *even though most of the child labor laws did not apply to the silk industry*. Together, these provide some confirming evidence for the role of capitalism-driven rising real wages as the cause of the reduction in child labor over the century. Even farm children saw their roles diminish, as improved farm machinery reduced the need for child labor and the increasing returns to farming enabled landowners to hire help from outside the family.

Critics of child labor during the Industrial Revolution also frequently overlook the fact that children worked before industrialization, but it was not for wages and it was in the organizational structure of the household (recall too our earlier discussion of putting out). The real change was children working for wages.[19] The same critics often tend to downplay the real dangers, rigors, and long hours of farm work and overplay the negatives, on net, of industrial work. Many, as Mintz (2004, p. 181) points out, even saw farm work as character building in ways that the more urban forms of labor were not thought to be. In the same way that women were to be sheltered from the unpleasantness of "filthy lucre," so were children.

There is no doubt that the conditions children worked under in factories were unpleasant by our own standards, but life on the farm was certainly no better and arguably worse. And if one accounts for the greater family income and greater access to resources, including medicine, that newly urbanized factory workers had, life was, overall, likely better for child factory workers than child farm workers of the generation before.[20] Nardinelli's (1990, p. 112) conclusion is worth quoting in full:

> The growing real income of nineteenth-century Britain was the most important force removing children from textile factories after 1835. Children worked in factories because their families were poor; as family income increased, child labor decreased. Indeed, as a given family's income increased younger children began work at a later age than had their older brothers and sisters. The well-known Victorian concern with children was in large part a reflection of rising income. One would therefore expect that, given the rapid rise in income in the last half of the century, the amount of child labor in textile factories would have declined in the long run without factory legislation.

Certainly the laws had some effect in pushing the process along, but the "most important force" remained the rise in real income that capitalism and industrialization had produced.[21] In contrast to claims by its critics, capitalism did not create unpleasant child labor, as such labor had always existed in the household and on the farm. Instead, capitalism was the proximate cause of the *disappearance* of child labor among the masses for the first time in human history, even if it first made child labor more visible by moving it out of the household and into the factories.

The economic changes of the nineteenth century provided another rationale for the withdrawal of children from the labor force: the rising opportunity cost of current labor in terms of foregone investment in human capital. Part of the spectacular growth of the nineteenth century was an increase in the demand for skilled labor. More complex machinery required both more skilled operators and more skilled thinkers and workers to invent and build such machinery. The returns to investment in the education and skills that constitute human capital rose very quickly. Combined with a declining need for child labor in the factories and in the household (due to new technology and declining family size, the greater availability of manufactured goods on the market, and the increased capital-intensivity of agriculture), the rising returns to human capital made educating children a better use of their time than having them working for wages. With more families able to support themselves on one adult income, the space for a new vision of childhood was opened up. Nardinelli (1990, p. 63) observes: "The rising opportunity cost of child labor in and out of the home may have been the most important long-term change in the economic role of children. It led to the emergence of a modern childhood devoted primarily to leisure and education rather than labor."[22]

This new vision of childhood is captured by the phrase the "sheltered childhood" (see, e.g., Macleod 1998). The doctrine of the separate spheres and the economic changes that were slowly removing the need for children to engage in wage labor combined to ensure that children in the home were integrated into the world of domesticity and the private, female sphere. The beginning of this process was the increase in sentimentality toward children that paralleled the rise of the love match in marriage. Just as premodern families could not afford to indulge the emotional sentiments of their children when marriage was on the line, neither could premodern parents afford excessive sentimentality toward their children when diverting resources away from other uses toward one child might undermine the entire household. The tradeoffs were much steeper at that time than by the Victorian Era. As Shorter (1975, p. 264) said of the premodern family, "[T]he stakes were too high to risk on the life of a single child." All of this changed with the economic growth that capitalism brought.

Perhaps most important, that growth "liberated mothers from [their] desperate need to employ their time elsewhere" (Shorter 1975, p. 264). Freed from the need to participate in market production, it was now possible for women to devote a significant amount of time toward household production, especially the care of children. This work was, as Shorter points out, not all that less taxing and unpleasant than work in the fields or factory, but it did have the important advantage that "in the end their children would live." Improved medical technology and scientific knowledge along with greater material resources and maternal time being devoted to children meant a reduction in infant mortality rates. As a result, children began to acquire a degree of sentimental value that they rarely had in the past. At one level, this was a result of declining infant and child mortality reducing the costs of sentimental attachment. When children were more likely to die, such attachment could be very costly; when they became increasingly likely to live, sentimentality could be indulged more fully. Again, this is not to say that premodern parents did not treat their children with *any* sentimentality; only that, on the margin, changing economic conditions made more sentimentality easier. At another level, this increased sentimentality reflected a change in children from being seen as potential producers for the household in the immediate future, to objects of investment for the long run as a way to increase the children's *own* well-being. With economic growth having lowered the opportunity cost of children staying in the home, parents adopted lower time preferences and greater altruism with respect to their children's contributions to market production (i.e., they became more concerned with what the children could do in the *long-run* and *after* leaving the home). Thanks to that same growth, they also had the resources they needed to engage in the care that would protect and nurture the investment that children now represented.

Childhood began to be reconceived as a time of innocence, play, and education, all taking place out of sight of the adult worlds of work and politics. The sheltered childhood was achievable most easily by the urban middle class, who had the ability to survive on a male income alone, but it was transmitted, as Mason (1994, p. 52) argues, through the burgeoning print media, especially women's magazines, to families far from the urban centers. More than just a norm that would be desirable to imitate, later Progressive Era reformers saw the sheltered childhood as an ideal against which the parenting practices of the urban working class, and immigrants in particular, were deemed unsatisfactory.[23] A good deal of turn of the twentieth century Progressive Era legislation involving children and families grew out of the desire to force working class and immigrant (and eventually rural) parents to adopt the urban, middle-class model of the working father with the mother at home caring for the nonworking children.

During the decades prior to that time, one notable shift in the law that promoted the sheltered childhood norm was the increasing tendency to give custody of children to mothers rather than fathers in cases of divorce or other disputes. For previous generations, children were seen as effectively property of the father, which is not surprising given the role of the father as head of the economic organization known as the household and the contributions to its output children made as productive resources. With children as economic assets under the stewardship of their father, courts followed suit by setting fathers as the default custodial parent. However, as the economic functions of the family changed and the separate spheres and the cult of motherhood and domesticity became the norm, children became increasingly likely to be given to their mothers not because they had legal rights to the children, but because "placing children in their mothers' care was in the best interests of the children" (Mason 1994, p. 53). This view of custody is consistent with both the sheltered childhood idea, in its concern with the child's best interest, and the separate spheres doctrine, in seeing that interest best served by mothers.

As part of the changes in the physical structure of the home we noted earlier, it was often the case that the first dedicated, separate space was a nursery for infants or play space for children, with children's bedrooms not far behind. These changes were architectural instantiations of the sheltered separateness of childhood. The growth in income and the extension of markets and mass production over the nineteenth century also made it possible for parents to purchase toys and holiday gifts for children. Our contemporary idealization of the domestic bliss of the Christmas season finds its roots here as well. Toys also had the effect of encouraging children to play inside the house, which continued the ideal of the sheltered childhood and also promoted the domesticity of the nuclear family (Macleod 1998). Many of the basic elements of childhood that we now take for granted in the modern family find their origins in the changes that took place over the nineteenth century.

Much of the intense focus on childhood was also couched in the typical Progressive Era language of science, which was especially evident in the popular child-rearing manuals at the turn of the twentieth century.[24] The titles alone provide a good sense of things: *The Care and Feeding of Children* by L. Emmett Holt and Mary West's *Infant Care*.[25] Both sound more like user's manuals for household appliances than guides to raising children. The content of both books lives up to that impression as both are full of supposedly scientific advice, much of which had the result of reinforcing the sheltered childhood norm by keeping infants and children isolated from the adult world and shielded from overstimulation (Macleod 1998, p. 37). Children were to be fed on rigid schedules, kept on very bland diets, and guarded against any contact with people or things that could introduce illness. Formula feeding was preferred as it could be measured and timed with the faux exactness of apparent science. As Macleod notes, "Despite the germ theory's presumed ascendancy, pediatricians found it easier to explain health problems in terms of nutrition and environmental influences rather than infection" (p. 36). One might view this scientific fascination with getting infancy right in particular as a reaction to the ongoing changes in infant mortality rates. With such rates on the decline, it was becoming harder and harder to accept the death of a child with the sense of inevitability seen in the premodern family, even though such deaths were still somewhat common. The result was an even greater push to try to control the conditions of infancy and toddlerhood in the hope that their own children would not be one of the fewer who died young.[26]

The intense focus on domesticity and childhood that emerged in the nineteenth century led to the sheltered childhood that characterizes most families of the Western world today. The ability to do all of this was a consequence of the economic growth brought on by capitalism. And the emergence of the sheltered childhood was on balance clearly a good thing. Not only did it become a cultural justification for keeping children out of the work force that was complementary to the changing economics of the decision, it also became a rationale for investing in children's education and trying to understand better the conditions under which children might flourish. These complementary economic and cultural processes made childhood a far more enjoyable stage in human development than it had ever been. Spared not just from the world of work, but increasingly from mistreatment, disease, and competition over limited household resources, children were better able to explore, learn, and grow. With fewer children, parents were also able to concentrate more resources on each. The ability to invest in human capital through formal and informal forms of education accelerated the virtuous cycle of wage growth and rising incomes. Each generation was able to command higher wages than the previous, which enabled them to provide even more human capital investment for their own children. In our own time, college-educated children spend the first quarter of their lives investing in their human capital, free from many of the worries of the adult world. This is a situation that our ancestors, for whom children were often a source of as much grief as joy, and whose own childhoods were ones of toil and sickness, could never have imagined.

## The Two Worlds at the Start of the Twentieth Century

It is worth pausing to see how far the family has come. For most of human history the family was hardly the Victorian domestic ideal. Children died young and those who did not were expected to work hard for the household and eventually leave to earn their own keep at what would to us be a young age. Like the cattle, children and women were seen as assets to be managed by the male head of the household. Often this meant that the needs of humans were less important than those of cattle or that the opportunity cost in terms of market production foregone of engaging in human labor-intensive forms of child care was simply too high. Chapter 3 documented the rather unpleasant environment of the family in the preindustrial era. This chapter has argued that capitalism began to change all of this almost completely for the better.

It is in this way that the evolution of the modern family is an application of Deirdre McCloskey's argument in *The Bourgeois Virtues*. Capitalism offered ways to earn income outside of the household and in doing so slowly eliminated the family's role as an institution of market production and thereby removed it from the realm of narrow economic calculation and "Prudence Only," or at least "Prudence Mostly." Without a need to treat family members instrumentally as parts of a production process, and with the means to treat them more frequently as ends in themselves now possible as a result of the higher incomes capitalism produced, the family became the focal point of the altruism of intimate associations. The improved economic and legal status of women and children, the gradual equalization of the marital relationship, and the ascendance of the virtue of Love as the basis for marriage and the parent-child relationship, all reflect the ways in which capitalism made possible and nourished other virtues. As Prudence began to spend more time out of the household and in the market, capitalism made it possible for Love (and perhaps Faith and Hope as well) to come in and take its full and rightful place at the family table. In making this transition possible, capitalism thereby humanized the family. The somewhat tragic irony is that capitalism is in our own time often accused of reducing interpersonal relationships and other higher ideals to naked, financial self-interest or narrow calculative rationality, when in fact it was *capitalism that humanized the most deeply interpersonal of all human institutions—the family.*

The changes brought by the economic growth of the industrial era also created the context for the two sorts of worlds at once problem that has been a running theme of this book. Although exchange and markets had both long been parts of the human experience, it is only with the late eighteenth century and the spread of capitalism that the market became the overriding social coordination process for an increasing proportion of the Western world. In the premodern world, markets existed more on the periphery of life in the small village, the farm, or the feudal estate. These face-to-face worlds and their long-standing rules of behavior defined the social landscape. Capitalism redrew that landscape by extending the interdependencies created by the Law of Association from the face-to-face world to the anonymous world of the market. Commercial relations slowly took their place alongside the community as important parts of people's lives, thanks to both laboring for wages as producers and purchasing more and more products on the market as consumers. The new world of the market also brought with it a moral code that differed from that of the face-to-face village, not to mention the even more intimate evolutionary environment in which our minds and moral instincts had developed. The evolution of the family we have outlined in this chapter can be seen through this lens as an ongoing struggle to come to grips with the fact that humans now had to move between the two worlds of the intimate family and the anonymous market.

The love match and the higher aspirations it brought to marriage, the development of the sheltered childhood, and the doctrine of the separate spheres all served to draw lines between the newly emerging commercial order and its more self-regarding morality and the older orders of the household and community and their more collectivist orientation. Although the premodern family did take a calculative approach toward the welfare of its members, at least the wives and children, it was nonetheless true that the survival of the household as a whole was the overarching goal. In turn, the household's economic fortunes were intimately linked with those of the surrounding community. The moral norms in this world were clearly about duty and obligation to kin and community rather than self-interest. As economic growth pushed aside the family's market production functions and the self-regarding commercial mentality became more widespread, the family kept itself shielded from that world by becoming the site of emotional and psychological fulfillment. Spousal love and the more general cult of domesticity became outlets for our evolved moral dispositions toward altruism and kin. In the face of a commercial morality that seemed immoral in contrast with our evolved preference for visible, intentional support for others, the family provided emotional connections that became outlets for those ingrained moral dispositions, replacing the family's internally collectivist economic connections that had previously served that function. Spousal love and the romanticized vision of home instantiated in the increasingly private, nuclear family could replicate to one degree or another the context in which our evolved moral instincts might be effective.

The sheltered childhood made the home a place where parental concern with the physical, intellectual, and emotional well-being of children became paramount. The very language of sheltering children from the adult world speaks to the two worlds framework. Children were to be protected from the self-regarding moral code of the commercial world for as long as possible. The gauze of sentimentality and innocence that began to envelop children was a curtain designed to shut out the uglier, less virtuous, adult world. Formal schooling also tried its best to keep children sheltered from that world.

As the doctrine of the separate spheres slowly locked into place over the nineteenth century, it became perhaps the most clear battleground for the struggle between the two worlds of the intimate associations and the anonymous Great Society. With capitalism having produced this larger, more anonymous network of social interaction that required a set of moral rules that would condone self-interested behavior and condemn long-standing forms of altruism, social institutions had to adapt. One solution to the two worlds problem was to, in essence, assign a gender to each world. The similarity of language between Hayek's two worlds formulation and the separate spheres of the Victorians indicates the ways in which they are two ways of seeing the same phenomenon.

The problem that the separate spheres idea attempted to solve was a real one, but as we shall see in the next chapter it was not a sustainable solution. By assigning women to the sphere of the world of intimate associations and men to the sphere of the world of the anonymous market and Great Society more generally, the Victorians were attempting to reconcile the tension between the two different forms of social interaction they represented. Not only that, they argued that the female sphere involved the higher morality of hearth and home. Both men and women came to see home and the women who ran it as places of virtuous refuge from the uglier, seedier world of the market and politics. The purity of women could arguably be seen as deriving from them being unsullied by participation in the other of the two worlds. Here too, the history of the family reflects McCloskey's argument that by the mid-nineteenth century the notion of bourgeois virtues was coming to be seen as a contradiction in terms. Virtuous behavior had to take place somewhere other than in the commercial world of the bourgeoisie. The Victorian cult of domesticity provided one such alternative in its attempts to shield women and children from that commercial world and to provide men with a morally superior respite from it.[27]

The separate spheres doctrine combined with the disdain with which the male sphere was treated provided women with a chance to extend their enlightened morality outside of the household: "For all its repressiveness, the early nineteenth-century definition of woman's sphere had given her moral responsibility beyond the household, a duty that easily shaded into social activism" (Coontz 1992, p. 153). In the words of a midcentury female author, "Let men enjoy in peace and triumph the intellectual kingdom which is theirs . . . The moral world is ours—ours by position, ours by qualification, ours by the very indication of God himself" (quoted in Coontz 2005, p. 162). The result was that women were often leaders in campaigns for moral purity in the larger Great Society. From antislavery activism to the temperance and prohibition movements to the child savers of the Progressive Era, women attempted to extend the moral authority they wielded in the intimate world into the more anonymous world outside the household. Sometimes this activism was designed to be legislative, other times it was just involvement in any number of social organizations, or Burkean little platoons, which were in many ways no more than nonfamilial intimate associations.[28]

One way of understanding the Progressive Era is as trying to extend the female sphere into the male. However, the more important change that began around this time was the shattering of the spheres themselves. As the next chapter will document, the underlying tension between the promise of equality embedded in the love match and Victorian domesticity, and the reality of the inequality of the male and female spheres, would eventually come to shatter the gender specificity of those spheres. The catalyst was in many ways the continued economic growth and evolution in morals that capitalism was generating. Slowly but surely job opportunities for women began to grow, technological substitutes for human labor in the household reduced the opportunity cost of women entering the labor force, and marriage itself took on more characteristics of a contract entered into by legal equals. Over the course of the twentieth century, men and women increasingly took on the responsibilities of the other sphere. What is important to note here is that, from a Hayekian perspective, the spheres themselves did not disappear, as there remained the distinct worlds of the intimate associations and the Great Society. What changed in the twentieth century was that both spheres were open to both genders. However, without gender to demarcate those spheres in a socially visible way, it was easy to forget that they still existed and that there were meaningful differences between them.

# CHAPTER 5

# Gender and Family in the Twentieth Century

## Introduction

Among the changes in the social structure that took place during the twentieth century, those involving gender and family are arguably the most significant. The legal rights and economic status of women were dramatically different at the end of the century than they were at the start. A time traveler would be astounded at the involvement of women in the public sphere, as well as the ways in which that involvement has transformed both the public and private spheres. The family as a social institution, though still recognizable to a time traveler, has changed in numerous ways involving both function and form. Perhaps foremost among those changes is a much broader set of forms and structures that would be counted as family. Sometimes referred to as the postmodernization of the family, this fragmentation of the dominant form does require keeping the distinction between form and function in the foreground in exploring this material.

The story of the evolution of women's roles and the changes in family is a well-known one. In most cases, the facts are not in dispute. However, what those facts mean and what the causal mechanisms were that drove these changes, and what implications all of these changes have for family policy and the status of women in the twenty-first century, are less commonly agreed upon. In this chapter, I offer a classical liberal interpretation of the expansion of women's roles and the changes in the American family that were so central to the social evolution of the twentieth century. The underlying theme continues the last chapter's emphasis on capitalism's role in changing the nature of work and providing a level of wealth that made possible new opportunities for women and a broader variety of family forms. In particular, I will focus on the changes in female labor force participation, both the rise in rates and the kinds of human capital investments women began to make. In combination with changes in birth control technology, these factors explain a great deal of the changes in women's role in the labor force and therefore the family. I will also look at the ways in which the growing separation of the family and market production that capitalism brought about made possible the development of homosexuality as an identity, which, combined with the development of the love-based marriage detailed in chapter 4, led to the development of gay and lesbian families and the more recent push for the legalization of same-sex marriage. Living in the shadow of the law, many gay and lesbian families are invisible, in that they *function* as families but their forms are such that we do not always see them. The same can be said of other family forms, and I will say a few words about some of them in this chapter and their relationship to the economic changes of the past century.

## From Status to Contract

In the mid-nineteenth century, Henry Maine (1861) described the "movement of progressive societies" as a shift "from status to contract" as the basis for social relationships. More specifically, Maine argued that this movement could be seen in the ways in which "individual obligation" was increasingly being substituted for "family dependency," leading to the individual as opposed to the household or family being the "unit of which civil laws take account." Maine accurately saw the changes that had already taken place in the Western world and were continuing to unfold during the nineteenth century. However, the ongoing substitution of the individual for the family did not really begin to reach married women until late in that century and on throughout the twentieth. The eighteenth and nineteenth centuries saw marriage move from status to contract as individuals gained the rights to decide who, when, and why they would marry. Once married, though, the law gave to men and women very specific roles and unequal status in the eyes of the law. A great deal about the specifics of the marital relationship was governed not by the preferences of the couple as a unit or by their individual desires, but by a whole host of legal limits and expectations that accompanied the status of being married, especially for women. The twentieth century would see a progressive reduction in those limits and expectations, making the status of being married less of a barrier to women's full participation in the Great Society. It also transformed marriage into something more like a contract, with both parties having independent standing with mutual obligations.

The prior chapter left off with the Victorian family solidly in place among the middle-class and above. Dad was responsible for market production and mom for household production, with children sheltered from the responsibilities of the adult world as they were educated and given time and space to play and explore. Percolating underneath the surface of the Victorian family (like the lava under the crust of a volcano, to use Coontz's [2005] image) were a number of tensions that would eventually break down the separate spheres and define the path that the family would take in the twentieth century. Although the doctrine of the separate spheres made it difficult for women to find success in the public worlds of the market and the polity, it was far from impossible. By the turn of the twentieth century, there were enough women succeeding in the public sphere to make it increasingly plausible and acceptable that others would follow them. Changes in the structure of the economy, most notably the rise of clerical and service work at which women could compete more evenly with men, also challenged the rigidity of the spheres. But the most fundamental tension was that between the substantive inequity of the separate spheres and the promise of equality implicit in the love-based marriage.

As we saw in chapter 3, the preindustrial family was legally and functionally under the control of the husband, with other family members being more or less assets or inputs into the household's productive activities. In that world, the relationship between husband and wife was dominated by considerations of *status*. The husband's legal position as owner of everything, along with his role as head of household production and the wife's corresponding inability to write contracts or own property in her own name, made the wife subservient to the husband. This subservience was not just metaphorical—in many premodern families, the wife served her husband and family and stood behind him as he ate, waiting until later to eat her own meal. Where the marital relationship was ruled by considerations of Prudence and structured by status, notions of equality between the sexes were not likely to be relevant.

As capitalism sowed the ground for the love-based marriage, the dominant role of status in structuring marriage and family would be challenged. With marriages being increasingly initiated on the basis of the emotional bond between the couple, the power dynamic of marriage began to shift. At the most basic level, the split between market and household production eroded some of the male's dominance over the household as he could no longer treat wives and children as inputs to the generation of household income. For all of the ideological uses of the idea of separate spheres, the rhetoric of equality associated with it also helped change marital power dynamics as women could at least invoke considerations of equality against male over-reach. The ability of some women to break into the worlds of the market and politics also began to challenge the old lines of status. Finally, and perhaps most importantly, the fact that husbands were more free to say that they loved their wives provided women with leverage against male dominance.

The two key events that changed the basis of the marital relationship from one of status to one more like contract were the end of coverture and women acquiring the right to vote and the associated rights of citizenship. Even as the spread of the love-based marriage in the nineteenth century began to create a promise of equality, and enact it to some degree in practice, the law still treated women, and married women specifically, in many ways no different from minors. Married women were legally subsumed (or covered) by their husbands. The tradition in English law was that upon marriage, the wife surrendered all of her rights to her husband; the couple *was* the husband. She could not make contracts, own property, sign other legal documents or even get an education or earn a living without explicit permission of her husband. Lord Blackstone, in 1765, went as far to note that a husband and wife themselves could not enter into any kind of covenant with each other as this would "suppose her separate existence" (cited in Coontz 2005, p. 186). The essential idea that a married woman had no separate legal or economic standing remained the underlying law in the United States and elsewhere through most of the eighteenth and nineteenth centuries.

By the end of the nineteenth century and into the early twentieth, the main manifestations of the idea of coverture slowly disappeared, though not without a struggle. Of the 27 states in the United States in 1840, none allowed married women to have rights to their own earnings and estates. In 1873 the Supreme Court did not help matters with its decision in *Bradwell v. Illinois* (1873). In an 8–1 decision, the court rejected the claim of Myra Bradwell that an Illinois law prohibiting women from becoming lawyers interfered with her right to practice a profession under the "privileges or immunities" clause of the Fourteenth Amendment. The court referred to the "natural and proper timidity and delicacy" of women as a reason they were unsuited for the bar. The majority opinion was explicit in saying that women's roles were as wife and mother as "the Creator" put forth.[1]

Despite this decision, or perhaps because of it, individual states began to grant women, especially married women, increasing legal and economic standing as the nineteenth century came to a close. In England, the end of coverture is usually dated by the Married Women's Property Act of 1882 and other legislation that followed. In the United States, much of this happened at the state level, as that is where most family law is based, so there is no single act to point to.[2] By the late nineteenth century, almost all of the 38 states allowed married women to have separate estates, while 31 enabled them to have control over their own earnings (Jacobsen 2007, p. 406). By the early twentieth century, every state had made these changes. This process was driven by a variety of factors, not the least of which was the promise of equality (even if distorted by the ideology of the separate spheres) that was embedded in the love-based marriage. The slowly increasing labor force participation rates of women, which rose from 8 percent in 1840 to almost 15 percent by 1880 and almost 19 percent by 1900, included more working married women who could press the case for their rights to property (p. 408). As economic and political rights were expanded to other groups, such as African Americans, the justification for denying such rights to women was hard to maintain. The economic forces set in place by capitalism were increasingly pushing Westerners to live up to the classical liberal language of equality promised by their founding political documents.

These important changes did not completely obliterate the underlying presumptions of the coverture laws. One of the key barriers to the completion of the move from status to contract in the early twentieth century was labor market protective legislation that limited women's employment options. These laws applied to women only and specified maximum hours, minimum wages, and working conditions for a number of jobs that had a significant female presence. Some jobs were also off-limits to women under any conditions.[3] For example, by 1909, 20 states had maximum hours laws and by 1919, 40 had such laws. Most of these laws limited women to somewhere from 8 to 10 hours per day, putting them higher than the nationwide scheduled average of 8.5 hours per day in 1919 (Goldin 1991, pp. 191–92). Jacobsen (2007, p. 415) points out that many of the first state-level minimum wages adopted around that time "applied only to women and minors." All of this legislation was claimed by many of its proponents to be about protecting women from more powerful, presumably male, employers. Proponents also argued that the physical labor of factory work was damaging to women's bodies and might threaten their fertility, necessitating protective legislation.[4] The laws were said to be in women's interests and were a different manifestation of many of the same beliefs that were behind the separate spheres thinking of a few decades earlier. Women had entered the public sphere, but still needed to be recognized as different. Clearly, these laws were limitations on women's ability to make contracts and were a continuation of the relative importance of status in defining the social roles of men and women. Their gradual disappearance over the course of the century was a victory for classical liberal notions of equality.

Claudia Goldin (1991, p. 192) sees two contradictory interpretations of these laws. The first is that they were a genuine attempt to protect the legitimate interests of women. The second is that they served the self-interest of male workers, especially unionized ones. The trade unions, not surprisingly, were generally in strong support of the limitations on women's employment, especially the minimum wage and the associated call to pay men a higher family wage to ensure that women would not have to work. Both policies would raise union members' wages in a way that would find support in places not normally supportive of union goals. The restrictions on female employment had the effect of preventing employers from hiring lower-wage competition rather than higher-priced union labor. Unions have long used a variety of tactics to achieve this result. Much like Goldin, but coming from the opposite vantage point, Coontz (2005, p. 175) notes with some surprise that many middle-class observers "not normally sympathetic to unionism" supported these proposals. These "observers" were presumably more conservative citizens who were motivated by the desire to protect women.

What Goldin sees as "contradictory" and Coontz sees as out of the ordinary is neither to anyone familiar with the "bootleggers and Baptists" phenomenon noted by Yandle (1983). Yandle argued that those who gain economically from making a particular activity illegal (e.g., bootleggers gaining from Prohibition) frequently find themselves on the same side with the moralists who wish to abolish their activity altogether (e.g., the "Baptists" supporting Prohibition). As a result, a number of government policies command significant political support because they serve the interests of both altruistic reformers and those producers who will materially benefit from their competition having higher costs or being legislated out of existence altogether. The two explanations Goldin sees for protective legislation are not contradictory but complementary. That very complementarity explains why the alliance should not be seen as out of the ordinary, as history is full of examples of this phenomenon.

It was not until much later in the twentieth century that two other sets of laws that reflected the idea that women had a different status than men were finally overturned in all of the US states and elsewhere in the world. The first was "head and master" laws that gave husbands the right to make important familial decisions without their wives consenting or even being consulted. For example, a man who was offered a new job in another state could force his wife to go with him even if she did not wish to. Such laws were slowly overturned in the latter half of the twentieth century. The second set was the laws around marital rape. As recently as the 1970s and 1980s, some US states still did not recognize the possibility that a husband could rape his wife. Much as coverture treated the wife as an economic extension of the husband, and thus precluded them from entering a contract or covenant with one another, the laws around marital rape treated the wife as a physical extension of the husband, thus removing the need for consent in their sexual relationship. Although the end of coverture proper was a major milestone in the pushing the marital relationship toward one of equals in a contract, rather than unequals tied by status, it took almost another century before the lingering presumptions behind it were completely overturned.

Plenty has been said in many other places about the importance of women's suffrage in advancing gender equality. I have nothing to add to that story other than to point out its connection with the changing economic circumstances of women. One of the running themes of the twentieth century's dramatic changes in the status of women was how often economic changes preceded cultural and political shifts. The turn of the twentieth century saw a dramatic increase in the number of women who attended high school and then college, with the number of female college students tripling between 1890 and 1910 (Coontz 2005, p. 192). These young women were not going to be satisfied with their mothers' lives, and the expanding economy of the period began to open up new job opportunities in clerical and service work. As this generation of women entered the public sphere of the market, their contact with the public sphere of the polity expanded as well, bringing into clearer resolution the importance of voting rights and forms of legal protection extended to male citizens but denied to them. Expanding economic opportunities and freedom created a demand for political change and, with it, cultural change in how women saw themselves.[5] Once women received the right to vote nationwide as well as other rights of citizenship, and broke through the walls of the domestic sphere, it became that much easier to push for further change. This process set off a virtuous cycle that promoted a more substantive notion of equality than the merely rhetorical equality of the separate spheres.

In all of these ways, the evolution of marriage that accelerated early in the twentieth century is a microcosm of the more general shift toward contract and consent as the basis for economic (and political) activity. Although marriage was not, and still is not, a contract exactly like others, it is still true that the commercial and contractual ethos of capitalism was crucial in generating the *idea* of contract as a new model for marriage.[6] Writing in 1922, Ludwig von Mises (1981 [1922], p. 82) captured this nicely:

> As the idea of contract enters the Law of Marriage, it breaks the rule of the male, and makes the wife a partner with equal rights. From a one-sided relationship resting on force, marriage thus becomes a mutual agreement; the servant becomes the married wife entitled to demand from the man all that he is entitled to ask from her. Step by step she wins the position in the home which she holds today... This evolution of marriage has taken place by way of the law relating to the property of married persons... as the idea of contract advanced in other fields of the Law of Property it necessarily transformed the property relations between the married couple.

Although Mises surely overstated the degree of equality present in the 1920s, the underlying point remains valid. For Mises, this change in the nature of marriage was also a further extension of the Law of Association that we discussed in chapter 3. The spread of market relationships not only took place across *households* but now began to take place across *individuals* as well. Just as trade had drawn more people into the ambit of the extended division of labor and the ethos of the market, so would the extension of the idea of contract into marriage now give women the right to participate in the market and join the peaceful cooperation of the Great Society. It would also enable women to meet men as equals both in and out of the home, reinforcing the idea of marriage as a form of contract.[7]

## The Sexualization of Marriage

In his discussion of the contractual basis of marriage, Mises raises another point about the changes in marriage that capitalism and the idea of contract brought about. The sexual component of marriage works best when men and women meet as equals and where they have an emotional bond between them. In, as he calls it, "the age of violence" (Mises 1981 [1922], p. 78), the lesser importance of that emotional bond made sexual enjoyment difficult, most obviously for the woman who was likely in the relationship against her will, but also for the man who might find sex with a partner with "a merely suffering attitude" not very enjoyable. Mises argues that if such men wanted sex to be enjoyable, they would have to court their partners to some degree, thus diminishing their apparently absolute power in the household. By contrast, where the idea of contract has permeated marriage, the parties meet as closer to equals and they come to the relationship because of the emotional bond between them: "In the modern contractual marriage, which takes place at the desire of husband and wife, marriage and love are united" (p. 83). The implication is that the sexual component of the marriage will be more powerful and more enjoyable because it requires love, and love "cannot exist when women occupy the position of contempt which they occupy under the principle of violence. For under this system she is merely as slave, but it is the nature of love to conceive her as a queen." In our own time, with marriage as a contract between equals, "the sexual act now requires a special psychic attitude to the sexual object," and that "psychic attitude" is love (p. 78).

By the time Mises wrote those words in the early 1920s, modern marriage had indeed become sexualized in ways that would have been nearly unrecognizable to those of a few generations before. Before marriage got there, however, it had to deal with the very serious tension between the love-sex-marriage connection and the ideals of the Victorian era. The doctrine of the separate spheres created a dramatic separation between the lives lived by husbands and wives. To the extent they stuck to their own spheres, their moment-to-moment and day-to-day existences had little in common. One result was that it was harder to achieve the sort of emotional intimacy that we associate with twentieth- and twenty-first-century marriages. Living very much in different worlds, it was hard to imagine one's spouse as a conversation partner who could empathize with the struggles and challenges of the typical day. This separateness also explains the predominance of same-sex recreation activities, from the craft groups of women to the pubs and sports of men. Seeking out same-sex social groups was a way to find others who understood what the finer details of your life were like.

This lack of emotional intimacy worked against the sort of sexual marriage that we now take as the norm. However, as Coontz (2005, p. 189) points out, there was a second issue that made matters worse: "While the doctrine of difference inhibited emotional intimacy, the cult of female purity in particular made physical intimacy even more problematic." The separate spheres doctrine saw the public world in which men operated, particularly the world of money and markets, as being a kind of necessary evil, or a dirty world which women were fortunate to not have to deal with. The veneration of the domestic sphere and women's role in it was extended to a more general belief in the purity and goodness of women that was then contrasted with the more base, animal nature of men. There was a "dirtyness" to both men's financial and sexual desires that was "beneath" the clean, pure Victorian woman. The result was that a good number of marriages of the Victorian era suffered from problematic sex lives where women thought that being outwardly sexual was inappropriate and where men, buying into the same set of beliefs, often found it difficult to envision their wives as sexual beings. Not surprisingly, male patronage of prostitutes was often a "solution" to such situations, as prostitutes had already undermined their own feminine purity by crossing into the commercial sphere, and doing so sexually.[8] The conflict of the mores of the two worlds was on full display in the differing treatment of marital and commercial sex.

These tensions manifested themselves during the Progressive Era's social purity and social hygiene movements. As part of the era's more general attempt to manage human interaction in more scientific ways, a tendency we saw with the child-rearing manuals of the time, reformers attempted to use some moral suasion, but more importantly the power of the state, to regulate the sexual behavior of the population. Their concerns ran from prostitution to sexually transmitted diseases, to the extraordinary panics over masturbation and child sexuality[9] that were the more extreme moments of the social hygiene movement.[10] Like the movement to make child-rearing more scientific, the hygiene movement tended to target immigrants and nonwhites disproportionately. The one upside of the movement was that it did bring discussion of sexual issues out into the open in ways previously unseen. By doing so, it may have inadvertently paved the way for the sexual freedom backlash of the post–World War I period.

As D'Emilio and Freedman (1988, p. 215) argue, the concern about the increased sexualization of American life during the Progressive Era was the product of the underlying changes in the economy, specifically the ongoing growth and spread of capitalism: "The entry of women into the work force, the breakdown of the separate spheres that underlay earlier norms, and the commercialization of much of American life (including pleasure) that came with the spread of capitalist social relations, all contributed to the crisis that fed the Progressive era's sexual politics." The increased presence of women in previously nearly all-male circles was the critical point. Women's entry into higher education, the work force, and, at least through their activity in various reform groups, the political arena meant that men and women, especially younger ones, "began to socialize on more equal terms" (Coontz 2005, p. 197). Rather than primarily socializing with members of the same sex, all of these changes shifted the primary form of socializing to be more mixed. With more sites of socializing available to both sexes, the young people of the early twentieth century began to sexualize their interactions in ways that undermined the old norms. Contributing a great deal to this process was the growth of the major cities, in which young men and women could both earn a living by working outside of the household economy and their families and could also exist in a relative degree of anonymity that made it easier to break the old rules around sexuality.[11]

Claudia Goldin (2006, p. 4) offers some data and analysis of the increased labor force presence of women during this period. From 1890 to 1930, women aged 25–44 saw their labor force participation rates climb 9.5 percentage points to around 20–25 percent and married white women aged 35–44 climbed from near zero to around 10 percent. These are not large numbers, but they are evidence of the increased presence of women in the market sphere. Women were also interacting more with men in higher education, with women's increased presence in college being a response to economic growth and the increase in service and clerical jobs it brought. Goldin, Katz, and Kuziemko (2006) show that for Americans born in the last 25 years of the nineteenth century, college enrollments were roughly equal between men and women by the time they reached age 35. Women were less likely to have bachelor's degrees as they were more likely to attend two-year teacher colleges. However, by 1925, only 22 percent of women in college were enrolled in all-women's schools of any sort.[12] Higher education, along with the world of work, were increasingly becoming public sphere sites of interaction between the sexes and ones that were free of parental oversight.

Reductions in parental oversight were also taking place in other venues, thanks to economic growth and new technology. By the end of the nineteenth century, the middle-class practice was that boys would be invited to "come calling" to the house of a girl with whom they wished to have a romantic relationship. The prospective couple would get to know each other at her house, under the watchful eye of her family. Coontz (2005, p. 199) points out that this practice gave the girl's parents a good deal of control over her behavior, as they provided the physical location as well as the hospitality. Boys, in fact, had to wait for permission to come calling. With the private sphere of the home being the site of relationship-building, it is not surprising that it was women, both the girl and her mother, who had power over the process. Clearly, with such relationships being built under those constraints, the opportunity for privacy and any sexual activity was limited.

By the 1920s, this process had been reversed. Our modern notion of a date, where the couple spends their time away from home in the public sphere, begins to take hold in the first decade or two of the twentieth century. A number of factors were responsible for this shift. Some economic explanations included the ongoing increase in wages that made it easier for young men to have disposable income to spend on a date and more growth-induced entertainment options for spending it in the public sphere (such as the advent of movies and the gradual proliferation of affordable restaurants). A key technological factor was the automobile, which made getting around the public sphere much easier and provided a form of privacy even within that public sphere. The privacy of the car combined with being out from under the watchful eye of parents made it a site of a great deal of sexual experimentation (which it remains to this day).[13] Perhaps most important in all of this was that the shift from calling to dating put boys in control over the terms of the relationship, as they were much more likely to have the economic resources now required to build a romantic/sexual relationship. Boys were now expected to be the initiator of relationships, and with their control of the hospitality, the question of what young women were obliged to provide in return hovered over the evolving relationship.

At the same time that opportunities for sexual experimentation were expanding, so was knowledge of human sexuality, reflected in increased public discussion of the subject. This change was the product of a combination of cultural, technological, and economic factors. Freud's work, despite all of its flaws, made it acceptable to discuss sexual behavior in ways not possible before, especially to the degree it complemented the Progressive Era's fascination with scientific solutions to social problems.[14] Advances in medical knowledge enabled a better understanding of sexuality, especially disease transmission and treatment, and increased literacy and education levels made more of that knowledge available to more people. Access to birth control, thanks to the persistent (if tainted by the stain of eugenics) work of Margaret Sanger, began to improve and public discussion of its role was more frequent. Changes in a variety of laws finally made condoms much more easily available in drugstores by the early 1930s. Finally, the new forms of entertainment such as radio and movies made the portrayal of sex in popular culture more widespread and visceral than did books alone. When combined with the growing role of sex in the advertisements in the burgeoning magazine industry, "popular culture became saturated with sex" (Coontz 2005, p. 198).[15] D'Emilio and Freedman (1988,

p. 241) summarize this set of changes as a movement "toward a view of erotic expression that can be defined as sexual liberalism," including the separation of sexual activity from procreation, which in turn made heterosexual pleasure "a value in itself" and put such pleasure at the center of what made for "personal happiness and successful marriage." It also broke the connection between sexual activity and marriage, which was the start of another central process in the evolution of the family in the twentieth century.

With sexual, political, and economic opportunities starting to become more accessible to women, they began to aspire to the same sort of independence and visibility in the public sphere that men long had. Labor force participation rates for single women continued to rise and rates for married women cracked the 10 percent barrier during the 1920s (Goldin 1991, p. 17), and, along with the right to vote, the growing independence of women was also transforming the relationship between the sexes. Coontz (2005, p. 201) points out that many contemporary observers worried whether this newfound independence and its corresponding challenge to existing gender roles would ultimately destroy marriage.[16] In particular, the fear was that growing female independence would make marriage less important to them and thus undermine the institution as a whole. At some level this fear was justified, at least in the long run, as the place that marriage holds in the longer-term life path of women certainly became less prominent by the end of the century. Some evidence for this transition in the early twentieth century is the data showing that young single women were gaining more years of formal schooling while continuing to participate in the labor force at the same or slightly higher levels. By implication, they must have been devoting less time to other activities, and Goldin (1991, p. 55) suggests it was "time spent at home," being socialized into, and learning the skills involved in, taking on the future role of wife and mother. Young women were beginning to shift their human capital investments from those associated with household production to those of market production. Most of the dramatic effects of this shift were still decades off.

With men and women starting to meet on more equal terms and with sexual compatibility and pleasure playing a larger role in defining a successful marriage, the expectations for what marriage should bring rose accordingly. Rather than defining a good marriage in terms of the yoke-mate work of centuries prior, or playing out the more rigid gender roles of the nineteenth century, the changes of early last century began to make personal happiness and emotional and psychological fulfillment the characteristics of a successful marriage.[17] The key to the immediate effects in the 1920s was that women's changing roles created more scope for the sort of emotional intimacy that marriage had lacked throughout prior human history. The new scope for emotional intimacy was particularly important given the loss of marriage's long-standing economic and political functions: "Because the progress of industrialization and democracy had weakened the political and economic constraints forcing people to get and stay married, such deep intimacy was now seen as the best hope for stability in marriage" (Coontz 2005, p. 203). Marriage and family in the twentieth century would increasingly take on emotional and psychological functions to replace the economic and political ones lost through the processes described in the prior two chapters.

Contemporary observers worried that the new emphasis on personal happiness and emotional intimacy would destroy marriage by making it a mere matter of personal preference rather than a crucial social institution that required the ongoing commitment of the partners. In the long run, their concerns were well-founded, but in the short-run, the reaction was an inward turn toward marriage, home, and the nuclear family. With the increased centrality of the emotional relationship between spouses and the ongoing expansion of the sheltered childhood, the other kinds of social bonds that had been part and parcel of adult life were slowly disappearing. For example, in earlier periods it was expected that married couples would keep close ties to their parents and care for them in their own homes late in their lives, but with the private, emotional life of the couple taking center stage, such ties to parents were seen as old-fashioned and disruptive of a healthy marriage (Coontz 2005, pp. 207–208). Prior patterns where same-sex social groups were part of the typical adult's experience also began to fracture, as husbands and wives increasingly expected to get friendship, intimacy, and fun with each other rather than friends from work or the community. The family was becoming increasingly nuclear as couples shed many of the bonds that connected them outside the family. Marriage began to pick up the social and interpersonal functions that those other social practices and groups used to fulfill.

## Female Labor Force Participation and the Shrinking Sphere of Household Production

The ways in which young women were allocating their time in the first few decades of the twentieth century presage the major changes that would come in the later decades. The spread of high schools and the expectation that girls would finish at least that level of education, combined with the increasing job opportunities for women in the growing service and clerical sectors, meant that more of women's time was devoted to investment in human capital and the deployment of that human capital in the world of market production. The result was that high school aged girls spent less time engaged in household production and developing the human capital that prior generations associated with the roles of wife and mother. At the same time, the technology of household production was changing in ways that began to reduce the labor hours necessary to engage in basic cleaning and cooking activities. This development was highly complementary to the increased education and work available to young women, but it had an important effect on the nature of the family as well. As capitalism and democracy squeezed out the role of the family in market production and the political sphere, the separate spheres doctrine of the nineteenth century filled the void in the family's functions with its emphasis on domesticity. The family was about creating that private space sheltered from the worlds of markets and politics and it was women's job to make sure that function was fulfilled, which required both physical and emotional labor to make the house a physical and emotional respite. Given the technology and expectations of the time, household production was a full-time job that replaced the time women in generations before had spent on market production, either on farms, in factories, or in cottage industries.

Goldin (2006) describes the evolution of female labor force participation in four phases driven by the terms of the relationship between the income effect of increased wages for husbands and the substitution effect of higher potential wages for wives. One would expect that, at least early in the twentieth century, as husbands' incomes rose, wives would be *less* likely to work, all other things equal. As the wages available to women rose, it would, again all else equal, make women *more* likely to work. The question is over the relative strengths of these opposite effects.

In the early twentieth century, the income effect largely dominated the substitution effect, as the social stigma of wives working in the market made their labor supply fairly insensitive to changes in wages and therefore changes in demand. The increases in the labor force participation of married women seen between 1890 and 1930, around 9.5 percentage points for women aged 25–44, "must have resulted largely from shifts in the labor supply function" (Goldin 2006, p. 4). Goldin also points out that given the strength of the income effect, these shifts in the supply curve had to have been fairly substantial to outweigh the income effect sufficiently to generate the increased labor force participation. As we have already noted, the factors that were pushing out the labor supply curve were more educational opportunities, the rise of less unpleasant work, such as clerical and service jobs, fewer children per family, and the slowly declining stigma associated with women working. Put differently, the increased labor force participation of married women early in the century was not a response to the higher wages they could earn there, but to changes in the factors affecting their preference for, or ability to, work in general.[18]

Over the period from 1930 to 1950, what Goldin (2006) calls "Phase II," married women's labor force participation rates jumped by 15.5 percentage points to 25 percent, for those aged 35–44. By 1950, 47 percent of employed women were married (p. 5). Explaining this increase involves both the demand and supply side of the labor market. The continued growth in office work and the larger percentage of high school educated women combined to mean that more young women had "nice" jobs prior to marriage, as well as skills that could be deployed in work in later years. As Goldin points out, most of these women left work at marriage in the 1930s and early 1940s due to social norms but also due to marriage bars that mandated that women leave jobs upon marriage. Marriage bars were often found in school districts, as well as in the private sector. They were particularly common in the 1930s, as the high unemployment rates of the Great Depression made it seem unfair that some families had two working adults when so many others had none. In 1932, Congress prohibited the federal government from employing two people in the same family. Coontz (2005, p. 219) observes that even though the language was gender neutral, "nearly all of the 1500 people fired in the first year were women." The marriage bars peaked in the early 1940s and declined as the Depression eased and as women's experiences in war production began to shift cultural norms. Despite the marriage bars, the need for clerical workers with education continued to push labor force participation rates upward.

The shifting norms around women's work, especially as husbands began to accept their wives working, began to reduce the negative income effect of male wages on female labor force participation. Goldin defines Phase Two of the evolution of female labor force participation as a transition period where the income effect began to fall (in absolute value) and the substitution effect began to rise. In other words, labor force participation rates for married women became increasingly responsive to the wages they could earn rather than changes in preferences. Goldin (2006, p. 5) points to the rise of part-time work in the 1940s as being a key factor. In prior decades, married women responded to changes in the market wage with an "in or out" decision in the labor market, and not a change in their hours, because the necessary flexibility did not exist. The growth in part-time work in the 1940s (and its even larger growth in the 1950s) changed that and allowed women to adjust on the margin of hours, making it possible for some married women to join the labor force who would not have, had full-time work been the only option.

All of this focus on human capital and wages needs to be supplemented by consideration of the alternative uses of married women's time and the functions that families and households must perform. The decision that married couples face about who will work and how much work they will do must recognize that, although market production can earn valuable income, the tasks of household production must get completed. Houses have to be cleaned, lawns have to be mowed, laundry has to be done, meals have to be prepared, and children have to be cared for. When there was no line between household and market production in the precapitalist economy, women were able to contribute to both processes with great fluidity as both took place in the home. With industrialization breaking the link between home and work, accomplishing the dual tasks of earning an income and managing the household became a more complex decision. Early on during industrialization, both husbands and wives (not to mention children) worked outside the home (or engaged in putting out inside the home), given that wages were too low for families to survive on one income. A strict division of labor between the market and household was simply not feasible.

As wages rose, and Victorian domesticity and the idea of the separate spheres grew along with them, children and women retreated to the home, creating the gendered division of labor between the market and household that was the norm in most Western households until recently. Men were assumed to be in the market and women in the household. The implication of this is that for most of the twentieth century, the decision facing households deciding whether the wife should work was dependent on their ability to find resources other than her time that would ensure that household production was taken care of. The option of the woman working and the man staying home to care for the house simply was not on the table. This was because of prevailing cultural norms and because the circumstances were so rare under which the wages available to the woman were high enough for such a decision to be remotely feasible (not to mention finding a man with the right human capital to be as productive as necessary at household production).[19] Women have been seen, at least until very recently, as the secondary earner, which means that their decision to work has been affected by the need to ensure that household production is still undertaken.

In general, households have three ways to substitute for (female) labor in accomplishing the tasks of household production. The first is to expect more from other household members, especially children. As more children attended school for longer periods of time over the twentieth century, this became less of an option. Other extended family members did sometimes present a viable alternative, especially with respect to child care. The other two choices are more salient, especially earlier in the century. The second option is to purchase more substitutes for household production on the market. Paying others to do laundry, mow lawns, or care for your children or make your meals (either at home or a restaurant) are all alternatives to applying household labor to those tasks. The final option is to take greater advantage of labor-saving technology. Rather than paying others to do the work, purchase appliances that reduce the amount of human labor required to accomplish the task. The best example here is the development of automatic clothes washers and dryers, which took a task that by some estimates consumed three days (and often prevented young girls from going to school so they could help with it) at the dawn of the twentieth century and reduced it to a matter of hours and allowed people to engage in other tasks while the machines did the work. As households decided whether it made sense for the wife to work in addition to the husband, historically it was the case that they would have had to ensure that one or more of these options for engaging in household production were feasible. Alternatively, the feasibility of these options was a key factor affecting the decision of married women to enter the labor force.

During the Phase Two period of 1930–1950, identified by Goldin, these factors were in play. The technologies noted earlier were spreading quickly among the middle and working classes in addition to even more basic ones such as refrigerators, running water, electric lights, and the flush toilet.[20] By reducing the amount of time necessary to engage in some of the most basic tasks of household production, these new technologies and appliances made the wage necessary to lure women into the labor force lower than it would be otherwise. In technical terms, this increased the elasticity of the aggregate labor supply curve for women, which meant that they were more likely to respond to an increased demand for their labor than in years past. Definitive data on time spent in household production going back that far is difficult to come by, but anecdotal and indirect evidence is fairly plentiful, and the evidence for the second half of the century is quite clear in demonstrating the decline in housework hours by employed women and married women (Jacobsen 2007, p. 111).[21]

At the same time, market alternatives to household production were becoming more common and, as men's and women's wages continued to rise, more affordable. Options for dining out expanded, and it is not coincidental that the rise of the diner as a cheap eating-out experience takes place in this period, nor that the 1950s and 1960s soon to follow saw the origins of the fast food restaurants that have enabled families to solve these problems into our own time. Even as early as the late 1910s, a majority of middle-income families had begun to use commercial laundry services and around 16 percent had household servants of some kind (Moehling 2001, cited in Goldin 2006, p. 5). In combination with the increasingly available labor-saving appliances, these market substitutes made labor force participation increasingly possible for married women.

One further factor is worth mentioning. The early twentieth century also marked a period of declining family size as the factors in play since industrialization continued their long-term trends. With fewer children in the household and with better birth control options available, allowing couples to space the children they did have, women had a greater ability to juggle children and work than they had in the past. Fewer children meant less time devoted to child care both at any point in time and in terms of the total number of years with young children at home. A desire for fewer children also meant fewer pregnancies, which led to fewer interruptions of any employment women might have, as well as a reduction in the health risks associated with frequent pregnancies. All of these together made it more likely that married women could work outside the home either with or without children. What was once an enormous sphere of responsibility was now beginning to shrink with these demographic changes, reducing the time required to fulfill functions of the family-based household and thereby also reducing the opportunity cost of female labor force participation. The continuation of these trends later in the century, in particular the development of even more effective birth control methods that women controlled, will be taken up later in this chapter.

The appearance of these various household technologies and market alternatives to household production is also a product of the wealth created by capitalism. The competition and technology that made these products and services affordable, along with the growth in capital that increased wages to the point where they could be afforded by increasing numbers of people, are all results of the institutions of the market economy. The effects that capitalism-driven economic growth had in liberating women by giving them (and men in more recent times) a set of real choices involving work and home cannot be understated, nor can the resulting effects on the functions and form of the family.

## The Misunderstood 1950s Family

Goldin's use of the word "evolution" to describe the ongoing growth of female labor force participation in the first half of the twentieth century is worth a deeper examination. A look at the growth in that participation rate reveals a steady upward march in the data, especially for married women, from early in the century until the numbers begin to plateau in the late 1980s and early 1990s. The slope of the trend lines do not markedly change, especially over the post–World War II era. The history of women's increased presence in the labor force does not show any distinct points at which participation rates changed dramatically.

The importance of this point is its relationship to common narratives about the 1950s and the women's movement that followed it in the 1960s and 1970s. One of those narratives, frequently associated with conservatives, points to the 1950s as a time when women largely stayed home with their children, forgoing the labor market while the children were young. The next decade, this narrative argues, saw the rise of the women's movement, which pushed women out of the house and into the labor market, undermining family stability and creating the conditions for the supposed fragmentation of the family in the past few decades. The assumption of this narrative is that the women's movement was the cause of a great exodus of married women into the labor market. However, the smoother progression found in the data tells a different story. Although it is true that the late 1960s marked the beginning of greater labor force participation for married women with young children, such women were not nonexistent during the 1950s and the growing labor force participation of older married women paved the way for the changes of the decades to follow.

In this section, I want to make a few brief points about the 1950s family, a subject on which entire books have been written (e.g., Coontz 1992). My focus will be on two elements: the ongoing changes in female labor force participation and the degree to which our perceptions of the 1950s family are the product of nostalgia and thereby cause problems for our understanding of the family's more recent history.

The labor force participation rates of married women grew steadily through the 1950s, led by women 45 and older, many of whom were employed during World War II and were able to keep their jobs after its conclusion. Younger married women saw the growth in their participation continue, and then increase somewhat more intensely toward the end of the decade. For married women aged 35–44, labor force participation rates "increased from 25 to 46 percent from 1950 to 1970" (Goldin 2006, p. 6). Goldin points out that this era saw the continued change in the relative importance of the substitution and income effects on women's work. Continued acceptance of married women working, surely helped by their roles during the war, dampened the income effect, and the fact that the average employed married woman was better educated than average married women as a whole suggests that educated women were responding to better wage opportunities. The end of marriage bars and the continued expansion of part-time work were also factors making the quantity of married women's labor supplied more responsive to changes in the wage rate. Changes in demand, Goldin argues, were mostly the cause of increased participation rates and hours of work. All of that said, "married women were still the secondary earners in their households," and they were largely segregated in a few jobs where the skills they already had were sufficient to get and remain employed (e.g., secretaries, teachers, librarians, etc.). Few of these women expected to have long-running careers. Most imagined themselves in more intermittent work and therefore did not invest in the human capital necessary for a genuine career.[22]

With approximately 35–40 percent of married women with their youngest child between 6 and 17 participating in the labor force by the end of the 1950s (and the numbers were higher for black women), the image we get from the TV shows of the late 1950s and early 1960s of stay-at-home mom caring for the children while dad does the market work was hardly universal.[23] Even 15–20 percent of married women with a youngest child under 6 were in the labor force over the decade of the 1950s (Jacobsen 2007, p. 102), and here too the numbers for black women were higher. Labor force participation rates for black married women with small children exceeded 40 percent (Coontz 1992, p. 30).

At the same time, women were marrying younger, with 1956 recording the lowest ever median age of marriage for both men and women at 22.5 and 20.1, respectively. These were the early years of the postwar baby boom as well, with the birth rate per thousand remaining well above the long-term trend line throughout the 1950s and early 1960s, even accounting for the steep decline in birth rates during the Great Depression (Jacobsen 2007, pp. 141–44). These two factors together are responsible for two elements of the 1950s. The first of those is that while all elements of female labor force participation grew, it was especially evident in the increased participation of older married women. Early marriage and high birth rates meant that one of the traditional sources of transient female labor, the young and unmarried, was in short supply. Combined with the continued expansion of the clerical and service sectors causing a large increase in the demand for labor, this demographic shift meant that firms had to reconsider their previous reluctance to hire married women. The marriage bars quickly fell and many of the same women who had been responsible for the rising participation of younger unmarried women in the 1920s were now returning to the labor force in their later years. Their employment had two important effects: it demonstrated to firms that hiring married women made economic sense and it offered a role model to these women's daughters with respect to their future choices about work and home. The labor force participation trends of the 1950s would set into motion many of the changes that would follow in the later decades.

The declining median age of marriage and high birth rate are also responsible for the sense in which our nostalgic view of the 1950s family has important elements of truth in it. It was a time during which marriage, children, family, and home became central to people's lives and identities, especially those of women, to a degree they had not before. We saw earlier how during the 1920s marriage increasingly took on the function of meeting the psychological, emotional, and sexual needs of the couple, leading them to focus more on themselves than on other social connections. The Great Depression and World War II interrupted that process, or at least slowed it, by the former pushing the economic functions of marriage and family back to the forefront as many struggled to make ends meet and by the latter separating couples either temporarily or permanently. The 1950s, however, not only revitalized the centrality of companionate marriage, it extended that norm to the whole range of features we associate with the family form of that era. The presence of television and other mass media enabled that norm to spread "like a steamroller that crushed every alternative view" (Coontz 2005, p. 229).[24]

So powerful was that steamroller that the features of the 1950s family have come to define what many see as the traditional family. In particular, the ideas that marriage should be entered into at a fairly young age and followed quickly by children, that family was about a nuclear existence largely independent of extended family and other social groups, and that, perhaps most importantly, it was the woman's role to stay home with the children and the man's role to earn a living all became defining characteristics of the so-called traditional family. Moreover, these features took on an incredible normative power that quickly defined other family forms as nontraditional or even deviant and established the TV family as the aspired-to image of the family for an entire generation, including those whose own families were very different. The role of the mass media in this development cannot be overstated. The advent of television enabled an idealized image of the family to be created and spread with unprecedented ease and reach. One need not see the media's convergence on this one family form as an intentional attempt to marginalize alternative forms to recognize the ways in which it had that effect. As Coontz and others have pointed out, although not *every* 1950s family looked like those on TV, more real-world families did indeed have these characteristics than ever had in human history. That media looking to appeal to a broad audience would choose that family form to portray as normal in both the descriptive sense as well as the prescriptive sense should therefore come as no surprise.

This TV-drenched perception of the 1950s family was primarily responsible for the mythology that this particular family form was traditional and normal in the prescriptive sense, which has had large and problematic implications for our understanding of the changes in the family since the 1950s as well as a whole variety of related family policy issues. The prior two chapters have provided ample evidence to contest the claim that the 1950s family was traditional in any meaningful sense of the term. About the most that could be said is that heterosexual marriage is the one element of that family that has been a near-constant in the history of the Western family. But all of the other elements, from companionate, sexual marriage, to the male breadwinner, to the family having emotional and psychological functions at its core, to the sheltered childhood are all ones that are postindustrial if not specifically twentieth-century phenomena. To universalize this family form as traditional is ahistorical, and by reifying the family form of one historical moment, it diverts our attention from the more important issue of exploring what functions families must perform in the social context they find themselves and how family forms and structures have evolved to perform them. One consequence is that discussions of family policy get overly focused on issues of form, with the implicit assumption that a particular family form, something akin to the iconic 1950s family, is the only one that is functional. The reluctance to explore whether, and how, various forms might be sufficiently functional is to a large part due to a mistaken belief about how traditional the 1950s family really was.

To the extent that a good number of families in the 1950s really did resemble the TV image, it was the result of a confluence of a set of unique historical factors, including a number of government policies rather than some long-term, natural state of the family. The historical factors were dominated by the continued growth that the market economy was producing, which was especially high-powered in the aftermath of World War II. Combined with an economy that was producing well-paid industrial jobs for even those with modest education and other human capital, and progressively cheaper consumption goods, the possibility that large numbers of families could live very well on one, male, income had never been greater.[25] The desire to return home that followed the war was certainly pushed along by the media and other cultural forces that made leaving the workforce and becoming a homemaker women's patriotic duty when the war ended.[26] The ongoing demise of the economic and political functions of the family meant that its newly acquired emotional and psychological functions, as well as the heightened importance of sexuality within marriage, would continue to rise in prominence, leading to a whole new set of expectations and responsibility for wives and mothers. They were expected to keep an immaculate home, be the doting mother providing the appropriately sheltered childhood for their children, and to be, simultaneously, their husband's emotional support and sexual companion. This confluence of historical factors was unique in human history and the family structure that it produced was much more a product of the times than some universal archetype or endpoint of social evolution, or even the only form of marriage and family suitable to an industrialized society, as some observers believed at the time (Coontz 2005, pp. 242–44).

Gender relationships and the family have hardly been the product of an evolutionary process devoid of political intervention, whatever one's judgment about the value of such interventions. And although the twentieth century saw the reduction or elimination of a number of such interventions, including particularly crucial ones such as limitations on married women's rights to property and contract and the various pieces of protective legislation, there were still plenty of government policies that were relevant for the emergence of the family. Government subsidies for education via the GI Bill and for the automobile via the construction of the interstate highway system surely contributed to important elements of the 1950s family, as the highways contributed to the creation of the suburbs by lowering transportation costs. Another whole series of subsidies were those related to homeownership, in particular those of the Federal Housing Authority, which insured private lenders, enabling them to give loans that required well under a 20 percent down payment. One could add a whole variety of subsidies and tax breaks for residential and real estate developments that also helped to create the modern suburbs as we know them. None of this is to say that such developments would not have happened through other means had these subsidies not been in place, but such a claim requires an argument rather than an assertion that the 1950s family and the conditions that produced it were only the product of some natural set of social forces.[27]

This point is worth making because, in retrospect, we know that the 1950s family did not last very long, as several events in the decade to follow would push the family in a number of new directions. Too often in discussions of family policy, however, the 1950s family is invoked as a standard of normality or the traditional family against which later changes are unfavorably compared. A longer historical perspective and a closer look at the contemporary factors in play in the immediate postwar era enable us to recognize that the 1950s family was a unique moment in time in which a particular family form dominated as never before or since. Part of the dominance of that form was the result of the family taking on new functions that had not been central in prior centuries. The twentieth century's emphasis on the emotional and sexual compatibility of the marital dyad, along with the long-run decline in family size, were beginning to put pressure on the long-standing centrality of procreation and child-raising to the functions of marriage and family. In the next decade, that pressure would expand enormously and, buttressed by a variety of economic and social factors that made the labor force participation of mothers of young children increasingly lucrative and possible, it would finally lead to the fragmentation of the 1950s family form into a whole new variety of structures. For classical liberals, these changes in family form reflect an increased level of individual freedom, especially for women. The next several sections explore some of the family forms these changes in the 1960s and 1970s produced.

## Breaking the Link: The Pill and the Revolution in Female Labor Force Participation

As noted already, the labor force participation rates of married women continued to grow in the 1950s, despite the image of the mom-at-home that has become the iconic representation of that era. However, that growth was largely the province of women returning to the labor force after their children were sufficiently grown and less so that of younger women entering the labor force directly after college. For most women at the time, and into the 1960s and early 1970s, their jobs were work rather than a career. For some it was about relieving the boredom of housewifery, for others it was about contributing to family incomes that would otherwise have felt too low. But for only a very few was their work deeply ingrained in their identity in the way it was for men and would be soon enough for a good number of women.

By the late 1970s, however, matters were very different. Through the 1960s and 1970s, the patterns of the 1950s continued in a more or less evolutionary fashion. And if one looks at labor force participation rates, other than the rapidly rising participation of married women with children under one, there are no obvious signs of any real change since the late 1970s. On the surface, things seem to have continued to evolve steadily. However, as Claudia Goldin (2006, p. 8) argues, the relatively stable growth in labor force participation rates masks important underlying changes in women's attitudes toward work that reflect something more of revolution. Specifically, Goldin points to three indicators: "horizon, identity, and decision making." Horizon refers to women taking on a longer-run perspective about their work and family decisions and, more important, *having more accurate expectations about their future work lives.* Identity captures the idea that more women were defining themselves in terms of their work and career and adopting many of the same values about their importance that men had long had. The combined importance of an expanded time horizon and a concern with identity was that it dramatically changed the kinds of decisions women made at younger ages, which in turn affected their work and family lives down the road.

The most powerful evidence for the longer and more accurate planning horizons is data from surveys of young women asking them what they imagine they will be doing at later stages in their lives. The National Longitudinal Surveys of Young Women and Youth asked young women in their late teens whether they expected to be engaged in paid employment at age 35. Those numbers rise from around 25–33 percent in the late 1960s to around 50 percent by the early 1970s and then over 80 percent by the early 1980s (see Goldin 2006, p. 9). Clearly young women were revising their expectations. Goldin points out that the 33 percent number was an accurate mirror of the likelihood of their mothers' labor force participation. The reality, however, was their own lives would be different. In 1968, 28 percent of white women aged 14–24 imagined themselves working at age 35. In 1980, 70 percent of those same women were, in fact, in the labor force.[28] Rising expectations eventually caught up to reality and young women now, if anything, slightly overexpect their labor force participation rates. The important implication of their increasingly correct expectations is that young women are now seeing their working lives as long-term commitments, which means making different human capital investments (which is consistent with rising female college attendance, including at the postundergraduate level, and converging patterns of college majors), all of which have implications for family life.

Clearly this is tied with issues of identity as well. Goldin (2006) reports on evidence from surveys of college freshmen that indicate convergence in the weights that males and females assign to the importance of peer recognition and career/financial success. The economic data bear this out indirectly, as both the income and substitution elasticities of women's employment "decreased substantially in (absolute) magnitude for all education groups" over the 1980s and 1990s (p. 12). This means that female employment is stickier in the sense that it takes a larger change in income or wages to cause women to change their labor force participation rates. The implication is that their work is more core to their identity than it used to be and less about more narrowly economic considerations.[29] Putting their more accurate expectations and increasingly work-related identities together helps to explain the different decisions young women now make with respect to their human capital and willingness to marry and raise children. The later ages of first marriage and first child since the 1950s, along with the continued decline in the number of children per family, reflect the shifting ways in which young women are using their time in response to a different view of their own futures.

A few things had to happen in the 1960s to generate this shift in attitudes toward work among American women. One important factor was the continued expansion of the economy, which increased the demand for labor and the wages that women could earn, which in turn continued to raise the opportunity cost of staying out of the workforce. The decreasingly physical nature of much work, along with an increase in the number of women with some amount of college education, also made the labor force more accessible to women and made it more likely they, and then their daughters, would imagine themselves engaged in more career-oriented work. Of course the more general increase in women's rights that took place during the 1960s and early 1970s matters here too, even if it was a response to an earlier cohort's experiences in the labor force.

But above all of these issues, it was the invention of the Pill that arguably had the most immediate and profound effect on the relationships among gender, work, and family. The birth control pill enabled women, really for the first time, to be in total control of their fertility with a device that was extremely effective if used properly. It was also a device the responsibility for which rested solely on the woman, freeing her from relying on a partner for providing and properly using contraception. The effect, as the Pill's use spread, was to reliably separate sexual intercourse from reproduction for the first time in human history for a wide swath of the population. The Pill was introduced in 1960 and first affected married women as numerous states had laws that made access to birth control difficult for single women. After the *Griswold v. Connecticut* (1965) decision overturned state laws prohibiting the sale of contraceptives to anyone, including married couples, a number of states enforced such laws against singles. Those laws were overturned in *Eisenstadt v. Baird* (1972).[30] By the early 1970s, the Pill was available to any woman who had a prescription. The delay in its spread to the young and unmarried is reflected in the time lag between its introduction in 1960 and its effects on the choices of young women, which really do not change substantially until a decade or more later.

The most important of these effects was the delay in the age of first marriage, with its rapid climb from the 1950s trough beginning in the mid-1960s and taking even a sharper turn upward by the mid-1970s (Jacobsen 2007, p. 141). As the Pill separated sex from pregnancy, it also separated sex from marriage (not to mention reducing the number of pregnancy-induced early marriages), which enabled young women to get a college education and begin a career without sacrificing romantic/sexual relationships along the way. The later average age of first marriage rose as a consequence.

With more time to devote to increasing their human capital through education and on-the-job experience, it is not surprising that young women began to put their professional identities ahead of any desire for marriage and children. The increased independence the Pill provided was complemented by a variety of other legal changes that put men and women, including husbands and wives, on a more equal playing field. The inclusion of gender in the equal rights legislation of the 1960s, along with Title IX of the Education Act of 1972, and, of course, *Roe v. Wade* (1973), all contributed to this process. Just a few years after *Roe*, "it became illegal to require a married woman to have her husband's written permission to get a loan or a credit card," and the various head and master laws that made husbands the primary member of the marital couple quickly followed into the dustbin of history (Coontz 2005, p. 255).

With new legal rights in hand, and the higher earning power that came from better human capital investments and a career-orientation, the married women of the mid-1970s and since have had a degree of leverage within the marriage that women in years past had only dreamed of. It is not coincidental that divorce comes to the forefront of social concerns around the same time. Divorce rates began their post–World War II ascent in the late 1960s, peaking around 1980 and very slowly declining since. At the same time we have seen changes in divorce law, especially the advent of no-fault divorce starting in California in 1970. Although I will have much more to say about the economics of divorce in the next chapter, a few comments on the cultural issues and effects on family are relevant here.

The rise in the divorce rate from the late 1960s to 1980s tracks the spread of no-fault divorce very closely. There is a raging debate in the economics and sociology literatures about the degree to which no-fault is the cause of higher divorce rates.[31] It might be more fruitful, however, to look at no-fault as the *consequence* of some of the changes noted in this section. That is, might the demand for a divorce process with lower transaction costs be a consequence of changes in the self-identities of women, increases in their economic independence, as well as the even greater centrality of psychological and emotional pleasure as a function of marriage? Where women see themselves as having an identity more independent of their husbands and families, and have the material resources to survive without them, and where unhappiness is socially accepted as a sufficient condition to end a marriage, it would be no surprise that women would want to find easier ways out of marriage. Many observers have argued that the rise in divorce rates in the 1970s was not the direct result of no-fault per se, but rather a kind of pent-up demand for divorce that was finally released once the transaction costs fell. These were marriages that were already bad.

One objection might be that the divorce rate should have then settled back down to its level before no-fault rather than falling as slowly as it has. In the next chapter, I respond to that with an argument about signaling: it may be that the revolution in women's labor force participation and self-identities made it harder for men to know what their prospective wives would be like in 10 or 15 years and harder for women to assume that such men were willing to be married to a career woman. The same sort of cohort lags that characterized the rest of the century's patterns of female labor force participation may be in play here, with younger people now beginning to overcome the signaling problem, leading to somewhat lower divorce rates. Census Bureau data bear this out somewhat as the percentage of men and women married in the late 1980s and early 1990s reaching their 10th and 5th anniversaries, respectively, is anywhere from 1 to 3.4 points higher than those married in the late 1970s, depending on gender (US Census Bureau 2007). So as gender roles and work/family preferences converge for men and women and stabilize, it may be easier for prospective marital partners to form accurate expectations, suggesting that the percentage of marriages ending in divorce will perhaps fall more rapidly than it has in the last couple of decades.[32]

Beyond these effects, the changes in the family that took place in the 1960s and 1970s, especially the break between sex and procreation, had cultural aftershocks that we continue to deal with today. Historically, the connection of sex, marriage, and family in some form or another has been a near-constant. Human infants require care, thus it was understandable that the activity that created said infants would be tightly connected with marriage, so that any infants produced would have parents to care for them. In early times, as we saw in chapter 3, the marital dyad existed in a broader band of kin from which child care could be provided, but even there, sex, marriage, and a broad notion of family all appeared together. The growing economic independence of women along with the appearance of reliable female-controlled contraception came together with the triumph of the sex-centered, love-based marriage to weaken all of these links.

By separating sex from reproduction, the Pill also destroyed the link between sex and marriage for good. With the fear of pregnancy pretty much eliminated, women were free to indulge in sexual experimentation in ways similar to what men had done for generations, and, there was no need for women, and therefore men, to wait until marriage to have sex and less reason to get married at all. Of course even with the low risk of pregnancy, there were still powerful emotional reasons why people would still be choosy about their sexual partners. Even so, with sex severed from reproduction and from marriage, marriage and reproduction took on a new relationship, especially when combined with the growing economic independence of women. One change was that women now had both sufficient cultural acceptance, or at least tolerance, and the economic resources to raise a child outside of a marriage. A second change was that with more women committed to careers, more marriages became childless (or had children at much later ages). In both of these cases, the idea that one key function of marriage was the emotional connection with a partner played a large role. If one wanted a child, there was no reason to get married unless the right partner was there and the psychological-emotional benefits were sufficient. Alternately, if a marriage itself was providing for one's emotional needs, there might not be any reason to have a child. In either case, the combination of the love-based, if not love-exclusive, marriage and the changes in contraception and women's economic status meant that the long-standing assumptions that marriage implied children and that having a child required a marriage had now evaporated.

The result of these changes was a fragmentation of family forms. The economic opportunities produced by the market, the improving technology of birth control, and the continued commitment to both equality under the law for women and an expansion of their individual rights with respect to reproductive decisions all reflected a more libertarian environment for family formation. In 1967, the Supreme Court, in *Loving v. Virginia* (1967), overturned state laws against interracial marriage, further opening up marriage to the realm of individual choice and expanding the range of family types accordingly. In the decades to follow, the range of family structures expanded even more, as single-parent households became more common and more economically viable, more couples chose to live without benefit of legal marriage, more marriages stayed childless, and high divorce rates meant more couples and children found themselves part of blended or step-families where more than two adults functioned as parents.[33] Recent developments in reproductive technology more deeply challenge the notion of children having no more than two parents, as it is possible that as many as eight adults could lay claim to some notion of parenthood, thanks to such technology.[34] By the end of the century, it would be hard to say that there was any family form that rivaled the dominance of the 1950s family in its time. Instead, there seemed to be almost as many types of families as there were people to create them.

## The Emergence of the Gay and Lesbian Claim to Family

The separation of sex, procreation, and marriage and the rise of the love-centered marriage gave rise to a whole other type of family form not mentioned earlier. By the 1970s, gay and lesbian couples were starting to demand their place at the table of marriage and family. When family was centered around marriage, and marriage was tied tightly to procreation rather than pleasure, and where procreation required male-female sexual intercourse, the notion that homosexuals could marry and form families understandably seemed absurd to many. But with the collapse of all of those assumptions in the twentieth century, the legalization of the close analogy of interracial marriage, and the more general multiplication of new family forms, the gay and lesbian demand to be included in the world of marriage and family is hardly as revolutionary as it first seemed. Much as it did for the other changes in marriage and family in the past 200 years, capitalism also had a starring role in the emergence of the gay and lesbian claim to family.

The key historical distinction that needs to be made first is between homosexual acts and homosexual identity. What is unique about the past 120 years or so of human history is not that some number of people have engaged in sexual acts with members of the same sex, but that a fraction of humanity has come to *define* themselves (or be defined by others) in terms of that aspect of their personhood. Literature and art and earlier histories inform us that homosexual acts have been a constant over human history. However, homosexuality, first as condition but now as an identity, is of recent origin. The word itself was first used in 1869 and didn't come into more common use until closer to the end of the century. What the term marked was the idea that some people were sexually attracted to members of their same sex and that orientation was an ongoing, if not permanent, part of who they were. Though first defined in terms of the sexual aspect of that orientation, the word has come, perhaps not surprisingly given the evolution of heterosexual marriage, to be more inclusive of the romantic component of attraction. Same-sex attraction is now thought to be not significantly different from opposite-sex attraction in its combination of love and sexual desire. The role played by capitalism was, as D'Emilio (1993) argues, that it transformed homosexuality from acts that some people engaged in to an identity defined by romantic-sexual attraction.[35]

The first way capitalism drove this process was through the spread of wage labor and the separation of market production and the family, which led to rise of the large city and its anonymity. D'Emilio and Freedman (1988, p. 227) summarize the process as follows: "Labor for wages allowed more and more men, and some women, to detach themselves from a family-based economy and strike out on their own; the anonymous social relations of the metropolis gave them the freedom to pursue their sexual yearnings." Where economic survival did not depend upon having a wife and children to be part of a household-based process of market production, individuals could indeed earn a living outside of the family unit and without marriage and children. The factory system began this process and the subsequent economic growth and urbanization expanded it, as the retail, service, and clerical sectors of the economy became new places for employment outside of the family.

By the turn of the twentieth century, many major US cities were supporting growing, if underground, homosexual subcultures. The size and anonymity of the city made living a gay or lesbian lifestyle possible. The sheer size of cities meant that the absolute number of gays and lesbians would be of a sufficiently critical mass to enable the emergence of a subculture and its associated institutions. Even today, rural gays and lesbians frequently find themselves traveling to the largest nearby city to find the elements of gay culture, much as, say, minority groups in smaller, more ethnically or racially homogeneous towns travel to nearby cities to purchase specific foods that cannot be found where the small extent of the market severely limits the profitability of such a fine division of labor. With size comes anonymity, and given that homosexuality was highly stigmatized well into the twentieth century, the ability to avoid everyone else knowing your business was a welcome change from small-town or rural living.

Closely related to anonymity was the transience of many of the most popular meeting places for gays and lesbians early in the century. Many such places also were already located outside of the acceptable culture for one reason or another. D'Emilio and Freedman (1988, p. 228) provide some examples and an explanation:

> Boardinghouses, waterfront areas where sailors congregated on leave, red-light districts, bohemian communities such as Greenwich Village, transvestite clubs paying the police for protection, military bases with soldiers far from home, YMCAs housing travelers, theatres that hosted touring companies: all of these constituted places freed from the bonds of family and community, able to tolerate deviance from the moral rules of acceptable society.

The cities that emerged from the advent of capitalism and industrialization, especially the port cities, became the gathering place for groups of people who were slowly beginning to be defined collectively in terms of their sexual orientation.

A second effect of capitalism on the evolution of gay identity is that this process was unfolding during the early twentieth century at the same time that the love match and the sex-centered marriage were fully conquering the heterosexual world, thanks to the economic and social forces I have identified. In addition to creating the direct economic conditions that made gay identity possible, for example, wage labor and urbanization, capitalism and its associated economic growth contributed to broader cultural changes that helped gays and lesbians see their sexual orientation as a form of identity. As sexuality in general was unshackled from its Victorian constraints and became an increasingly central part of how a satisfying heterosexual relationship was defined, and as the institution of marriage came to be understood as first and foremost about love and emotional attraction, rather than procreation, it became less strange to view one's choice of emotional and sexual partners as important to one's self-identity. Of course in the world of the early and mid-twentieth century, it was still nearly impossible to live a public life identifying oneself as gay or lesbian. Whatever changes might have taken place in the broader culture that would allow gays and lesbians to see *themselves* differently, the sexualization of marriage and the rise of its emotional functions were still understood solely in the context of heterosexual love, and imagining marriage and family-like relationships outside of the context of procreation was not on the table, given the weight of history.

The changes of the 1960s and 1970s discussed in the last section were instrumental in enabling gays and lesbians to move out of the shadows and more into the mainstream of American culture. The civil rights movement, especially the women's movement, along with the sexual liberation of that period brought together the combination of sexuality and discrimination in ways that eventually exploded in the Stonewall riots in 1969 in New York City. The fight for gay and lesbian rights and recognition had been ongoing, but a very explicit attempt to raid a well-known gay bar in Greenwich Village brought the anger and activism to a breaking point, as patrons fought back against the police. The ongoing scuffles lasted for several days, galvanizing the gay and lesbian community and bringing their concerns into public discourse. Stonewall is generally recognized as the birth of the Gay Liberation Movement and the modern fight for gay and lesbian rights.

At the same time as these events were unfolding, the effects of the Pill, increased female labor force participation rates, and rising divorce rates were changing the face of the heterosexual family in a variety of ways. Falling birth rates associated with rising wealth and (misplaced) concerns about over-population decreased the centrality of children to our understanding of family. More people got married (or decided to live together long-term) just to be together as a pair. The nationwide legalization of abortion contributed this trend as well. Rising divorce rates led to an increase in single-parent families, and for more women, having a child without a husband became an economically feasible choice rather than an accident. Remarriage created complex blended families complete with step-siblings and step-parents of various degrees of involvement in any of the families they might be part of. Adoption became more common, as a result of both fears of over-population and loosening of restrictions on international and inter-racial adoptions. Advances in medical technology opened up opportunities for surrogacy and egg and sperm donations, further complicating our notions of parenthood and family.

With this diversification of family form and the increased public visibility of gays and lesbians, it is not that much of a surprise that gays and lesbians would want to find ways to lay claim to the concept of family.[36] For some it was through parenting, sometimes with biological children from a failed heterosexual marriage and sometimes through adoption, especially in those few states that allowed a same-sex partner to adopt the other partner's child or allowed both do so jointly.[37] For others it was trying to create a dyadic relationship that looked like a heterosexual marriage and to campaign for it to be legally recognized as such. For still others, creating "families we choose" (Weston 1991) was a political act that challenged heterosexual concepts of family through their collaborative arrangements with larger groups of other gays and lesbians to share living arrangements, expenses, and care for one another.[38] Even those who wanted to challenge prevailing understandings of family, still, in some sense, wanted to be able to use the word.

Over the last two decades of the twentieth century, these demands for inclusion were increasingly successful. On the legal front, more and more states began to allow gays and lesbians to adopt and to serve as foster parents, and laws that would deny visitation or custody to divorced gays and lesbians also began to disappear. Culturally, gays and lesbians found themselves more able to be out of the closet, and popular culture helped in that process with more TV shows and films featuring gay and lesbian characters or themes in positive ways, demonstrating, as we saw in the 1950s, the power of mass media to portray particular families in ways that helped them politically. The increased visibility and cultural acceptance of gays and lesbians as actually *having* families had economic effects, as employers could no longer afford to ignore the ways in which such couples looked increasingly like their heterosexual employees' families. The result was the progressive extension of benefits to the partners and children of gay and lesbian employees in the private then public sector. These formal recognitions of the ways in which gays and lesbians had families were clearly based on the idea of family being defined in terms of what people do (i.e., the functions families perform) rather than any particular form. With the fragmentation of the modal form as noted earlier, there were already a variety of structures that were clearly families. And as firms sought to draw the lines of eligibility for partner benefits, they normally looked for evidence of sharing and caring, such as long-term cohabitation, pooling of income, and sharing of expenses. Over this period, family, at least as far as employers were concerned, had little to do with a male-female dyad and children, rather it was about the emotional, psychological, and economic relationships shared by people.

With this increase in the ways in which gays and lesbians were asking to be included in our understanding of family, and the successes it was having, the current debate over legalizing same-sex marriage was very much a logical next step. As Stephanie Coontz has argued, whatever its merits, same-sex marriage is not a revolutionary change; the real revolution was the love-based marriage. Everything since then is just another step along the road that began there. Putting on hold until chapter 10 the question of whether legalizing same-sex marriage would be a good or bad thing from a classical liberal perspective, it is worth noting now that the desire to legalize it is, in many ways, the result of forces set in motion by classical liberal ideas and institutions. We have noted the ways in which capitalism created the economic structures, urbanization, and wealth that made gay and lesbian identity possible, not to mention the love-match marriage. Classical liberalism's demands for equality under the law and a constitutional "presumption of liberty" (Barnett 2004) can also be invoked as part of the desire to legalize same-sex marriage, particularly in light of *Loving v. Virginia* and, more recently, *Lawrence v. Texas* (2003). To the degree that same-sex marriage is seen as feasible, it is because it looks less different from heterosexual marriage than it used to. This convergence is because heterosexual marriage has shed most of its political and economic functions and because we, as a society, have broken the links among sex, marriage, and reproduction.[39] This whole set of social changes has emerged from, and is consistent with, the ideas and institutions underlying classical liberalism and capitalism.[40]

## Invisible Families

The story of the evolution of gay and lesbian claims to family raises a broader issue for the analysis of the family in the twenty-first century. With the greater variety of forms that characterize families in our time, we have increasingly come to understand what a family *is* in terms of what people claiming to be families *do*. For most of human history, especially in the past 200 years, it was easier to identify families by the way a group claiming to be family was structured. This is not to deny the existence of a variety in family forms in the past, but it is to say that then-modal family form of the man, woman, and children was more common than the modal form today. To the extent that we now increasingly define a group as a family by what they do, or by the degree to which they fulfill particular functions we associate with contemporary families, it makes some families hard to see as we have to actually explore how they function to know if they really are what we would want to call family.[41]

Although gay and lesbian *couples* are perhaps the most obvious example of this point, the argument goes well beyond them. There are numerous other instances of groups of people functioning as families in ways that do not match the modal form of the 1950s. Gays and lesbians have frequently established the sorts of "families we choose" mentioned in the last section, where the number of people involved in performing the functions we associate with the heterosexual, nuclear family might extend well beyond two adults. For gays and lesbians with children, financial support and parental care might come from a couple at the center of the family unit as well as the biological parent(s) of the child(ren) and other friends and relatives of the couple. This might be true even if the only romantic/sexual relationship is the couple at the center. In other cases, such familial units might not be centered on a specific couple, but perhaps one individual with children and an extended network of support, or even a more flatly organized group without a clear central pair. Weston's (1991) book offers all kinds of examples of these sorts of families.

Among heterosexuals, there are a number of cases where we might have more than two adults who are involved in some combination of legal and romantic relationship in which they are performing the functions of a family, especially, though not only, with respect to children. The most obvious example of what we might call multiparent families are step-families. Children of divorce might have as many as four adults, and perhaps more, who perform the functions of a parent if their original parents have both remarried after divorces. Looking only at the household in which such children reside (primary physical custody) will give only one picture of parental functioning as it leaves out the contributions of the other legal parent, whatever those might be. Even including his or her contributions leaves out any contributions from the noncustodial parent's partner or spouse. It certainly can be the case that all of these adults are genuinely interested in the welfare of the children and make material and emotional contributions to it. To understand who comprises those children's family, we need to look at the actions the various adults are taking rather than focusing only on whose household the children are in most often, or who has the relevant legal parental rights. Making these invisible relationships more visible in the eyes of the law would offer children some important protections, but doing so is complicated by the assumptions built into the law that no more than two adults can have parental rights and that such rights can only be acquired as an indivisible set.

These questions will undoubtedly become more pressing as one of the next steps in the social evolutionary process that expanded our notions of marriage and family seems to be the uptick in the visibility and acceptance of polyamorous relationships. If we think of marriage as most often having been both heterosexual and a dyad, it should not surprise us that once the assumption of heterosexual exclusivity began to crumble, the assumption that it need be only two would be next. The apparent increase in polyamorous relationships and their heightened visibility in popular culture suggest that polyamory might be the next step in the evolution of marriage. I leave the legal question of plural marriage to chapter 10 and simply note here that should such relationships produce children, whether in the context of marriage or not, polyamorous parents will have to deal with the same assumptions about the nature of parental rights as do step-families.

Similar considerations might also apply to children who are the products of various forms of reproductive technology, surrogacy, or open adoptions. In all three cases, more than two adults could quite easily have a claim to parenthood, and in some cases, the legal parents might choose to allow any of those other adults to play a role in the child's life. If the question is "who is this child's family?" and the answer depends on who acts in ways that perform the functions we associate with family, the family may be composed of people who neither live with nor have legal rights to the child. Like step-families, these other ways of forming families, many of which are a product of the technology and wealth created by capitalism, have evolved more quickly than policy and the law, not to mention our understanding of what family is, have been able to change to accommodate them. This has made invisible important parts of how they function.

A third example of invisible families is the way in which many African-American families have been, and continue to be, structured. The classic treatment of this issue is in *All Our Kin*, Carol Stack's (1974) ethnography of life in a poor, urban, black community in the late 1960s. Best read as a response to the claims of the Moynihan Report (Moynihan 1965) that the black family was more or less utterly dysfunctional, Stack's book offered a detailed look at the ways in which the residents of this community fulfilled the functions of families, sufficiently if not perfectly, with very few of them resembling the two-parent, nuclear family held to be the ideal form. What Stack argued is that looking only at family form was not enough; one had to see how such families actually interacted to understand how they ensured that children were cared for and that people had the material resources they needed to survive.

Several elements of her story are worth mentioning here, although this brief discussion cannot fully capture the richness of the book.[42] One way in which folks survived with many single-parent families and few resources was through various types of "swapping." This could be as simple as sharing items of clothing or household appliances or as complex as finding ways to share modes of transportation. The most fascinating, and perhaps uncomfortable to contemporary readers, form of swapping was the exchange of children to ensure they were cared for. Parents who were temporarily unable to care for a child would find another adult, sometimes an extended family member but sometimes not, who was willing to take on that child's care, often for a period of months or years. Like the other forms of swapping, asking someone else to care for your child established a kind of social indebtedness that could be called upon later by the other party.[43] Various forms of ostracism, especially through gossip, were used to discourage free-riding on the goodwill of others.

What all of this swapping did was to extend the usual economies of scale of a single household across an entire community. Rather than clothing being used by one or two members of a particular household, it became a kind of community resource that a large pool of people could draw upon. Clothing sitting in a closet unworn might be a luxury that individuals or households in better-off communities could afford, but in an impoverished neighborhood, its usefulness to others, and therefore its implicit value as part of the swapping credit process, would outweigh the more private service of being "available" that clothing in a closet represents. The same could be said of parenting services, especially when we recognize that for adults already raising children, the marginal cost of an additional child is notably less than the average cost. Temporarily giving up one's child to an adult in another household was a way of actually extending or combining households to take advantage of those economies of scale. As Stack (1974, p. 62) described it:

> The expansion and contraction of households, and the successive recombination of kinsmen residing together, require adults to care for the children residing in their household. As households shift, rights and responsibilities with regard to

> children are shared. Those women and men who temporarily assume the kinship obligation to care for a child, fostering the child indefinitely, acquire the major cluster of rights and duties ideally associated with "parenthood."

In the context of this community, parenting is seen as a collection of rights but also a collection of functions that need to be performed, and both the rights and the functions can be de facto, but not de jure, unbundled and split among various individuals and households. As a whole, children are cared for, both emotionally and materially, but looking only at individual households or even individual adults will only reveal part of the picture.

Even where children did not change households, other adults could have significant parental roles in children's lives. Anthropologists distinguish between natural and social parenthood, which roughly correspond to de jure (or perhaps biological) parenthood and de facto (especially if understood as functional) parenthood. Closely related is the concept of fictive kin, where people invoke terms of kinship, such as aunt or brother or sister, to describe adults or friends who are not family members but who earn the fictive kin title through the nature of their relationship to the individual. Stack's description of the community of The Flats offers a number of examples of multiple adults playing parental and other familial roles in children's lives, often according to complex and subtle divisions of parental functions among them. Stack (1974, p. 83) explicitly contrasts the middle-class ideal of the mother who performs all of the functions we associate with that term to the families of The Flats where the residents, especially the women, "do not expect a single person, the natural mother, to carry out by herself all of the behavior patterns which 'motherhood' entails."[44] Various aunts and other female relatives may have very specific roles they play with respect to a particular child. In addition, where a natural mother decides to no longer care for the child, these other women will frequently acquire greater or full parental rights in the eyes of the community even if such arrangements "are often in conflict with the publicly sanctioned laws of the state" (p. 89). In contemporary African American communities, women other than the natural mother often play parental roles as "othermothers," and, as Lehr (1999, p. 114) notes, this is also one way that lesbians have entered into the world of parenting and child-raising.

All of these invisible families share two things in common: by not matching the more typical family forms they are frequently overlooked in discussions of families and how they work, and despite not looking like more typical forms, they manage to function to one degree or another. They do so because they find ways to work outside of those traditional forms, and the laws and policies that were made with those forms in mind, to find the structure that works best in the contexts they find themselves. Lehr (1999, pp. 113–14) nicely summarizes this process in response to claims about the dysfunctionality of single-parent families in the African American community:

> While this discourse of blame has been developed and promulgated, the reality that many African-American children are successfully raised in single-parent

> families goes ignored. So, too, do the support systems within communities that have allowed for this success... The network of support that allows for the growth and development of children is more complex than what conservatives... care to see. Because they view two parents who live together as the ideal for children, [they are not] inclined to ask—rather than ignore or vilify—how social policy might better recognize and respect these extended relationships.

This point is applicable to all of the invisible families discussed in this section.

The big question this brief look at invisible families leaves unanswered is the degree to which such family forms are, in fact, functional. The quote from Lehr asserts the claim that "many" African-American children are raised successfully in such families, but what about gay and lesbian families and step-families or single-parent families? I will briefly explore these questions in later chapters, but for now I just wish to note that these families exist and need to be part of what we talk about when we discuss the modern Western family. Moreover, I would argue that such families are functional in the sense that most of their children do get material and emotional support and most do manage to make it to adulthood relatively unscathed. Whether they do so *better* than other family forms remains a matter of contention, as does the question of whether what we should expect from families is meeting some minimum standard of care or whether it should be a matter of policy to try to push the maximum standard of parenting and family functioning possible—or whether something in between is more appropriate. That is the question we need to answer before we declare particular family forms to be failures, and especially failures that might suggest a need for government intervention or disincentives.

These invisible families also present other interesting questions for classical liberals. Although there is little doubt that government policies have contributed to the variety of family forms that we have discussed, I would argue that effects of those policies are small compared to the more secular forces of economic and political change. The wealth and technology that capitalism has brought, along with the expanding sphere of individual freedom that has marked the past 150 or more years, are the powerful, long-run causes of the increasing variety of family forms. If these family forms are insufficiently functional, particularly in raising children who are socialized into respecting the rights of others and sufficiently educated and skilled to contribute positively to a market economy, then the fruits of classical liberalism may contain the seeds of its own downfall. After a more in-depth discussion of marriage and divorce in chapter 6, I turn in chapter 7 to look at the family at the start of the twenty-first century and explore, among other questions, the issue of the functionality of the multiplicity of forms that marks the contemporary family.

# PART III

## *The Twenty-First-Century Family*

# CHAPTER 6

# Marriage, Divorce, and the Market Process*

## Introduction

The discussion so far has largely kept to the side one of the most notable changes in the family over the past 40 years, namely, the increased frequency of divorce and its effects on marriage, family, and children. Although the divorce rate has leveled off, and perhaps even declined very slightly, in the past decade or two, it remains at a level that is historically very high. Understanding the reasons behind higher divorce rates is best accomplished by setting divorce in the broader context of a number of the changes in marriage and the family that were touched on in chapter 5. Changes in the frequency of divorce are both a cause and consequence of changes in the institution of marriage as well as changing gender roles, both of which were focal points of the prior discussion. In this chapter, I explore a number of issues relevant to marriage and divorce in the early twenty-first century by bringing to bear the framework of the Austrian school of economics. The Austrian approaches to disequilibrium, plan formation under uncertainty, and human capital can be combined to illuminate a number of historical changes and empirical puzzles surrounding modern marriage and divorce.

A salient feature of Austrian economics is its attempt to incorporate and account for endogenous change. Some of the best Austrian works in the past 40 years have explored the effects that social and economic institutions have on the patterns of economic outcomes and the ways in which institutions continue to change. As distinct from standard neoclassical economics (with which it shares much in common), recent work in Austrian economics has given special attention to decision-making in conditions of real-world uncertainty (radical, genuine, as opposed to parametric, uncertainty). Starting with individuals who form expectations in particular institutional environments, informed by their own particular knowledge-base, Austrian approaches recognize that expectations, and the plans and valuations to which they lead, may differ among individuals, giving rise to a situation of plan disequilibrium. The market process approach associated with the Austrian school allows for imperfect information, structural uncertainty, and disequilibrium outcomes. This approach has gained relevance lately because of the variety, extent, and rapidity of the changes in social institutions that have characterized recent history. There is generally a growing recognition in economics of the need to include and account for changes in the underlying institutions within which transactions of various types occur.[1] It is this perspective that informs my analysis of marriage and divorce.

## Families and Firms

Traditionally economics distinguishes between households and firms, although the household economics that has been developed in the past several decades could be interpreted to imply that the household is merely a special type of (small) firm. Though there are important similarities between firms and households, such an interpretation obscures the essentially distinct characteristics of households and their role in the broader institutional context. Households produce goods and services for their own consumption and not for the market. This is a defining characteristic and is what distinguishes them from firms, which are organizations that specialize in production for the market.[2] This distinction has important implications.[3] Because they produce for the market, firms exist in a competitive environment in which organizational form and fitness represents one aspect of their general capabilities. Firms jealously guard their competitive advantages and the capabilities that produce them. Households do not exist in an environment that could meaningfully be called competitive in this sense, and therefore do not find imitation a threatening prospect.[4] Quite the contrary: the prospect of generally peaceful, prosperous, and stable households is of benefit to all.

To the extent that successful household forms and practices are valued and can be imitated, they might be expected to proliferate in the population. The still crucial, though less so than in the past, role played by reproduction in the family strongly reinforces this fact, and the values of the offspring can often be presumed to be strongly correlated with those of the parent(s).[5] Evolution in a stable institutional and economic environment could, therefore, be expected to produce stable family forms (Bergstrom 1996). Given that we have seen dramatic changes in family structure take place over the past half century, it seems reasonable to look first for explanations of these changes in the increasing pace of change in the economic and institutional environments. Some of the changes in these environments (expanding work opportunities for women, technological advances in household production, the availability of convenient and inexpensive birth control, etc.) have already been discussed in chapter 5. In this chapter, I shall pay special attention instead to aspects of the legal and social environment that have not received as much attention or have not achieved the same degree of consensus (such as the advent of no-fault divorce and the awarding of child custody). In so doing my focus will be on the effects of changes in the legal structure within which the family is formed, exists, and is dissolved. Much of the literature focuses on uncovering the essentials that characterize families and on comparing them cross-sectionally across populations, income-groups, or other relevant features. The focus here will be on big-picture, long-term changes that have occurred and are occurring over time and how particular environmental changes have both altered the incentives for members of the family to acquire certain types of human capital and the effects those decisions have on observed outcomes. Specifically, I will argue that changes in the legal and social environment have created coordination-reducing uncertainty, leading in turn to more plan disequilibrium in the realm of marriage and family.

In exploring the economics of the family, some historical context is required. As I have argued, the family is arguably the oldest, and perhaps the most important, of all social institutions, and over the course of its long history, it has varied markedly in size, composition, and form. Until recently, however, it was almost invariably characterized by the existence of marriage, where marriage connoted not only the presence of a strong (implicit and explicit) contractual obligation between a man and a woman, but also, importantly, the achievement of an enduring and differential social and legal status, that of a "married person" (Rowthorn 1999). To the extent that, in more recent years, the distinction between a married person and an unmarried person has been blurred, important social and economic consequences have followed, not least of all for the family itself.

Like the firm, the family is an organization that engages in joint production. Family members combine their resources and efforts to produce outcomes that they value. The most obvious is children; others are love and companionship, a clean home, insurance, nutrition, education, and training (and various other types of human capital). The fruits of family production depend, as with production generally, on the scope for the division of labor. In general, the more specialized family members are and, more importantly, become over time, the greater the rewards to household production in comparison to alternatives. In this way, greater advantage can be taken of differences in any natural or acquired comparative advantage between family members. The degree of specialization of family members, specifically of husband and wife, has dramatically decreased as, from one side, women have entered the workforce in large numbers, reducing the advantages of having a specialized male bread-earner around and, from the other, as substitutes for household production have become more numerous and affordable, reducing the advantages to having a specialized female responsible for household production. The benefits of producing certain goods and services with in the household, as opposed to on the market, have been declining. These two trends are also self-reinforcing: as families are increasingly benefiting from two incomes, they can both afford to purchase market substitutes for household production, and the additions to the labor force have helped make such substitutes more widely available and affordable. One of the ironies of this remarkable trend is that a fair number of women entering the labor force are engaging in labor (e.g., teaching, health care, accountancy, and other personal services) quite similar to what their mothers or grandmothers might have performed, except that they are performing those tasks in the market rather than applying them directly to household production.

Marriage is also occurring later and the incidence of marriage has declined at all ages. The median age at first marriage for men has risen from 23.0 in the immediate post–World War II period to 27.1 by 2003. For women, the change is from 20.3 to 25.3 over the same period.[6] The 2003 figures represent a later age than even the relatively high ages of first marriage witnessed in the late nineteenth century. Jacobsen (2007, p. 143) also documents the decline in the percentage of men and women married at various age groups. (The big exception to this decline are those 65 and over, who, due to longer life spans, are now more likely to be married rather than widowed.) Likewise, and more remarkable,[7] the incidence of divorce has risen dramatically in the past 100 years, and the fertility rate has fallen dramatically. Although the internal organization of firms (not to mention the role of any individual firm within the market) is becoming more specialized, that of families is becoming less so.

The rest of the chapter first considers the relationship between marital dissolution and human capital investment, then takes a closer look at the rise in the divorce rate. Insofar as it is possible to make such a distinction, the first discussion looks at the *consequences* of a rising divorce rate while the latter sections looks at its *causes*. The chapter ends with some general conclusions and a brief discussion of the future of the family..

## The Effects of the Declining Benefits of Marriage on Human Capital Acquisition

An important aspect of a market process approach is its understanding of capital. The resources that become inputs into the production process, and the intermediate goods that are produced prior to the final product, are characterized as capital. Decision-makers form capital combinations in pursuit of gain (utility, profit, etc.). Because production plans take time to unfold to their expected results, the entire process of production through capital combinations is assumed to take place in a world of fragmentary knowledge and structural uncertainty. The producer combines the resources he *believes* will be most suitable for producing the output he *believes* that consumers will want.[8]

In the eyes of the producer, the production process represents an integrated and complementary capital structure. Each of the capital items is believed to fit with the others in a structure that will produce the desired output. Frozen in time at the onset of the production process, this complementarity characterizes the structure created by the producer. The producer is in an individual equilibrium with respect to the capital structure he has created and the plan he hopes to execute. The equilibrium here is not with respect to the objective conditions, but rather the relationship between the capital structure and the goal of the plan.

The Austrian approach to capital emphasizes the heterogeneity of capital resources. Capital goods are seen as being specific to a range of uses, with the degree of specificity varying across the economy. Capital is not understood as an undifferentiated, homogenous lump of stuff that can be applied with equal effectiveness to any production plan. The very complementarity of a firm's production plan depends upon its ability to fit together heterogeneous capital inputs into an integrated and complementary structure (Lachmann 1978 [1956]). The multispecific nature of capital also means that the refitting of capital goods (or the retraining of human capital) is not costless and that the capital-using decisions of firms must take this into account. Where the capital structure of the firm must evince complementarity, the use of capital across the whole economy is characterized by degrees of substitutability. When production plans fail, changes must be made and new combinations must be created out of existing capital from elsewhere in the economy.

This analysis applies with equal force to nonhuman and human resources. For the purposes of my argument, almost all that is true of nonhuman capital holds for human capital as well. Each individual is a producer of a structure of human capital that includes all of the various skills, knowledge, education, experience, and the like that each has acquired over a lifetime. The choices made by individuals about the skills and knowledge they acquire will differ, and any attempt at an integrated production plan that includes human actors will have to take account of the heterogeneity of human capital. Human actors will also have to consider the gains and losses of the particular human capital investments they make, facing the same sort of uncertainty faced by market entrepreneurs who are attempting to invest in physical capital. Seen from this perspective, a marriage (and by implication, a family) is an attempt to create an integrated structure of human capital within a household that is consistent with the plan the couple has to engage in the market and household production necessary to sustain the household. That plan can either succeed over time or fail, just as in a firm.

In a world of structural uncertainty, the possibility of one's plan being executed to perfection may well be small. The unfolding future holds genuine surprises that must be dealt with along the way. At each step in the production process, the possibility of plan failure arises. From a market process perspective, plan failure is evidence of disequilibrium. If things do not turn out as planned, there were erroneous expectations by at least one market actor, implying that we could not have been in economy-wide equilibrium (Hayek 1937). Producers who see profits below expectations, or losses, or even unplanned negative cash-flows, must make adjustments in the face of this evidence of plan failure. *Disequilibrium entails equilibrating adjustments.*

Divorce can be seen as evidence of plan failure. Plan failure is linked to the reliability of expectations, which is in turn related to the degree of uncertainty that producers face. In an environment of faster change, for example, there may be more uncertainty and more plan failure. Of course producers will try to respond to the increased number of failed plans by hedging against uncertainty, perhaps by using (human) capital that is more versatile (i.e., less specific) and that can therefore be applied to a larger range of production processes, or possibly by shortening their planning horizons if they believe that uncertainty increases with the length of the planning horizon. If uncertainty is great, we would expect these sort of adaptations to take place and to see evidence of them manifested in a variety of market outcomes. We might also see changes in social institutions that reflect new ways of enabling actors to coordinate their behavior when uncertainty is greater, or different in kind. Later, I will argue that ongoing demographic changes surrounding marriage and the family can be interpreted as reflecting similar rational responses to heightened uncertainty in the social world.

Within marriage, the most important (but not the only) dimension along which human capital can vary is that of (labor) *market-oriented* human capital versus *household-oriented* human capital. Market-oriented human capital (MHC) may, of course, be firm-specific or more general in nature, but it is more useful in the labor market generally than it is in the household. It is oriented to the earning of income, so it aids in household production only indirectly. By contrast, household-oriented human capital (HHC) is oriented primarily toward direct household production. The most obvious and important type of HHC consists of the skills associated with childcare, but it would also include skills for house cleaning, gardening, laundry, car-pooling, cooking, and the like. Since human capital accumulation takes time and effort, and thus has an opportunity cost, specialization in household production involves specializing also in the accumulation of specific human capital.

As we saw in chapter 3, the earliest human families/households were sites of both market and household production. In this world, the contributions of the two marital partners were less distinct than would be the case immediately after industrialization. Still, the marriage was a matter of complementary human capital combinations. Women needed men's comparative physical strength and their contribution to creating wealth in the form of children; men needed women's labor in the fields and their contributions to household production, as well as their contributions to child creation. But without a firm line between the market and the household, and with a limited range of productive activities, individual men and women were not that different from other men or women in the skills they had. The result was that it was easier to form marriages because human capital was far less specialized than in modern times. With human capital being much more general, and the range of outputs it could be devoted to being very narrow, the odds of not finding sufficient complementarity to have a reasonably successful human capital combination were fairly low. In such a world, plan failure in marriage was much less likely.[9]

Given that the household as a production unit requires inputs in the form of market-earned income combined with household human capital, most of human history has seen household members specialize in one or the other, with men in the labor market and women in the household as the historically most common combination in the industrial world.

The pattern of specialization may follow actual or perceived comparative advantages, as, for example, when it is believed that women have a comparative advantage in childcare, and small initial differences in comparative advantage may, through the accumulation of specific human capital, become magnified over time as human capital accumulation is subject to increasing returns via learning by doing (Becker 1981). Some human capital is also marriage specific in that it has more value inside a particular marriage than outside of it. That is, HHC may be specialized to a particular household (i.e., *relationship or marriage-specific*) or it may be more generally applicable (see figure 6.1).[10]

The human capital investment decision is thus influenced by family members' expectations of the duration of the marriage. A marriage of unexpectedly shortened duration, either because of early death of either spouse or because of an increased likelihood of divorce as the marriage unfolds, implies a shortened payoff period and increases the danger of a capital loss from the accumulation of HHC and especially marriage-specific human capital. Thus anything that engenders the expectation of a higher probability of marital dissolution is likely to inhibit the accumulation of HHC. This process is enhanced by the falling gains from specialization in the household. In the rest of the chapter, I consider the effect of known high and rising divorce rates on the human capital structure formed in households. Then I consider the effect more generally of the increased uncertainty associated with marriage. The analysis proceeds from the assumption that the amount and type of human capital a person has and the specialized activities in which a person engages are mutually determined within the household.

There is a self-reinforcing process at work here. As we saw in the last chapter, women's workforce participation has increased steadily in the past half century. At the same time, the gains from marriage that are achieved by home or market sector-specific specialization have fallen. With lower potential gains from marriage, both husband and wife tend to reduce marriage-specific investments

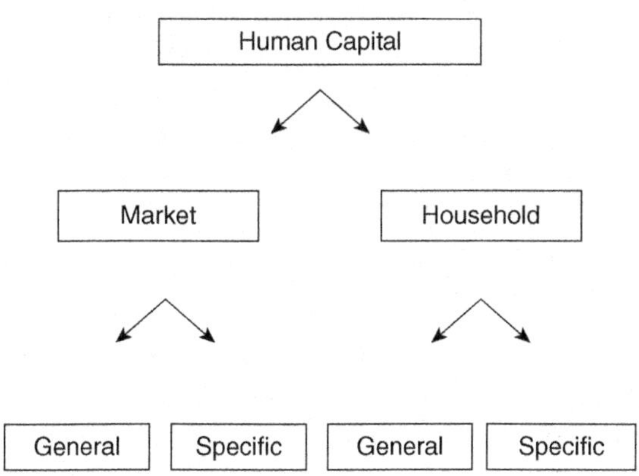


**Figure 6.1** Types of human capital.

in human capital, which in turn lowers the cost of divorce. The lower cost of divorce results from the reduction of the losses associated with marriage-specific human capital that is near-useless after a divorce, due precisely to its overspecificity and the corresponding high costs of "retraining." The lower cost of divorce therefore increases the incidence of divorce. A rising divorce rate implies a higher perceived probability of divorce, and this produces important and different reactions in husband and wife regarding the accumulation of human capital. Those reactions, in turn, further reduce the costs of divorce, themselves making divorce more likely.

Although the gender division of labor within households has become more equal in recent decades, it is perhaps surprising that even as wives have entered into previously predominantly male occupations, husbands have not, to the same extent, taken on more typically female dominated household tasks. This is particularly true of child care, but also other household chores that constitute what Arlie Russel Hochschild (1989) termed the "second shift." Married men increased their hours spent on housework from 4.5 hours per week in 1965 to 11.1 hours in 1985 and 13 in 2005. That improvement is notable, but that 11.1 figure compares to 22.4 hours per week for married women in 1985 and 17 hours in 2005 (Jacobsen 2007, p. 111). The analysis further offers an explanation for the fact that women have made significant progress toward equality in the market, but somewhat less so in the division of household labor. This lack of progress is what Hochschild (1989, p. 45) refers to as the "stalled revolution." Central to that analysis is the influence of children on the prospect of marital dissolution.

The parent who gets primary physical custody of the children will have to be ready to engage in an increased amount of household production. This is true even for a parent with substantial means to be able to afford to pay for child care, since child care is to a great degree "relationship specific."[11] In the modern industrialized societies of the West, the majority of divorces involving children result in child custody going to the mother.[12] This may be because it is generally accepted that because of innate or acquired differences between men and women, the latter are more able and willing to take care of the children, and this has become entrenched in the law.[13] If parental care is an especially relevant concern when children are young, the fact that most divorces occur early in a marriage when the children are younger is likely to combine with the bias toward maternal care to produce maternal physical custody as a frequent outcome. The divorce-rate age profile tends to be bimodal: the divorce rate declines with the duration of marriage, as bad marriages are weeded out and others are locked-in by specialized human capital investments, and rises slightly toward the end of the life cycle when the children are out of the home.

Given that divorce is likely to occur early in marriage, and given that custody is most likely to be awarded to the wife, an increased probability of divorce is likely to increase the bargaining power of the husband and weaken that of the wife with respect to the allocation of household tasks and investment in HHC. (I ignore for the moment the possibility of negating this by a prenuptial contract.) Wives are pulled in two directions by the joint prospect of divorce and single parenthood:

1. As the probability of divorce increases, they are inclined to accumulate more MHC than they otherwise would as a form of insurance against being unable to provide for themselves and their children. Johnson and Skinner (1986) found evidence that women tend to increase their labor supply in the years immediately prior to a marital separation. This evidence supports the view that the women in question are rationally increasing their market-oriented human capital as a form of insurance when they perceive that the likelihood of divorce has increased significantly. As Jacobsen (2007, pp. 114–15) points out, some research has argued that this increase in market-oriented human capital is a way to offset the lack of compensation for marriage-specific investments at divorce. Others have argued that it is a way to offset reductions in market-oriented human capital directly, as those losses do not get compensated at divorce. Either story could be true in particular cases.[14]
2. On the other hand, in anticipation of having to take care of their children without a partner, women might be more likely to agree to specialize in household tasks, especially in a marriage that looks rocky, and thus accumulate more HHC than they otherwise would. Or, in what amounts to the same thing economically but not socially, men anticipating a divorce have less incentive to engage in household production if they assume that their wives will have custody of the children most of the time.

Thus even as women are accumulating additional MHC as insurance against the risk of being a single mother, the relative burden of household production is likely to shift toward them as well. These effects are true both in individual marriages where a divorce increases in likelihood and with respect to marriages in general in an environment of relatively high divorce rates.

A first response might be that increased child support payments by husbands, or the expectation thereof, could address this problem. Doing so may dampen the incentive to acquire more market-oriented human capital, but it will have little effect on the incentives to focus on household-oriented human capital in anticipation of custody. In fact, to the extent that better child support payments may be anticipated, married women need not invest in as much, or as high quality, MHC to maintain a given standard of living as their market wages will be supplemented by the larger child support. On the margin then, better child support payments after divorce, given the likelihood of maternal physical custody, might lead women to spend more time with their children or engage in other forms of household production before the divorce. Higher or more reliable child support payments may well increase women's economic well-being after a divorce but could feed back to have the effect of worsening the inequalities of the second shift in the predivorce household.

In general, married women are likely to have a less market-oriented human capital structure than their husbands, even though the increase in the probability of divorce, ceteris paribus, increases their rate of labor force participation. More specifically, although married women participate more in the workforce than they used to, their MHC structure is likely to be more general and less specific in nature than that of their husbands. This is because the accumulation of more specific MHC involves a greater sacrifice of HHC, which remains relatively more valuable to them to the degree that the cultural expectation remains that women shoulder a disproportionate burden of household production including postdivorce child custody. The point here is not that these differences in human capital structure between men and women that the cultural norm generates are immutable. Cultural changes could indeed help to reduce those differences. The point here, however, is that these differences in human capital, and their relationship to the inequalities of the second shift, are reinforced by current divorce and custody law.

For example, a rise in the probability of divorce in a specific marriage involving children would be likely to discourage the wife from spending time acquiring training for specific types of MHC. Although we might expect to see women in such situations attempt to increase their more general forms of MHC (such as computer skills, or perhaps finishing off a college degree), it would be less likely that they would be willing to invest in acquiring very time-intensive specialized skills. This point is reinforced by the fact that single mothers are also likely to prefer jobs that offer them flexibility in scheduling and other compensating differentials. Such jobs are more likely to involve more general forms of MHC (such as retail positions or clerical work) rather than fairly specific ones (such as a professional job that demanded a great deal of travel or that had a high decay rate in the MHC necessary to keep current in the field). It also remains to be seen what the effects of the rise in telecommuting are on this argument. To the extent that child care and market work can be combined more easily to take advantage of economies of scope in a single mother's time, it might make it more likely that women anticipating divorce will be able to invest in MHC that would enable them to acquire jobs where they can work out of the home, both during the marriage and afterward. An increase in the ability of divorced mothers with small children to earn good incomes while working at home would further reduce the benefits of marriage and thereby reduce the losses associated with postdivorce custody. As working from the home becomes easier, women's bargaining position (given the likelihood of having postdivorce custody) with respect to household production improves, and we might well see a further reduction in gender differences in housework.

The incentives facing married men reinforce these conclusions. If married women are expected to get the children in a divorce settlement, and if we focus on the costs of custody, then the loss from a divorce is likely to be greater for them than for their husbands. This ignores the loss to husbands who desire custody, which could be substantial and which may in some cases outweigh the cost savings.[15] I will assume that such cases are rare (although I note one such example later) and that, in general, husbands gain from the wives taking on the majority of the child care. In any event, given the way custody usually goes, men are unlikely to plan for having to engage in any significant increase in child-related household production after a divorce, whatever their feelings about custody. *Given the labor market participation rates of women, a rising divorce rate thus works to reduce the amount of HHC that husbands accumulate.*

In an earlier era, when the household division of labor was more specialized, there was little incentive for men to acquire HHC, and with the decline in that specialization, men have indeed acquired more than they used to, as the data presented earlier on time spent in housework would indicate. A strict application of economic theory would suggest, as McKenzie and Tullock (1975) predicted 40 years ago, that as men's and women's wage rates equalized, their opportunity cost of doing housework would equalize, thus the hours each devoted to that activity would equalize. Men's contributions to household production, while increasing, have not equalized to the degree that wage rates have. The discussion here is offered as a possible answer to that puzzle, as the effects of the higher divorce rate and the likelihood of the mother getting physical custody could be causing a reduced effort in household production by men that partially offsets the increase coming from the lower relative opportunity cost (i.e., the smaller gains from specialization) of men engaging in household production.

This is true even for families that do not end in divorce. In this way, the discussion resembles the separate spheres noncooperative bargaining model of Lundberg and Pollak (1993). Married women, facing a rising probability of divorce and a strong likelihood that they will get custody, have less leverage over married men to get them to invest in HHC than they might have if divorce rates were lower or if physical custody were more equally shared. As a result, women are more likely to live with an imbalance in the gender division of labor in the household, where they continue to shoulder the bulk of the household duties in spite of working full- or part-time in the labor market and in spite of the fact that married men are likely working fewer hours than their fathers did.[16] The expectation that divorce is more likely is sufficient to generate the changes in each spouse's human capital structure.

In Arlie Russel Hochschild's (1989, Chapter 4) *The Second Shift*, she recounts the story of the Holt family, which is struggling with many of these same issues. The couple has a small child and both parents work outside the home. Though the wife works somewhat fewer hours than the husband, he does very little to contribute to household production, with the burden of the second shift falling mainly on her. She tried and failed at getting him to do more around the house. As the work of the second shift piles up, especially given his greater leisure time, she considers leaving him. However, she is not sure she can make it on her own with a small child and convinces herself things are not that bad: "It's not worth breaking up a marriage over a dirty frying pan." As Hochschild points out, women in this situation either need to live with the reality of this imbalance or construct a narrative by which the objective inequality does not seem so unequal. The Holts do the latter by dividing the household chores in a way that has a superficial element of equality to it, but where in reality, the wife still is doing the vast majority of the work.[17] The wife clearly knows this arrangement is unequal but accepts it as a necessary myth to keep the marriage together. Seeing her husband's lack of contribution as just a matter of a "dirty frying pan," and then acquiescing in a myth that lets him off the hook for not contributing more equally, indicates the kind of weak bargaining position in which married women frequently find themselves. This analysis offers one explanation for such an outcome.

The incentives for working mothers to accumulate household-oriented human capital and the corresponding incentives that lead working fathers to see little reason to acquire those skills, provide an explanation for the unequal contributions to the second shift by husbands and wives. Furthermore, the process that produces the inequality of the second shift and that also produces the resulting leisure gap between husbands and wives (favoring the former) is self-reinforcing. If women fearing the joint prospect of custody and divorce have the (intrinsic or acquired) comparative advantage in child rearing, such fears will tend to be reinforcing as that advantage makes it more likely that they will be awarded custody. Legal and cultural institutions have evolved from, and perpetuate asymmetry in, the awarding of child custody, and this provokes asymmetry in the investments, which, in turn, reinforce the asymmetry in child custody awards.

## No-Fault and the Spoils of Divorce

Is this situation remediable? Could not husband and wife anticipate these inequities and contract around them? A premarital payment (a bride price), for example, to the wife (or her family) might serve this purpose as it did centuries ago in the West and still today in other parts of the world. Alternately, the marriage contract may incorporate the contingency of divorce and specify payments between the parties in proportion to their contribution to the human capital of the family as a unit *and according to who is judged to be at fault*, thus providing a disincentive for opportunism (see, e.g., Rowthorn 1999, p. 670). To the extent that this is possible (and it may be only to a limited extent owing to the intrinsic incompleteness of contracts), it will tend to encourage increased specialization in either household or market production, since it reduces the risk of divorce and the perils to husbands and wives of being locked into an unprofitable human capital structure. However, the recent and widespread trend in divorce law has been toward unilateral (no-fault) divorce, implying that any party may leave the marriage for any reason, coupled with a reluctance to apply considerations of fault in divorce settlements. This tends to raise the risks of divorce and puts a greater burden on prior contracts to safeguard the financial position of the abandoned spouse, thus explaining the rise in the use of prenuptial agreements in the post-no-fault era.

The term "no-fault divorce" is used to describe a system that in fact includes two elements, only one of which is the absence of a finding of fault. As Parkman (2000) points out, the current divorce system in almost every state in the United States is one where divorce is both *unilateral* and *no-fault*. Unilateral divorce refers to the ability of either party to decide they wish to end the marriage without the consent of the other. No-fault divorce refers to the fact that such a divorce can be for any reason that either party wishes to invoke and that it need not involve a claim that either party is at fault. Prior to the advent of no-fault, divorces, in the United States anyway, were normally granted only if one spouse or the other could prove abuse, abandonment, or adultery on the part of the other. Simply being unhappy, or deciding that one's spouse was not living up to other expectations associated with the marital partnership, was not enough for the law to grant a divorce. Spouses who were just unhappy had to concoct phony evidence of one of the legal grounds for divorce, which entailed significant costs (which tended to work in the man's favor), not to mention undermining the integrity of the judicial system. Fault-based systems did, however, have one major advantage: they allowed for bargaining between the spouses as both needed to consent to the divorce in cases where abuse, abandonment, or adultery were not present. This tended to benefit women, at least financially, as they could ensure a better settlement by withholding their consent. It is important to keep in mind for the discussion to follow that one could continue with no-fault but still require that both parties consent to the divorce, whatever the reasons for wanting to terminate the marriage.

There is some disagreement on the effects of the introduction of no-fault divorce.[18] A complete contracting model would suggest that the parties would contract around any such effects in the long run through side payments. Thus a spouse contemplating abandoning the marriage may be deterred from doing so by a contract that divided the spoils according to the relative contributions to the net worth of the marriage by either spouse.[19] The classic case is that of a husband whose wife's earnings has put him through medical school, prior to her having children and staying at home with them, and who now finds a younger more attractive woman (Cohen 1987; Grossbard-Schechtman and Lemennicier 1999). Should the husband be liable to compensate the wife for her contribution to his human capital investment, including the long-term earnings she has forgone by not accumulating extra market-oriented human capital (as she was working and could not continue her education)? A suitable contract would negate the effects of a no-fault law by requiring a degree of compensation that would, in effect, transform it into a consensual divorce.

This argument is an application of what is known in economics as the Coase Theorem. Coase (1960) argued that if property rights were well-defined and transaction costs were sufficiently low, parties to a contract can always find a suitable arrangement under which the damaged party is compensated such that he or she is indifferent between the damage plus compensation and the status quo ante. Coase pointed out that, again absent transaction costs, it did not even matter who held the property rights in such a case as long as they were well-defined. Imagine the resident of an apartment complex who starts up his noisy motorcycle every morning at 6:30, awakening some number of other residents. There are two possible solutions: either the residents pay the motorcyclist to move elsewhere to start the bike or to acquire a better muffler, or the motorcyclist compensates the residents for disturbing them. At some price, either option will solve the problem. Furthermore, if transactions costs are very low, it does not matter who has the rights (the motorcyclist or the sleeping residents), as in either case, the costs being imposed can be neutralized through a contract with suitable compensation. Given clearly defined rights and very low transaction costs, costs imposed on third parties can be contracted around ex ante.

If the conditions specified by the Coase Theorem hold with respect to marriage contracts, there should have been no long-term effect on the incidence of divorce from the introduction of a unilateral/no-fault divorce system and the abandonment of a consensual one. Spouses could find ways to create contracts that mimicked the outcomes of a consent-based system. In the short-term one would expect a bump in the divorce rate as some spouses took advantage of the new law that had not been anticipated in the marriage contract.

The evidence on this is mixed (see Peters 1992 and Allen 1998 for opposing views) but seems to support the case for a positive effect on the divorce rate (see the survey by Rowthorn [1999, pp. 671–78] and Parkman 1998). This evidence suggests that such effects cannot be contracted around because transaction costs are positive, and perhaps significantly so, and because people are very reluctant, or find it impossible, to take fault into account in divorce settlements. Given that the history of the move to no-fault was a reaction to couples having to either fake faults or engage in costly monitoring of each other's behavior to prove fault, the change was a clear transactions cost reducer. Women trapped in potentially abusive marriages might also be very willing to sacrifice the need for consent and the financial superiority of alternative regimes for the ease of the current divorce law.

However, rather than being an exogenous cause of a reduction in the permanence of marriages, no-fault divorce was more likely an endogenous result of the changes in the institution of marriage that I have documented in earlier chapters. Recall that by the 1950s and 1960s, marriage had changed from a primarily economic and political institution to one centered around human happiness and psychological/emotional goals. As a result, marital partners, especially women, wanted out for reasons beyond abuse, adultery, and abandonment. They wanted to leave because they simply were not happy. Given the change in preferences that this represented, the existing constraints proved too binding. No-fault can therefore be seen an endogenous response of legal institutions to this change in the institution of marriage. That change has, however, opened the possibility of the sort of opportunistic behavior noted earlier, which in turn has reduced further the benefits of marriage.

If one thinks of marriage as, at least in part, a contractual obligation, it is perhaps surprising that no-fault divorce as a norm would gain wide acceptance. Contractual obligations in general are predicated on the notion of performance and responsibility, with penalties for default. This is an important basis for a classical liberal society. It is not clear why one would think a marriage contract to be so different as to not operate in a similar fashion. Without the teeth that come with most contracts, as Rowthorn (1999, p. 663) has remarked, it becomes difficult for the parties to make *credible commitments* to each other, which in turn discourages the type of investments that make marriage attractive and durable. If partners to a marriage cannot be assured that the other will live up to the terms of the contract, they are less likely to invest in the sorts of relationship-specific forms of human capital that are necessary to sustain the marriage and the larger family that might result. It is here where the analogies to the firm make some sense: only where employees believe that their relationship with the firm will be ongoing will they be willing to invest in firm-specific forms of human capital.[20] Such investments must be undertaken in an environment that promises a continuing relationship because firm-specific human capital investments make employees less marketable outside the firm.[21] In an environment where the probability of divorce is greater, marital partners have less incentive to do the very things necessary to sustain the marriage.

With the rising economic opportunities for women and increased market substitutes for household production that characterized the twentieth century reducing the net gains from marriage, perhaps the weakening of the ability of partners to make credible commitments to each other is not quite so problematic as it would have been a couple of generations ago. One way in which the marital contract differs from others is that the parties to the contract may well have legal obligations to third parties that emerge from the contractual relationship (e.g., children). In the current environment, opting out of the marriage contract might be relatively costless for the contracting parties but might have high costs for the children they are raising. No-fault divorce might well have been an understandable outcome of changes in the institution of marriage in terms of the preferences of husbands and wives, but the impact on children is not so clearly neutral. More generally, this discussion points out a paradox at the heart of the current cultural status of marriage: any specific marriage can be dissolved largely at will, but there are clear benefits to somehow continuing the institution in one form or another. The concern is whether the incentives that lead to more frequent divorce are also threatening the whole institution.

The incentives created by no-fault do not necessarily apply only to the case of women afraid of being abandoned. Such a law may result in overly generous divorce settlements to the party who is primarily responsible for the break-up of the marriage. If there are children involved, and women are most likely to receive custody, the husband may find himself "deprived of his family home and paying a large part of his income to support a family from which he has been effectively expelled... [M]en will [thus plausibly] become increasingly mistrustful... Any system which makes generous, unconditional awards following divorce is inviting abuse" (Rowthorn 1999, p. 671).

Rowthorn (1999) notes a legal initiative that would appear to preserve the option to make marriage a more binding contract. In the late 1990s, the state of Louisiana introduced a twin-track system allowing couples to choose the kind of marriage they wanted. One type allows speedy, unilateral, no-fault divorce; the other is "covenant" marriage, which is harder to terminate and for which speedy divorce is only available in the case of fault at the request of the injured party. The definition of fault is narrowly drawn. Couples can convert from no-fault to covenant marriage, but the reverse is not allowed (p. 685). This form of marriage is now an option in Arizona, Arkansas, and Kansas as well. In Louisiana, the percentage of couples taking this option has been consistently around 1 percent, with the other states being even lower.[22] A plausible interpretation is that couples desire the flexibility of current no-fault divorce law, even though it might work to the pecuniary disadvantage of women and create problems for children. Again, there may well be strong nonpecuniary reasons that women wish to be able to leave marriages with the fewest transaction costs possible.

The new dilemma that women face is that while they can make a go of it in the market by themselves and in that way do not need marriage as before, what they may well need is a partner for household production, especially child care. If they do not have sufficient income to purchase the kind of child care they want, they may look to marriage to provide the complementary HHC, or at least for enough MHC in a mate that enables married women to engage in household production and still have significant income, or for the couple together to be able to afford market substitutes for in-home child care. Put somewhat differently, the decline in the benefits of marriage have mostly been in terms of the loss of uniqueness of men's market incomes and the increased ability to purchase the outputs of household production on the market rather than having to produce them within the household.

Child custody laws and norms and rising divorce rates are thus ancillary and partial explanations of both the rise in labor force participation of married women and also of the persistent gender wage gap. If, statistically, either party were equally likely to obtain the children (or if it were a matter of circumstance and fault), labor force participation rates among men might be more variable and overall more similar to those of women, implying that human capital structures would be more similar and so also would earnings patterns. Under the current institutional environment, married women invest in less and/or different types of MHC. As a result they tend to crowd into different kinds of jobs: those that are more flexible, requiring less specific human capital and which allow them to continue to accumulate HHC. Due to these compensating differentials, these jobs tend to be lower-paying. The circumstances surrounding divorce and custody will tend to lead women to invest in MHC that is less likely to generate large incomes and to look for jobs with flexible work conditions that allow them to continue to accumulate HHC.

## Explaining the Fall in the Number of Marriages

The story of the past half century is one of fewer marriages, fewer children, and more divorces. In other words, fewer marriages are occurring and more are failing. Although the demographic and economic developments usually offered in this context seem to explain satisfactorily the falling rate of marriage, it is not clear that rising divorce rates, some consequences of which we have noted earlier, have been equally well-explained.

Marriage may be looked at as a contractual project with an uncertain lifetime. It may terminate because of the death of either spouse or because of divorce. The longer the expected duration of the marriage, ceteris paribus, the higher the expected benefits from a good marriage (or the losses from a bad one—which is a contributing factor to the increase in time spent searching for a suitable mate). Thus, the substantial increase in life span has tended to increase the benefits from marriage, but also makes it more likely that divorce rather than death will be the terminating factor. In addition, the cost of divorce has fallen. The advent of no-fault rules and the disappearance of the stigma of divorce have made it easier for either party to dissolve the marriage in the face of a relevant unexpected outcome. Ceteris paribus, a fall in the cost of divorce would decrease the benefits from marriage because, as already noted, the credible commitments that are necessary for the joint production process that are often central to a marital household are more difficult to make. The effect of a reduction in the cost of divorce works both directly and indirectly, through its effect on the accumulation of marriage-specific HHC, to increase the number of divorces and the probability of divorce.

The cost of divorce, considered as an independent variable, could by itself be expected to account for part of the explanation of the decline in marriage benefits and the rise in divorce. A fall in the cost of divorce implies a rise in the incidence of bad marriages. Looking only at the falling cost of divorce, people should be more inclined to enter into riskier marriages, since the cost of a mistake (the discovery at any point of time that the benefits are less than expected) can be more easily undone. Thus, a decline in the cost of divorce by itself should produce an *increase* not a *decrease* in the number of marriages because the cost of entering a bad marriage has gone down. Some evidence for this can be seen in the rise of so-called starter marriages, where people in their twenties get married and then divorce after a few years, normally before children are present. This has been characterized as a way for the partners to test marriage as an institution. These sorts of marriages are what one would expect with the lower costs of divorce. However, they have not been so frequent as to outweigh the effects described later that are causing reductions in the number of marriages. The lower cost of divorce considered alone should also reduce the search time for a suitable marriage partner (which runs counter to the effect of increased life span mentioned earlier). However, both of these arguments that suggest lower divorce costs would increase the number of marriages run counter to the empirical reality that marriages are occurring less often and later. Of course, the decline in the cost of divorce is not an exogenous event. It is plausibly the outcome of political and other initiatives in response to the perception that marriage benefits have declined, with no-fault divorce being one obvious example (Rowthorn 1999, p. 676).[23] So one may logically extend the search for more ultimate explanations.

Perhaps the most ultimate of causes is the expansion of opportunities for women in the labor market that has accompanied the increasingly complex division of labor and capital that are part of economic development. Labor-saving technological advances in household production would explain greater workforce participation by women, including married women, but it does not imply a decrease in the benefits of marriage. To the extent that the same degree of specialization could be accomplished without the household labor of the wife, the benefits of marriage might be enhanced (with the addition of the wife's income and the extra home time available) and not reduced. A two-income household can take advantage of pooled income and economies of scale and scope in production and consumption to have differential benefits over two single-person households. In addition, the availability of household labor time from two adults might also be a net benefit, depending on whether or not the demand for household production increases more quickly than the supply grows when the household expands. Furthermore, to the degree the benefits of marriage are now mostly in terms of complementary consumption preferences, these more narrowly economic considerations may be less important.

To explain the decline in marriage benefits, one must appeal to a relative rise in the wage rate available to women and the accompanying increase in the cost of her time in the home. This indeed implies a reduction in scope for the division of labor in the home. *The increased division of labor in the economy as a whole, by increasing labor-market opportunities available to women, has reduced the division of labor within the family.* This is another way of looking at the increase in purchases of market substitutes for household production. The very same economic forces that have provided women with labor force opportunities in eateries, child-care centers, and the household appliance retail sector, not to mention the professions, have also reduced the degree of specialization necessary in the family. The scope of household production has shrunk as the scope of market production has widened. Changes in household technology and the availability of market substitutes for household production (and the increased income needed to afford them) have continued the long historical trend of more and more productive activity taking place outside of the household rather than in. With fewer things needed to be done within the organizational form of the household, the material benefits of marriage, the primary way in which households are formed, have declined substantially, leading to fewer and later marriages. With sex and emotional satisfaction more available *outside* of marriage, and many employers offering fringe benefits to various forms of partnerships, the marginal benefits of marriage over cohabitation have become significantly lower.

Another self-reinforcing process is in play here: a perception of a decrease in the benefits of marriage (to which one may be committed for a longer time because of the increase in life span) plausibly leads to changes in the legal and cultural environment that reduce the cost of divorce, and this, in turn, further reduces the benefits from marriage and raises the probability of divorce. This also explains the decline in the incidence of marriage and the increase in age of (first) marriage. Given that it is in their twenties and thirties that people accumulate a great deal of the MHC necessary to pursue a long-term career, it is during this period when the opportunity cost of marriage rises most rapidly. If marriage means children, it is likely to reduce the MHC acquisition and labor force participation rates of one or both parents, more likely the woman. With more women in high-paying jobs that require ongoing MHC investments, it is not surprising that we see fewer and later marriages, along with fewer children and later ages of parenthood, given the higher opportunity cost in terms of MHC that marriage (and children) in one's twenties and thirties implies.

The dramatic increase in labor market opportunities for women has, therefore, two effects on the marriage rate. First, it increases the opportunity cost of marriage by increasing the opportunity cost of time spent in acquiring HHC rather than MHC, especially very specific forms of MHC. This cost is especially high in the early years in the job market where such forms of MHC are especially valuable on the margin and declines with the decreasing net benefits of further specific MHC as women (and men) age. Second, it reduces the direct benefits of marriage by shrinking the sphere of activities that need to be done through household production. The finer division of labor that the presence of more women has brought to the marketplace has helped to create the very substitutes for household production that reduce the net benefits of marriage.

## Uncertainty, Plan Failure, and the Causes of Divorce

The larger relative wage of women, the increase in female labor force participation, the decline in fertility, and the decline in the cost of divorce thus combine (and interact) to explain a great deal of the dramatic changes in the structure of marriage and the family over the past four decades. There is, however, an additional factor at work in this dynamic: the level of uncertainty produced by the rapid social and economic changes that have occurred over this period. Since at least the 1970s, there have been far-reaching and fundamental changes that have affected the workplace for both men and women and that have implied a loss of certainty with regard to lifetime careers that, not surprisingly, may have affected the ability to plan family life as well. This may be an ancillary and an important influence on marital dissolution and, indeed, the rise of single parent households (including those with never-married parents).

Divorce may be said to occur in one of the following two circumstances:

1. The benefits from marriage turn out to be lower than expected, such that the net benefits of continuing the marriage are negative.
2. The benefits from marriage, though they turn out as expected, become exhausted, so that the marginal net benefits of continuing the marriage are negative.

In the second case, it seems difficult to argue that divorce is an instance of plan failure. As average life spans continue to grow, we should not be surprised to see marriages exhausting themselves. Given that marriage as being centrally about romantic love took hold in the eighteenth and nineteenth centuries when life expectancies at the age of marriage were shorter, it may well be the case that the institution is just incompatible with "until death do us part" when death might not take place for 50, 60, or 70 years after marriage. This point is even more telling when we look at the evolutionary long-run and recall that for the vast majority of our biological history, human life spans were even shorter than in the eighteenth and nineteenth century. There may be evolutionary reasons why 50 or 60 years of pair-bonding is difficult to achieve. If sustaining the intensity of the marital relationship beyond a certain number of years becomes increasingly difficult (especially as the expectations of the degree of that intensity continue to be high), we would expect to see more divorces late in life, and there is some evidence to support this expectation.[24]

Longer life spans might also contribute to the delayed entrance into marriage, as that becomes a way to avoid being alone or miserable at the end of one's life by trying to ensure that the marriage will indeed reflect until death do us part. Given any reasonable discount rate, a willingness to give up current marital benefits for ones in the distant future suggests that the net benefits of marriage at a young age are quite low and/or that the benefits of marriage at the end of life are quite high. The former is compatible with the arguments about rising female wages advanced earlier, and the latter seems intuitively plausible as the companionship and joint resources of marriage would become more important when people retire from market production and return to the home, and potentially face illness and rising medical costs, toward the end of life.

Another possibility is that we may well see the rise of "serial marriages." Paradoxically, it is conceivable that divorce could be planned, like short-term ventures in business. It could be, that with declining benefits from marriage, people plan shorter marriages. This too is not at variance with the observed behavior in the marriage market. If there is an upper time limit on the sustainability of marriage, we might well begin to incorporate that into our plans, leading to more marriages, but of shorter length, as well as more divorce. However, neither these serial marriages nor late-life divorces need necessarily be seen as plan failures. Do note, however, that the expectation of engaging in serial marriages would imply a much lower payoff for investments in relationship-specific human capital and thus would increase the likelihood of divorce and the prevalence of multiple short-term marriages. In terms of Austrian capital theory, the rise of serial marriages means less investment in specific forms of human capital, which in turn reduces the fineness of the complementarity of the household production plan, creating a less well-integrated combination of human capital, reducing the productivity of the household plan it contributes to. More general human capital is, ceteris paribus, less productive, especially in the intimacy of the marital relationship.

Although in these sorts of cases it may not be a very surprising event for the husband and wife, divorce is nevertheless surely an instance of plan failure in the eyes of the nonadult children of the divorcing family, even if (as is often the case) it may be preferred to the continuation of a bad marriage. Whatever the plan, it is hard to argue that, in general, divorce is the best-case scenario for the parties involved. So, even if we take a probabilistic approach, and note that although divorce in general has a substantially higher probability than heretofore, and is therefore less unexpected, specific divorces are never fully expected and are therefore still, relative to the best-possible outcome (a successful continuing marriage), an instance of plan failure. Either way then, conditions may have conspired to render the environment more uncertain in a way that makes divorce more likely.

Anything that has made planning a successful marriage more difficult is a candidate in this regard. Douglas Allen (1998) suggests that no-fault divorce became more valuable after 1970 in part because of a significant change in the degree and type of work done by women after World War II. The variance in female work patterns became greater and more difficult for potential mates to predict, so that more marriages occurred where mistakes in partner selection were made. Difficulties in predicting the wife's working pattern implies the related difficulty of predicting how well integrated the human capital of the married couple will be and therefore how "productive" the marriage will be (p. 133). Allen argues that "the variance in the type of marital contribution of women as wives has increased over the last fifty years" (p. 135). In other words, during the 1970s, it began to become more difficult for men to know exactly what a given woman's contributions to market and household production would be, given the flux in gender roles and opportunities that were taking place and continue today.

The changes in workforce behavior among women took place in a context where the difference in the number of people holding traditional views about the roles of women and the number holding more progressive views was not large. To the extent that these expectations were not communicated accurately or did not remain constant, they created problems in estimating the value of future productivity within marriage. Allen (1998, p. 136) writes, "Hence when a man is assessing the marital contribution of a woman, he is more likely to make a mistake than in the past, since larger variances in expectations and actual work behavior increases the noise in estimation." He continues, "On the other side of the marriage market, women have not experienced a large change in problems of estimating the productivity of future husbands." This may be true, but labor market changes involving men certainly may have made it more difficult for women to find reliable spouses with whom to form a stable marital union. This may be the case particularly at the bottom of the economic and educational scale and among minority groups where the earnings of young males are lower and unemployment rates are higher than that of whites (see Coontz 1992, Chapters 10 and 11).

Allen's discussion complements nicely one by Gillian Hadfield (1999). Hadfield conjectures that the distribution of labor-market jobs by gender may be a matter of the coordination of human capital investment planning, as potential mates use the labor market as a signaling device. By observing the job in which a potential mate is engaged, one receives a signal about the degree to which that person's human capital is complementary to one's own. Cross-cultural comparisons reveal that what emerge as male jobs and female jobs are highly variable and largely unrelated to any intrinsic characteristics of the job.

> [E]ven in a world in which both men and women are equally adept at learning how to grow wheat or bake bread, if each of these skills requires substantial human capital investments before an individual knows with whom they will be breaking bread, there is a strong tendency for an economy to become organized along gendered lines: either men farm and women bake or vice versa. Trying to

> break out of these gendered categories, which are ultimately arbitrary from an economic point of view (on the assumption of zero differences between men and women) puts an individual at great risk of not finding a partner with whom he or she can combine skills so as to have bread to consume. (Hadfield 1999, p. 143)

To the extent that men and women use labor market patterns to make accurate predictions about the beneficial human capital complementarities necessary for a successful marriage, and to the extent that gender workforce patterns have undeniably become more variable, successful mate selection is a more difficult task. That increased difficulty helps account for the long-term rise in the divorce rate.

This sort of social uncertainty has made it more difficult for people interested in marriage to create accurate production plans, as the human capital complementarity that is central to such plans is harder to predict accurately. This is the social equivalent of noisy price signals for physical capital. Just as noisy price signals are more likely to produce failed production plans, noisy signals about human capital will produce more divorces. And such divorces are fruitfully understood as plan failures. One can also see the rise in Internet dating applications and websites, such as Match.com and Eharmony.com, as examples of new institutions that evolved to reduce the transaction costs of finding a romantic partner with whom one's expectations align more closely. These dating sites are perfect examples of the bottom-up emergence of transaction cost reducing institutions that enhance social coordination in response to increased uncertainty. In that regard, they may well be contributing to the more recent slow decline in the divorce rate. We may be seeing fewer, but better, marriages.

From this perspective it is entirely possible, perhaps plausible, that the notable changes in the family that we have discussed earlier, may be the manifestation of a society in short-term transition, a disequilibrium situation.[25] Clearly, the US economy is undergoing a restructuring during which the nature of work and the workplace is changing radically. The advent of the new information-based economy has transformed the career-track and the relationship between worker and employer and has rendered much accumulated human capital obsolete. It has also upset the ideal typical expectations that are central to social coordination, thus rendering accumulated social wisdom equally obsolete. In a society in this sort of economic and social transition, it becomes harder to predict accurately the behavior of others with respect to work, family, and gender roles, thus making plan failure more likely. The decline in marriage rates and later average age of first marriage may be ex ante responses to both lower average benefits of marriage early in life and greater variance around that lower mean, due to the uncertainty associated with cultural and economic transitions. The higher divorce rate may be an ex post response to the same factors.

It is equally possible that the data noted earlier indicating falling divorce rates among those married in the 1990s is some evidence of the social signaling process becoming less noisy. As young people, particularly men, increasingly shed the assumptions about work, marriage, and family that characterized prior generations, and marriage itself transitions away from production issues to consumption ones, it may be the case that the uncertainty that has characterized the past 40 years is slowly diminishing. The empirical data suggesting that recent marriages have a slightly lower divorce rate is consistent with such a reduction in ex ante uncertainty and/or the effects of the uncertainty ameliorating dating websites. From a market process perspective, those websites can be seen as endogenous institutional responses that are forms of equilibrating economic and social entrepreneurship.

## Conclusion

From an evolutionary standpoint, the current average family strategy of late marriages, frequent divorces, and, most importantly, few children cannot be a stable or dominant one. Logically, something must eventually replace it. It would, for example, certainly be overwhelmed eventually by a persistent natalist strategy dedicated to the production of at least three children who are, in turn, dedicated to the same strategy. A society that is not committed to at least replacing itself will eventually disappear, though, of course, it would take many generations. Similarly, a society that began with only a small proportion of its families dedicated to its replacement would take many generations to become overwhelmed by them. As Bergstrom (1996, p. 1912) has noted: "Perhaps the low birth rates currently observed in the West do not represent long-run equilibrium . . . In most countries of Western Europe and North America, low average birth rates have been present for only three or four generations—far too short a time for vertical transmission [across the generations] to replace the low-fertility norm." Two questions remain. First, as economic development spreads worldwide, will the human race as a whole settle into fertility patterns that are sustainable in the long-run? Second, will the recent changes in work, family, and gender roles in the Western world ever settle into patterns that will reduce the current uncertainty, or will even more new social institutions develop to help actors navigate that uncertainty should it continue?

This chapter has taken a broad look at some diverse aspects of the changing scenery surrounding modern family life. Much remains to be done to understand fully the momentous changes that have and are occurring. And, it is clear, whatever diagnosis one finds persuasive, there is no going back. The family will never be the same. Families have changed all throughout human history. They have varied in size, duration, composition, and function. They will continue to change. What the future family will look like is difficult to predict. I have suggested that the current trend toward smaller families of shorter duration may not be a stable evolutionary strategy. To the extent that families have a comparative advantage in the transmission of certain types of valuable human capital across generations and to the extent that such families are held together by altruistic behavior manifesting in the desire for and care of children in numbers large enough to reproduce the family unit, one may expect such behavior to eventually overwhelm other, more individualistic behaviors.

The possibilities for future developments, portending a rise in the fertility rate, are many. One possibility is that the relative importance of the income and substitution effects may flip back in favor of the income effect as overall wealth grows. Families may decide that the consumption benefits of more children, or perhaps the status associated with being able to signal wealth by having more children, are large enough so that they outweigh the marginal costs, including any opportunity costs, of having larger families.[26]

The fundamental challenge that faced families in the industrial era was that work and home became geographically separated, creating the need for a more distinct division of labor between market and household. In agricultural families, work and home were most often the same place, enabling wives to contribute both to the market work of the farm and the household production of the home (although this was mitigated by the larger number of children associated with rural families). In a world of telecommuting, where work and home are once again converging, but without an economic need for large families, we may well see families that blend work and child care in creative and idiosyncratic ways. To the extent such changes lower the cost of child care, it may well bring fertility back up. That is, if women can work more easily while pregnant and if either parent can work more easily without purchasing child care on the market while the children are very young, it may well increase family size. The postindustrial era may recapture the blurred lines between work and home of the preindustrial era but with enough wealth to enable families to reproduce themselves and invest the human and financial capital necessary to prepare those children for the lives they will lead into the future.

# CHAPTER 7

# The Family in a World of Abundance

## Introduction

The history of the Western family discussed in chapter 3 began by exploring the emergence of the family as a social institution in a world of extreme scarcity. Chapter 4 discussed the ways in which capitalism and industrialization transformed the Western family by changing the relationship between work and home and by producing an extraordinary increase in the level of material wealth. The last two chapters have brought that historical narrative up to the present by documenting the profound changes that took place in the twentieth century and by offering an economic interpretation of some recent trends in marriage and divorce. This chapter and the next look at the family in the world of the early twenty-first century. In this chapter, I explore the functions and forms of the modern family in the world of abundance that characterizes the twenty-first century. In the next chapter, I look at the debate over parenting styles in the United States and consider how the increasing intrusiveness of parents in their children's lives might cause problems for the sustainability of classical liberal institutions.

## The Abundance of the Twenty-First-Century West

Despite the significant economic troubles that have affected Western economies since 2008, life for the average Westerner as measured by a variety of socioeconomic indicators has never been better. The process of economic growth that was kindled by the Industrial Revolution has continued and has not only provided new technology that has improved human well-being, it has also made such technology increasingly affordable to more and more people. We live, in the words of Brink Lindsey (2007, p. 18), in an age of "mass affluence," or an "age of abundance," to take directly from his title. The average American has available to her a range of goods and services unimaginable to the rich of several decades ago, not to mention the nobility of centuries ago. Unlike the peasant of those centuries past, the average American does not worry from day-to-day where his food, clothing, and shelter will come from, nor is the average American's income subject to any significant uncertainty from everything from weather to crops to illness to politics. The average Westerner increasingly lives in a world of abundance, where the lack of life's necessities does not impinge on our day-to-day living in the way it has done for all but a few decades, or at most a century, of the several millennia of recorded human history.

Of course in saying that we live in a "world of abundance," Lindsey does not mean to say that we have conquered scarcity in the way in which economists use the word scarcity. Goods and services, not to mention knowledge and time, are still scarce in the sense that all have opportunity costs. To get any of them, we must sacrifice something, hence they remain economically scarce.[1] However, it is certainly true that the vast majority of goods and services have become *considerably less scarce* over the course of the past century and especially the past few decades. At the same time goods and services have become cheaper, human labor has become more valuable, and both results are part of the same pattern of dynamic long-term economic growth. There are a number of ways to demonstrate empirically the increasing abundance of modern life, and this chapter explores some data that do so.

Perhaps the most fundamental measure of the relative abundance of modern life is the decline in the amount of work time it takes to earn the income to purchase the basic goods and services we use on a regular basis. Because time is the ultimate scarce resource in human life, it makes sense that we should measure the real cost of goods in terms of the work time it takes to purchase them. Comparisons of such data over time can give us a sense of the relative abundance of the modern world. Cox and Alm (1999, p. 43) present a variety of data that show the various amounts of time that a worker earning the average private sector hourly wage would have had to work in order to earn income sufficient to purchase various goods. They provide a useful overview how many hours of work it cost to purchase several basic goods, such as a loaf of bread, a gallon of gasoline, or 100 kilowatts of electricity, as well as less basic ones such as air travel and computing power, over the course of the twentieth century. In every case, the clear trend was a dramatic reduction in the labor time cost of these goods. The smallest declines by 1997 still represent a reduction in cost to about a third or a quarter of the 1920 figure, and several goods fell to mere fractions of their earlier costs. Another set of data making the same point is presented in table 7.1.

Boudreaux (2006) used the same methodology as did Cox and Alm to derive the work time data. He also points out that it was not easy to find directly comparable goods, as the some of the goods available in 1975 were not offered in the same form in 2006. For example, the 1975 garage door opener was a quarter-horsepower model and Sears sells nothing less powerful than a half-horsepower model today. So for the over 50 percent drop in the labor time cost of the bottom of the line garage door opener one should also note that the

Table 7.1 Labor time cost of Sears catalog goods

| | *1975 (hours)* | *2006 (hours)* |
|---|---|---|
| Freezer | 79 | 39.8 |
| Answering machine | 20.43 | 1.1 |
| Garage door opener | 20.1 | 8.57 |
| High-priced work boots | 11.49 | 8.26 |
| Top automobile tire | 8.37 | 2.92 |
| Low-priced gas mower | 13.14 | 8.56 |

*Source:* Boudreaux (2006).

bottom of the line was twice as powerful in 2006. If we measured the labor time per unit of horsepower, the decline is almost 80 percent from the 1975 cost. One could make similar points about the quality of almost any consumer good available today in comparison to years past. For example, major purchases such as household appliances are far more energy efficient and have more features than in years past. What these data demonstrate is that the real cost of goods and services to the average wage earner has fallen, and fallen a great deal, over the past several decades.

Perhaps our discussion of the average obscures some distributional issues that make these impressive benefits less available to poor households. In fact, the data show that poor households over the past 35 years have had increased access to the goods considered basic to modern, Western understandings of comfort. This increased access has been so significant that poor households in the United States today are more likely to contain many consumer goods than was the *average* household in 1971. As table 7.2 indicates, the only categories where the poor have become worse off are in freezers (likely because more are built into refrigerators) and telephones, which have been replaced by the increase in cell phones. Stoves are down slightly, but that too could be due to swapping regular stoves for microwaves or even toaster ovens. In any case, the decline is pretty small. These data also do not take account of things like advances in medical technology that have become more affordable for more Americans.[2] The point of these data is not to ignore or downplay the fact that there remain real pockets of poverty in the modernized West, nor is it to suggest there are not steps that could be taken to alleviate that poverty. It is only to make the point that we live in a world where, even among the statistically poor, many of life's basic creature comforts are well within reach.

One other data point that indicates the degree to which most people no longer have day-to-day concerns about life's basics is the percentage of income spent on food, clothing, and shelter. Cox and Alm (1999, p. 15) report: "Among households below the poverty line, outlays for food, clothing, and shelter were down to 37 percent of consumption in 1995, compared with 52 percent two decades earlier, 57 percent in 1950, and 75 percent in 1920."

**Table 7.2** Frequency of various consumer goods in households below the poverty line vs. all US households

| *% Households with:* | *Poor 1984* | *Poor 1994* | *Poor 2003* | *Poor 2005* | *All 1971* | *All 2005* |
|---|---|---|---|---|---|---|
| Washing machine | 58.2 | 71.7 | 67.0 | 68.7 | 71.3 | 84.0 |
| Clothes dryer | 35.6 | 50.2 | 58.5 | 61.2 | 44.5 | 81.2 |
| Dishwasher | 13.6 | 19.6 | 33.9 | 36.7 | 18.8 | 64.0 |
| Refrigerator | 95.8 | 97.9 | 98.2 | 98.5 | 83.3 | 99.3 |
| Freezer | 29.2 | 28.6 | 25.4 | 25.1 | 32.2 | 36.6 |
| Stove | 95.2 | 97.7 | 97.1 | 97.0 | 87.0 | 98.8 |
| Microwave | 12.5 | 60.0 | 88.7 | 91.2 | 1.0 | 96.4 |
| Color TV | 70.3 | 92.5 | 96.8 | 97.4 | 43.3 | 98.9 |
| VCR | 3.4 | 59.7 | 75.4 | 83.6 | 0.0 | 92.2 |
| Personal computer | 2.9 | 7.4 | 36.0 | 42.4 | 0.0 | 67.1 |
| Telephone | 71.0 | 76.7 | 87.3 | 79.8 | 93.0 | 90.6 |
| Air conditioner | 42.5 | 49.6 | 77.7 | 78.8 | 31.8 | 85.7 |
| Cellular telephone | | | 34.7 | 48.3 | 0.0 | 71.3 |
| One or more cars | 64.1 | 71.8 | 72.8 (2001) | | 79.5 | |

*Source*: US Census Bureau (2007).

Lindsey (2007, p. 29) cites a figure of 90 percent of income devoted to food, clothing, and shelter for working-class households in New York City at the end of the nineteenth century. He also notes that household income of working-class families was from a fourth to a third composed of the earnings of their children. The comparable decline in the percentage of income spent on food, clothing, and shelter for middle-class and upper-class families is likely to be even more impressive, especially with the breaking of the housing boom. Obviously, the smaller percentage of income taken up by those basics, the more scope families have for purchasing other goods and services to make their lives better. With a lower percentage of income going to those basics, families were able to save more and thereby be able to continue to purchase those basics if their income declined over any significant period of time. When 90 percent of one's income was spent on basics, and when child labor was required to get you to that level, there was, as Lindsey notes, little margin for error.

One final way to illustrate the abundance of the modern West is in terms of available leisure time. Thanks to a later average age of starting work, an earlier average retirement age, and longer life expectancies, as well as shorter work days and work weeks, the average American has seen an ongoing decrease in hours spent at market production. This decrease is in both absolute and percentage terms over the past 125 years, and there is a less dramatic decline in hours devoted to household production. The result is a significant increase in leisure time over the same period. For example, the average American in 1870 had 299,315 hours of leisure over a lifetime. That number grew in later years as follows:

| | |
|---|---|
| 1950: | 444,972 hours |
| 1973: | 488,106 hours |
| 1990: | 519,736 hours |
| 1996: | 528,386 hours |

In other words, lifetime leisure hours grew by over 75 percent over the whole period and almost 10 percent between 1973 and 1996, years that many claim reversed the material gains of the average American over the decades prior. The vast majority of those decreases came from reduced hours on the job rather than reduced hours in household production, which only declined by about 17 percent over the whole period, while hours at work fell by about 56 percent (Cox and Alm 1999, p. 57).

As Cox and Alm go on to demonstrate, this increase in leisure time combined with the increase in wealth that made such leisure possible has provided Americans with the opportunity to have time for everything from "symphony to softball." The increase in leisure time is best understood, in terms we used in chapter 5, as the dominance of the income effect over the substitution effect in labor markets as wages rose over the period in question. Rather than respond to higher wages and the higher opportunity cost of leisure by working more hours, workers began to use the higher income implicit in those higher wages to purchase additional leisure time. By itself, that choice is a sign of progress in the battle against scarcity as it suggests we can get what we want without spending more hours at work. Last, having both the time and resources to spend on things other than basics has meant that more and more people are able to pursue hobbies and other activities that would have been seen as frivolous by preceding generations. This increase in leisure time is particularly relevant to discussions of the family as it should translate into more opportunities for families to do things other than market and household production, which in turn suggests changes or additions to the functions of the family and perhaps even changes in its form as a result.

## Abraham Maslow's Hierarchy of Needs and the Modern Family

In Brink Lindsey's (2007) book, he argues that many of the dramatic cultural changes that have taken place since World War II can be understood as a kind of society-wide climb up the psychologist Abraham Maslow's (1943) famed "hierarchy of needs." In the process of putting forward "A Theory of Human Motivation," Maslow argued that humans have a hierarchy of needs starting from the "lowest," most basic to the "higher," more abstract ones, and that, generally, they attempted to satisfy the more basic needs first. Once those needs are sufficiently satisfied, they can turn their attention to the needs at the next level up. For Maslow, those needs were, from lowest to highest: the physiological needs, the safety needs, the love needs, the esteem needs, and the need for self-actualization. Maslow says that this is not a strict hierarchy, in that people do not need to satisfy completely one need before climbing to the next higher one, nor will every person put the needs in exactly the same order. A few people will reverse elements of the hierarchy (though the order presented will apply to most people) and, as Maslow put it, "[a] more realistic description of the hierarchy would be in terms of decreasing percentages of satisfaction as we go up the hierarchy" (p. 388). Finally, he noted that the higher needs in some sense only emerge when the lower order needs have been sufficiently satisfied.

Lindsey takes Maslow's framework, which was intended to explain individual behavior, and analogizes it to the United States as a whole in the twentieth century. For most Americans, the economic growth of the postwar era has meant that their day-to-day concerns about meeting their physiological needs and needs for basic safety are minimal. As a result of having largely conquered the basic needs of life, Americans and others in the developed world are able to spend time and resources achieving more abstract goals, best illustrated by the flourishing of entertainment, sports, and recreation/vacation opportunities in the postwar era, and the ability and willingness of Americans to spend on them.[3] Lindsey argues that these new patterns of expenditure reflect an increasing focus on needs that are higher up Maslow's hierarchy. More and more of our labor and consumption is geared around activities that involve our needs for esteem and self-actualization rather than our basic physiological or safety-related needs.

Lindsey (2007, p. 67) notes the central role that changes in the family played in this collective climb: "The transformation of the family from a unit of production to a unit of consumption had enormous consequences." He goes on to quote the retailer Edward Filene's observation that now that the father did not control the way in which families earned income, he would be "relieved of many ancient responsibilities and . . . prerogatives." As we have already seen, the course of the twentieth century saw an increased focus on the family as a site of personal fulfillment and consumption expenditure, as well as an object of psychological fulfillment and concern. Family relationships, along with other aspects of human interaction, were increasingly seen in terms of mental well-being and personal happiness. This same period saw the development of pharmaceutical treatments for psychological and psychiatric disorders. There was a society-wide emphasis on being happy and fulfilled. And as 1950s television so clearly portrayed, the conjugal, nuclear family was in many ways the centerpiece of that quest for esteem and self-actualization at the top of the Maslow hierarchy.

The transformation of the family documented in earlier chapters can be seen as an example of the broader trend that Lindsey identifies. For most of human history, the primary functions of the family were concerned with the two needs at the bottom of the Maslow hierarchy: the physiological and safety needs. The family provided the house as physical shelter, providing for both kinds of needs, and it provided parents, who fulfilled those needs for helpless infants. Consistent with Maslow's point that we need not completely satisfy one need and then move on, families today still fulfill the lower-order needs, but doing so takes up much less space in the whole range of activities that families engage in and the needs they fulfill. The data presented on the percentage of household income taken up by food, clothing, and shelter provides a proxy for the size of the role played by satisfying the physiological and safety needs in the whole set of activities in which families now engage.

Historically, the family also provided for physiological needs through its economic function as the site of production. Given the primacy of addressing those needs, families tended to take on forms that best fulfilled those functions. Examples discussed in earlier chapters include: large numbers of children to work the land or the early factories and provide for parents too old to work, marriages based on compatibility as "yoke-mates" or even arranged by parents, the use of wet-nurses or older relatives to care for children so that healthy women could immediately go back to the land, the treatment of children and women as near-property, and a tolerance of community intervention to ensure their obligations to others. Where familial functions primarily addressed the lower Maslovian needs, particular forms followed.

The advent of capitalism began a process by which the production-oriented economic functions of the family were slowly made less central. As capitalism made it possible for people to meet their basic needs through extra-familial processes such as the market, and as it made meeting those needs even easier through the higher wages that it brought in its wake, capitalism reduced the centrality of meeting the physiological and safety needs to the family's day-to-day existence. As those needs were either met through other institutions or met more easily in the family, the family was able to take on additional functions that involved meeting needs that were higher on the Maslow hierarchy.

After the physiological and safety needs comes the need for love. The historical record matches this nicely as the earliest stages of industrial capitalism largely align with the time period in which affection becomes the central rationale for marriage among a notably wider range of people (Coontz 2005, p. 5). The centrality of love to marriage and family grew alongside the economy during the nineteenth century, with increased sentimentalization in the form of the sheltered childhood making love increasingly central not just to the marital dyad, but to the parent-child relationship as well. For adults, marriage and family were now increasingly about loving relationships with both one's spouse and one's children.

Next up Maslow's hierarchy is the need for esteem. By the late nineteenth century, the doctrine of the separate spheres served as a rhetorical trope to convince women that their esteem needs were being met within Victorian domesticity. However, as noted in chapters 4 and 5, it was a very thin veil over the increasing dissatisfaction of women with what was clearly the consolation prize of the private sphere. A good portion of the first wave women's movement of that era can be seen as women deciding that love in the family was not enough. A love-based marriage was at least implicitly premised on equality between the spouses, and the objective inequalities women were facing in the public sphere were so inconsistent with that presumed equality that they could no longer be tolerated. Voting rights, the end of coverture laws, and some increased protection against domestic violence made it more possible for women to meet their esteem needs. This was most obviously achieved through an increased presence in the public sphere, but also in the family, as their more equal public status gave them more power with which to demand increased equality and respect in the home. By the early twentieth century, the family was legitimately a place where women could far better meet their needs for self-esteem. Increased legal rights and protections, as well as the beginning of their integration into the labor force, gave them political standing and slightly more economic leverage. To the degree that the subordinate status of women was a holdover from family-based organization of production in the precapitalist era, the increased individualism made possible by capitalism and wage labor, and the wealth they produced, are important causal factors in this change in the functions of the family.

At the same time, the increased focus on the legal status of children provided children a parallel kind of satisfaction of their esteem needs. New concerns about children's rights, and the mid-twentieth-century incorporation of "the best interests of the child" into constitutional limits on parental rights (e.g., *Prince v. Massachusetts* in 1944), all reflect a sense in which the family was supposed to be concerned with the child as a being with interests and needs of its own, including those of respect and self-esteem.

The family's integration of the esteem needs into its functions did not have a major effect on family forms, other than through the internal dynamics of the household where the husband/father's ability to exercise authoritarian control was clearly attenuated. From the outside, the family largely looked the same even as people increasingly saw it as a way to meet their esteem needs.

The pinnacle of Maslow's (1943) hierarchy was the need for self-actualization. By this he meant the ability "to become actualized in what [one] is potentially" (p. 382). As Maslow pointed out in his original article, the ability to meet this need in an effective way depended upon the other needs being satisfied beforehand. People who have fewer worries about their physiological needs, their safety, being loved, and having self-esteem can then aspire to self-actualization. It would seem as though men and women over the twentieth century, and especially in the early twenty-first, have seen their own needs for self-actualization as a primary reason to marry and form families in the first place. Whereas for most of human history the purpose of marriage and the functions of the family were largely about lower Maslovian needs and obligations to the community, marriage and family are now much more seen in terms of what they will do for the individual, where "do" refers to the higher Maslovian needs. Family is no longer necessary to ensure physical survival and safety at least for adults, so it can be a site of self-actualization.

Decisions about when and who to marry, whether or not to have children and, if so, how many, and the ongoing conscious decision to stay married in a world of easier divorce, are all often understood in terms of how they meet the highest emotional and psychological needs of the individual. Marriage and family have been, as it were, divorced from the more material needs of economic survival.[4] Given that both men and women can survive economically outside of marriage and a family, and given that children are no longer needed for direct productive purposes or as a form of old-age insurance, the pressing material reasons to marry and procreate have largely disappeared, making these decisions clearly a matter of deciding how they will serve the higher Maslovian needs of the individuals involved. Marriage and having children are worth doing if they will make the individuals involved happy and help them "become actualized in what [they are] potentially."

## Two Applications

Viewing the contemporary family as a vehicle for the self-actualization needs of the adults who form families sheds some interesting light on a number of contemporary family phenomena. We can take a quick look at divorce and same-sex marriage through this Maslovian lens. A third issue that can be very fruitfully explored through this perspective, the contemporary concern with hyper-parenting and our over-protected children, will get an extended treatment in the next chapter.

The rising divorce rate since World War II has clearly been, as noted in the last chapter, a result of the increased economic independence of women. However, that was not the only factor in play. In the language of economics, we can view the rising divorce rate as the consequence of changes in both *constraints* and *preferences*, where both changes worked in the direction of a higher divorce rate. Constraints in this context refer to the objective economic circumstances facing women, while preferences refer to their subjective desires.

Chapter 5's discussion of women's growing economic well-being makes the point that the constraints facing women shifted dramatically over the past few decades. Many marriages that would have stayed together in years past are now being dissolved simply because women have the ability to survive without a husband in ways they did not before. Even if there was no change in women's beliefs or expectations concerning marriage, we would predict a rise in the divorce rate as a result of that change in constraints. However, looking at marriage from the perspective of the current chapter, we can see that changes in preferences reinforced the effect coming from the loosening constraints.

The increased expectations that marriage and family now bear in a world where they are expected to be part of self-actualization would predict that the threshold for a happy marriage has probably risen over that same period. Both men and women have higher expectations about the benefits that marriage is supposed to bring to them. As the love-based marriage has conquered most of its competition in the West, and even as marriage becomes less central to the life-course of many people, the expectations about what it will deliver have become even greater. To the extent marriage is not necessary in the way it once was, it has now become much more a matter of choice and therefore it must deliver sufficient satisfaction to be worth choosing. Seen through Maslow's perspective, marriage has moved from mostly being about satisfying the lower needs to satisfying the higher ones. We now invest marriage with the power of self-actualization, as seen in the ways we talk about soul mates and life partners, and put romantic love's transcendent power at the center of marriage.

With these higher expectations, it is understandable how more marriages might fail in the sense of being unable to deliver what either or both spouses expect from it. Notice that I am not suggesting that marriages are in some objective sense weaker than before. They might be, but for the sake of this argument, they need not be. Even if marriage itself had not changed over the course of the past 100 years, as our expectations of it rose, it was inevitable that more marriages would be below the bar in terms of meeting the expectations of either or both members of the couple. To flip the earlier point around, even if women had not made substantial economic gains, rising expectations about the psychological satisfaction marriage is supposed to provide would predict a rise in the divorce rate. Empirically, however, two things are probably true: (1) the size of each of these effects probably differ, with the change in constraints having a greater effect than the change in preferences; and (2) the two factors cannot be totally separated as the same underlying aggregate economic growth caused both the increase in women's economic independence and the higher expectations for marriage. Analytically, however, we can separate these two effects and observe that cultural changes that portray marriage as about the highest psychological needs of the spouses will continue to raise people's expectations about marriage and will, by themselves, keep the divorce rate higher than it was for most of human history.

We can also take a brief look at the demand by many gays and lesbians to be fully included in the institutions of marriage and family by understanding that demand as the result of self-actualization becoming the central psychological need that those institutions fulfill. As the heterosexual family has become less focused on the needs it used to fulfill, such as market production and procreation, and more focused on those needs associated with the top of the Maslow pyramid, gays and lesbians have also not surprisingly wondered what the difference might be between heterosexual marriage and families and their own relationships. That is, once marriage and family become understood as meeting needs for love, esteem, and self-actualization, why is there a need for the marital dyad to be of different sexes? The romantic love of homosexual couples, they might argue, is no different from that of heterosexuals, nor is their desire to have their higher Maslovian needs satisfied through the benefits of a lifelong love recognized through a public ceremony, so on what grounds should they be excluded from legal marriage or from parenting?

At a time when marriage and family were about the lower needs in the hierarchy, especially when procreation was central to economic survival, one could at least imagine the response to a demand for same-sex marriage as focusing on the needs that marriage and family fulfilled and arguing that it would be frivolous to think in terms of anything but the urgency of survival. In a world of poverty, any marriage based on the personal needs of the individuals involved, no matter their gender, would not, and did not historically, get much sympathy. In a world of greater abundance, however, where the level of wealth has enabled us to meet the more basic needs more easily, we can afford to make marriage about our own needs as individuals. In such a world then, the "what exactly is the difference?" argument becomes a much stronger one, and it is understandable why many gays and lesbians would see their exclusion from marriage and family as nothing more than prejudice. Even if one is not interested in drawing any particular policy conclusion about the legal status of same-sex marriage, viewing marriage and family as now fulfilling needs higher in Maslow's hierarchy can shed much light on why the demand for such change has emerged at this point in history and why its proponents often couch their arguments the way they do.

## The Functions of the Family in a World of Abundance

Given this Maslovian perspective on the twenty-first-century family, I want to revisit the prior discussion about the function and forms of the family. In this section, I will briefly explore the functions central to the twenty-first-century family, keeping in mind our Hayekian insights from prior chapters. In the next section, I will turn back to family form and briefly address the concerns of many that the increased variation in family forms of the past few decades, especially the high divorce rate, has led to a decline in the functionality of families.

In many ways, the family in the world of abundance has many of the same basic functions that families have always had. First and foremost is taking care of the basic needs of any children that are present.[5] The biological fact that human infants are helpless for the first year or two of life, and strongly dependent on parental resources and protection for a number of years to follow, remains at the core of what it is that families do. From an evolutionary perspective, these features of human infancy and childhood are connected with our ability to learn and engage in higher mental functioning than our animal kingdom relatives. However, it does mean that children need caregivers, and we saw in an earlier chapter that there are strong reasons to think that, all else equal, those with (closer) biological ties to the children are best equipped to provide that care. Children's basic physical needs for food, clothing, shelter, safety, and the like (the ones near the bottom of the Maslow hierarchy) will continue to be a core function of the family, and families will continue to be the central institution by which children are cared for.

Beyond those physical needs, children have emotional and developmental needs that must be met. The psychological literature is clear that simply providing for the physical needs of children is not enough to ensure their ability to thrive as adults. Children require education, training, and various forms of socialization that go beyond physical needs and speak to the broader concept of child development. Children need adults who can provide for these needs, and there are reasons to believe that, all else equal, family members will do so best.[6] Families, specifically the relationship between children and primary caregivers, enable both children and adults to develop the necessary psychological attribute of secure attachment bonds (Bowlby 1973; Hartup 1989).[7] Attachment can occur in both the child-caregiver relationships and the romantic relationships that comprise families. Young creatures across the animal kingdom, including humans, instinctively seek physical proximity with objects that have certain sensory characteristics and will quickly show a strong preference for such objects (Bowlby 1973, p. 42). For humans, this is normally with the infant's primary caregiver. The two points that matter for the psychological health of the child are that such attachment bonding takes place and that the bonds are secure. Children require what is called the secure base that attachment to a caregiver provides. Having that relationship with a caregiver provides the foundation for the learning behavior of childhood.

Children between 12 and 24 months will exhibit that "proximity seeking" behavior if those attachment bonds are secure. The other distinctive characteristic of attachment behavior is that it is usually exhibited by a "young or subordinate individual towards an older or more dominant one" (Bowlby 1973, p. 43). I will note later the way attachment can and does occur between adults. When children are in the company of a caregiver with whom such bonds have formed, they will move closer to that person if placed under stress and will cry or become visibly agitated in other ways if left alone. Even if left with an adult other than the primary caregiver, they will not demonstrate the same level of comfort and security as they do in the presence of the caregiver. When reunited with the caregiver after an absence, they will normally immediately seek that person's presence and attention. This is proximity seeking behavior.

Secure attachment bonds serve two purposes in child development. First, they create a context for learning and exploration. Children who are securely attached will be more likely to investigate strange surroundings or play in less self-conscious and more open-ended ways than those who lack such bonds. The knowledge that they *can* return to the caregiver if need be, even if that need never actually arises, is the source of the secure base from which they can investigate the new and unknown (Bowlby 1973, pp. 44–45). One sign of child development is that the need for the proximity associated with attachment becomes progressively more abstract. Children do not necessarily need physical proximity, but simply need to know that the caregiver will, for example, return from running an errand eventually. The child begins to understand that just because the caregiver is out of sight, he or she has not disappeared forever.[8] This secure attachment leads to higher-order sorts of learning in the preschool years, as children become capable of exercising increasing levels of independence in accomplishing more and more complex tasks. We see this process in adulthood when we feel drawn toward the security of being back in our parents' home, for example, during the holidays. The elasticity of attachment bonds enables children to develop and grow into independent adults who nonetheless remain rooted to the secure base of their parents in these sorts of ways.

It is important to note that attachment is not a one-sided, uni-directional phenomenon. It is not the same as dependency. Healthy attachment is characterized by reciprocity in that we create and sustain these relationships with those who give something back to us.

Attachment bonds between parent and child also serve as a working model for creating attachment relationships with peers throughout one's life (Hartup

1989, p. 123). Relationships with other adults become modeled after the way in which our attachment relationships with our parents evolved (Bowlby 1973, p. 43). This includes romantic relationships such as the marital dyad. Psychologically healthy people are those with secure attachments to others, and the family both provides and models those relationships as part of the child development process. For example, both partners in a romantic relationship benefit from the attachment relationship they might share, as do both parent and child.

When we ask why families exist, focusing on children is the natural place to start. However, families also include marriages and other sets of adults where there are no children present. What are the functions of these families? In fact, they share an important function with families that include children: the psychological and emotional needs of the adults, including the kinds of attachment bonds discussed previously. Adults have needs for love and companionship, as well as sexual pleasure, that can be met through marriage or other forms of partnership that are the ways we form families. Healthy romantic relationships also provide a secure base for our navigation through the challenges of adulthood. In childless marriages, the partners can provide for a wide variety of needs of this kind, and they can enable each to rely on the extended family of their partners for various forms of emotional, psychological, and perhaps even financial support. The same things are true in families with children, as the adult relationships in such families also serve to meet the needs of those adults, as well as modeling healthy relationships for children. In thinking about the functions of the modern family, we should not neglect what families do for adults, especially given the extraordinary focus on the needs of children that has become so central in the popular discourse on parenting and the functionality of families in the twenty-first century. This point is worth remembering in the next chapter's discussion of parenting.

A Hayekian perspective can add to this discussion of the contemporary Western family's functions. The discussion of "living in two sorts of worlds at once" from chapter 2 is the starting point. With this insight in mind, one central function of the family is the way that it enables people, and especially children, to learn the rules of both the intimate or micro-orders of face-to-face interactions and those of the larger, anonymous macro-order of the Great Society. Because the family is an environment with people who care about their children and know them well, it enables children to learn these rules and their applicability, in a more collaborative learning process. Such an environment also enables adults to design learning processes, and any reward and punishment systems associated with them, in ways that are customized to individual children to the greatest degree possible.

At the core of Hayek's view of human action and social order is the idea that humans are primarily rule-following animals. Given that parents care about their children and know them well, the family is an irreplaceable social institution for the effective transmission of the discipline of rule-following. Other institutions can perform this function, but only in ways that supplement the family. It is within the secure base of the family that children can learn both explicitly, through instruction, and implicitly, through experimentation, the rules that do and should govern behavior in both intimate and anonymous social orders. In particular, the family can be understood as a school for learning tacit social norms. A child's first interactions with other humans are with family members, and those interactions, and the relationships they create, can serve as models for other intimate relationships and the more anonymous relationships of the Great Society.

The role played by families in transmitting the explicit rules of the modern world is perhaps obvious. Parents spend much of their time instructing children about general notions of right and wrong and helping them to learn what constitutes appropriate behavior in a variety of social contexts. Many of the fundamental ethical rules and obligations that are required for people to exist in a cooperative, civil social order and to engage in the social cooperation of the market are learned in the family in just this way. Ideas such as a general respect for the property of others, a reluctance to initiate coercion or force, a respect for individuals as individuals, tolerance of difference, the rules of etiquette, and the ability to make assessments of trustworthiness are central for individuals to be able to function in the Hayekian Great Society, not to mention ensuring that such a society contains a minimum of friction and maximum of social cooperation. The family is a superior, although not the only, site for learning these rules of behavior.

The *explicit* rules of social interaction are only one element of the socialization process as seen from a Hayekian perspective. A central part of Hayek's theory of cognition and its relationship to his conception of the social order is that many of the rules of the social order are tacit, in that we often act according to rules of which we are not consciously aware. These tacit mental rules are at work in the very structure of the mind, as the mind is a complex of rules and attendant dispositions that the mind itself is unable to completely articulate (Hayek 1952). As we saw in chapter 2, the mental rules that guide behavior evolve and become encoded through the various forms of social interaction that children encounter early in life. The literature in psychology demonstrates that early childhood experiences can in many ways affect children for life and that the development of attachment bonds is particularly central to a healthy developmental path. In terms of Hayek's theory of mind, those attachment bonds affect the mental map that humans develop to guide their behavior. These rules of behavior may or may not be social, in the sense that they deal with the behavior of others. Such rules may, for example, have to do with our interactions with the physical world. What is central here is that learning these guiding rules will be facilitated by a family environment that encourages children to explore the world around them, but shields them from the physical harm that might result from mistaken exploration. Children need to learn the way the world works as part of the process of mental development, and the knowledge and love that parents bring to that process put them in a superior position to ensure that this development takes place.

Parents frequently model the more tacit rules of the social order through their behavior in a variety of social contexts. An obvious example here is how children learn to behave appropriately in restaurants. There are some rules that parents can explicitly convey to children (e.g., "don't eat with your hands—use your silverware"), but there are others that parents may not even be aware of themselves that their actual behavior communicates to children. Interacting with wait staff might be full of all kinds of subtle and tacit norms that parents cannot articulate but children can learn through repeated observation supplemented by parental praise and criticism. This sort of imitation is an important form of learning for humans, and the social institution of the family provides numerous and repeated opportunities for parents to consciously and unconsciously model for children the rules of the social order.

These explicit and tacit norms can also be learned in nonfamily social institutions. Schools, religious organizations, other social organizations, and even just playing without adults present, are all ways in which children can and do learn through imitation.[9] The argument, however, is not that families are the *only* way to provide such learning. Rather it is that families are able to do so particularly well and are necessary, if not sufficient, to ensure that such socialization takes place. Children who are exposed to a variety of such learning opportunities will likely be better able to navigate the world than those who have fewer. In this sense, it is true that "the village" helps to raise children. But recognizing that truth does not mean that the family can be *replaced* by the village. The family remains *necessary*, though probably not sufficient, as part of the process of Hayekian socialization, even as the other institutions of civil society play valuable roles in enhancing that process.

## Is This the End of Marriage?

Despite living in an age of abundance where the family's struggle to provide so many of the basics of life has been eliminated by the forces of market-driven economic growth, many people are quick to point to the numerous problems faced by modern families. There are indeed problems, but it is helpful to put those problems in a larger historical perspective. Perhaps the most discussed of those problems is the role that historically high level of divorce rates might have on the overall health of the family as a social institution. With divorce rates still high, marriage rates low, and the average age of first marriage continuing to climb, as well as the recent growth of interest in polyamorous relationships, there is concern in many quarters that marriage as an institution may be under the siege that will finally be its downfall. This concern is an old one, as every major change in marriage as institution has led to the very same worry that *this* change was the one that would destroy marriage.

Even those sympathetic to the ongoing changes to marriage and family recognize the possibility that these changes might be of greater significance. For example, Coontz (2005, p. 23) argues that once marriage became the embodiment of so many emotional and psychological hopes, it also created the possibility of this sort of self-destruction:

> People expect marriage to satisfy more of their psychological and social needs than ever before . . . Never before in human history had societies thought that such a set of high expectations about marriage was either realistic or desirable . . . [T]

> he adoption of these unprecedented goals for marriage had revolutionary consequences that have since come to threaten the stability of the entire institution.

We can understand those heightened expectations as deriving from the movement up the Maslow hierarchy. As marriage and family both have increasingly concerned themselves with the self-actualization needs, the expectations of what marriage is supposed to deliver have risen accordingly. When the expectations associated with marriage are set so high, many more marriages are likely to be perceived as failures, with divorce being the outcome.

In addition to a high divorce rate, high expectations might well make young people choosier about marriage in the first place, perhaps especially among those who saw their parents unable to live up to those expectations. In the United States, marriage rates continue to drop to record lows for reasons that have already been explored, such as the declining benefits of marriage and the increasing availability of alternatives such as cohabitation. The rise of open relationships and some forms of polyamory might also be part of this resistance to marriage, even in its most contemporary form.

As history suggests, marriage is a lot more resilient than the critics give it credit for. Social institutions in general have ways of adapting their form as their functions change and responding to changes in the economic or political context in ways that enable them to continue to perform their core functions. Here is where evolutionary thinking can be of some help as well. At one level, we know that the family as a social institution cannot completely disappear. Helpless human infants will always require care from a basic biological perspective, and human beings still have the same built-in drive to reproduce that other animals do. Changing social norms can certainly temper that drive, but they cannot completely erase it. As long as the desire to reproduce is there and the infants it produces require care, some social institution will have to exist to structure those processes.

If it also true that, all else equal, two parents are better than one, the odds of single-parenthood completely replacing the two-parent family seem slim. The odds of plural marriages of any sort also being significant in number seem equally slim but for different reasons. From an economic perspective, the coordination costs of having multiple persons with responsibility for the household, and especially any children, rise dramatically as more adults are included into any marriage-like relationship. Perhaps there will be a small number of people who can make such an arrangement work, but the likelihood that marriages of more than two would overtake the standard dyad is very small. It is important that these alternative forms of marriage play on as equal a playing field as possible, especially with respect to single parenthood. Government subsidization of any particular form of family makes it more difficult to figure out which forms really do fulfill the functions of the family best.[10]

The challenge in trying to understand what these trends mean is the question raised at the end of chapter 6: are these part of a disequilibrium adjustment process to the rapid change of the past 30 or 40 years that will eventually reverse itself, or have we settled into a new longer run equilibrium of fewer, though perhaps better, marriages? Furthermore, do fewer but better marriages reflect the end of marriage as an institution, or are they simply another phase in its ongoing evolution? Even with the distortions caused by current policies, history still suggests that marriage as an institution is not likely to crumble in the face of recent changes. The forms marriage might take, including the possibility of serial marriages as noted in chapter 6, might be as hard for us to foresee as contemporary marriage might have been to our great-grandparents.

## The Nirvana Fallacy and Effects of Divorce

No discussion of divorce would be complete without addressing the question of whether divorce causes more problems than it solves. Few family issues are more contentious than this one and few have been subject to more empirical examination than the effects of divorce. A chapter section can hardly do justice to this complex and voluminous literature, so my goal here is to provide a quick look at some of those results and a framework within which we might think about them. At the very least, I want to provide some reasons to think that the historically high rate of divorce of the modern era is not a major reason to fear for the well-being of children or the future of marriage as an institution.

The argument I wish to make is that although we might all agree that a world without divorce, assuming this is also a world where all marriages work very well, would be the ideal for both the marriage partners and their children, we do not live in a world where that is possible. The real world is one of imperfect marriages where the question of the effects of divorce have to be understood in a comparative context. Moreover, any attempt to calculate the benefits and costs of divorce *must* take into account divorce's effect on the marital partners and not just the children. In other words, analyses of divorce must not fall victim to what the economist Harold Demsetz (1969) termed the "Nirvana fallacy," whereby an unpleasant and imperfect reality is compared to an idealized, perfect alternative that is, unfortunately, not achievable.[11]

The essence of the argument is that the choice facing couples considering divorce is always between an imperfect marriage and an imperfect post-divorce reality, especially when children are involved. Critics who wish to make divorce tougher too often focus on the damage that divorce does to children as support for their position. There are three problems with this approach. First, in assessing the damage done to children from divorce, it is necessary to know the size of the effects involved. It might matter a great deal to our assessment if the negative effects on children are comparatively small or large. If the effects are large, then any benefits of divorce and/or costs of remaining married must be sufficiently large to overcome those negatives. If, however, the effects are small, even if they are statistically significant, then the comparative questions look different.[12] Second, any calculation of the costs and benefits of divorce must take into account the costs and benefits to the adults involved. Divorce, especially under a no-fault regime, has not produced good financial outcomes for women. However, the ease of divorce under no-fault has allowed a number of women to leave marriages that involve abuse or other serious problems, including financial troubles caused by husbands. Even if the problems are not severe, any increased utility men or women get from leaving an unhappy marriage should be part of the discussion.

Stevenson and Wolfers (2006) found that the introduction of no-fault divorce had significant effects on the well-being of married adults. For example, the number of women murdered by their intimate partners declined by 10 percent after the introduction of no-fault. In addition, the female suicide rate dropped significantly, as did rates of domestic violence. Stevenson and Wolfers add that the decline in rates of domestic violence was "large enough to imply that domestic violence was reduced not just by ending violent relationships, but by reducing the violence in extant relationships as well" (p. 269). By reducing the costs of exit, a legal regime of no-fault divorce provided women with alternatives to staying in violent relationships or exiting them via suicide. As one considers the costs and benefits of more liberal divorce laws, the benefits associated with a reduction in harm to adults has to be factored in alongside the effects that a higher divorce rate might have on children.

Finally, and perhaps most important, is the question of alternatives. If the effects of divorce on children are negative and they are large enough to matter, the question becomes "as compared to what?" What is the alternative to divorce, especially if the parents are deeply unhappy? Critics of divorce argue that the parents should do whatever it takes to work out their problems "for the sake of the children." But what if the continuing in-home conflict is at least as much of a problem for the children as are the negative effects of divorce? A substantial body of research in psychology and sociology suggests that children of high-conflict marriages are frequently made better off by divorce, as the conflict poses more of a problem for their long-term development than does the divorce and its consequences.

Amato, Loomis, and Booth (1995) used 12 years of longitudinal data to study the effects of both marriage and divorce on a sample of over 2,000 married persons and a subsample of their children. What they found was that "in all cases, the adverse outcomes associated with a high-conflict parental marriage that does not dissolve are more severe than those associated a with high-conflict parental marriage that breaks up" (p. 909). Interestingly, these children did better than those from low-conflict marriages that ended in divorce. What this suggests is that the costs associated with divorce may be relatively constant, but the benefits may vary by the level of marital conflict. The children from the high-conflict marriages benefitted a great deal from getting out of a high-conflict home, and the loss of exposure to the conflict was enough to overcome the costs associated with the divorce. The authors conclude:

> When conflict between parents is severe, divorce removes children from an aversive and stressful home environment. Under these circumstances, the decline in stress may well outweigh the loss of other resources, resulting in an overall positive outcome. On the other hand, when overt conflict between parents is not excessive, children are unlikely to anticipate or welcome divorce. Under

> these circumstances, divorce represents a loss of resources for the child with no compensating gain. (pp. 911–12)

The implications of this study are that not all divorces are bad for children and that divorces that end high-conflict marriages are actually good for children. To the degree that liberalized divorce laws have made doing so easier, they have improved those children's lives. As Amato, Loomis, and Booth also observe, ending low-conflict marriages can be problematic for children, especially if the divorce comes as something of a shock.

Later research by Yu et al. (2010) confirms this basic result in the context of adult children of divorcing parents having various levels of conflict. They offer two conclusions. First:

> These findings support the stress relief hypothesis (Wheaton, 1990) that contends that parental divorce, even as a stressful life event, may actually ameliorate some of the negative effects of marital conflict on children's adjustment if divorce presents escape from the more stressful environment of a high-conflict family. (p. 290)

Children can benefit from the dissolution of a high-conflict marriage because the exit option provides a way to reduce the stress associated with that conflict. Divorce has stresses of its own, of course, but the evidence suggests that the gains in stress reduction from ending high-conflict marriages outweigh the increased stress associated with the divorce itself. Yu et al. also find that

> the group differences in factor loadings of parents' marital conflict suggested that physical violence was more likely to characterize the divorced couples. This result supports the assumption that after leaving a violent or abusive marriage, mothers may be more physically and mentally healthy and thus more able to establish a healthier relationship with their children. (p. 290)

Divorce that ends high-conflict marriages is not just good for the children directly, it can also enable mothers to reduce *their* stress, which will improve outcomes for their children through better mother-child relationships. The implication of these results is not that divorce is always benign or beneficial. Instead, the point is that in considering the effects of divorce, and therefore the desirability of a lower-cost divorce regime such as no-fault, we have to engage in a comparative analysis and avoid assuming that the costs all take place after the divorce. Bad marriages can be worse than divorces, and that is true for both the adults and the children. To the extent that the historically high divorce rate reflects an easier exit option from bad marriages, it represents a strengthening of marriage as an institution, not a weakening.

This brief discussion cannot cover all of the complex issues raised by high divorce rates. My goal here is simply to raise a number of questions that emerge from my earlier analysis and that should play a larger role in discussions of the costs and benefits of divorce. As marriage and family continue to be increasingly concerned with the needs at the top of the Maslow hierarchy, divorce is not going to disappear. We need to be sure we are considering all of the relevant factors as we discuss its social impact and any possible changes to public policy we might adopt.

## Capitalism, the Family, and Human Flourishing

Whatever the scientific merits of Maslow's hierarchy of needs, it serves as a useful heuristic to capture the upward progress of humanity over the past two or three centuries. From millennia of poverty in which ensuring the basics of food and physical safety were day-to-day challenges for the vast majority of humanity, an increasing proportion of the population has reached a point where those struggles are largely nonexistent. In the Western world, the overwhelming majority of the population do not worry moment-to-moment about their physical safety or where their next meal is coming from. The percentage of people living on less than one or two dollars a day continues to fall, and fall rapidly, while people in other parts of the world continue to climb close to Western levels of wealth and comfort. Pulling ourselves out of poverty is perhaps humanity's greatest achievement. Creating a world in which a substantial majority of the seven billion people on the planet live at least relatively long lives of reasonable comfort is a feat sometimes overlooked.

Even among those who recognize this accomplishment, few recognize that the institutions of market capitalism and respect for trade and profit that it requires are the main reasons for that upward climb. Understanding how capitalism has met our material needs is one thing, but as I have argued, as we more easily meet our material needs, we open up the ability to pursue all kinds of nonmaterial values. The less we must spend on life's necessities, the more we have to spend on things we want simply because we enjoy them. Consider again how much of the income of the average American is spent on things other than food, clothing, and shelter. We indulge our toys and our hobbies like never before. We give gifts and we travel. Even what we spend on the necessities can be spent on not just items that are merely functional, but on those that please us aesthetically. Our expenditures on food are on vastly better food than a century, or even a generation ago.

More generally, this expansion of wealth has freed us to engage in quantities of education, art, and leisure that were possible only to a tiny fraction of humanity for most of our history. Even relatively poor Americans can get a college education and have access to books, music, and art that the wealthy of generations past did not have. For others, the expansion of wealth is an opportunity to *create* knowledge, music, literature, and art that would not have been available generations before. That so many young people spend the first 18–22 years of their lives just learning and not engaged in much in the way of economic production is a luxury of the wealth capitalism has produced.

Consider these points in light of the frequent complaint that capitalism makes people overly materialistic and focused disproportionately on money and profit. By contrast, I would argue that market capitalism has freed us from a focus on the material and the narrowly economic by producing *so much* material well-being and economic growth that such concerns can be less central to our daily lives. Capitalism has freed us to pursue an ever-expanding range of nonmaterial interests and values. The story of the family told so far aligns with that observation. The changes in economic activity and the wealth that capitalism brought have freed the family from a concern with material survival and have opened the space for it as the site of our deepest nonmaterial aspirations. We look to the family for love and emotional satisfaction rather than sheer survival.

The places that have adopted the classical liberal institutions of private property, contract, exchange, the rule of law, and sound money, and the corresponding norms of peace, tolerance, equality before the law, and respect for work and profit are places where humans, both inside the family and out of it, have not just survived but flourished. They are the places where humans have extended their lives, treated each other well, expanded literacy and learning, created more technology and art, and lived in peace. The institutions and norms of classical liberalism and capitalism have made that possible and made the family into a far more humane institution. However, like all such accomplishments it cannot be taken for granted. I have argued that the family is the central way in which we pass on the values and rules of the liberal order. It is worth asking whether the abundance of the modern world has made it easier or harder for families to achieve that goal. How well societies at the top of the Maslow hierarchy are able to sustain that position may depend greatly on how we raise our children and whether they are ready to take on the responsibilities that a liberal society requires as a condition of the wealth it produces. That is the issue explored in the next chapter.

# CHAPTER 8

# Why Parenting Matters: The Importance of Play, Risk, and Failure for Classical Liberalism

## Introduction

Last chapter's discussion of the family's climb up Maslow's hierarchy of needs painted a fairly rosy picture of where the family has evolved early in the twenty-first century. Even if one believes that many of the changes in the family have been either benign or positive, one can still recognize that there remain a variety of problems facing the modern family. Divorce can create real problems for children even if it is the right decision for all concerned. There is certainly an exhaustive literature on other pathologies, such as abuse, that are part of the reality of family life in the twenty-first century. Even so, on the whole, family life is a far better place today than it was in even the comparatively recent past of 100 or 200 years ago.

However, the sentimentalization of childhood along with Freudianism and the more general increase in what we might call the "psychologization" of parenting has created another set of potential concerns, as modern parents have become more and more worried about getting parenting right. The belief seems to be that there is, in fact, a right way to parent and that parental mistakes can cause lasting psychological harm to children. Such worries are yet another luxury of Western wealth—parents who were busy trying to scrape a living off the land could hardly afford to worry about whether incorrectly potty training their children would scar them for life. With the functions of the family turning more and more inward, it is no surprise that nervousness about raising children properly would increase at the same time. As the psychological functions displaced the economic and political ones, as psychology became increasingly seen as scientific, and as science in general became a more powerful social force, it is no surprise that a central concern of parents became figuring out how to parent scientifically and to manage children in the same way humans were increasingly controlling nature.[1] It is also not surprising that parents would turn more frequently to supposed experts to help them parent properly, displacing the informal knowledge that had passed down by word of mouth and imitation, and sometimes in written form, through prior generations.

One result of all of these forces is the development of what might be called an increasingly child-centric family. With parents having fewer children and investing more in them, and with the continued concern about parenting correctly, it perhaps is not surprising that children's needs have become the focus of family life over the past few decades, with the parents' needs, and even their marriage, pushed to the periphery. In the extreme, the increasingly child-centric family has produced the phenomenon known as "hyper-parenting," sometimes called "helicopter parenting," in which parents are deeply involved in every aspect of their children's lives, even through their college years and beyond, often as a way of protecting them from any perceived danger or possible failure. The cloak of sentimentality that has slowly covered childhood since the Victorian era has morphed into a straight-jacket imposed by parents out of fear of their own mistakes and their misperceptions of the dangers of the world outside the family. Rather than being seen as a robust creature who could, and did for centuries, withstand all kinds of unpleasantness that modern parents could never abide, the modern child is now treated as fragile and delicate in ways that require constant parental monitoring and protection.

Although this view of children is hardly universal in the Western world, it has certainly become much more widespread, especially in the United States. Its commonality raises the question of whether such hyper-parenting is a cost of the luxury of being at the top of Maslow's hierarchy. Is hyper-parenting just a personal choice of parenting styles, or might it have implications for the family's role in passing on the cultural and social capital necessary to maintain a broadly liberal social order? If, as Mises, Hayek, and other classical liberals have argued, the family is the major conduit for ensuring the survival of liberal values, then perhaps choices about parenting might have implications for the likelihood of families doing this job well. The debate over hyper-parenting has come to a boil in the past decade with the emergence of a clear backlash movement. In this chapter, I explore this debate by focusing on two of the backlash books: Hara Estroff Marano's (2008) *A Nation of Wimps* and Lenore Skenazy's (2009) *Free-Range Kids*. Marano's book documents the ways in which hyper-parenting has made children fragile and less resilient, while Skenazy's offers an alterative approach to parenting that avoids the pitfalls that Marano identifies. I will also discuss Amy Chua's (2011) *Battle Hymn of the Tiger Mother*, which can be read as a backlash to the backlash with its defense of a philosophy of very involved parenting.

The overarching question is the degree to which changes in parenting, and the family more generally, are raising concerns that have potential implications for the socio-political order. We tend to view these changes in parenting as distinct from political questions, but if the family is the conduit of central cultural values that might or might not help to sustain the desired political and economic institutions, then the link is there. And if parenting is the primary way families pass on those values, parenting is a legitimate object of discussion with respect to the survival of liberal societies, and classical liberal values in particular. Classical liberals, who believe in economic and political freedom and individual responsibility, should have every reason to be concerned if changes in parenting and families are undermining those values that are core to their beliefs and that are required for their institutions to function well.

## What Is the Problem with Families?

There are a number of ways to characterize the problems families are facing. The symptoms are often quite recognizable, but it is not always as clear what the underlying disease is. The stories and anecdotes about the helicopter parent are everywhere. The media are full of stories of moms and dads who hover over their children, directing every aspect of their lives just about every hour of the day. A conversation with any K-12 teacher or college professor will bring forth even more such tales. Often this type of parenting manifests in the form of children whose schedules are full of activities both in and out of school, from music lessons to sports to volunteer work or any of several dozen things that the parents have decided they need. This drive to overschedule, like so much else with this phenomenon, may well come from a good place, namely, the parents' desire to see their children succeed combined with the assumption that meaningful success requires all of this preparation from day one. It is not hard to imagine, mostly because they are real, the parents who fret over their children not getting into the right baby day care because it will shut them out of the best preschool, which means the child will not get into the top private primary school, which in turn means that he or she will not get the preparation and connections necessary to get into that Ivy League college, which is, of course, the only way the child will ever be a success. These parents also tend to be the ones Marano (2008, p. 19) calls "snowplow parents," who attempt to remove every obstacle in the way of their children living out that life-path, while simultaneously giving the children very little responsibility, or choice, in the matter.[2]

At the same time that these parents are overscheduling and hyper-managing the details of their children' lives, they are also protecting them from any risk of danger or failure. We are all familiar with the stories of parents fearing all of the horrible things that can happen to their children, demanding hand sanitizers everywhere, removing traditional playground equipment, or driving their children two blocks to school for fear of what might happen if they walk by themselves. Add to this parental fears about everything from online predators to poisoned Halloween candy to what chemicals are in plastic sippy cups and you get children who are constantly being bubble-wrapped for their own protection.

Aside from the fear of the lurking dangers, real or imagined, this hyper-parenting often takes the form of an unwillingness to allow children to experience the pain and discomfort of failure. More generally, in an analogy to how markets work, hyper-parenting refuses to allow children to suffer the psychological equivalent of profits and (especially) losses that help them learn how to navigate the world successfully. The snowplow parents who clear the road of obstacles are denying their children the feeling of psychological profit that comes from accomplishing something themselves. As a result, such children do not learn as effectively how to deal with challenges and novel situations that require them to work hard and figure out solutions. Those parents who attempt to cushion every one of their children's failures, whether in the trivial form of second-winner trophies for losing sports teams, or in the more serious form of aggressively pushing school officials to change grades or override a coach's decision to cut their kid from a sports team, are denying those children the chance to feel the psychological loss that comes from failure and is necessary for learning what *not* to do. Trying to bail out children from every possible failure has the same effect as bailouts do in the economy. Such bailouts lock in inefficiencies and waste resources by cutting short the process by which we learn what to do and what not to do. Just as bailed out firms can become economic zombies, economically dead but still wandering around consuming resources, so do bailed out children stumble through late adolescence and early adulthood unable to be resilient in the face of failure and creative in the face of roadblocks.[3]

Another way of looking at these phenomena is that they represent the sheltered childhood and its sentimentalization taken to an extreme. The concept of the sheltered childhood was originally concerned with creating a space in which children could become educated, play, and learn without having to worry about the ugly reality of the adult world of work and the public sphere more generally. Sheltering children within the worlds of family, school, and houses of worship, and in the process really creating childhood and adolescence as we know them today, was an understandable reaction to the long history of children having to work on farms or factories as part of the family's role in market production. It was not intended to protect children from every possible danger or even to cushion them from failure in the way that too many parents do today. It seems as though there is no risk to children that is worth tolerating, at least if parents or policymakers become aware of it. Steven Pinker (2011, p. 444) aptly said of this phenomenon that "[t]he historical increase in the valuation of children has entered its decadent phase."

An economic perspective can shed some light on this view of childhood. One way to understand hyper-parenting is that if each and every child is viewed as infinitely valuable, his or her safety or happiness cannot be traded off against any possible risk. Notice how many of the safety-related concerns of parents deal with very low probability outcomes, though they are often ones that would have very large negative effects if the very low probability event were to occur. Included here would be fears of kidnapping and online predators, the risks of which are greatly overestimated by most parents, especially since crimes against children in general have fallen significantly over the past few decades.[4] If the activities that incurred these risks had no benefits, then it might be sensible to not accept any level of risk. However, as I will argue later on, many, if not most, of the activities that are seen as too risky for children do indeed have benefits associated with them, which might make them worth engaging in since the risk is so small. However, not enough parents and policymakers seem to be willing to talk in terms of costs and benefits or acceptable risk when it comes to issues involving children.

In the language of economics, it is as if some parents can only think in terms of a "corner solution" when it comes to risks and their children. This terminology refers to the way economists think about trade-offs. We tend to depict trade-offs using something like the diagram in figure 8.1. For almost any example one can think of, there is a trade-off between safety and the reward one gets from the activity. Almost anything we do has some element of risk to it, such that the only way to obtain the reward is to accept some amount of risk and thereby reduce one's safety in the broadest sense of the term. The curve depicts that trade-off by showing how increasing the benefit from the activity also means reducing its safety (increasing its risk). The term "corner solution" refers to point A, which lies at the corner of the curve and the axis, indicating that there is no trade-off being made. At point A, the person prefers all the safety that can be obtained, which implies no reward whatsoever. (And we could put a comparable corner solution point at the other axis, reflecting someone who had no concern for safety whatsoever.)

Many parents might well say "yes, when it comes to my child's safety, no risk is worth taking." Such parents probably believe this as well, yet their actions suggest otherwise. If parents really believed this, they would never choose to put their child in a car (car seat or not). Car accidents are a major killer of children, yet parents are very willing to take *that* risk, but far less willing to, for example, allow their children to eat Halloween candy from strangers even though there is not one verified incident of poisoned Halloween candy on record (Skenazy 2009, p. 62). At one level, this concern about keeping children safe is problematic because parents appear to misjudge what choices really put their children at risk. A concerned parent might respond by saying, "well of course I put my children in the car—after all I have to transport them to various places and

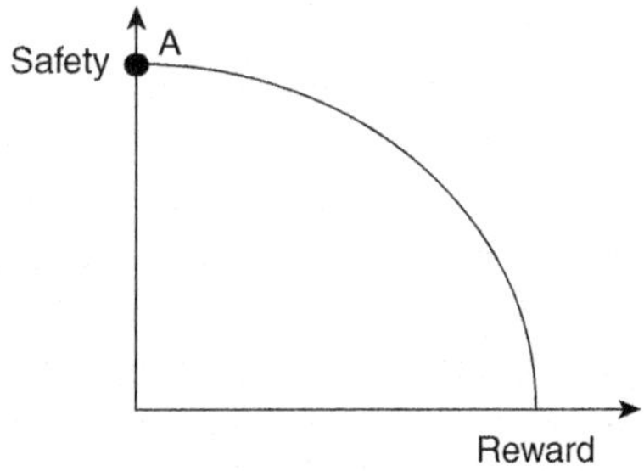


**Figure 8.1** Corner solution thinking.

they cannot walk everywhere." True enough, but it also makes the point: some risks are worth taking if there is a benefit to the risky activity that more than compensates for the risk. Parents do, in fact, understand that corner solutions are not optimal in many situations.[5]

We see this same corner solution mentality at play in the policy world as well, where concern for how some policy or some private sector action affects children is almost guaranteed to inspire new laws or regulations.[6] Perhaps the most obvious example of this attitude is the way in which the fear of sexual abuse by strangers has led to everything from various proposals to regulate the Internet to public schools requiring parents to demonstrate they are not pedophiles before being allowed to enter school property.[7] We see a similar mentality in the way in which every time something bad happens to a child, politicians, egged on by the victim's family and friends, pass a law to try to prevent a repeat of the event and then name the law after the dead child. Even if the odds of this particular tragedy happening again are very, very low, we feel like we need a law, even if such laws might well have unintended consequences that make matters worse for children.

The question of why we are seeing these developments is a complex one. One possible explanation is that parents are more likely to see their children as a reflection of their own merit or accomplishments. There are two possible sources for this explanation. First, as the functions that families perform have moved up Maslow's hierarchy, more and more of family life becomes about self-actualization for all of the members of the family. So adults see their family lives as contributing to them becoming the sort of people they wish to become above and beyond their basic needs. Families, and especially the children within them, become a reflection of parents' highest aspirations and who they are as people. It is a short step from there to parents who see their children's accomplishments as a public signal about the parents' value and worth as people. The common bumper sticker advertising that "my child is an honor student at" is some evidence consistent with this explanation. Given our more general youth culture, parents may well see their children as an opportunity to make choices that they themselves did not or could not make. In short, parents are trying to create "trophy children."

The second form that children's new status as a reflection of the parents' own worth might take derives from the way in which parenting has been overpsychologized and professionalized over the past generation or two. After thousands of years of mostly successful parenting without expert help, parenting has become the province of various experts and their guidebooks and newspaper columns. From pregnancy to potty training, and from toddler to teenager, parents are besieged by experts telling them what to do and what not to do. This is problematic in a variety of ways, but the most fundamental problem is that parents are taught to think that there is a clear right and wrong way to accomplish each individual parental task and that their choices about parenting will make or break their child's development. The effect of this view is that children's successes but *particularly their failures* will be seen by their parents as a reflection of the parents' own ability and moral worth. If one's child does not get into the prized private school or Ivy League college, it presumably indicates failures on the part of the parents. The same would be true of misbehavior in school or any other sort of problem with their children. To the degree that parents really do believe that they are the primary cause of their children's success or failure, and the popular parenting literature has given them ample reason to believe that they are, they will see their children's outcomes as a reflection of their worth as parents. This will lead them to be both highly directive and, perhaps, very averse to any risk with a significant downside, no matter how infrequent the bad outcome is. It also might explain why parents are so quick to push back at institutions like schools when their children do not succeed. Failure must be seen as the school's fault, because if it is the child's fault it may well be the result of bad parenting, which in turn reflects poorly on the parents.

A second broad explanation might come from changes in the roles of women. With more women in the workplace in general than a generation or two ago, and with significantly more women having more responsibility at work and working for a number of years before having children, it may be the case that they, as well as their husbands, are bringing their workplace mentality to the task of parenting. It is at least possible that the more laid-back forms of parenthood of generations past, especially when parenting just one or two children, are simply not sufficiently challenging to women (or men) used to the modern professional workplace. If so, seeing the task of raising children in the same light as an office project, and bringing the same managerial mentality to it, is not so much of a stretch. The outcome is a very results-oriented approach to parenting that can only see the value of time spent doing certain things in terms of how they explicitly forward the ultimate goal. Everything the child does must be tightly related to some educational or other highly valued purpose that will help to ensure their eventual success. Ignoring for a moment the significant evidence discussed by Caplan (2011) on how little parenting matters for most individual children's outcomes by adulthood, it might also be the case that less structured and more open-ended childhood activities do more for the child's maturation than highly structured, results-oriented ones.[8] This possibility might well run against the deeply ingrained instincts of modern parents used to the highly goal-oriented workplace. If true, this argument hardly suggests that parents should give up the world of work. Instead, it becomes another version of the Hayekian "two sorts of worlds" argument that has framed this study from the start: what works in the anonymous world of the market, or even in the complex modern firm, may not be effective in the more intimate world of the family.

## A Nation of Wimps?

The result of all of this overprotection of children is that we may well be raising what Hara Estroff Marano (2008) has termed "a nation of wimps." Marano's fear is that by wrapping our children in protective bubbles that prevent them from suffering any physical or psychological harm at all, we are raising a generation that will struggle to exercise independence and not know how to deal with inevitable failure. Although the term "wimps" may be overly strong, the concern of Marano and other psychologists is that young people are being made unnecessarily fragile as a result of having been shielded from having to accept and respond to disappointment. As Marano reports, the empirical research in psychology is pretty clear that resilience is a key part of psychological health as people who have that quality are better able to deal with disappointment and failure. There is evidence to suggest that we are born with the ability to be resilient in the face of failure but that it can be unlearned if we do not have the opportunities to make use of that trait. The research also indicates that one of the ways that people develop more resilience is to have successfully responded to disappointment and failure in the past. In other words, we gain two things from our mistakes: we learn what we should avoid doing and we develop the confidence to know that we can fail and not only survive but come back stronger. Without the experience of not just failing but *overcoming* failure, we would be very fragile in the face of those inevitable failures.

In addition to young adults who might struggle to respond to failure, the sort of overparenting that we often see these days may well raise children who find independent decision-making to be challenging. To the extent that parents have overprogrammed children's lives in order to engineer some type of ideal childhood, these young people will find the freedom of early adulthood, or college, to be an enormous challenge. Unused to deciding for themselves, particularly with respect to more major decisions, they will be more likely to make bad choices or to continue to turn to mom and dad for help. Surveys of college students report, and the anecdotal experience of many professors and administrators certainly confirms, that many students are in very frequent contact with their parents, and it is not unusual for them to be on the phone with one or more parent while meeting with an advisor or trying to sort out a problem with residence life staff. Reports of parents accompanying their college graduate children on job interviews are not uncommon either. No doubt in some cases this is a desire on the part of the parents to continue to engineer their children's lives, but some young adults might actually *want* their parents there. If so, such dependency is arguably the result of kicking birds out of the nest without giving them enough experience at flying solo.

If this argument is reasonably accurate, then parenting practices have implications for social order, particularly the viability of a liberal social order. The costs of this sort of parenting are not isolated to the parents themselves, though the costs on them are significant. As Bryan Caplan (2011) argues, "parents count too," and engaging in the sort of intensive parenting that risks producing fragile children is extraordinarily costly for parents and has almost no, and perhaps some negative, return on the margin. Trying to do everything for one's children leads to tired, stressed, unhappy parents, and this sort of "secondhand stress" is a major complaint that *children* have about their parents. Caplan discusses survey results indicating that one thing that many children wish for is not that their parents would spend more time with them (which is what many parents expected their children to say), but that their parents would be less tired and stressed (pp. 32–33). As Caplan also points out, parents might believe it's all worth it if their time-intensive parenting were producing better children. However, Caplan marshals a large amount of empirical evidence to suggest that parenting matters much less for long run individual outcomes than do genetic factors.[9] So all of the costs that parents bear for this type of parenting might be mostly in vain, as they will not produce the results they hope for, and they will run the risk of producing children who will struggle unnecessarily into adulthood.

Beyond the parents themselves, the costs of hyper-parenting fall on others across society. At a fairly trivial level, many other adults wind up bearing the costs of overparented children, whether as professors or staff members at college or managers in the workplace.[10] The standard argument in economics about the ability to externalize costs may well apply here. To the extent that parents do not pay the full cost of these parenting strategies, they will likely engage in more of them than they would otherwise, much as firms who do not pay the full costs of their polluting activities will pollute more than those who do pay the full costs. If parents believe they also *gain* from such parenting strategies, they are that much more likely to continue to practice them and to continue to externalize some of the costs. If parents believe this sort of hyper-parenting is necessary to ensure their children's success, or if they simply enjoy being that involved in their children's lives (or even living vicariously through them), then these practices are also likely to continue. Caplan (2011) explicitly argues that such parenting strategies do not have the benefits parents think they have and that, therefore, the costs are simply not worth it. Caplan hopes to persuade parents that effective parenting is less costly than they think. This will inspire them to have more children, or at least to have the number of children that is genuinely aligned with fully informed preferences. He is less persuaded that we are producing a nation of wimps than that we are producing a nation of unnecessarily tired and stressed out parents who are not having as many children as they would really like to have. However, if we *are* producing a nation of wimps, then one advantage of Caplan's argument is that if people accept it, we might reduce the external costs of hyper-parenting on innocent third parties.

Of more direct importance for the relationship between the family and the liberal order is whether hyper-parenting affects the ability of children to accept the responsibilities of such an order. Is there a link between parenting styles and how children come to view the political world at the broadest level? For example, if we raise children who are used to having things done for them, and who are not used to suffering the consequences of their mistakes, will they have the tolerance for risk that is necessary to produce the entrepreneurship that is essential to economic growth in a market economy? Can children who have not been trusted to wander more than a block from home, or to organize games unsupervised by parents, or to go the playground without safety gear, become adults who are willing and able to take economic risks? Will they tolerate others taking such risks, including standing by when those risks do not pan out? The liberal order cannot survive without a willingness to take risks, particularly in the economy but also in terms of what John Stuart Mill 1985 [1859] called "experiments in living." Path breakers with new ideas have to be willing to accept the risk of rejection, whether in the form of social condemnation or economic losses, if liberal societies are to progress. If there is a link between having been parented in a way that protects against all such risks, or at least from suffering the full consequences if they did not pan out, and how one views risk taking in the broader social order, then not only might we be raising a nation of wimps, but also a nation unprepared to take on the tolerance for risk and failure that is essential in a liberal society.

Perhaps an even worse outcome than young adults afraid to take risks would be young adults who are *too* willing to take risks because they are used to getting bailed out if they fail. Hyper-parenting might produce a generation that wants more and more freedom with less and less responsibility when their choices do not pan out. Rather than a nation of wimps, we get a nation of excessive risk takers who want to externalize the responsibility for their mistakes onto other individuals or institutions rather than accepting responsibility for their choices and their corresponding risks. Will such young adults be willing to tolerate the verdict of the market when firms, whether their own or others, fail and are headed for bankruptcy? Or will they prefer the economic equivalent of "everyone gets an award" and argue that bailouts are in order? Will a nation of bailed-out children produce a nation of bailed-out firms? If the discovery process of the market is an essential element of a liberal society, and if that process requires that actors bear the economic consequences if their plans fail to create value, then constantly bailing out money-losing firms will destroy the learning process of the market. Without that learning process, we will be stuck in a world where resources are consistently misallocated, impoverishing many, and where other resources get devoted to battles over the political distribution of bailouts and other forms of favors and subsidies designed to soften the blow to firms that cannot create value.[11]

This question is perhaps even more pressing in the context of the Great Recession and especially groups like Occupy Wall Street and others concerned about the "1 percent." Even as some of the protestors complain about the privileged 1 percent, survey data indicates that about half of the protestors thought the bailouts of the banking system were necessary.[12] A sizeable number of young protestors have also argued that their college loan debt should be forgiven, which amounts to their own request for a bailout. Whatever the legitimacy of their complaints about the power of corporations and the failures of the political class, the frequent refrain that their college degrees did not ensure them their dream job, or that their debt should be forgiven, is at least consistent with a generation that was raised with a great deal of freedom, but far less responsibility for bearing the negative consequences that can come with it.

Perhaps it is a stretch to connect parenting styles with political *gestalt*, but liberal thinkers have long argued that families are central transmitters of important cultural values and norms, so we should not be surprised that when family structures and parenting styles change, so do the values and norms people bring to their understanding of politics. The running Hayekian theme that liberalism requires us to supersede our atavistic, altruistic moral instincts honed in eons of existence in small kin-based groups is relevant here. If the family has one key function in the Great Society, it is perhaps that it can teach by example the ways in which a liberal society must accept failure and learn from it. Of course no parent should allow his or her child to risk serious physical harm, but to the degree that we continue to prevent children from feeling any pain, disappointment, or frustration, we risk creating a society in which people either demand freedom without responsibility, or constantly wish to restrict the freedom of everyone in the name of either safety or self-esteem. Either outcome is a recipe for disaster.

## Or of Free-Range Kids?

In response to the overprotectiveness of parents potentially raising a nation of wimps, we have seen a backlash in what has become known as the movement to raise "free-range kids." The phrase comes from author Lenore Skenazy (2009), whose book by that title makes the case for getting away from the hyper-parenting model. Skenazy came to this argument when she wrote a newspaper column about allowing her then nine-year-old son to ride the subway alone from Manhattan to their home outside the city. The reaction to her column was nearly uniformly negative, with many calling her "America's worst mom" for, in their view, putting her child in so much danger. Part of Skenazy's point in giving her son that freedom and responsibility was to demonstrate that most of the fears that parents have about the dangers to their children are exaggerated and that children are happier and better off when raised with a lighter hand and allowed to explore the world more freely.[13] She also argues, as Caplan does, that parenting this way dramatically reduces the time demands and stresses on parents in addition to the benefits for children. In response to all of the negative publicity, she began a blog and a book project dedicated to an alternative view of parenting.

In contrast to the extreme risk-averseness of hyper-parenting, Skenazy (2009, p. 41) argues that "some risks are worth taking." Too often, she argues, parents are trapped in a "just in case" mentality that causes them to prepare for the worst possible thing that can happen to their children, rather than to assess real risks more accurately. This worst-case scenario thinking is what she refers to as "thinking like a lawyer" in that parents are trying to protect children against any possible negative outcome that could potentially cause any kind of harm. In contrast, she counsels parents to think in terms of risk-reward rather than just risk. Although she does not phrase it this way, she is asking parents to think like economists and to consider the marginal benefits and marginal costs of the choices they make for and with their children. In contrast to the earlier discussion, she wants parents to avoid settling on the corner solution that involves reducing risk as close to zero as possible.

Critics often respond by asking why it's worth taking *any* risk when it comes to something as precious as a child. The reality, however, is that even parents who claim to be highly risk-averse take risks with their children all the time because there are some activities whose benefits are so obvious that we choose to accept the risk. Take the earlier example of transporting children in a car. In *that* case, parents intuitively understand that the risk is worth the benefits. Skenazy's point is that there are many more activities that have benefits that outweigh the risks if parents can both recognize the benefits and have a clear understanding of the risks. Like Caplan, she attempts to provide better information so that parents can make better decisions and ones that will improve both their lives and those of their children. So, for example, Skenazy argues that parents should encourage their children to walk to school if at all feasible rather than be driven. Parents might say that letting their children walk alone exposes them to "stranger danger," but, as Skenazy points out, the real risk of a child being abducted on the walk to school is extremely small, especially when we recognize that the vast majority of child abductions are by family members known to the child. "But," says the parent, "why should I even take that minimal risk?"

There are two responses here, both related to thinking like an economist. First, what's the alternative? Driving the child to school also has real risks of getting in an accident, and those are likely larger than walking to school. Second, children who walk to school alone benefit, just as Skenazy's nine-year-old riding the subway alone did. Children who are given the freedom to explore the world on their own are more likely to develop a sense of independence and competence, as well as responsibility, than those who are unable to explore the world in this way (Gray 2013). Rather than seeing all choices where children are given freedom as being filled with risks, Skenazy is asking parents to both consider how big the risks really are and to recognize that the often minimal risks do come with important benefits. We expose children to real risks of one sort or another every single day. Keeping them wrapped in a bubble simply is not possible, nor is it desirable. Given that some risk is unavoidable, parents should make better informed decisions about the real risks of various activities and the potential benefits they bring.

To be clear, the point is not to take on *any and all* risks, but to take ones that are rationally assessed and that have clear benefits. Risk is also contextual. Letting a child who has never been out of his small town ride the New York City subway by himself is not a smart risk, nor is letting a city child wander around in the woods at night. The important point is that it is individual *parents* who are, or should be, in the best position to know what risks are worth taking. We need not impose a take-no-risks rule of parenting, or use the law to prevent others from taking such reasonable risks. Skillful parenting adapted to the tacit and contextual knowledge that parents have of their children and the situation at hand is the way to manage risk. One-size-fits-all zero-risk corner solutions are not. That said, it is worth repeating that some risks are just out of bounds, such as ones that expose children to a high chance of severe injury. The message here is not one of complete benign neglect. Instead, parents should practice what Gray (2013) calls "trustful parenting." Children will want to make really dumb decisions and parents, at least at the extremes, can and should prevent them from doing so. But where the downside risk is reasonable, and the benefits exceed the risk-adjusted losses, children benefit greatly from parents giving them the freedom to make choices and take the consequences. Skenazy's book and blog are full of stories from parents about how their children gained in confidence and responsibility once the parents let up and gave them the opportunity to exercise meaningful choice. That seems the kind of parenting to engage in if one desires a liberal order of free and responsible adults.

Free-range parenting also requires that children be responsible with the freedom they are granted. When children mess up, the responsibility for dealing with it should fall on their shoulders whenever practicable. To take one example from economist Donald Wittman (2005): suppose your middle-school aged kid forgets to bring his lunch to school. It is tempting to want to engage in the bailout of bringing it to school for him, but this has two problems. First, your child has externalized the costs of his mistake onto you when you feel as though you have to spend the time and energy to bail him out. Second, bailouts, both of children and firms in the market, create what economists call "moral hazard." The more you bail him out of his mistakes, the less likely he is to remember his lunch in the future, knowing full well that you will bail him out. Instead, Wittman argues that the child should bear his own costs: do not take him any lunch and let him go hungry. No child is going to be seriously harmed by missing a meal. The child will pretty quickly get the message that he is responsible for his lunch, and the costs to you are near zero. The same applies when children have minor problems in school or with friends. It should be *their* responsibility to attemt to resolve them whenever possible. Of course it is also okay for parents to cushion outcomes in more extreme cases, but what constitutes such a case is best left to parental discretion.

From an economic perspective, part of what Skenazy and Wittman and others are arguing is that parents should not allow their children to impose the costs of their misbehavior back on parents. Parents who feel as though they have to drop everything and run that lunch back to school are letting their children externalize the costs of their forgetfulness on the parents. Like the external costs of raising a nation of wimps, smaller-scale parenting decisions that let children engage in actions where the social costs are larger than the private costs will lead to those actions being produced excessively. Instead, parents should be looking for ways to internalize costs back on children where possible. Letting that child go a little hungry will likely solve the forgetfulness. Making siblings find a way to solve their own problems, rather than dragging parents into endless battles over "who started it," is another such example. The same can be said for disputes among friends, at least where the stakes are relatively low. Not only does this reduce future attempts to externalize the costs, it makes parenting easier in the short run by extracting parents from having to solve every problem their children have.

Parenting should be about ensuring that children are exposed to a profit and loss system of maturation. When children get it right, they should reap the benefits, but when they mess up, they should also pay the price. If we continue to grant children greater freedoms, but continually prevent them from experiencing the psychological equivalent of losses, we will have denied them a crucial part of the learning process and, in so doing, potentially weakened their ability to navigate effectively the liberal order. Just as privatizing profits and socializing losses in the economy leads to misallocation and moral hazard, so will parenting that socializes losses lead to children who find the reality of the extended order of the Great Society puzzling and unacceptable. If the liberal order depends crucially on people acquiring certain values and norms, and understanding that the liberal order differs from the intimate orders of the family, parenting needs to take into account how best to inculcate those liberal values. Allowing children to experience the real risks associated with freedom and the profit *and loss* such freedom might bring is one way to do so.

## Why Parents Misjudge Risk?

Central to both Skenazy's and Caplan's books is the task of reminding parents that their perceptions of what is dangerous to their children are often at odds with the statistical facts. The things that we often think are dangerous, like Halloween candy and stranger abduction, are really not meaningful dangers at all. Misperceiving risk is hardly limited to thinking about parenting issues, and misperceiving statistical frequency is a common human problem. For example, we forget that the most dangerous part of air travel is driving to the airport. We are far more likely to be killed on that drive than on the plane, yet our beliefs about which is riskier are often at odds with that fact.

Cognitive psychologists and behavioral economists have a number of explanations for why we are so bad at thinking like statisticians. These explanations are often termed *cognitive heuristics*, which is just another way of referring to mental shortcuts. We use heuristics all the time when our information is incomplete. For example, we infer that person who is smiling at us is trustworthy. It does not always work, but it is right much of the time. Using these sorts of heuristics, however, introduces biases into our thinking. The previous example might lead us to be wrong about smiling people being trustworthy in specific instances, as experiences with car salespeople with big toothy grins might indicate.

One of the most important of these biases for the issues facing parents is *availability bias*. A common shortcut we use when our information is incomplete is to rely on the information that is currently available to us. This is particularly the case when information that is relevant to the question at hand has been recently acquired. So when a friend says, "Does it seem to you like everyone's getting divorced these days?" you immediately think about the two or three divorces that you just heard about and quickly nod your head. But the fact that those examples are easily available does not mean that the divorce rate is, in fact, any higher than it used to be. Human minds are biased toward the information that is immediately available and we make statistical inferences from those examples, not the total set of relevant information.

Consider the following example from Kahneman (2011). If you ask people to come up with 12 examples of their assertiveness then rate themselves on how assertive they are, they will likely rate themselves lower than if they are asked to provide only six examples. Why? Because getting the first few examples is easy, but then it gets harder, and when we go to self-rate, we remember the struggle to find those examples and those bias our self-rating downward. With only six, we struggle less, and that counter-experience is less available and therefore does not bias our judgment.

If we consider how parents judge things like the risk of a stranger abduction or other childhood dangers, one of the main sources of available information is media coverage. If parents do not know the real statistics, they will grab for information that is available, and that is often that story on television about the little girl who was kidnapped from her bedroom (or that plane that crashed last week, or that story about some rare disease). As Skenazy (2009, Chapter 2) points out, the media, both through the news and through dramas like *CSI* or *Law and Order*, focus on the extreme and on the rare, and because our experience of the media dominates our own store of recent information, it feeds right into availability bias. Looking to make a judgment about our children's safety, we are ripe for falling for that cognitive bias.

Availability bias can lead to what some behavioral economists have termed the "availability cascade." Media stories that create exaggerated perceptions of risk start generating emotional reactions in the public, and those emotional reactions themselves become newsworthy. The media coverage intensifies and now the issue becomes a major cultural concern. As various media outlets compete for attention, the risk involved gets exaggerated even more and people begin to dredge up other available examples of the apparent phenomenon. Those who try to provide evidence of the real risk are shouted down and are often labeled as cold-hearted. It is but a short step from this point to calls for political action, and the result is often wasteful and misguided public policy based on a false perception of risk. One need only think of the overwrought media and policymaker reactions to child abductions and related events that fit this pattern perfectly.

Parenting issues can add one more element to the availability cascade. Parents react to the misperception of risk by engaging in costly preventative steps that, like bad public policy, end up harming the very people they are intended to help—their children. The availability bias leads to overprotected children who are denied important skills they need to effectively navigate the adult world. Plus, these misperceived risks put inordinate demands on parents' time for very little in the way of benefit, creating stressed-out parents and children. This is why it is crucial for parents to try to push back against the availability bias and for citizens in general to recognize the way that availability cascades lead to bad policy and overprotective parenting.

To some extent the availability bias is a product of evolution. Many of the shortcuts that our minds take are ones that proved themselves effective in the context of the early evolution of our minds and human social behavior. Because they worked, they become our quick reaction to many situations. As we saw in chapter 2, this is part of what Kahneman (2011) calls "System 1," or our automatic reaction of "thinking fast." In the face of the ways in which System 1 reactions can mislead us, Kahneman argues that we need to engage our slower thinking "System 2." System 2 double checks the automatic reaction of System 1 and slows us down, looking for things like the availability bias and helping us to calculate the real risk at hand. System 2 is the product of needing to engage the more complicated risk assessment of the Great Society rather than the more straightforward risks of the more intimate orders of our evolutionary past. The way in which things like the availability bias make it harder for us to assess risk accurately is another manifestation of the challenges of living in two sorts of worlds at once.

### Why Not the Tiger Mom? Because Parents Matter Too

Amy Chua's (2011) *Battle Hymn of the Tiger Mother* appeared not long after the Marano and Skenazy books. Although it was not a direct response to Marano's concerns or Skenazy's call for a lighter parenting touch, it certainly made the case for a very interventionist parenting style that both pushed children to excel in exceptional ways and demanded much of parents in the process. Putting aside the question of whether Chua's parenting style is distinctly Asian, that style can be analyzed on its own terms within the framework developed in this chapter.

Chua (2011, p. 8) starts by claiming that Chinese parents have higher dreams for their children than do Western parents, and higher regard for them, by understanding just "how much they can take." With that background, the book tells the story of her attempts (and notably, they are mostly hers and not that of her husband) to turn her two daughters into elite musicians. The girls are forced to practice endlessly, often while being subject to strong verbal criticism from Chua, to the exclusion of any other sort of typical childhood or adolescent activity. Chua devotes hours of her own time per week, not to mention a lot of financial resources, to trying to make the girls into elite concert musicians. The book is full of stories of her driving them to practices, her dissatisfaction with various private instructors, and her constant demands on the two girls, including her attempts to deal with the resistance of the younger one. There is much one could say about the details of Chua's parenting philosophy, but the general idea is that she believes that the job of parents is to ensure that their children reach the very top of whatever they do, and what they do should only be things of overarching value. She also believes that "to get good at anything you have to work, and children on their own never want to work, which is why it is crucial to override their preferences" (p. 29). She also argues that it is important to be unafraid to respond to "substandard performances" by one's child with excoriation, punishment, and shame (p. 52). Even as she raises some important questions about the supposed laxity of Western parents, some of which parallel the concerns of Marano, her alternative is not to give children more freedom and responsibility, but less, and to respond to failure with "excoriation, punishment, and shame" rather than letting children take the consequences alone.

As a parenting strategy, the most obvious point to raise is that engaging in Tiger Mom parenting requires a great deal of time and material resources from the parent. Chua has a job that enables her to have the time and resources to parent the way she does, not to mention a husband who is mostly willing to tolerate, if not support, what she is doing. These opportunities and resources are not available to a large number of parents, making Chua's views on parenting much less widely applicable, at least with her level of intensity.

Readers of the book might wonder whether her daughters are really happy being parented this way. At one point Chua says that children parented the Chinese way are no less happy than ones parented the Western way. That may be so, but it misses an important point, and one raised by Caplan in the context of his discussion of parenting: children are not the only ones whose happiness matters. What might be troubling to some readers of Chua's book is how unhappy *she* appears to be so often. There is no doubt she is very proud of her daughters' accomplishments, but there is a great deal of fighting, yelling, and conflict, much of which Chua clearly dislikes, in order to get her daughters to where she thinks they should be. The question raised is why parenting should be so miserable *for the parents*. Caplan argues that the advantage of a lighter parenting touch, which he believes is justified by the much stronger influence of genetics on children's long-run outcomes than parenting behavior, is that it makes for happier parents who have more time to do the things they *and their children* enjoy. That in turn, he argues, makes for happier children because, as noted earlier, they do not experience highly stressed parents all the time.

Parents who recognize the limits of their own influence (as Caplan argues) and who recognize the benefits of giving their children more freedom and responsibility (as Skenazy argues) are parents who will have more time to sleep and more time to engage in the activities *they* enjoy. Perhaps most importantly, they will have the time to keep their marital relationship strong, rather than one or both parents centering their lives around their children. One of the other things one might take away from Chua's book is what happened to her relationship with her husband. Many readers might wonder what sort of marriage it is where the wife's life is nearly completely devoted to furthering her children's potential careers at the cost of the possible neglect of her relationship with her husband. Like the previous chapter's discussion of divorce, it is a mistake to not take into account the preferences and needs of parents when thinking about good parenting.

As noted at the outset of this chapter, the modern family has become extraordinarily child-centric. When the supposed needs of children trump everything else, parents are engaging in another form of corner-solution thinking. The result is that the needs of parents fade away, both as individuals and in their role as a married couple. Parents who devote their entire lives to their children run the danger of neglecting their own needs and ability to grow, in addition to possibly neglecting the needs of their spouse. If one of the keys to successful parenting is a family with a solid adult partnership at the center of it, then parenting strategies that make it easier to lose sight of the importance of maintaining that relationship are likely to backfire. Children need the model of a healthy adult relationship, and they are troubled when the adults in their lives are unhappy and constantly under stress.[14] This is what is missing from Chua's vision of parenting. Parenting should not have to be an act of suffering and martyrdom. Unhappy and stressed parents will not do the job as well. And if Caplan's review of the behavioral genetics literature is correct, most of that unhappiness and stress will be for very little gain for most parents. Instead, a lighter touch will not only raise children at least as well-adjusted for adult life, it will also reduce the costs on parents both early on in the child's life and later in adolescence when their children can more responsibly exercise independence.

Chua's vision of parenting also raises the question of whether what this is all about is trophy children. At various points in the book, Chua speaks of being a "junior partner" to her children's success. That is at least suggestive that part of what she cares about is not really her children's success per se, but instead how that success is a reflection of her superior parenting skills. She seems to be just the sort of high-powered professional who would bring the skills of the business or professional leader to the project of parenting. If so, it brings an interesting twist to families being child-centric. It may be that in many families where it looks like the child is at the center of things, due to the time and resources parents devote to their success, what is actually happening is that parents are spending on themselves in a form of consumption. All of that work is really not about the children per se, but about how the children reflect back on the parents. Rather than doing the things that might really forward their children's happiness and success, they are doing the things that make themselves look good as parents. We might call this a social signaling approach to parenting. By contrast, free-range kids may appear to be not at the center of parental attention from moment to moment, but those parents might well be doing more for their children in the long run by giving them more freedom and responsibility and focusing their own time more on themselves. In other words, we should judge how child-centric a family is not by resources, attention, or parental intentions, but by whether parenting strategies really empower children to be free and responsible adults. In economic terms, the value of any productive activity is determined by whether the combination of inputs creates an output with more value, not by the value of the inputs themselves. It is not at all clear that the Tiger Mom strategy is successful, and it *does* seem clear that it makes for unhappy and stressed parents, which matters too.

## Unsupervised Play, Ostrom Moments, and the Liberal Order

A recent poll indicated that 68 percent of Americans think there should be a law that prohibits children aged nine and under from playing at the park unsupervised, despite the fact that most of them no doubt grew up doing just that. In the same poll, 43 percent supported a similar law for 12-year-olds.[15] In other words, almost half of Americans would like to criminalize all preteenagers playing outside on their own. This is despite abundant evidence that childhood has never been safer than it is today. Between these unfounded fears about child safety and the belief that parenting needs to be incredibly intensive, even if not to the extreme Chua takes it, children have lost the ability to engage in unsupervised play. As it turns out, this loss is more important than it might seem. It has implications for both child development and, I will argue, the health of liberal societies.

Denying children the freedom to explore on their own takes away important learning opportunities that help them to develop not just independence and responsibility, but a whole variety of social skills that are central to living with others in a free society. In his *Free to Learn*, Peter Gray (2013) documents the ways in which the ability to truly play is central to how children learn and how it thereby contributes to their growth into functional adults.[16] In particular, he focuses on what he calls "free play," or "play in which the players themselves decide what and how to play and are free to modify the goals and rules as they go along" (p. 7). He adds that "free play is nature's means of teaching children that they are not helpless" and that "in social play, children learn how to negotiate with others, how to please others, and how to modulate the anger that can arise from conflicts" (pp. 17–18). One other element that defines play is that it continues only with the consent of those playing: "the ultimate freedom in play is the freedom to quit" (p. 141). This matters because it means that the playing will only continue if those engaged in it can resolve conflicts and mollify complaints in ways that keep everyone interested in playing.[17] This is one way in which the social skills are taught: if children want to play, they have to learn to keep everyone sufficiently happy.

The kind of play Gray is focusing on here is very different than the structured play of something like Little League baseball. There the rules are imposed and disputes are settled from the outside by adults. Children, once they get involved, cannot as easily quit that type of game as they can quit true play. This alternative institutional environment removes the bottom-up ways in which children learn to create and enforce their own rules and makes them nearly completely dependent on adults.[18] Gray also argues that free play causes children to develop an important kind of empathy, as they have to be able to "see from others' perspectives, to understand what others want, and provide at least some of that for them" (p. 159).

All of these skills developed by play, Gray argues, are central to child development and enabling children to be functional adults. He notes that these skills also have important social implications. One way to integrate these insights into the argument of this book is to observe that the ability to engage in group problem solving and settle disputes without the intervention of outsiders is a key part of the liberal order. Think about all of the social interactions people have during the day that involve some minor disagreement or dispute: Whose turn is it at the copier? Who should clean up the coffee area? Who gets that parking space? Think about how often these disputes get settled without violence or acrimony. Or think about how we design rules and procedures in small informal groups, again mostly without violence or acrimony. Think of the ways we put up with annoying or obnoxious behavior of others, or the ways we adjust our own behavior to the needs and wants of others. When one seriously considers all the moments in a typical day that have potential for conflict and get resolved through conversation and negotiation, or just plain tolerance, it is actually somewhat astounding how smooth social life is.

In a liberal society, these sorts of moments can take place in a variety of institutional contexts. Even in the context of the market, which is certainly structured by rules that are largely external to the players, there are still numerous moments of human interaction that demand that we accommodate others without clear, explicit rules to guide us. Outside of the formal market, we engage in voluntary interactions with a large number of other people during the course of our days where, again, there may be no explicit rules to guide us in how to behave. Yet we manage to find ways to avoid conflict or resolve those that arise. If we were to lose the skills necessary to do so, it is not hard to imagine that people would quickly turn either to external authorities like the state to resolve them, or would demand an exhaustive list of explicit rules where such a list might not be possible.[19] One key to maintaining a society in which the role of either public or private coercion is limited is a citizenry that has the skills to solve such problems consensually. The ability of the people involved to design a set of rules for resolving potential conflicts is at the center of how free people can create institutional solutions that reduce the level of coercion. Like play, such solutions rest on the consent of the players and must be created in ways that keep everyone sufficiently happy. When we understand play as a consent-based activity structured by rules created by the players, learning to play becomes the way we practice the skills we need for the very real world of social and political interaction.

Thinking in terms of play shines an interesting light on the work of Elinor Ostrom (1990). Ostrom's scholarship focuses on the ways in which people solve common-pool resource problems without the formal structures of either the market or the state. She argues that those are not the only two institutional forms available to communities as they figure out how to "govern the commons." Many situations are more amenable to the members of the communities involved developing their own institutional solutions for managing common-pool resources, and she shows through many case studies the variety of forms such solutions might take. For our purposes, Ostrom's work is a useful example of the sort of bottom-up problem solving that can characterize how free people avoid and resolve conflicts without resort to external authorities. More interestingly, Ostrom draws on some basic game theory to make her arguments and claims that "[i]n the most general sense, all institutional arrangements can be thought of as games in extensive form" (p. 23). The leap from games to play is a very short one.

Although Gray is very clear that true play is "mentally removed" from real life, many of the elements of play can be seen in the ways in which people construct and make use of the institutional arrangements that resolve social conflicts. Like play, the ways a community might decide how best to manage a common grassland or waterway ultimately rests on developing a set of rules that everyone will consent to. The same skills of compromise and empathy, and the same need to keep people sufficiently happy so they consent to play the game (i.e., adopt and follow the institutional rules), that characterize childhood play are necessary for developing real-world institutional solutions for the management of common-pool resources. What Ostrom calls "the possibility of self-organized collective action" (p. 25) could usefully describe what Gray calls "free play." The key difference is that real world institutional solutions, because they are in the real world, are focused on particular ends, unlike play, which has no specific goal of its own. The kinds of institutional arrangements that interest Ostrom are ones that solve specific problems. Nonetheless, those arrangements do take on many of the characteristics of play, and as her work demonstrates, human communities are able to develop amongst themselves a wide variety of institutional solutions in the face of common-pool resource problems.

Although Ostrom's work focuses on larger-scale social problems that require collective solutions, the same potential for conflict exists in all of the smaller scale kinds of situations we noted earlier. Conflict is a constant feature of human interaction. It is possible that these little "Ostrom moments" get resolved peacefully because so many of us have had experience from childhood at having to engage in the sort of rule-making and rule-enforcing that is so critical to a liberal society. As Ostrom (1990, p. 14) observes:

> Instead of presuming that optimal institutional solutions can be designed easily and imposed at low cost by external authorities, I argue that "getting the institutions right" is a difficult, time-consuming, conflict-invoking process. It is a process that requires reliable information about time and place variables as well as a broad repertoire of culturally acceptable rules.

Liberal societies are ones in which individuals have learned how to problem solve in these ways without the need to invoke violence or some sort of external threat. Developing these skills is a central, if largely invisible, foundation of the peaceful human interaction and cooperation that keeps liberal societies as liberal and free as they are.

If we did not have these skills, we would inhabit a world where many more social conflicts, or interpersonal slights, led to anger or violence. Imagine a world where rather than trying to settle conflict through conversation and negotiation among the parties, we immediately went to the police or lawyers. We are seeing more and more of this in modern America. It might be the result of an increasing number of young people who have not sufficiently developed the skills to resolve conflict peacefully on their own because they simply did not have the opportunities as children to engage in the unsupervised play that allows them to learn those skills.

If this argument is correct, parenting strategies and laws that make it harder for children to play on their own pose a serious threat to liberal societies by flipping our default setting from "figure out how to solve this conflict on your own" to "invoke force and/or third parties whenever conflict arises." A society that weakens children's ability to learn these skills, denies them what they need to learn smooth social interaction. The coarsening of social interaction that will result will create a world of more conflict and violence, and one in which people's first instinct will be increasingly to invoke coercion by other parties to solve problems they ought to be able to solve themselves. Unsupervised play is a key way that children learn the skills necessary to engage in social cooperation in all kinds of social spaces, both within the market and especially outside of it. If we parent or legislate in ways that make it harder for children to develop those skills, we are taking away a crucial piece of what makes it possible for free people to be peaceful, cooperative people.

This argument fits right into Lenore Skenazy's insistence that we need to consider both the benefits and risks of childhood activities. She also deplores the decline of unstructured play among children as it too has risks worth taking. As Gray's book demonstrates, unstructured play has tremendous benefits associated with it, especially when we think about the role that childhood learning can play in preparing children for the liberal order. Children who only know structured, supervised games and play enforced by adults will likely become either risk-averse uncritical external rule followers or people too quick to invoke coercion because they will find creating and enforcing their own rules very difficult. When children are free to invent their own games and rules, they learn invaluable skills in negotiating and cooperating with others, in thinking about the relationship between rules and fairness, in learning how to enforce agreements with others, and in responding when things do not work out the way they hoped. Such unstructured play has risks, particularly those associated with the variety of mean things children can do and say to each other with no parents nearby, but learning to deal with those negatives is a *benefit, not a cost of engaging in unsupervised play.*

Marano's (2008, p. 91) description of the benefits of such play is particularly Hayekian and provides one other way in which childhood play might matter: "[P]lay is the true preparation for adulthood. At its heart, play is rule-bound activities in which the outcome is unknown. It's the way we learn to handle the unexpected. Play sharpens the wits and makes mental processes nimble—resilient and ready for whatever life throws our way."

This description of play could apply equally to competition in the market process. It too is a rule-bound activity whose outcome is unknown, and it too is about helping us to handle the unexpected, as well as increasing the mental skills of those who are competing. Thinking about play this way provides additional texture to Hayek's (1977, pp. 115–20) description of the market as a "game of catallaxy" or exchange. Thinking of markets as, in these ways, a form of play opens up some interesting possibilities for how we think about game theory and competition and their relationships to child development. It also reinforces this chapter's theme that parenting, in this case allowing children to engage in unsupervised play, is not unrelated to the sustainability of liberal institutions.

It is worth asking whether the demise of unsupervised play will have major effects on the broader society by undermining the development of the negotiation and cooperation skills needed to resolve conflicts on our own. So much of our interaction in the liberal order is in spaces neither fully defined by formal rules nor enforced by formal mechanisms. Without practice at dealing with such situations, young people may struggle and ask for formal rules and enforcement, which will likely smother the ability of those informal spaces to function well. Solving social conflict through informal norms and negotiation is a central, if underappreciated, feature of liberal societies. It is particularly important if one is committed to a libertarian vision in which both public and private coercion is to be minimized. The ability for the parties involved in low-level conflicts to solve them through peaceful means reduces private coercion and thereby reduces the demand for more public forms of coercion. Free societies rest on a bedrock of informal conflict resolution, and the skills necessary to make that kind of resolution happen may well be developed through forms of unsupervised childhood play. Parenting strategies that declare such play to be too risky are fraught with risk.

# PART IV

## *Classical Liberalism and Family Policy*

CHAPTER 9

# Knowledge, Incentives, and Parental Rights: A Framework for Classical Liberal Family Policy

## Introduction

Classical liberals and libertarians have not had a lot to say about issues of family policy and children's and parental rights. Though there are probably many reasons for this lack of attention, the most likely one is that children pose particularly difficult challenges for classical liberalism. Children pose difficult challenges for *any* political philosophy, as such systems are usually centered around some idealized picture of what rational adults would do. Classical liberalism's commitment to the sanctity of the choices of such adults makes the question of children that much more vexing because classical liberals, like others, also believe that all human beings have a minimal set of rights worth protecting, even if they are not the full set of rights extended to rational adults.

Like any other realm of public policy, there are multiple interests at play in family policy. This is often framed as a triangle involving individual liberty (of both the parents and the children), the best interest of the child, and the interests of policymakers, normally understood as a concern with the public interest. Although that is one way of looking at matters, a view more informed by contemporary political economy might be skeptical that the public interest is foremost in the mind of policymakers. Instead, the argument of this chapter makes use of a somewhat different triangle: the rights of parents, the rights of children, and the best interests of the child. One way of framing the question of this chapter is "who is in the best position to decide what is best for children when they are unable to decide what is best for themselves?" This question presumes that some degree of paternalism is required, as after all, the question is about the parent-child relationship. The core question is how far the rights of parents extend. That question implies the related ones of what rights children have and when those might trump the decision-making rights of parents. This set of questions in turn leads to the policy-relevant question: what combination of rights for each will best serve the best interests of the child, and what role should the state, the extended family, and the institutions of civil society (e.g., houses of worship, community organizations, or even neighbors and friends) play when those interests are not being served?

For example, what if the choices of parents appear to violate the rights of children? Cases of clear mental and physical abuse are somewhat easier to deal with, as such parents can be treated pretty straightforwardly under criminal law as having violated their children's basic rights as humans. Here we might not hesitate in arguing that the parents have given up their decision-making rights over their children in the same way that any lawbreaker gives up her rights, especially if we recognize, as I will argue later, that parents have taken on the obligation to care for their children when they acquire those rights. But these are the easier cases.

What about the tough cases, such as one that I will return to at the end of the chapter: what can classical liberals say about parents whose religious practice forbids them from providing their children with medical treatment without which the child is likely to die? How do we resolve the tension between the parents' presumed right to do what they see as best for their child, who classical liberals might argue is not sufficiently mature to decide for herself, and the child's presumed right to life, which might entail certain obligations for the parents? Does the state have a role here, even within classical liberalism's general skepticism about what states can and should do? At what point might, if at all, the exercise of parental rights violate the rights of children? And how should such cases be handled, and by whom? *Who gets to decide*?

In this chapter, I wish to think through the principles that might guide classical liberals in addressing these issues of family policy.[1] My purpose is not to provide a foolproof template for making policy or to provide pat answers for the tough cases like the one earlier, but to explicate a framework for thinking about these issues that can be applied to a variety of policy questions. In particular, I want to argue for a strong notion of parental rights and make use of a number of standard tools of classical liberalism in doing so. Parents should have a very broad range of rights with respect to how their children are raised and treated because the parents are the ones with the strongest incentives to act in the child's best interest and the local, often child-specific, knowledge to know what that interest might be and how best to achieve it. The incentives to act in a child's best interest facing state actors are weaker and they are less likely to possess the knowledge relevant to discerning the best interest of the child. Even in recognizing that parents are not infallible, I will argue that parents are less fallible than the state and that the burden of proof resting on the state should be high in order to demonstrate why parental rights should be overridden.[2]

Finally, my use of the word "parent" in this chapter should not be taken to necessarily have any biological content to it. I am concerned with the rights of those who are legally responsible for the child, regardless of their biological relationship to the child or to another parent. The question of whether such rights could be unbundled in ways that might allow more than two people (e.g., step-parents) to possess them when all are performing parental functions is an important question that is beyond the scope of this chapter.[3] The question here is what should be the rights of those who are legally entitled to be the child's parents under the current general legal framework.

## Establishing Parental Rights in the Constitution

The evolution of constitutional jurisprudence on the question of parental rights is in many ways a microcosm of the more general changes in the Supreme Court's approach to the relationship between legislative decisions and individual rights over the course of the twentieth century.[4] By the mid-1920s, there was a strong presumption in favor of parental rights with a high barrier to the sorts of legislation that could override them. Legislatures had to demonstrate a very compelling rationale for second-guessing parents' rights to make decisions about their children. By the end of the century, the burden of proof had begun to shift, as it did in so many other areas of constitutional law, such that as long as legislatures had some "rational basis" for claiming that the "best interests of the child" justified overriding parental rights, whatever they might pass through the democratic process would be constitutionally acceptable. Although the court continues to hold that the early-twentieth-century decisions establishing parental rights were basically good law, recent cases appear to have established that the hurdle that legislatures have to leap is somewhat lower than in years past. A review of the major cases establishing parental rights reveals all of these trends.

The whole concept of a constitutional parental right is a peculiarly twentieth-century phenomenon. Perhaps the best way to understand it is that the question of whether such a right exists is only relevant if governments see intervention into parent-child relationships as one of their legitimate functions and when people recognize that having limits on such intervention might be desirable. For most of the history of the West, areas that we would now describe as "family law" were, for the most part, dealt with in the common law, and not seen as areas to be addressed by the administrative law of the state. As noted earlier, even the very notion of the family as "separate" from kin, community, church, and the state was not relevant for most of human history. Questions of constitutionality cannot arise until we have a constitution and until the family becomes more nuclear and private in the ways that it did in the eighteenth and nineteenth centuries.

With the growth of government in the late nineteenth century, and the Progressive Era's romance with using government to "fix" families in particular, questions arose about the limits of the state's ability to make decisions that had been previously the domain of parents. The irony here is that it was state intervention that required that we define the boundaries of the family with respect to the state. Stephanie Coontz (1992, pp. 145–6) put it this way: "Western notions of privacy and family autonomy developed as corollary to the new claims of an expanding state over the public sphere; both family privacy and individual autonomy were increasingly guaranteed by the state." Coontz also notes that these same developments were part of the longer-run trend of trying to extract the family from its embeddedness in other parts of the community, as we saw in chapters 3 and 4. The whole notion of family privacy and parental rights as we understand them today is indeed a creature of the economic and political changes that pulled the family away from the oversight of the community and the political and social changes that legitimated the possibility of state intervention into families.

The two cases generally credited with establishing the idea of the constitutional rights of parents are *Meyer v. State of Nebraska* (1923) and *Pierce v. Society of Sisters of the Holy Names of Jesus and Mary* (1925). Both cases, interestingly, dealt with educational issues.[5] In *Meyer*, the State of Nebraska had passed a law in 1919 that prohibited the teaching of children in "any language other than the English language" before the completion of the eighth grade. The plaintiff, Meyer, was found guilty of teaching German to a ten-year-old in 1920 and appealed the conviction. The school he was teaching in was a parochial one and the statute in question explicitly applied to "any private, denominational, parochial, or public school" in the state. The law was as much a possible infringement of the right of contract of the parents and school as it was about parental control over their children. The issue in *Pierce* could also be seen this way.

In fact, Justice McReynolds, speaking for the majority in *Meyer*, framed the question before them as "whether the statute, as construed and applied, unreasonably infringes the liberty guaranteed to the plaintiff in error by the Fourteenth Amendment" (399). He continued by noting that the Court had not historically defined with any "exactness the liberty thus guaranteed." However, that liberty was more than:

> merely freedom of bodily restraint, but also the right of the individual to contract, to engage in any of the common occupations of life, to acquire useful knowledge, to marry, establish a home and bring up children, to worship God according to the dictates of his own conscience, and generally enjoy those privileges long recognized at common law as essential to the orderly pursuit of happiness by free men. (399)

Then followed a long list of citations to previous decisions in the tradition of "substantive due process," about which I say more later. McReynolds next indicated that the "established doctrine" is that the liberty defined under the Fifth and Fourteenth amendments "may not be interfered with under the guise of protecting the public interest, by legislative action which is arbitrary or without reasonable relation to some purpose within the competency of the State to effect" (399–400). He also noted that it is the Court that has the final decision as to whether such exercises of the police power are proper.

After a discussion of why the law in question was not, in the Court's view, addressing a legitimate concern of the police power, McReynolds noted that even though the state may "go very far indeed" in attempting to "improve the quality of its citizens," it is still the case that "the individual has certain fundamental rights which must be respected" (401). Furthermore, even if a particular end were desirable, it "cannot be coerced by methods which conflict with the Constitution—a desirable end cannot be promoted by a prohibited means" (401). He then illustrated the point by quoting from Plato's *Republic* and noted that the scheme for raising children there might have had salutary effects, but it would not be permissible in the United States because it does "violence to both letter and spirit of the Constitution" (402). Here the Court is clearly laying out a view of the Constitution very much consistent with the jurisprudence of that era.

The role of *Meyer* in establishing constitutional protection for parental rights is linked with McReynolds' majority opinion in *Pierce* two years later. Taken together, these two cases are considered to have established the necessary constitutional foundation for parental rights. The facts in *Pierce* were similar to those in *Meyer*. The State of Oregon had passed a law in 1922 requiring that as of September 1926 all children aged 8–16 attend a public school in the district in which they reside. There were a few minor exceptions allowed, but the law was intended to apply statewide. A religious and a private school challenged the law before its implementation on the grounds that the law "conflicts with the right of parents to choose schools" for their children and "the right of schools and teachers therein to engage in a useful business or profession" (532). The private school explicitly claimed that the law "contravenes the corporation's rights guaranteed by the Fourteenth Amendment" (533). The lower court had ruled against the State, arguing that the law deprived the schools "of their property without due process of law." It made clear that the schools' right to sell their services was a form of property and that "parents, as part of their liberty, might direct the education of [their] children" (533). The State of Oregon appealed that decision to the Supreme Court.

McReynolds's majority opinion began by noting that this case has no implications for the State's more general attempts to regulate teacher qualifications or curricula or the like. He then pointed out that private and parochial schools are an "undertaking not inherently harmful" and that, in fact, they are seen as "useful and meritorious" (534). He then referred to *Meyer* as having established "the liberty of parents and guardians to direct the upbringing and education of children under their control" and that "rights guaranteed by the Constitution may not be abridged by legislation which has no reasonable relation to some purpose within the competency of the State" (534–5). He then even more clearly established the notion that parents have a powerful set of rights grounded in a broader theory of liberty:

> The fundamental theory of liberty upon which all governments in this Union repose excludes any general power of the State to standardize its children by forcing them to accept instruction from public teachers only. The child is not the mere creature of the State; those who nurture him and direct his destiny have the right, coupled with the high duty, to recognize and prepare him for additional obligations. (535)

This passage is the one generally quoted in later cases as indicating where the existence of constitutionally protected parental rights were established, especially when combined with *Meyer*'s list of liberties protected by the Fourteenth Amendment.[6]

Before discussing the ways in which the rights of parents have since been articulated and attenuated by the Court, it is worth putting these two decisions in some historical context. *Meyer* and *Pierce* are still considered good law today. They were at the tail end of a series of decisions that found in the Fourteenth Amendment protection for a whole variety of rights not specifically enumerated in the Constitution. In the late nineteenth century, these rights were largely grounded in the "Privileges or Immunities" clause of the Fourteenth Amendment. As Barnett (2004, p. 66) argues, the accepted meaning of that phrase at the time of the amendment's adoption referred to "both natural and inherent rights as well as those particular 'positive' rights created by the Bill of Rights." However, not long after the Amendment's adoption, this phrase was gutted of this meaning and its expansive protection of liberty. In the *Slaughter-House* cases of 1873, the Court adopted a very narrow conception of the Privileges or Immunities Clause that tied it to the rights of "national citizenship" rather than the more general civil rights that Barnett argues were intended by its authors.

However, the notion that the Fourteenth Amendment still somehow protected those unenumerated rights persisted and the emphasis shifted to the Due Process Clause instead. The clause was originally understood to refer to the *process* by which laws were adopted, but in a sleight of hand perhaps necessitated by the *Slaughter-House* decisions, later courts took to viewing the clause as referring to not just process but the content of the laws in question. More specifically, the Due Process Clause was interpreted as protecting rights of contract, particularly in labor markets. As we saw in *Meyer*, McReynolds listed some of those and provided citations to a variety of cases from prior decades that had established that precedent. One of the most famous of the cases from that era was *Lochner v. New York* (1905) in which the Court overturned a New York law establishing maximum hours for bakers on the grounds that it unconstitutionally interfered with the right of contract of the bakery and its employees.[7] The *Lochner* case was also notable for Justice Holmes's famous dissent in which he accused the majority of trying to read the Constitution as enacting Herbert Spencer's *Social Statics* and its defense of laissez-faire capitalism.[8] *Lochner*'s fame now is as the representative case of this whole class of decisions that were to be subsequently rejected during the New Deal, as the post-1935 Court sought to find constitutional justification for the greater willingness of Roosevelt and the Congress to intervene in a variety of private economic arrangements. "*Lochner*-era thinking" is now a pejorative among most constitutional experts, reflecting their belief that using the Due Process Clause to defend *unenumerated substantive economic rights* stood in the way of the greater economic role for government necessitated by the Great Depression and New Deal.

Despite the general rejection of such jurisprudence, *Meyer* and *Pierce* remain good constitutional law, even as their main conclusions have been softened in subsequent cases. Those two cases were crucial to establishing that the Due Process Clause's defense of unenumerated substantive rights could be applied outside the economic realm. Even as the Court overturned the use of the Fourteenth Amendment to protect economic rights, and had to devise somewhat convoluted arguments to defend an unenumerated right to privacy in places *other* than the Fourteenth Amendment, these two parental rights cases are still recognized as binding precedent, right down to the specific source of those rights being the Due Process Clause.

The next major parental rights case facing the Court was *Prince v. Massachusetts* (1944). The case involved a nine-year-old girl who, accompanied by her legal guardian Sarah Prince, was selling religious magazines on the streets of Brockton, Massachusetts. Prince was arrested and charged with violations of the state's child labor law, which prohibited boys under twelve and girls under eighteen from engaging in such sales on the street or in any public place. Prince argued that the law violated both her First Amendment freedom of religion and her Fourteenth Amendment protection of parental rights. The decision was read by Justice Rutledge and began with a now-famous summary of the Court's position on parental rights:

> It is cardinal with us that the custody, care and nurture of the child reside first in the parents, whose primary function and freedom include preparation for obligations the state can neither supply nor hinder [citing *Pierce*]. And it is in recognition of this that these decisions have respected the private realm of family life which the state cannot enter. (166)

The next sentence, however, brings the "but." Rutledge then catalogs the ways in which the family has nonetheless been subject to "regulation in the public interest," including requiring school attendance, regulating and prohibiting child labor, and others. Rutledge then concludes "the state has a wide range of power for limiting parental freedom and authority in things affecting the child's welfare" (167), including issues of religious practice.

The Court went on to make the case that a child of such "tender years" preaching on the public street would be exposed to numerous threats to her welfare, from "emotional excitement" to "psychological or physical injury" (170). Even though the parent or guardian might be present, she can at best "reduce, but cannot eliminate entirely, the ill effects of the prohibited conduct" (170). The Court also made clear that it was not creating a precedent for *any possible* state intervention into parental rights in the name of the best interests of the child; rather it was limiting such interventions to "the facts the case presents" (171). Despite that protest, *Prince* is now frequently seen as establishing the ability for the courts to weigh the best interests of the child against parental rights in establishing the constitutionality of legal interventions into the family. It is also worth noting, in light of earlier chapters, that the Court's language leaves little room for trading off *in practice* its perception of the welfare of the child to protect the rights of the parents.[9] The belief that state intervention is necessary because parental supervision alone cannot "eliminate entirely" the perceived dangers posed to the child suggests that the goal here is the "elimination" of such dangers. But is this realistic? How far is the state allowed to go to create a "danger-free" world for children, if that is indeed the implied standard? How much protection for parental rights does this really leave us with?[10] In subsequent cases, the Court certainly has not applied such a standard, but the underlying logic behind the idea that because parents cannot eliminate entirely the dangers to which children are exposed, state intervention is ipso facto justified is alive and well in much family policy today.

## Parental Rights in the Post-New Deal Constitution

The move the Court made in *Prince* was consistent with the general direction of constitutional jurisprudence in the New Deal era. Many of the unenumerated rights that had been protected by the much-maligned *Lochner*-era Court began to fall by the wayside in the face of shifting cultural beliefs about the necessity of greater government intervention, especially in the economic realm. Put most simply, the burden of proof of constitutionality underwent a significant change from what Randy Barnett (2004) calls a "presumption of liberty" to a presumption of constitutionality. Until the New Deal era, the burden of proof lay on the state to demonstrate that a challenged law was within the defined powers of the legislature and did not violate the presumed and broadly read liberties of the people, including rights not explicitly enumerated in the Constitution. Since then, the presumption has been that laws passed by the democratic process (assuming "due process of law") are constitutional unless the challengers can demonstrate that such a law violates the rights enumerated in the Constitution or those that have been established by the Court to be "fundamental" even if not enumerated. The result has been the gradual extension of state power and erosion of liberties, except in those areas explicitly enumerated (such as the Bill of Rights) or that the Court has chosen to define as fundamental (e.g., privacy or various protected classes).

The key to this reversal of the constitutional burden of proof is found in *United States v. Carolene Products Company* (1938). In several decisions earlier in the decade, the Court had begun to undo the *Lochner* approach of putting the burden of proof on the state to show that legislation was "necessary and proper" and was explicitly authorized by the Constitution and did not override accepted unenumerated rights. By *West Coast Hotel Co. v. Parrish* (1937), the reversal was largely complete with the Court appearing to defer totally to the democratic process to a degree that the notion of judicial review itself might be rendered superfluous (Barnett 2004, p. 229). In *Carolene Products*, the Court pulled back from that precipice and began to define the terms under which it would proceed for a number of decades.

The relevant passage is the famous "Footnote Four" in *Carolene Products*. In the text of Justice Stone's majority decision, the Court argued that the legal restrictions on the market for the milk substitute at the center of the case should be presumed to be constitutional "unless in the light of the facts made known to or generally assumed it is of such a character as to preclude the assumption that it rests upon some rational basis within the knowledge and experience of the legislators" (152). Stone then qualified that presumption of constitutionality in the first part of Footnote Four: "There may be narrower scope for operation of the presumption of constitutionality when legislation appears on its face to be within a specific prohibition of the Constitution, such as those of the first ten amendments, which are deemed equally specific when held to be embraced within the Fourteenth" (152). As Barnett (2004, p. 230) summarizes it, we now have the post-1941 theory of constitutional rights:

> Adopt a loose conception of necessity and presume all acts of legislatures to be valid, except when an enumerated right listed in the Bill of Rights is infringed (or when legislation affects the political process of discrete and insular minorities), in which event the Court will employ a strict conception of necessity and put the burden on legislatures to show that their actions were both necessary and proper.

As long as the legislature could construct an argument that the legislation in question was reasonably perceived to able to solve some problem (and that it did not violate one of the enumerated fundamental rights noted in Footnote Four), then it would pass the test of constitutionality. This gave, if not carte blanche, at the very least a wide latitude to the legislature and substantially weakened the grounds from which the courts could overrule it.

The Footnote Four approach stood for over 20 years until it was attenuated somewhat further in *Griswold v. Connecticut* (1965), which dealt with a state law making the sale of contraceptives illegal for both the parties to the exchange and anyone who assists in the exchange. The law was challenged and the Court agreed that it was unconstitutional. What was important about the case was the way in which it reached that conclusion. Justice Douglas had to find a way to avoid going back to *Lochner*-type arguments, yet still find protection for activities that were not explicitly enumerated as rights in Bill of Rights or otherwise fit the criteria laid out in Footnote Four. The Court concluded that the law violated the "right to privacy," which, of course, is found nowhere in the text of the Constitution. The Court did so, interestingly enough, by relying on the decisions in *Meyer* and *Pierce* as precedent for such an unenumerated right.

The problem, therefore, was how to ground that right constitutionally without going back to the Fourteenth Amendment, which would both violate the procedure laid out in Footnote Four and open the door to the unenumerated economic rights of the *Lochner* era that were overturned during the New Deal. Douglas's solution was to find the right to privacy in the "penumbras, formed by emanations" of the various rights protected in the Bill of Rights. By the logic of Footnote Four, this was not a right deserving of presumptive protection and the high burden of proof on the state that would accompany it. Nonetheless, the Court had established this right to privacy, and 27 years later in *Planned Parenthood of Southeastern Pennsylvania v. Casey* (1992), the Court would solidify it by referring to a "realm of personal liberty which the government may not enter." It again referred to a number of cases including *Meyer* and *Pierce* to substantiate that view.

Barnett (2004, p. 233) argues that *Casey* "exemplifies the current approach to constitutional rights." In this approach, what he calls "Footnote Four-Plus," it is the Court that decides which of the unenumerated rights in the Constitution are worthy of being declared "fundamental rights" and getting the higher level of protection demarcated in Footnote Four. This puts the Court in the position of making "moral assessments of different exercises of liberty" (p. 233). Generally, the liberties associated with noneconomic activities have received the protection of being "fundamental," while economic ones have not. Of course, as Barnett notes, there are exceptions, such as the lack of protection for the liberty to ingest marijuana. Nonetheless, the Footnote Four-Plus approach has allowed the Court to pick and choose among liberties guided, presumably, by any particular set of Justices' sense of which rights are deserving of such protection at the particular time in question. Barnett rightly points out that this approach is better than the original Footnote Four jurisprudence that did not recognize unenumerated rights at all, but it suffers mightily from the appearance of capriciousness.

That perception of capriciousness may well lie at the center of debates over "judicial activism," in the sense that when the Court defines those liberties associated with the majority's own ideological predispositions as "fundamental," this causes those with other beliefs to charge "judicial activism." When the Court defines those liberties a group likes as fundamental, then the Court is just perceived to be doing its job in preventing legislative overreach. With Footnote Four and the stigma of the *Lochner* era having pushed the Court down a path where it has to protect noneconomic unenumerated rights in a way rightly seen as capricious, it is no surprise that the Supreme Court has become a lightning rod in the culture wars, including a variety of issues related to the family.[11]

Since *Prince* in 1945 there have been several noteworthy parental rights cases and I want to take a brief look at two of them to see where the rights of parents stand in the Footnote Four-Plus world. As the continued reliance on *Meyer* and *Pierce* as good constitutional law would suggest, parental rights have largely been deemed sufficiently fundamental to garner a fair degree of protection. The two cases I will explore are both ones in which parental rights were upheld against claims of the state, though not without having to demonstrate that such protection was warranted under the current approach.

In *Wisconsin v. Yoder* (1972), the Court was faced with an Amish family in violation of a Wisconsin law that required children to attend a public or private school until the age of 16. The Amish saw no need for education beyond the eighth grade and removed the children from school at age 14 and 15 in order to work on the family farm. The children did not object to this decision. The family argued that the law violated their rights under the First Amendment. The

Supreme Court of the State of Wisconsin agreed and the Court upheld that decision. Most of the Court's opinion, written by Justice Burger, focused on the reasons for the Amish's objection to schooling and whether this was harmful to the children. The Court noted early on (213) the importance of requiring public schooling but that it could be "made to yield to the rights of parents to provide an equivalent education in a privately operated system," citing *Pierce*. In line with the Footnote Four-Plus approach, the Court noted:

> Thus a State's interest in universal education, however highly we rank it, is not totally free from a balancing process when it impinges on fundamental rights and interests, such as those specifically protected by the Free Exercise Clause of the First Amendment, and the traditional interest of parents with respect to the religious upbringing of their children. (214)

Implicit in this sentence is the idea that the government's interest is presumed to be constitutional, unless it "impinges on fundamental rights and interests." That is, the burden of proof is on the side of those asserting a particular liberty to demonstrate that it is among the protected categories. This contrasts with the approach in *Meyer* and *Pierce*, in which the government was expected to demonstrate some compelling reason to exercise the police power that would override the presumption of parental rights. Even here, the parental right is not seen as a given against which a piece of legislation must be deemed necessary and proper to reach a particular goal. Rather it is one of a limited list of rights deemed sufficiently fundamental to be "balanced" against presumptively constitutional legislation.

After establishing that the Amish's religious beliefs were not mere "personal preferences," but deeply rooted practices of hundreds of years, the Court then noted that no social harm appears to have come to Amish children who lacked the additional two years of education, nor were they under any risk of serious harm working on the family farm. The latter point was particularly important in distancing this case from the facts in *Prince*, where the claim was that the selling of religious magazines on a city street constituted a physical danger to the child. In the end, the Court did indeed hold the Wisconsin law unconstitutional, arguing that the high burden posed by the parental right as a fundamental right was not met in this case, as there was no harm being imposed on the children (and the children were in agreement with the parents' decision). The Court was also very careful to lay out the limited applicability of the case to the context of groups such as the Amish with this long-standing set of beliefs. Mere parental preference not to educate children all the way to age 16 would not have been sufficient to invalidate the law in the name of parental rights.[12]

The most recent major parental rights case in front of the Court was *Troxel v. Granville* (2000). This case involved a pair of grandparents suing for visitation rights to their deceased son's children over the objection of the children's mother. The State of Washington had a law that permitted "any person" to petition for visitation rights and that allowed courts to "order visitation rights for any person when visitation may serve the best interest of the child whether or not there has been any change of circumstance" (2). The Washington Supreme Court overruled a Court of Appeals decision that denied that the Troxels (the grandparents) had standing to seek visitation, but also ruled that the law itself was an unconstitutional violation of parental rights. The decision was based on two claims: the law did not require a demonstration of actual or potential harm, which should be necessary to override the parents' wishes, and the law's language allowing "any person" to get visitation rights if it only serves "the best interests of the child" was too broad, as it gave the state inappropriate power to decide upon the proper rearing of children. The US Supreme Court's decision upheld that finding, with Justice O'Connor writing the opinion.

The Court's (6) review of the precedents began with the Fourteenth Amendment's Due Process Clause having a "substantive component" that protects "certain fundamental rights and liberty interests" (quoting *Washington v. Glucksberg* [1997]). The "liberty interest" associated with parental rights was then described as "perhaps the oldest of the fundamental liberty interests recognized by this Court" with citations to *Meyer*, *Pierce*, and the language of *Prince*. O'Connor then noted the "breathtakingly broad" nature of the law in question and its clear implication that the parents' wishes are irrelevant, which "places the best-interest decision determination solely in the hands of the judge" (8). In fact, that is what happened when the Washington Superior Court ordered visitation rights for the Troxels. There was no finding that the mother was an unfit parent in any way. Rather the judge simply decided that it was good for the children to spend time with their grandparents, *regardless of their mother's preferences*, given that there was no reason to think such visits would adversely affect them. As the Court pointed out, this put on the mother the "burden of *disproving* that visitation would be in the best interest of her daughters." This flips the notion of parental rights on its head in a way that, perhaps unsurprisingly, parallels the switch in burden of proof in constitutional law: the burden shifts to those claiming the rights to show that there is a reason their rights should not be violated rather than being on the violators to show reason why they should be overridden.

The Court put its conclusion rather plainly: "the Due Process Clause does not permit a State to infringe on the fundamental right of parents to make childrearing decisions simply because a state judge believes a 'better' decision could be made" (14). O'Connor quickly added that in holding the law unconstitutional because of its breadth, the Court was not considering the issue of whether the constitutional protection of parental rights "requires all non-parental visitation statutes to include a showing of harm or potential harm to the child as a condition precedent to granting visitation" (14–15). The Court thereby refused to overturn specific nonparental visitation statutes per se. So here too, the scope of the decision is somewhat limited, with the Court making clear that the constitutionality of such statutes depends on the "specific manner" in which the laws and their associated standards are applied.

## Parental Rights and the Ninth Amendment

At the moment, the constitutionally protected rights of parents in the United States are generally considered a "fundamental right" under the approach Barnett labels "Footnote Four-Plus." That is, the rights of parents are nowhere enumerated in the Constitution including the Bill of Rights, but are nonetheless protected as fundamental by the long tradition of recognizing them as implicit in the Due Process Clause of the Fourteenth Amendment. Strictly speaking, they are not among those rights that Footnote Four alone would protect given that they are unenumerated. But faced with the pre-*Carolene* precedents of *Meyer* and *Pierce* that are still considered good law, even as economic liberties that had once been protected by the same clause were seen to be no longer worthy of protection, the Court had to find a way to continue to offer such protection. The solution, interestingly enough, has been to define them as "fundamental" and to do so under the idea of "substantive due process" without any real embarrassment about the rejection of that doctrine in other areas.

Put differently, it is something of a mystery that *Meyer* and *Pierce* remain good constitutional law and serve as the binding precedent for later parental rights cases and, as discussed in the next chapter, cases involving the right to marry. Faced with the Footnote Four approach, the Court in *Griswold* felt it necessary to cram the square peg of privacy into the round hole of a Bill of Rights that never mentions such a right in order to avoid two unpalatable alternatives. The first was to find such a right in the Fourteenth Amendment, arguing that a right to privacy had the same standing as the right to marry or parental rights under the Due Process Clause. That alternative was likely rejected for fear of a return to rediscovering unenumerated economic rights as in *Lochner*, yet no such fear accompanies declaring as good law the very same argument made in the parental rights cases. Perhaps it is the finding of new rights in the Due Process Clause that is the problem?

In a fascinating overview of the history of parental rights and constitutional law in the context of education, Gilles (1996) offers an alternative way to ground parental rights: the free speech provisions of the First Amendment. His argument is that the right of parents to direct the upbringing of their children at least in the context of education, as laid out in *Meyer* and *Pierce*, is essentially a right of free speech, both in terms of what parents may teach their children and the rights of parents to not be coerced into exposing their children to speech the parents dislike. One reason he likes this approach is that it relies on an enumerated right of free speech, allowing the Court to avoid the entire messy issue of unenumerated rights. Based on this argument, Gilles defends a very strong conception of parental rights, again at least in the realm of education. It remains questionable whether this approach would pass constitutional muster if attempted, but even if it did, it does not seem to be an effective way to ground a conception of parental rights that extends to issues other than education that would be hard to fit under the umbrella of free speech.

Another approach, and one that was available to the *Griswold* Court, was outlined in Justice Goldberg's concurrence: make use of the Ninth Amendment.[13]

As Barnett (2004) argues, taking a second look at the Ninth Amendment's explicit discussion of unenumerated rights provides us with a way to both undo the damage to the Constitution's protection of rights done by the post-New Deal courts and to find a way to protect unenumerated rights that does not rely upon the Court having to pass judgment on the very contentious issue of which unenumerated rights are fundamental and which are not. Relying on the Ninth Amendment can resolve a number of the constitutional puzzles in which the parental rights cases play a curious role. It could also offer a better grounding for parental rights themselves. A brief exploration of Barnett's case for reviving the Ninth Amendment is in order as a concluding thought on the constitutional history of parental rights.

The text of the Ninth Amendment is straightforward enough: "The enumeration in the Constitution, of certain rights, shall not be construed to deny or disparage others retained by the people." Barnett argues that the historical context of the amendment was a concern that a Bill of Rights that specified certain rights that people had might be interpreted as an exhaustive list. Many present at the drafting of the Bill of Rights wanted to avoid that interpretation and make it clear that just because they had listed a whole series of rights in what are now the first eight amendments, later generations should not take that list as exhaustive. The people "retained" a whole variety of rights that they had prior to entering into the constitutional "contract" that gave certain specified powers to government. Barnett claims that the historical context out of which this argument rose was one in which people were believed to possess certain natural rights prior to the creation of a constitution and government. Even as they agreed to institute a government for the purpose of enforcing those rights, they did not give up those rights to the state. Rather, they accepted limits on those rights necessary for the limited powers of government, but retained all of the other rights they possessed previously. Barnett believes the Ninth Amendment confirms this view.

The importance of unenumerated rights is clear every time that debates erupt over whether or not a certain right is in the Constitution. This is certainly obvious in the debate over contraception and abortion as to whether a right to privacy that is never explicitly stated in the Constitution can really be said to exist. The same could be said of the decision in *Lawrence v. Texas* (2003), which was interpreted by Justice Scalia as finding a "right to sodomy" that appears nowhere in the Constitution. Barnett's view of the Ninth Amendment gets around these problems by providing a textual location for unenumerated rights. Yes, there is no explicit right to privacy in the document, but that is equally true of any of a million individual rights that one could list. The whole point of the Ninth Amendment is to respond to this argument by shifting the burden of proof so that courts approach constitutional interpretation with Barnett's "presumption of liberty" and expect the state to show where the powers it wishes to exercise are explicitly granted, or necessary and proper.

Historically, this was never better articulated by the Court than in Justice Goldberg's concurring opinion in *Griswold*. He there makes the case for grounding the right to marital privacy and the consequent right to purchase contraceptives in just this sort of reading of the Ninth Amendment. After both explaining the history of the amendment and the Court's earlier protection of the right to marry and raise children in *Meyer* and *Pierce*, he makes the case for using the Ninth Amendment to ground those rights:

> Although the Constitution does not speak in so many words of the right of privacy in marriage, I cannot believe that it offers these fundamental rights no protection. The fact that no particular provision of the Constitution explicitly forbids the State from disrupting the traditional relation of the family—a relation as old and as fundamental as our entire civilization—surely does not show that the Government was meant to have the power to do so. Rather, as the Ninth Amendment expressly recognizes, there are fundamental personal rights such as this one, which are protected from abridgment by the Government, though not specifically mentioned in the Constitution. (495–96)

Goldberg still frames the discussion in terms of those fundamental rights the Court has decided to protect, but he also notes earlier in his concurrence that such rights must come from a broad social and historical understanding of our institutions, rather than the personal preferences of judges.

Goldberg's concurrence and the larger intellectual framework provided by Barnett provide a way to ground parental rights in the Constitution in a manner consistent with both the unenumerated noneconomic rights currently protected by the Due Process Clause of the Fifth and Fourteenth Amendments, in some cases, and by the emanations and penumbras of the Bill of Rights in others. Uniting all of these unenumerated rights, including parental rights, in the language of the Ninth Amendment would have three salutary effects. First, it would provide a grounding in the actual text of the Constitution for the idea that unenumerated rights are deserving of constitutional protection. This might have the consequence of avoiding the charge that judges are inventing constitutional language that does not exist in the text. Second, it would bring all of these rights into an intellectually consistent framework rather than picking and choosing which part of the Constitution applies in which case. Third, it could provide a framework, as Barnett argues, for reestablishing the existence of constitutionally protected, yet unenumerated, economic rights and liberties.[14] Bringing all of these unenumerated rights under the Ninth Amendment would solidify each by the presence of the others. Even though parental rights do not seem to be under any serious constitutional threat, the possibility is always out there and any steps that could ground them more firmly would be desirable. More generally, the Ninth Amendment could serve as a defense of classical liberal rights in a whole variety of areas in which they could use stronger support.

## Children's Rights and Parenting as Stewardship

It might be tempting to see the argument for a strong constitutional protection of parental rights as somehow being antithetical to the welfare of children.

That temptation is one to be avoided. The assumption behind most calls for taking parental rights seriously is that the interests of parents and their children are sufficiently congruent to ensure that protection for parents' decision-making rights will be the way to do best by their children. In other words, a strong case for parental rights remains the best way to ensure the rights of children are protected. In this section, I unpack this argument and provide some reasons for believing it to generally be the case. I do not believe that those interests are *always* congruent, as plenty of real world examples of various forms of abuse would demonstrate, and that is precisely why we need some conception of children's rights beyond the rights of the parents. However, as I will argue in the next section, the imperfections of parental behavior do not make for an ipso facto case for the state abrogating their rights. Just as modern political economy realizes that so-called market failures and other imperfections of the market do not *by themselves* mean that state intervention is a superior solution, so it is with parental rights. Any theory of parental rights and the role of state intervention into the family has to take seriously the possibility of "government failure." Both parents and the individuals who work for the state in places such as Child Protective Services (CPS) are imperfect and flawed. The question is which group of people, given the knowledge and incentives available to them by each one's institutional context, are more likely to get it right more often and learn from their mistakes so as to avoid egregious errors. I will argue that the case for parents is strong enough to justify a high burden of proof upon the state before its agents intervene in the family.

Thinking of children as their parents' property is a very tempting move for both economists and classical liberals. The usual response is to very quickly point out that truly owning another human being is a practice classical liberals have long fought against and would lead to monstrous results if taken literally. However, the underlying intuition is not necessarily misguided. Parents do, and I will argue *should*, have the right to boss their children around and make decisions for them in ways that we would never allow in noncontractual adult relationships. In those ways, children look somewhat like property. At the same time, parents frequently treat their children much like assets in which they are investing in hopes of a future return (which is rarely financial), at least for the children themselves if not for the parents directly or indirectly. This too looks like the way people might treat a valuable piece of property that they hope will appreciate.

Given that the de facto behavior of parents makes children look like property in important ways, and given that we would reject treating them fully as property, is there way we can capture the former without stumbling into what we would reject? The concept of "stewardship" might provide the answer. One definition of stewardship is "the careful and responsible management of something entrusted to one's care." The advantage of talking in terms of stewardship is that all the definitions make clear that the object of that stewardship is not something that the steward owns. The object in question has simply been entrusted to the steward's care. For physical objects, this presumably implies that they are owned by someone else who has done the entrusting, but in the case of children, we can alter that understanding. Parents choose to entrust *themselves* with the task of "careful and responsible management" by accepting legal parenthood of a child, either through birth or adoption. The child, like a physical object of stewardship, is not the property of the parents, but they accept the responsibility of caring for it by accepting the legal rights of parenthood.

There are few extended discussions of children's and parental rights in the libertarian literature. George Smith (1991) offers an overview of children's rights in political philosophy. His discussion of Jeremy Bentham's view that the parent-child relationship is akin to a "guardian and ward" is very close to my use of stewardship. Smith (1991, pp. 284–5) writes, "A guardian exercises power over another person for the benefit of the ward, rather than for himself." He quotes Bentham describing the guardian's obligation as governing the ward "precisely in the manner in which the latter ought to govern himself." Smith summarizes Bentham's view this way: "The parent has duties as a guardian and rights as a master; the child has rights as a ward and duties as a servant" (p. 285). What is useful about this summary is that it emphasizes the way in which children's rights imply parental duties/obligations and the way in which parental rights imply children's duties/obligations. Put differently: parental rights and parental duties are part of the same package when we consider a guardian or stewardship model.

Murray Rothbard's (1998) discussion in *The Ethics of Liberty* also offers a conception of the rights that parents have with respect to their children that is similar to stewardship, but differs on a key implication. He argues that parental "ownership is not absolute, but of a 'trustee' or guardianship kind" (p. 100). Rothbard rightly argues that children, once out of the womb at least, possess a right of self-ownership by virtue of being potential adults. This prevents them from being treated strictly as the parents' property. So far, Rothbard's trustee concept parallels my notion of stewardship. However, Rothbard further argues that, although the child's right of self-ownership prohibits anyone, including the parents, from aggressing against it, thereby distinguishing it from property, that right does not create a "*legal obligation* to feed, clothe, or educate" the child (p. 100, emphasis in original). The trustee conception of parenthood prevents the parent from actively aggressing against the child, but still gives the parent "the legal right *not* to feed the child, i.e., to allow it to die. The law, therefore, may not properly compel the parent to feed a child or keep it alive" (p. 100, emphasis in original).[15] To put it in different language, parents cannot abuse their children, but they can neglect them.

The key premise in Rothbard's (1998, p. 100) argument is that if parenthood implied an obligation to feed and clothe, it would mean that the parents were being coerced into doing "positive acts... depriving the parent of his rights." Because Rothbard's version of libertarianism is rooted in natural rights and begins with what he calls the "non-aggression axiom," any situation in which the state coerces a person (who has not initiated force him or herself) into acting in a particular way constitutes a violation of that person's fundamental right not be aggressed against. The natural response is that parents have somehow voluntarily accepted that obligation to care for the child by creating it in the first place, so that having a child creates a form of contractual obligation for the parents. If so, then ensuring that parents do not neglect their children is a matter not of coercion, but legitimate contract enforcement.

Rothbard's (1998) response to this criticism is to raise a number of counter-examples that aim to show the absurdity of what he calls the "creation argument." He rightly asks how this can be true of a child conceived in a rape (p. 102). But then he also asks how step-parenting, foster parenting, or guardianship can be legitimate if those people did not participate in creating the child. What he seems to miss in this discussion is the idea that the obligation to care for a child does not come from the act of sexual creation per se, but from the assumption of the legal rights associated with making the child "one's own." In most cases, sexual creation and the assumption of rights take place together, as the birth parents take actions to establish that they wish to keep the child and thereby consent to the obligations that come with it being theirs.[16] However, adoptive parents, more so than do birth parents, must take affirmative steps in the legal system to acquire stewardship of the child, which makes it even more clear that they have consented to the responsibilities for the child that come with parenthood. All of the other examples Rothbard mentions are amenable to the same sort of analysis. For example, accepting foster parenthood of a child involves a different set of rights and responsibilities. The same could be said of step-parenthood, although as noted at the outset of this chapter, the way in which the law limits parental rights to a maximum of two adults prevents step-parents from more easily accepting both rights and responsibilities with respect to the child.

In another discussion of these issues, Wendy McElroy's (2012) argument faces problems similar to Rothbard's.

> As a legal matter, neglect and cruelty present a problem. Common decency rebels against abusing an infant, even non-violently. But the fact remains that the bad treatment is non-violent. If a parent does violently aggress against a child, then it is criminal matter and a third party has the same right to intervene on the child's behalf as on the behalf of someone being mugged in an alley.
>
> The uncomfortable fact, however, is that libertarianism does not recognize positive legal obligations except as established by agreement. That is to say, there is no positive obligation that legally forces a parent to provide sustenance or shelter. Only if the parent has entered into an agreement with the infant can such positive obligations be enforced. But, clearly, until the infant reaches the age of consent, an agreement with it is not possible. Positive obligations cannot be enforced.

The problem here is that the parents' obligation to care for the child is not about making an agreement with the child, and the lack of such an agreement with the child does not mean the parents have no obligations. The parental obligations come when parents engage in the positive act of treating the child as theirs by asserting their parental rights and thereby accepting the corresponding obligations. "Treating the child as theirs" is a kind of public declaration of the exercise of parental rights, and those rights come with corresponding responsibilities and obligations.

In this sense, taking a child home from the hospital is analogous to homesteading: the parents are declaring *to others* (*not* to the child) that this child is theirs and that they thereby accept the responsibilities to care that come with exercising those parental rights. If people bring a child into the world and do not wish to care for it themselves, they have an obligation to arrange for its care by finding someone else who wants to acquire those rights.

Children must be cared for, and they are unable to consent to who becomes their caregivers. Therefore the agreement parents enter into is not with the child directly, but with "the rest of us" by engaging in de facto exercises of parental rights that then create de jure obligations to care for (or to arrange for the care of) those children. And this is the reason that all forms of abuse or cruelty, and extreme forms of neglect, *should be* actionable in a libertarian world. Infants are helpless, and this is relevant not just because it means they cannot consent to who gives them care. It is relevant because it means that accepting parental rights, but refusing to accept the corresponding obligations to care for a helpless child, is a form of breach of contract. Again, the contract is not with the child, but with "the rest of us." Given the helplessness of infants, *someone* has to provide that care, and those who act in ways that exercise parental rights are simultaneously announcing their willingness to accept the obligation to care.[17]

In essence, exercising parental rights and accepting parental responsibilities is one or more adults publicly saying to the rest of the adults: "I/we am/are agreeing to care for this child." Throughout history, we have seen various religious traditions capture this idea through ceremonies such as baptisms, baby-namings, and namakarans.[18] Those have endured because of the importance of that public declaration of acquiring parental rights and accepting parental obligations.

What Rothbard's and McElroy's arguments rely on is the centrality of *consent* in the classical liberal tradition as a justification for rights and responsibilities. The paradigmatic example of consent is the *express consent* that we see in a written contract associated with a negotiated exchange. However, as Bell (2010) argues, that form of consent lies at one end of a scale of graduated consent *and unconsent* whose ability to justify the validity of an action will vary. Bell's scale runs from "express consent" to "implied consent" to "hypothetical consent" and then continues with hypothetical, implied, and express unconsent. That list is in order of their justificatory power from strongly positive to strongly negative. Just as contractual language that indicates both parties' agreement to take specific actions is the strongest form of consent, so is express contractual language that indicates an *unwillingness* to accept particular actions the strongest form of unconsent.

Bell's framework of graduated consent gives us a way of talking about the process by which parents accept the rights and responsibilities of parenthood.

Adoption has many of the characteristics of express consent, as parents take affirmative legal steps to acquire the rights of parenthood. By contrast, conceiving a child and bringing it home from the hospital does not involve the express consent of the legal process of adoption. But here is a clear case of implied consent, as the combined decision to conceive the child, see the pregnancy through, and take it home indicate an acceptance of the parental rights and corresponding responsibilities. As Bell (2010, p. 29) points out, express consent remains the "standard for judging such surrogates as hypothetical and implied consent [and] the closer those alternatives come to mirroring express consent, the better claim they have to our respect." One could argue that the express decision to attempt to conceive a child along with the express decision to continue the pregnancy, and then the express decision to keep the child in one's house after the birth, all add up to a very strong form of implied consent that comes close to express consent, even if there is no specific moment at which the parents explicitly agree to the legal rights and responsibilities of parenthood.

The graduated consent approach also allows us to avoid Rothbard's logically consistent (given his premises), but unpleasant, conclusion that parents should be legally able to neglect their children. Unpleasantness per se is not a reason to reject an argument, but many people, classical liberals or not, would probably be more persuaded by an argument that both defended parental rights and implied that parents had some positive responsibility for the care of their children. Intuitively that is how most parents understand what they have signed up for as parents.[19] Once we recognize that consent is not a binary choice between express consent or no consent, we can construct a view of parental obligations to their children that derives from the parent(s)' express or implied consensual acceptance of those responsibilities via a variety of forms of actions they undertake. Having taken on those responsibilities through forms of consent that are strongly justificatory, failure to discharge them would be legitimate grounds for legal action.

Jan Narveson (2002) provides one of the few other attempts at addressing this set of issues in the libertarian literature. His argument is more consequentialist than Rothbard's, centering on the idea that moral obligations emerge as agreements among rational agents as a way to allow us to disagree about the nature of the ends we wish to pursue, but agree upon the means by limiting our interference with the plans and projects of others. For reasons different from those articulated earlier, Narveson comes to a similar conclusion to my own that parenthood implies both a wide scope for parental discretion and an obligation on parents to care for their children in the ways Rothbard denies they must. For example, Narveson points out that viewing children in some sense as property does not mean that parents can do *anything* with them because all property involves limits on what owners can do with it in that they must respect the rights of others. For Narveson, this is not so much about what the parents must do for their children directly, but more about the obligations parents have to steward their children in ways that do not lead the children to violate the rights of *other adults*. Narveson (1999, p. 269, emphasis in original) makes this point as follows:

> Our rights *against each other*, as adults, are the proper sources of rights for children. Children are potential adults. To treat them well is to set them on the road to being the sort of adults we want to have around; to treat them badly is virtually to invite them to become the sort of people we don't want around. Parents who fail toward their children are parents who fail their neighbours and fellow humans, as well, of course, as the adults those children become when they grow up.

The advantage of this approach is that it recognizes both the obligation not to abuse but also the obligation not to neglect. It would seem to imply at least a minimal standard of education and socialization that is required of parents and can therefore be seen as rights of children.

Narveson's (1999) commitment to pluralism and the classical liberalism that it implies politically leads him to want to respect a wide variety of parenting strategies and parental authority over children that might be compatible with this minimal standard. He concludes: "A rational view of morals will leave parents largely in charge, to be shown right or wrong when their children emerge into the world as fellow grown-ups" (p. 276). Though Narveson does not mention it, I would emphasize our ignorance about both how much influence parents really have on their children and what parenting strategies work best. Given a commitment to pluralism and a recognition of our ignorance, Narveson's argument is a strong one and is consistent with my own argument for stewardship and a robust conception of parental rights.

Having made the argument for a conception of stewardship that involves both rights and responsibilities, we must recognize that one additional rationale for those responsibilities is that children differ from other objects of stewardship in that they eventually become "owners of themselves."[20] The parents' responsibilities are fixed neither in kind nor across all time. Parents remain responsible for their children until either the children emancipate themselves through a recognized legal process or they reach a state-enforced age of majority. This implies that part of the responsibility parents have is to help children take on the responsibilities of adulthood, or at the very least, not engage in behavior that significantly and intentionally retards children's ability to do so. Therefore, in accepting stewardship of a child, parents agree to limit the choices they can make with respect to the child as well as agreeing to some general obligations that may require them to make certain sorts of choices. In the extreme, their obligation to exercise "careful and responsible management" means that physical or emotional abuse of the child would not be permitted.[21] Even as we have argued that parents do not have the legal right to neglect their children, the question of what constitutes neglect is much trickier, as the line between neglect and simply lacking resources to meet some preset standard of care is often difficult to ascertain.

Qua humans, children have the same negative rights against bodily injury and forms of abuse as do adults. However, as children, they acquire a different set of rights obtained both by their nature as incomplete adult humans and as the obverse of the responsibilities acquired by those adults who accept the rights associated with parenthood. Part of what it means to have the rights of a parent is to both abstain from injury and abuse and to affirmatively provide the minimum necessary to ensure that children do not impose costs and burdens on nonconsenting adults.[22] How this cashes out in detail is a set of questions beyond my scope here, but, as I argue in the next section, the failure of parents to meet whatever the minimal standard might be is not ipso facto evidence for the necessity of state intervention.

## Incentives and Knowledge as a Rationale for Parental Rights

I do not wish to construct a full-fledged philosophical theory of parental rights. I do, however, want to offer reasons to justify the view that parents have the strongest claim to the stewardship rights and responsibilities toward children and that, therefore, the bar the state must hurdle to abrogate or terminate parental rights is a high one. The argument I will make is a Hayekian one: *it is parents who have the right incentives and best relevant knowledge to know what is best for their children*. This argument explains both why, in general, a child's parents rather than others are in the best position to do what is best for them, and why the state, specifically, is unlikely to improve on parental stewardship in the vast majority of cases. As noted in chapter 7, one of the key Hayekian functions of the family is its role in socializing children for the task of living in "two sorts of worlds at once." There I argued that families help children understand the rules of both intimate orders such as the family or a firm and the anonymous order of the Great Society, as well as the differences between the two. A child's parents and the broader institution of the family, as opposed to other people or institutions such as the state, are best positioned to provide this particular aspect of socialization.[23]

The key to the family's advantages in doing so is its very intimacy. In contrast to the challenges we face in the Great Society in getting knowing other people in a very deep way, the intimacy of the family provides parents with deep, and often tacit, knowledge of their child that can be deployed in finding the most effective ways to transmit social rules and norms. In addition, at least in healthy families, the parents have the best incentive to make sure that such behaviors are learned, as the family remains a major site of social interaction where appropriate behavior will make such interactions smoother and because other family members may suffer negative external reputation effects due to the misbehavior of children.[24] Children who do not learn the rules of social interaction will cause their parents to suffer both directly and indirectly, thus providing parents with an incentive to ensure that such rules are learned. Here is the link between Narveson's defense of children's rights and the incentives facing parents. Children's rights come from the responsibility of adults to not raise children who impose costs on other adults. To the extent that children who do misbehave in those ways impose reputational costs on their own parents, the parents have an incentive to behave in ways that respect their children's rights by providing them with the minimal standard of socialization.

As we move out from the nuclear family to the more extended family, many of these same incentives remain in place, though weaker in degree. Grandparents, for example, will still have an interest in making sure grandchildren are well socialized in these ways, though not to the degree that parents will, given that the costs and benefits do not fall as heavily on them. This argument also suggests that other children might have an interest in the socialization of their siblings to the degree they have to live with the consequences of good or bad socialization. Of course only older children would be in much of a position to act on that interest. It might, however, enable us to see even minor sibling complaints about each other's behavior as more than an attempt just to annoy parents. Instead, this might be the way one child attempts to raise the cost of the other's behavior so as to reduce the external costs involved.

In addition, there is an evolutionary explanation for parents' desire to transmit such rules to their children: children who are better able to navigate the social world are more likely to survive and pass on the parents' genetic material. This point has increased in importance as social competition has come to dominate biological factors in determining success in the extended order of the modern world. If one assumes that having better skills at navigating the social world generally translates into greater economic success, and greater resources to ensure the survival and success of one's own children, then each generation of parents has a strong incentive to ensure the social success of their children for the results it has on both their children and their grandchildren. In a world where biological advantages and disadvantages play a much smaller role in the ability to pass on one's genes, the incentives facing parents to socialize their children well are very strong.

I have argued earlier that a great deal of the parent-child socialization process works through imitation. This same imitative learning process might be at work in the context of learning how to develop the social connections of the various intimate orders. Consider the discussion of attachment from chapter 7. How to create these attachment bonds cannot be explicitly taught. Rather, it is parental behavior and proximity that enables children and parents to form such bonds, as children learn through experience what it means to be attached to someone. As they develop, they deploy that learned experience in creating such bonds with others. How one creates a friendship or romantic relationship or the working relationships involved in face-to-face social institutions is not something that can easily be articulated. That process is learned through experience and imitation and may be imprinted very deeply within the mind. Not only do children learn the rules of social interaction of the extended order through an imitative process greatly facilitated by the intimacy of the family, but they can also learn the rules of intimacy themselves in a like fashion. Again, the family is a *discovery process for learning the explicit and implicit rules of social interaction of both the intimate microcosmos and the anonymous macrocosmos.*

The family's role in this Hayekian socialization process is complemented by schools, houses of worship, and the other elements of civil society. However, none of them can replace the family at the core of this process. Placing the stewardship responsibility for child-raising in the hands of parents gives those with the most knowledge and greatest social and biological incentive the right to make the relevant decisions about the children. Those decisions might include asking others to take on those stewardship responsibilities some of the time (e.g., child care or school). The implicit or explicit contractual nature of such an arrangement provides for a solution of the implied principal-agent problem via either "voice or "exit," ensuring that it is still the parents who are ultimately the stewards. Where children have clearly defined stewards and where those stewards have the necessary knowledge and incentives, they will be more likely to engage in the sorts of modeling of, and explicit instruction concerning, social behavior that are the key Hayekian functions of the family. Where responsibility is diffuse, and where those in charge lack the necessary knowledge and incentives, we would expect the same sorts of commons problems we are familiar with in other realms. Allowing "the village" to raise children is no more likely to succeed than has allowing "the village" to run agriculture or industry.[25]

This approach to parental rights can also be seen as an application of the "robust political economy" approach of Pennington (2011) and Boettke and Leeson (2004). At the core of robust political economy is the question of how sensitive the claims of theories of political economy are to their assumptions about the actors who populate their models. Models that hold across a wide range of people will be more robust than ones that will not work if the behavioral assumptions change. In particular, will theories be very sensitive to the assumptions made about the omniscience and benevolence of the actors? Too often theorists create idealized models of human behavior that at least tacitly assume that the actors in their theoretical model will both demonstrate a high degree of benevolence toward others and have a degree of knowledge that enables them to generate the model's results, but that might not correspond to the knowledge of the typical human actor. The robustness of various models will translate to a degree of robustness in real-world political-economic systems that look like those models. So were we to translate models in which predictions of rational resource allocation are highly dependent on strong omniscience assumptions about actors into real world economic institutions and then discover that people are, in fact, not that omniscient, we would expect those institutions to fail to produce the results the model predicted. In other words, such a model would not be robust.

Boettke and Leeson (2004, p. 103) argue that every set of political-economic institutions must deal with questions of knowledge and incentives. Does an approach to political economy adequately explain how actors will acquire the knowledge they need to produce the desirable results associated with the model of that system? Does an approach to political economy adequately explain whether actors in that system will have sufficient incentives to undertake the actions necessary to produce the model's desirable results? A robust model that generates a robust political economy is one that can answer both of those questions in the affirmative. The argument earlier suggests parents do indeed have the requisite knowledge and incentives. In addition, if approaches that give the state a large responsibility for doing what is best for children are very sensitive to the omniscience and benevolence of political actors, robust political economy would suggest that giving the state that responsibility is likely to produce less desirable outcomes.

If parents have stronger incentives and better knowledge to do what is right for their children than do others, we have a pretty good prima facie argument for a strong notion of parental rights. However, the superior position of parents does not mean they are infallible. The newspapers are full of stories of parents who have made choices that clearly do not have the best interests of their children in mind. One need not think that children are the only thing that matter to believe that many of these cases seem to require some action on the part of the state or others to stop the parental behavior in question. The question, however, is always a comparative one: even if parents are imperfect, will the state or other institutions that intervene in the family necessarily improve upon the imperfect parenting?

## Comparative Institutional Analysis

Robust political economy is inherently comparative. The questions it asks about omniscience and benevolence must be seen as questions of comparative institutions. No set of social institutions will perform perfectly across the whole range of knowledge and incentives facing human actors. Instead, we must look for those that work better, and particularly those that have built-in and powerful ways of informing actors of their mistakes and providing them the incentives to correct them. Mere imperfection in one set of institutions is not automatically a reason to adopt an alternative. We must ask whether the alternative can actually improve upon the mistakes of the first. We can apply that framework to the issue of imperfect parenting and the role of the state.

The problem of the imperfect parent should sound familiar to those who know something of the history of twentieth-century economics. Over the course of the century, economists developed progressively more sophisticated, though less realistic, models of how markets achieved equilibrium and optimality. These models were often used as the basis for policy recommendations, especially when real world markets failed to match the optimality properties of the models. Such situations were labeled "market failures," and the general conclusion for much of the century was that such failures called for government intervention as the cure. To take the classic example, where markets produced significant costs on third parties who were not part of the market (what economists call "negative externalities"), the models predicted that actors would produce too much of the good in question, given that they could shift the costs onto others. The implication was that government was necessary to correct this problem by taxing the producers and using the revenues to compensate those bearing the costs. As economists drew it on the blackboard, this would lead to the optimal quantity of the good being produced.

The problem with this story is that economists never asked whether, in fact, the political process could or would produce the result their blackboard models said it should. While the theory of the market relied heavily on the belief that market actors were self-interested and would respond to incentives such as higher taxes or the ability to externalize costs, the implicit theory of politics used in suggesting solutions assumed that political actors were all-knowing and selfless and lived in a world where incentives were irrelevant. Analysts did not ask the questions raised by robust political economy.

The pioneering work of James Buchanan and Gordon Tullock (1962) sparked an entire approach to the political process known as the "economic theory of politics" or "public choice theory." This theory and subsequent empirical work demonstrated that just as the real world economy "failed" in comparison to the abstract and unreal models of the economists, the government interventions intended to correct those failures themselves failed in comparison to the abstract models of the economists. The combination of looking more closely at the actual incentives facing political actors and the limits to the knowledge such actors might possess (recall the discussion in chapter 2) provided economists with a theory of "government failure" to put up against the market failure theories that dominated the discourse mid-century.[26]

The result was that no longer could economists make what might be termed the "ipso facto leap:" market failure could not be said to ipso facto make a case for government intervention to solve the problem. Once the idea of government failure was taken seriously, determining whether the state should act became a matter of comparative institutional analysis. Political economists had to understand the consequences likely to be produced by markets or other voluntary processes of civil society in general versus those likely to be produced by political processes in general. They also had to explore the specifics of the issue or policy in question to determine the degree to which those general insights were likely to hold. As I have argued throughout this book, there are strong reasons to believe that the decentralized, voluntary cooperation of the market and other classical liberal institutions of civil society are likely to produce desirable unintended outcomes on a regular basis. Taking a closer look at the incentives and knowledge facing political actors suggests political processes are far less likely to do so.

How would this framework apply to family policy? First take a simple case where comparative institutional analysis can be applied. Imagine a case of child neglect, though not physical abuse. The parents are not sufficiently caring for the children in terms of consistently providing warm clothes or regular, nutritious meals, or medical well-care. They also leave the children home alone and unsupervised quite a bit and none of them are older than ten. Assume that the children are in no immediate physical danger. It might be tempting to call this a case of "parenting failure" and ask Child Protective Services to intervene, perhaps even removing the children from the home. The first question worth asking is "and do what with them?" Is the alternative that the state will offer for the children really better, on net, than their current situation? Suppose that alternative is foster care. There is enough empirical evidence on the problems with foster care, especially short-term placements where the incentive to really behave as a steward for the child is weaker, to be skeptical that it would be an improvement. When we account for the psychological effects on younger children of being taken from their parents and placed with strangers, the comparative analysis suggests the case for intervention is even weaker.

Finally, just as we might ask with apparent market failures whether there are ways to improve the rules of the game such that market outcomes might be even better, or whether there are forms of voluntary cooperation other than traditional private property rights that might address the situation (see, e.g., Ostrom 1990), we can ask in the case of parenting failure whether there are other institutions that could be brought into play to help these parents perform better (e.g., a religious institution, a neighborhood group, extended family members, etc.). In the specific case of neglect, the problems are often financial, rather than bad parenting per se. Parents may be too poor to afford what others would see as an adequate level of care and/or they may be working so many hours that supervising children is challenging, as is finding the time to cook, shop, or get them to a doctor. In such cases, the sorts of civil society solutions noted earlier are far more likely to be appropriate than removing the children from the home of what are otherwise well-intentioned parents. One of the problems facing state intervention is knowing all of the fine details of each particular case sufficiently to come up with a solution. In general, those closest to the family are in the best position to understand the problems at hand, imagine an effective solution, as well as having an incentive to act on that knowledge. Bureaucrats with dozens of cases or more are unlikely to come close to the knowledge and incentives possessed by those in the family's local sphere.[27]

The choice here is not between just the nuclear family and the state; there are myriad other ways that humans can solve their problems through voluntary cooperation even if it does not look just like our idealized vision of the nuclear family. Ostrom's work points us in the direction of distinguishing between the *form* that solutions to social problems take and the *function* that those particular solutions perform. As Boettke (2009) has argued, voluntary, bottom-up solutions to a commons problem or other apparent market failures do not have to take the *form* of traditional private property rights to perform the *functions* that such rights perform, that is, ensuring efficient use that does not destroy the commons. This distinction maps directly on to the very same form versus function distinction made throughout this book about the way families work. Good comparative institutional analysis not only recognizes the possibility of government failure. It also recognizes that alternative institutional solutions in civil society come in a variety of forms, not just things like private property or families, strictly speaking.

Beyond the possibility of nonstate solutions to problematic parenting that come from outside the family, the incentives facing state actors are such that they are likely to err in intervening too often into families, for fear that they make a much more costly error of omission by not acting when they should have. This follows a more general pattern we observe with political actors: they will try to avoid making choices where being wrong involves a very visible cost and will prefer choices where the costs of an error are less visible, more subtle, and often long run. Consider the risks facing Child Protective Services in situations of possible abuse. If they do not act, they risk the children being injured or possibly killed. Should that happen and it becomes known that they were involved and chose not to act, the cost to CPS in terms of bad publicity is significant. If they do intervene and it turns out that the possible abuse was exaggerated or nonexistent, they will certainly take some heat for over-reacting, but not nearly what they would for the error of omission involved with children being injured or killed. In addition, the other costs of their erroneous intervention fall not on them but on the parents and children, mostly in terms of less visible and longer-term psychological damage to the children or to the functioning of the family. Faced with these alternatives, it is no surprise that CPS is likely to intervene more often than is justified so as to avoid making the mistakes that are more costly to them. When added to the usual public choice arguments about government agencies trying to maximize their own budgets, which is not forwarded by actually solving the problems they were created to address, this aversion to large, visible errors provides yet another element in the cost-benefit calculations that should be part of a comparative institutional analysis of family policy.

Given the problematic incentives facing political actors and given the limits on their ability to acquire the fine grained knowledge needed to know when and how to intervene in families, we have yet another reason to put a very heavy burden of proof on the state when it is considering intervention in families. Lacking the sorts of local and tacit knowledge we outlined earlier and having to consider the political consequences of their choices means that the failures of agencies such as CPS are more likely to be damaging than the failures of parents, especially when we consider that there are other, nonstate, resources available to families facing a variety of problems.

That said, it remains the case that in a world where the state is charged with the responsibility for protecting individual rights, there is a role for it to protect children from truly abusive parents. Any such action will face the dangers noted earlier, but there are several principles that might be applied in order to reduce unwarranted interference with parental rights:

1. The constitutionally protected status of parental rights, along with the arguments we have made for the superior knowledge and incentives facing parents, should place a heavy and high burden of proof on the state in order to justify intervention.
2. Intervention should generally be limited to clear and present physical danger to children.
3. Removal of children should take place only with the agreement of a judge and only after a good-faith attempt is made to interview the parents.

4. If children are removed, if at all possible they should be relocated to extended family members or religious or community organizations with a connection to the family.
5. In cases deemed to be short of clear and present physical danger, the state should step back and allow community organizations or extended family to work with the parents to address the problems.

These principles are hardly a detailed set of policy guidelines, nor will they stop every possible mistake by even well-intentioned state actors. Nor will they prevent every real case of abuse from happening, but neither does the existing process. No institutional arrangement will be perfect, but more severely limiting the state's ability to remove children by focusing on the clear and present danger of physical abuse and ensuring some checks on the process will improve matters. Rather than pursuing parents who fall short of an ideal, resources can be devoted to those children who really are having their rights violated and those parents who are doing the violating. We can also place more emphasis on how extended family and community organizations can improve the way families function so that the state's role can be reduced, or not needed at all. Placing the solution in the hands of community organizations also increases the flexibility and responsiveness of the process while using already-established connections to the family to help address whatever the problem might be. More completely respecting parental rights need not come at the expense of dealing with genuine cases of abuse if the right sorts of principles and processes are in place. The goal of family policy should not be to punish families for failing to reach an unreachable ideal (just as we should not use the same metric in judging the performance of real-world market competition), but instead should be seeking ways to help families who really need it from, as it were, "below" through institutional change and the institutions of civil society.[28]

## The Tough Questions and Cases

If the discussion in this chapter has been at an unsatisfactory level of abstraction and generality, it is because many of these issues are crying out for more attention from a classical liberal perspective. It is unfortunate that classical liberal thought remains disproportionately dominated by economists, philosophers, and political/legal theorists, with few psychologists, sociologists, historians, and educational theorists who might be very helpful in thinking through many of the topics this chapter has touched on. Even with so many scholars thinking about political economy and constitutional issues, how they apply to children and family policy remains underdeveloped. My presentation here is intended only to put a number of considerations on the table for others to run with in directions that I would not pretend to prescribe. In this last section, I wish to raise what I think are some of the tough questions and cases for classical liberals to think about.

Many of the questions raised by children for classical liberalism are extremely difficult, as they are for most political philosophies. I have deliberately side-stepped the question of how children's rights might be protected in a world without government, and this remains a very underdeveloped topic in the various works by the anarchist libertarians. Thinking about nonstate solutions to those problems is particularly difficult, in my estimation, but this is a challenge that libertarians have risen to in other areas, especially as they have thought more seriously about institutions other than the state and the market. I do not have any special wisdom to dispense on these questions, other than to point out that I do not think either of two solutions is viable: (1) children *cannot* be treated as the mere property of their parents and thereby denied all of the meaningful rights that adults have; (2) children *cannot* be treated with the full set of rights that adults have. Children clearly have some rights as human beings but not all of the rights of adult human beings.

The problems with the two extremes should be obvious enough to not require too much argument. The hard part is, of course, deciding what are the minimal set of rights all humans have by virtue of being human and then determining the criteria by which that minimal set of rights evolves into the full rights of adulthood. In our own world, we use a variety of government-imposed age-related rules, often buttressed by attempts to gauge maturity. There are legitimate concerns about the arbitrariness of age-related rules in general (e.g., we all know 16-year-olds who could handle adult responsibilities and 30-year-olds who cannot), and there are a whole variety of inconsistencies that seem to make little sense (e.g., a 15-year-old girl can often get an abortion without parental consent, but not a tattoo, and a 17-year-old boy can drive a car but cannot buy a utility knife at a hardware store in New York State).[29] There are admittedly advantages to the state's ability to draw universal lines in that they do reduce a variety of transaction costs. However, they come at the large cost of both our strong intuition that the issue is not age but maturity and the predictable amount of rent-seeking and other special interest behavior that leads to the inconsistent set of rules that the state actually produces. It is difficult to imagine a legal system, even without a state, not having to make use of some rules of thumb in this area. Deciding the maturity of children on a case-by-case basis would seem to be extraordinarily unwieldy. Anarchist libertarians will need to think through exactly how to determine which rights which children will have and articulate reasons for thinking it will improve on the far from perfect, though not totally disastrous, idea of universal age minimums as proxies for maturity. Whatever nonstate solutions anarchist libertarians might develop must recognize this intermediate status of children.

A related problem facing more anarchist-oriented libertarians is the question of how to deal with physical abuse of children. If we assume that this is a violation of those children's rights (i.e., children are not completely their parents' property), the question then is how to protect those children in the absence of the state, especially if we recognize a strong prior notion of parental rights. By what process and with what authority would anyone be able to press a claim on behalf of the children against the parents? Rothbard (1998) argues that neglected children would be less likely in his libertarian utopia if only because a more open market in trading parental rights would enable those who do not wish to care for children to transfer their rights to those who do at a suitable price. Why just leave a child to die when one can earn some income in selling the parental rights, perhaps to an intermediary such as an adoption agency? This is a plausible argument from an economic perspective, but still leaves open the question of what to do about parents who want their children but neglect them in ways that are clearly damaging to the child's ability to ultimately exercise her rights and liberties as an adult (e.g., not feeding a child enough such that the child is physically damaged).[30] Do such parents at some point cease to be de facto parents, thereby giving up their de jure parental rights and making them available for the equivalent of homesteading? This would seem to be a solution consistent with the approach favored by anarchist libertarians, but it surely needs further development to explore its strengths and weaknesses.

Even in the world of the limited state where we are willing to give it a role in protecting the rights of children, we face a number of difficult cases from a libertarian perspective. Again, I cannot treat these exhaustively and will raise one of them to suggest the kinds of questions that a more complete consideration of parental rights should be prepared to address.

Consider the case of the parents whose religious beliefs are such that they are unwilling to provide medical care to their severely ill child. They might refuse blood transfusions or other interventions that medical professionals deem necessary to save the child's life, preferring instead to engage in their own attempts to treat the child through prayer or other means, such as folk remedies.[31] Is their refusal to treat their child with modern medicine a form of abuse or neglect, or is that within the scope of their parental rights? A first response might be that such a decision *does* constitute abuse or neglect, given that it might well lead to either severe damage or the death of the child. However, what if the parents truly believe that prayer or folk remedies work better than medical science? In such a case, their intentions are to help their child and those intentions are followed up with specific actions that they believe will address the problem. It becomes harder to view their decision as neglect when they wish to do what they see as the right thing and use what they see as appropriate means to that end. It is perhaps even harder to see it as abuse, since they are not taking any *active* steps to worsen the child's well-being and because they do wish to see the child's condition improve.

The question in some sense is where the line is between "a difference of opinion over the appropriate treatment of an illness" and making a choice with a much lower probability of saving the child's life. These cases raise several difficult questions. How confident are we in the power of science to declare it so superior that alternative healing methods are to be viewed as forms of abuse or neglect? Does that confidence automatically become a justification for the use of force? How do we decide what sorts of scientific procedures are then "certain enough" such that refusing to use them would be actionable? Would the same sort of logic apply to other kinds of parental beliefs and decisions also? Could parents with unorthodox views about other issues related to caring for their children also be second guessed and with what standard or burden of proof? Are there dangers of slippery slopes once we open the door to second-guessing parents?[32]

The framework developed in this chapter supports the idea that parental intentions matter a great deal and that the bar for second-guessing them should be high. Although parents are hardly infallible, if it is true that they have strong incentives and notably better knowledge with respect to serving the interests of their children, then the claim that they should be allowed to care for them in ways they see fit should be seen as the strong, though rebuttable, presumption in place. As with so much public policy, there are no absolute solutions, only trade-offs. Taking a strong position like this will undoubtedly lead to cases where children are exposed to harm or even death in ways that were perhaps preventable.[33] But the trade-off to a more aggressive policy is opening up the family to a degree of state intervention that many would find unacceptable and might create a larger number of dysfunctional families than it prevents. One of the essential elements of classical liberalism is the commitment to rules rather than discretion when it comes to government policy. As we saw in an earlier section, discretionary policies might be able to solve the problems on the blackboard, but in practice, discretion faces serious incentive and knowledge problems that prevent it from working the way an abstract model might suggest. Limiting discretion means giving up even the possibility of fixing every wrong. However, it brings with it the greater gain of avoiding errors of commission that would outweigh the benefits of trying to right all wrongs.

Like all other areas of public policy, family policy offers us no perfect solutions. The classical liberal tradition gives us strong reason to think that even though a strong defense of parental rights will risk harm to some small number of children, the damage to parents, children, the family as an institution, and society as a whole that would result from giving the state the power to override those rights and try to fix every family would be significantly greater. Binding ourselves to such a rule is difficult when the costs of doing so are so visible in the form of harm to children, while the costs of discretion are often in the more subtle form of longer-term damage to children and families.[34] This difficulty is especially powerful in our own time, when our sentimental view of children and childhood has dramatically reduced our tolerance for any sort of harm to children. "What about the children?!" has become the rallying cry for public policy corner solutions whose proponents refuse to think seriously about opportunity costs and trade-offs. Trying to lash the state to the mast in the area of family policy is at least as much of a challenge as it is elsewhere, but it is a crucial battle to win given the importance of the family as an independent institution in the liberal order.

CHAPTER 10

# Classical Liberalism and the Contemporary Evolution of Marriage

## Introduction

The history and analysis of the family presented so far, along with the framework for libertarian family policy offered in chapter 9, can be deployed in tackling the issue that has been at the center of political and cultural debate over the family for the past two decades: same-sex marriage. As this chapter was being written, the Supreme Court had just granted certiorari on four cases from Kentucky, Michigan, Ohio, and Tennessee that raised a series of questions concerning whether individual states can either ban same-sex marriage in their own states, or refuse to recognize same-sex marriages that were performed in other states. The Ohio case *Obergefell v. Hodges* (2015) was listed first in the Supreme Court's order and became the title for the decision that encompasses all four. The ruling turned out to be a clear-cut statement of the unconstitutionality of state-level prohibitions on same-sex marriage, rather than the Court having to walk a knife's edge to gather any kind of majority by, for example, deciding only that states cannot constitutionally refuse to recognize same-sex marriages performed in other states.

Whatever the outcome of those cases had been, the ways in which the issue of same-sex marriage has arisen as a cultural phenomenon, and the variety of constitutional and policy issues it raises, have opened up a broader discussion of the nature of marriage and the relationships among marriage, sexual orientation, and the state. This discussion is closely related to several issues central to this study and to classical liberalism more generally. As I argued in earlier chapters, marriage and family have evolved over the course of human history, and they have done so at a more rapid pace since the advent of capitalism. If social institutions arise to solve certain problems, or fulfill certain functions, then the form such institutions take will likely change as the nature of those problems, or the currently relevant functions, change. We have seen the forms of marriage and the family evolve from arranged to consensual and love-based, or from the male dominance of coverture to the equality of the era of no-fault divorce, or from nearly exclusively same-race to the post-*Loving v. Virginia* world, or from many children and extended family members living in the same home to one or two children and perhaps just one parent living together in many cases today. I have argued that this evolution was driven by changes in the functions of marriage and family, especially those associated with the economic changes that capitalism and industrialization brought in their wake. Is same-sex marriage a fundamental break with this evolutionary process, or is it just another part of that process? Is there anything about *this* change in the institution of marriage that should trouble classical liberals more than those of the past 200 years? If, as I have argued, the long-term trajectory of the evolution of marriage and the family is the result of classical liberalism and is consistent with classical liberal institutions and values, is there any reason to think that this time the change is different?

The same-sex marriage question has also caused libertarians to think in more depth about the question of whether the state must be involved in marriage *at all*. Given the disposition of libertarians to seek private and civil society alternatives to state action in other areas, their willingness to explore whether marriage can be separated from the state should not come as a surprise. Libertarians who strongly favor full legalization of same-sex marriage and those who are more skeptical have all been asking what stateless marriage would look like, and often finding it more desirable than either the status quo or nationwide legalized recognition of state-granted same-sex marriage licenses. Whatever side of that debate one lands on, the questions it raises are well worth asking, as marriage and the state's involvement in marriage continue to evolve.

In this chapter, I examine these issues through the lens of the theory and history developed so far.[1] I will argue that although finding ways to separate marriage and the state is a worthwhile long-run goal for libertarians, and may well be one direction that the ongoing evolution of marriage is headed, an idealized vision of the future should not be the enemy of potential improvements. In the meantime, extending the constitutional right to marry to same-sex couples is consistent with the long line of classical liberal thought and does not represent a problematic extension of the state into the family or other forms of private decision-making. In particular, I argue that the long-standing classical liberal emphasis on "equality before the law," which was part of classical liberalism's very origins, demands that rights available to some should be made to all similarly situated, particularly when the extension of such rights causes no harm to third parties. This version of classical liberal egalitarianism has been pushed to the background in modern libertarian discussions that focus on freedom from state intervention. Such discussions often overlook the point that such freedom is a means to the end of human flourishing and not an end in itself, leading classical liberals to ignore obligations existing states have to treat their citizens equally, which is yet another means to that end.

One way of seeing the evolution of the form of marriage over the past few centuries is that the law has increasingly recognized that marriage is subject to the same concerns about equality before the law that have animated classical liberalism from the beginning. From the end of slavery, to the end of coverture, to the end of marriage bars in government employment, to the end of antimiscegenation laws, to the end of laws denying the existence of marital rape, and to the advent of no-fault divorce, the law has increasingly treated marriage as a relationship between equals in which two people who wish to be married can be married and will be treated equally by the law while married and if they so choose to end that marriage. Given our story of the way the functions of marriage have evolved to now focus on the psychological and emotional benefits associated with romantic love, it is not at all clear to an increasing number of people why the gender of the parties matters. If the law is to treat equally all those who are similarly situated, the love of two men or two women seems less and less a reason to treat their desire to marry differently. The same-sex marriage issue provides a unique opportunity to recapture classical liberalism's commitment to equality before the law and show how modern libertarianism can support policies that enhance both liberty and justice.

## The Fundamental Right to Marry

The US Supreme Court has a long history of rulings on the "right to marry" that can inform our perspective on the ongoing evolution of marriage. The Court has long recognized the existence of a fundamental right to marry that puts the burden of proof on the state to demonstrate why there is a need to violate it. It has also progressively extended that right to a wider range of people and restricted the state's ability to limit that right to a narrower number of situations. The Court's articulation and expansion of the right to marry has been a process very much consistent with classical liberal principles.

The Supreme Court's jurisprudence on the right to marry comes out of the same substantive due process tradition as does the parental rights jurisprudence discussed in chapter 9. That discussion began by looking at the first articulation of the idea of parental rights in *Meyer v. State of Nebraska* (1923). In the famous section in which Justice McReynolds described the nature of the liberties protected by the Due Process Clause of the Fourteenth Amendment, he included the right to marry in his list of the relevant liberties that are not explicitly mentioned in the Constitution:

> [Such liberties include not] merely freedom of bodily restraint, but also the right of the individual to contract, to engage in any of the common occupations of life, to acquire useful knowledge, *to marry*, establish a home and bring up children, to worship God according to the dictates of his own conscience, and generally enjoy those privileges long recognized at common law as essential to the orderly pursuit of happiness by free men. (399, emphasis added)

As Evan Gerstmann (2004, pp. 74–76) points out in his history of the right to marry, the Court had decided a number of cases involving marriage issues through the nineteenth century, but had never used the language of a "fundamental right" or a liberty that was protected by reference to an explicit part of the Constitution. Marital issues were considered part of state law, though the Court did recognize the role of the federal government in defining exactly what constituted marriage, as is clear from the debate over polygamy in the late nineteenth century. However, seeing the federal government as legitimately exercising its powers in defining the terms of the marriage contract is not the same as recognizing a constitutional right to marry. The latter could not happen until the very category of unenumerated rights was given legitimacy by the Court's Fourteenth Amendment jurisprudence at the turn of the twentieth century, including, as noted in the last chapter, the *Lochner* case in 1905.

The same story we told in chapter 9 of the relationship between parental rights and the evolving constitutional status of unenumerated rights is at work with the right to marry. *Lochner* established a short-lived constitutionally protected liberty of contract, and *Meyer* extended that use of substantive due process rights into the realm of the noneconomic. As Gerstmann (2004, p. 76) says of the mention of the right to marry in *Meyer*, "The constitutional right to marry was present at the very birth of noneconomic substantive due process rights." Like most of those noneconomic rights, including parental rights, the right to marry has continued to be recognized by a variety of Supreme Court decisions in nearly one hundred years since *Meyer*. Even as the post–New Deal shift in constitutional interpretation outlined in chapter 9 eviscerated unenumerated economic rights, the Court has continued to find ways to rescue unenumerated noneconomic rights such as the right to marry from the same fate that befell liberty of contract.

The post–New Deal Court was largely committed to a form of judicial restraint that presumed the validity of democratically enacted legislation that did not violate either explicit constitutional language or recognized "fundamental rights."[2] One of the first major cases involving marriage to face the post–New Deal Court was *Griswold v. Connecticut* in 1965. Chapter 9's discussion of *Griswold* focused on the unenumerated "right to privacy" that Justice Douglas used as the basis for his decision and the ways in which he had to avoid relying on substantive due process so as to not return to the *Lochner* era. In the context of marriage, it is important to see that the right to privacy in question was, in Douglas's mind, connected to marriage. The Connecticut law in question did not specifically limit itself to prohibiting married couples from purchasing contraceptives. Nonetheless, Douglas imagined the state invading marital bedrooms in search of contraband contraceptives and found this to be a violation of the "notions of privacy surrounding the marital relationship." For him, those notions of privacy were "older than the Bill of Rights" (*Griswold v. Connecticut*, p. 486). And as noted in the prior chapter, Douglas's decision relied on the precedent of *Meyer* for establishing those unenumerated rights.

Two years later, the Court decided the most famous case involving the right to marry, overturning the remaining state bans on interracial marriage in *Loving v. Virginia*. Some scholars interpret this decision as being narrowly about race given the use made of the Fourteenth Amendment in Chief Justice Warren's decision. In addition, there is not a lot of talk about unenumerated rights and the right to marry in the text.[3] On this reading, the decision is simply about racial inequality and says nothing in particular about the right to marry. Gerstmann (2004, p. 81), by contrast, argues that a closer reading of the decision indicates one of the precedents relied on by the Virginia state court upholding the ban saw marriage as an area that should be left completely up to the individual states. Warren's opinion rejected that line of argument because it violated the Fourteenth Amendment. Warren cited *Meyer* as one precedent for the relevance of that amendment. Of course race was not an issue in *Meyer*, which suggests that Warren saw this case as resting on those fundamental but unenumerated rights that McReynolds listed in *Meyer*. If the right to marry is fundamental, it trumps state-level laws designed to limit it, regardless of race. That *Loving* was *also* about race, and that therefore other Fourteenth Amendment considerations could be brought to bear, is another reason to think the case was correctly decided. That is not the same thing as denying that it is *also* a reaffirmation of the fundamental right to marry. Put differently, applying the Equal Protection Clause because the case was about race does not preclude also applying the Due Process Clause because the case was about the right to marry.

This reading of *Loving* is consistent with Justice Marshall's decision in a subsequent case *Zablocki v. Redhail* (1978) in which the court overturned a Wisconsin law that prohibited remarriage for anyone who was ordered by the court to support a minor child unless judicial permission was obtained. The law was intended to ensure that the person wishing to marry met his or her financial obligations. The Court's decision granted that the goal was a reasonable one but that the means for achieving it "unnecessarily impinge on the right to marry" (388). The Court relied on *Loving* as precedent. Gerstmann (2004, p. 82, emphasis in original) notes that Marshall "made it as clear as possible that *Loving* was based on two rationales: racial equality and an *independent* constitutional right to marry." Marshall wrote that *Loving* was decided on both the Equal Protection and Due Process clauses of the Fourteenth Amendment and emphasized the various Court decisions that had established the right to marry. A later case, *Turner v. Safley* in 1987, made the constitutionally protected right to marry even more clear when the Court overturned a Missouri prison regulation that effectively prohibited marriages among inmates. That decision clearly delineated the status of the right. Not even concerns about prison security could trump it.

As this book was being written, the same-sex marriage issue was in front of the Court. The history of the fundamental right to marry rightly played a role in the decision. However, in order to garner the necessary majority, the Court also made use of the Equal Protection Clause to make the case to overturn state bans on same-sex marriages. Both the fundamental right to marry and Equal Protection clause were invoked. There is enough precedent for treating sexual orientation within the scope of discrimination law to combine it with the long-standing right to marry to reach that decision. In addition, Justice Kennedy's opinion in *Lawrence v. Texas* was deployed because it relies on *Meyer*, *Pierce v. Society of Sisters*, and *Griswold* as precedents for thinking about the ways in which the Fourteenth Amendment Due Process Clause protects unenumerated rights such as the right to marry, or what Kennedy calls "the substantive reach of liberty" (564).[4] With *Lawrence* making clear that homosexual conduct falls within that "substantive reach," it was difficult for a majority the Court to find reasons to resist what seems to be the logical conjunction of those three arguments: overturning the state-level bans on same-sex marriage.[5]

## Classical Liberalism and Equality before the Law

One of the challenges in addressing the same-sex marriage issue from a libertarian perspective is that those who think laws that prohibit it should be overturned are normally making arguments based on equality. Equality-based arguments are not ones that many libertarians are comfortable with if only because they are often made in the context of economic regulations that libertarians, and classical liberals more broadly, find objectionable. Libertarians, unsurprisingly, prefer to argue in terms of liberty. A related concern is that overturning bans on same-sex marriage nationwide would create "special rights" or "new rights" for gays and lesbians. Interestingly, this argument seems to be an equality-based one in that it implies that such a change would create an unacceptable inequality. Untangling these issues begins by recognizing that concerns with equality are as much a part of the long classical liberal tradition as are concerns about liberty.

At the core of classical liberal arguments, especially in the nineteenth century, was what Peart and Levy (2005) have called "analytical egalitarianism." Classical liberals, going back at least as far as John Locke, began their analysis of the social world by assuming that human beings were equal both in their moral standing (everyone's preferences count equally) and in their capacity for making economic decisions. As Adam Smith phrased it, there was no difference between the street porter and the philosopher.

Peart and Levy contrast this "analytical egalitarianism" with what they call "analytical hierarchicalism," in which some people are thought to be different from others and, in the view of those at the time, therefore superior or inferior. Such differences might be attributed to any variety of in-born traits, from race, to ethnicity, to gender. By contrast, people like Adam Smith, John Stuart Mill, and other classical liberals believed that the observed differences among human beings were not due to inborn traits and capacities, but factors such as incentives, luck, and history (Peart and Levy 2005). There is no inborn trait or capacity, in the view of most of the early classical liberals, that consigns some groups to inferiority or elevates others to superiority. In understanding the social world, we must treat people as equal for the things that matter for theories and therefore the policy conclusions that emerge from them.

As Levy (2001) showed, one's view on analytical egalitarianism mattered at a practical level in the nineteenth century debates over racial equality. It was the classical liberals such as Mill who were on the side of racial equality because they believed that race was irrelevant to people's moral standing and capacity for choice. Classical economics assumed its models applied to all human beings, including the theorists themselves. Their theories argued that a free market and liberal society were desirable because all people were equal and capable of purposeful action, leading to the peaceful and prosperous world they promised. By contrast, many of the Romantic critics of capitalism hated it for exactly those reasons. Their starting point was the assumption of hierarchy, specifically among the races, and they understood correctly that free markets would undermine that hierarchy, which is why they opposed them. This argument is, as Levy (2001) demonstrates, also why the Romantics called economics the "dismal science"—they saw a future without hierarchy as a dismal one.

If there really were morally relevant differences among human beings, or if some groups were unable to engage in purposeful action, then it would be easier to construct an argument that these humans should be subject to the rule of their superiors. This is precisely what a good number of critics of classical liberalism did. They wanted the state to treat some people differently from others because some groups were not equal to others in their capacity for free choice, as we saw in chapter 5 and in the discussion of Progressive Era protective legislation.

The classical liberal argument for freedom was premised on equality, both in people's moral worth and in their capacity for free choice. In other words, the arguments for equality came first, and the desirability of liberty followed from them. Classical liberalism's critics denied that people should be free because they denied that people were equal. It was classical liberalism that defended both the principle of equality and the principle of freedom.

No doubt the concept of equality has been altered in the past 150 years. Too often it is used to mean equalizing outcomes via government policy, as opposed to treating people equally and accepting that unequal, but just and socially desirable, outcomes will result. Libertarians who defend such inequalities of outcomes need to recognize that those outcomes are only possible in a world where the assumption of analytical egalitarianism operates and where the state treats all humans as having equal moral standing and equal capacity for free choice. Hayek (1960, p. 87) made this point clearly:

> From the fact that people are very different it follows that, if we treat them equally, the result must be inequality in their actual position, and that the only way to place them in an equal position would be to treat them differently. Equality before the law and material equality are therefore not only different but are in conflict with each other; and we can achieve either one or the other, but not both at the same time. The equality before the law which freedom requires leads to material inequality.

Freedom requires equality before the law, which should serve to remind libertarians that equality was one of classical liberalism's foundational concepts.

Modern libertarians often get overly focused on the question of the size and scope of government. This perspective is understandable. Modern libertarianism grew out of a concern with what was seen as an overreaching government in the middle of the twentieth century, and the US federal government today is many times the size of what it was back then. However, the modern emphasis on shrinking the state has overshadowed the principle of equality before the law.

The ongoing legalization of same-sex marriage at the state level, and now a federal decision by the Supreme Court, has brought these tensions to the surface. Libertarians seem split as to whether they are celebrating this development. On one side is a smaller group arguing that the real problem is that the state is involved in marriage at all and that legalizing same-sex marriage just gives government more power. Therefore, they seem to be arguing, we should oppose this development (or at least be indifferent about it) and work instead to separate marriage and the state. On the other side are those who (might) agree that the long-term goal is the separation of marriage and the state. Given how unlikely that is anytime soon, they also think that we have to accept the state's role in marriage for the forseeable future and ask what the state's obligation is under classical liberal principles. That obligation, given the history of classical liberalism, is that the state must treat all of its citizens as equal before the law.

For most of human history, political leaders acted with near total discretion and could pick and choose among the citizenry for the distribution of both benefits and costs. One of the most important accomplishments of the liberal movement was to try to subject those with political power to the constraint of rules. From the Magna Carta up through the democratic revolutions of the eighteenth century and the constitutions they produced, liberalism has worked to create a society ruled by law and not by men. Since the eighteenth century, the liberal movement has also worked to ensure that *all* citizens, by virtue of being adult humans, had their rights fully respected. The liberalism of the nineteenth century was antislavery; it was antiracist, and it was part of the earliest movements for women's rights. It powerfully combined the commitment to human liberty with a commitment to human equality to make the case for the liberal order.

The same principles apply to same-sex marriage. If government grants certain privileges to those who are married, it must grant those to all of its citizens equally. In the same way that prohibitions on interracial marriage were wrong on classical liberal grounds due to their violation of equality before the law, so are the existing prohibitions on same-sex marriage. As I will argue, there is no credible evidence to suggest that overturning bans on same-sex marriage will harm innocent third parties, and there is no relevant functional difference between same-sex marriages and the marriages the state licenses among heterosexuals.[6]

To see this point, consider the following analogy. Suppose the United States had a Social Security system into which all residents of the United States paid taxes, but from which only white residents received the benefits. Would the libertarian position be that we should continue to deny people of color access to Social Security benefits on the grounds that giving the benefits to them would "extend federal power?" Should libertarians continue to insist that the only libertarian position is to argue for the elimination of Social Security for *everyone*, even though the existing system continues to benefit only whites? If the principle of equality before the law is as fundamental to classical liberalism as I have suggested, then the state must treat all citizens equally and libertarians ought to be outraged by such a discriminatory Social Security system. In the context of the same-sex marriage debate, the same concern with equality before the law should be paramount.

Another way to see this is that the right to marry, as elucidated earlier, is not a special right being conferred onto same-sex couples. As the prior section demonstrated, that right has long been recognized in US constitutional law as a fundamental right under the Due Process Clause of the Fourteenth Amendment, even though it is not explicitly enumerated in the Constitution. Extending that right to same-sex couples gives them no more rights than are possessed by heterosexual couples. It recognizes that government has an obligation to ensure that all persons equally situated have the same rights and privileges. Rauch (2004, p. 96, emphasis in original) puts it this way: "Equality before the law does not oblige the government to apply the law without regard to individuals' or groups' needs or circumstances. It does mean this: in a liberal democracy, 'democracy' refers to government by the consent of the people, but 'liberal' requires the government to *treat similarly situated people in a similar way*."

There is no formulaic way to determine what counts as equally or similarly situated. Just as the progressive elimination of distinctions based on race arose as persons of different races were seen by the American people to be equally situated with respect to things like public education or marriage, so has cultural change made it possible to see sexual orientation in the same way with respect to marriage.

One final point of concern to many classical liberals is whether nationwide legalization of same-sex marriage will mean that antidiscrimination laws will be used to force people with religious objections to same-sex marriage to provide services to gay or lesbian couples wishing to marry. This concern has emerged in recent cases involving service providers such as wedding photographers and bakers in which same-sex couples have sued businesses run by individuals whose religious beliefs led them to refuse to provide their services for the couples' weddings.[7] Some libertarians have also been concerned that antidiscrimination laws might be used to force religious groups to perform same-sex weddings. All of those concerns are legitimate ones. Legalizing same-sex marriage is about the secular and legal status of marriage and should not impose any requirements on the religious element of marriage. If churches, synagogues, and mosques wish to not perform same-sex marriages, they should be left alone by the law to act as they please. Membership in such organizations is voluntary and same-sex couples who wish to have a religious ceremony have a number of options within all of the mainstream religions for finding a house of worship that will provide it. The refusal of any given religious organization to perform same-sex ceremonies still leaves available a large number of alternatives for those who want to marry.

A similar argument applies to the trickier case of private sector service providers. Current antidiscrimination law forbids businesses from denying service based on race or gender, so why should the case of a clash between religious values and same-sex weddings be treated differently?[8] I think there are three different reasons why many people perceive relevant differences here. First, we treat claims of religious liberty with a much higher degree of respect than we would the claim of a businessperson who denied someone service on the grounds of pure racial hatred. The freedom to worship as one pleases is encoded constitutionally in the First Amendment in a way that other freedoms are not. Second, the issue at stake is the relatively narrow one of wedding-related services. Given the deep historical relationship between religious practice and marriage, which predates the government's involvement in marriage, one can make a case for treating religious liberty claims about marriage specifically as requiring even a higher degree of respect than other sets of beliefs, including other religious liberty claims. Finally, as with religious organizations, the market for wedding services is highly competitive. Being refused service by any particular photographer or baker or florist hardly denies same-sex couples of the possibility of obtaining the service at all.[9] This might distinguish such cases from other forms of service denial.

In addition to those three reasons, there is the more general observation that discrimination, including discrimination on the basis of race or gender, does not pay in a reasonably competitive marketplace. Economic theory (Becker 1971) has long argued that firms that discriminate in hiring or service provision are passing up potential profits from the higher productivity or additional purchases of the targeted group. If firms really are profit maximizers, then discrimination comes at a cost. In a reasonably competitive market, bypassing sales to same-sex couples means that firms are paying a price for their discrimination. If couples have other options, is the discipline of the market not sufficient to punish those firms? In a world of instant communication and social networks, this argument is even more powerful. Any seller who engaged in any form of discrimination would likely have its name splashed all over social media and sites like Yelp or TripAdvisor. With polls showing strong majority support for same-sex marriage, and with those numbers even higher among younger people who are both more likely to be getting married and be users of those sites, discriminating firms would likely see a more significant loss in business.[10] The power of competition is not just narrowly economic, but extends to broader social processes and the way they can affect reputation. In the modern world, the concern that those who invoke religious liberty considerations to refuse service to same-sex couples are somehow seriously denying them options seems not especially strong. Recognizing the validity of the concerns about preserving religious liberty also reduces one objection to same-sex marriage in a way that is consistent with classical liberal principles.

## Is There Any Harm?

The concern with individual equality before the law is only one of two kinds of concerns that classical liberals have had about the role of the state. The other is the liberty of the individual. Both classical liberals historically and libertarians today have wanted a world in which individual liberty was maximized subject to individuals respecting the equal liberty of others. One way of putting that desire into practice is to recognize that individual liberty cannot permit harm to third parties. This was most famously captured in John Stuart Mill's *On Liberty* and his use of the "Harm Principle" to decide what sorts of acts should be permitted or prohibited. Mill (1985 [1859], p. 68) argued that "[t]he only purpose for which power can be rightfully exercised over any member of a civilized community, against his will, is to prevent harm to others." There has been much subsequent debate over how to define harm, but in the case of same-sex marriage we can at least ask whether legalization might cause harm to other parties in ways that concern us, even if the marriage itself is consensual.

Most of the objections to same-sex marriage on grounds that might qualify under the Harm Principle have been about the damage such marriages would supposedly do to the institution of marriage or to children. The potential damage to the institution of marriage is normally framed as a fear that allowing same-sex couples to marry will somehow cheapen or undermine the uniqueness or solemnity of marriage in such a way that heterosexual couples will be less likely to marry, or perhaps more likely to divorce. Other concerns include the claim that legalizing same-sex marriage will lead to more births outside of marriage. Given the ways I have argued that families are a necessary institutional feature of a liberal society, if same-sex marriage did undermine the institutions of marriage and family, there would indeed be cause for concern. That possibility is a reason not to dismiss quickly the concern about damage to the institution of marriage as a whole.

The most obvious response to this line of argument is to flip it on its head: does not the fact that millions of people want to *enter* the institution of marriage suggest that the institution is not only in good shape but will be strengthened by these new (same-sex) marriages? It is not clear how a new group of people choosing marriage somehow weakens it in the eyes of those who have already chosen it or are contemplating it. Even if the argument is that the male-female combination has so uniquely defined marriage throughout human history that opening up marriage to same-sex couples will undermine the institution, the history of marriage and family gives us reasons to be skeptical. The evolution of marriage over the past two hundred years has changed elements of the institution that many once thought had the same unique status as the modern critics of same-sex marriage attribute to it being exclusively heterosexual. Every generation over the past century or two has seen changes in the nature of marriage, and each of those generations has also predicted that *their* change would be the one that destroyed the institution.

Marriage based on love, married women's property laws, the increased labor force participation of married women, and the relaxation of divorce laws are all instances where social critics predicted the demise of marriage as an institution. Each of those steps in the ongoing evolution of marriage changed the institution in important ways, but none of them ended it. Human institutions, especially ones that perform the kinds of important functions that marriage does, will find ways to adapt their forms as their functions slowly shift. Changes in economic, political, or social factors that might affect the function of social institutions will matter much more for the survival of the institution than will attendant changes in form. Economic changes, for example, do not happen overnight, which means that changes in function unfold over time, giving people the opportunity to try out new institutional forms that might better fulfill the newly emerging functions (or discard forms that are not needed as old functions recede). This has certainly been the story of marriage and the family told in the prior chapters. The changes in form that have marked the past century or two of their history have been responses to changes in function deriving from economic and other changes. Because marriage has moved from an economic institution to one centered around psychological and emotional needs, the form has changed accordingly, all without destroying the institution.

Same-sex marriage is but the latest change in form that those more fundamental changes in function have made possible.[11] Just as the changes in function do not happen instantaneously, neither do the changes in form that are responses to those new functions. Although it may seem like the increased discussion of the possibility of same-sex marriage has been a very fast social change, the ground was first plowed by the Stonewall riots and the rest of the civil rights movement, as I described in chapter 5. Once same-sex relationships in general were viewed as not only acceptable but also as roughly equivalent to heterosexual ones, the desire to instantiate them in legal marriage was not a large step. The whole process has taken place over a generation, and the institution of marriage has and will continue to adapt in the face of it. The fears of institutional collapse are no more real than they were when married women's property rights were recognized or when married women with children began to work in large numbers.

There is also empirical evidence to support the contention that same-sex marriage is unlikely to damage the institution of marriage. Eskridge and Spedale (2006) provide an overview of the experience of the Scandinavian countries after they started treating same-sex relationships as equal to heterosexual ones during the 1990s. In response to critics who point out that those countries have seen ongoing declines in their marriage rates and children born inside of marriage since the legalization of same-sex unions, they argue that those trends, as well as the rising divorce rate, were already well underway before legalization. If legalization of same-sex marriage were an independent cause of the collapse of the institution, all of those indicators should have worsened at faster rates since legalization. The evidence Eskridge and Spedale present indicate that in Denmark, Norway, and Sweden, not only has there not been an acceleration of those trends, in a number of cases the trends have stopped or even slightly reversed themselves. Even in cases where the trends have continued, they have done so more slowly than before legalization. The evidence from that part of the world suggests that offering gays and lesbians marriage equality has not undermined the institution and may even have strengthened it in precisely the ways I have argued earlier. The explanation for the longer-term trends in those indicators is the liberalization of marriage, which was ongoing before any changes in the status of same-sex couples. Legalization of same-sex unions did not worsen matters.

The concern about children is also a real one. One need not fetishize the safety of children in the ways discussed in chapter 8 to acknowledge that potential harm to children must be considered in changes of this sort. One long-standing line of argument that I will not address is that the normalization of homosexuality in general is a danger to children because gays and lesbians are more likely to abuse children or turn them into homosexuals. There is no evidence to support the first claim, and the second claim is equally false, though even if it were true, it is not clear what the actual harm is there. The more substantive concern is that nationwide legalization of same-sex marriage will mean that same-sex couples can adopt on equal terms with heterosexual couples, or that they will use various forms of reproductive technology to have children at least partly biologically connected to them, and that these children raised in same-sex households will have worse developmental outcomes than those from heterosexual households.

In many ways, the argument is the same one raised about divorce in chapter 7, although very few voices are claiming that worse outcomes for children is a reason to make divorce *illegal*. Instead, those supposed worse outcomes are reasons to make divorce legally harder or socially more discouraged. Like the discussion of divorce in chapter 7, the claim that children raised by same-sex couples will have worse developmental outcomes overlooks two things: the desires of the adults and the fact that worse outcomes on average do not mean unacceptably bad outcomes. Both points are valid in discussions of same-sex marriage as well. Even if it were true that outcomes for children raised in same-sex marriages were somewhat worse than those for children raised in intact heterosexual marriages, that does not mean they are necessarily so much worse off that we should be concerned. Worse on average does not mean all children in same-sex households are worse off than all of those in heterosexual ones.

In addition, we have to recognize the other relevant comparison: children who are adopted into same-sex households may well be coming from foster care or other institutional care in which their outcomes would likely be significantly worse than being raised in any kind of family, same-sex or otherwise. As we noted in chapter 9, engaging in judgments about the desirability of any particular family form should be an exercise in comparative analysis. When we ask about the effects of same-sex marriage on children, we have to ask "what is the realistic alternative?" Even if it were true that outcomes for such children were somewhat worse compared to the children of married heterosexual couples, that is the wrong comparison if the children being raised by same-sex couples would otherwise either not exist or be in institutional care of some sort.[12] If same-sex marriage enables more loving couples to adopt children who would otherwise languish in foster care or orphanages, such marriages would be a clear improvement in child welfare, even if being raised by a same-sex couple was marginally worse for children than being raised by a heterosexual one.

But, as it turns out, these fears are misplaced. The outcomes for children raised by same-sex couples are not significantly different from those of children raised in heterosexual households. For obvious reasons, there has been a great deal of research around this issue, and there is not space to cover all of the literature here. A recent, and reasonably authoritative, source on the topic is a technical report of the American Academy of Pediatrics (AAP) that appeared online in March of 2013 (Perrin, Siegel, and the Committee on Psychosocial Aspects of Child and Family Health 2013). That report offers an overview of 30 years of research on the children of gay and lesbian parents. They acknowledge earlier work by the AAP that claimed that two-parent families provide the best environment for children, but that no particular family form ensures good outcomes or makes bad ones inevitable. The report (e1380) goes on to review the literature on same-sex parenting and here is its general conclusion:

> Although studies of uncommon and varied phenomena are difficult to perform and yield incomplete and imperfect results, there is an emerging consensus, based on an extensive review of the scientific literature, that children growing up in households headed by gay men or lesbians are not disadvantaged in any significant respect relative to children of heterosexual parents. Indeed, the fact that most data suggest that children grow up successfully in families created by gay and lesbian parents despite the almost-universal family disruption and social stigma they have experienced attests to the resilience of these families. Greater acceptance and support of these families will provide an environment even more conducive to successful social and emotional development. Over the past decade, 11 countries have recognized marriage equality and, thus, allow marriage between two partners of the same gender: Argentina, Belgium, Canada, Denmark, Iceland, Netherlands, Norway, Portugal, Spain, South Africa, and Sweden. There has been no evidence that children in these countries have experienced difficulties as a result of these social changes.

It is worth emphasizing the point that these families successfully raised children despite the social stigma they still face, as well as the fact that many such families did not have the same protection of the law afforded to heterosexual couples during the period being studied. There is every reason to expect that the full legalization of same-sex marriage will reduce the social stigma associated with being a child raised by same-sex parents and will provide a framework of legal stability, both of which will improve outcomes for children of same-sex couples that much more.

There is strong evidence to suggest that legalization of same-sex marriage will harm neither the institution of marriage nor the children of same-sex couples. The experiences of the Scandinavian countries as well as the scholarly research on children of US same-sex couples both indicate that there are no serious harms to be expected from legalization. One last point to note is that many of the discussions of the possible harm from same-sex marriage are forms of single-entry bookkeeping. They focus almost exclusively on the harm to heterosexual marriage and often ignore the benefits that marriage rights would bring to gay men and lesbians. Rauch (2004) offers one of the most comprehensive arguments for those benefits, a number of which have been noted earlier. Most important is the way in which full marriage rights will provide gays and lesbians with the full protection of the law for both their own relationship and the relationships that they have with any children they might be legally responsible for. Bringing gays and lesbians into the institution of marriage, and the legal rights and safeguards it provides, will significantly improve their lives and the lives of their children, independent of any other benefits or harm it generates. Given that there is no harm to be expected, these gains to same-sex couples and their children provide a strong case that, by the standards of classical liberalism, full legalization should pose no concerns.

## What About Plural Marriage?

One argument made by both critics of same-sex marriage and by classical liberals in favor of it is that once that prohibition is removed, there is no logical reason for the state to prohibit various forms of plural marriage. If marriage is but a consensual agreement among people who love each other, why should that be limited to *two* people who love each other?[13] Of course the critics of legalizing same-sex marriage see this argument as a slippery slope reason to reject same-sex marriage: if we permit same-sex marriage, we will have to permit *that*. The classical liberals who see this connection are often arguing *in favor* of legalizing plural marriage. Much as someone in favor of same-sex marriage could read Justice Scalia's slippery slope argument in his dissent in *Lawrence v. Texas* as a reason to support that decision, so can one see the critics' belief that legalizing same-sex marriage will lead to legalized plural marriage as a reason to support same-sex marriage.

The argument developed in this chapter might cut both ways with respect to legalizing plural marriage any time soon. The argument in favor is the basic classical liberal commitment to peaceful acts among consenting adults. If three (or more) people claim to love each other and want to live together as a married group, the burden of proof should be on those who object to demonstrate why such a choice is a problem. By analogy, the majority of human beings might prefer to engage in sexual activity with only one other person, but classical liberals would object strongly to a law that said doing so with two or more other people should be banned. The commitment to voluntary choice trumps the fact that the practice in question is uncommon or thought to be unusual.[14] If the right to marry is older than the state's attempts to regulate it, what compelling reasons might there be to deny it to groups of three or more?

From a classical liberal perspective, I think this basic logic is hard to deny. Rather than deny it, I want to raise two questions that would need to be answered before the classical liberal case could be as strong for plural marriage as it is for same-sex marriage. As with same-sex marriage, we have to answer the challenge of the Harm Principle: would legalizing plural marriage create harms, and harms in excess of any benefits? For example, polygyny (i.e., plural marriages with one male and multiple females) has been shown to lead to a variety of problems for the women involved, as well as for children raised in such households.[15] Hall (2014, p. 92) points out that the competition by men for females in such societies leads to a lowering of the first of age of marriage and a general imbalance of power in favor of men. Compared to societies in which polygyny, or other forms of plural marriage, were more the norm, legalized plural marriage in the United States would likely be attractive to only a fraction of a percent of all marriages. If the numbers were that small, our judgment about the severity of the social harm might look different. Nonetheless, these questions are worth pursuing, because part of what has made possible the ongoing legalization of same-sex marriage is that enough people have been convinced that there is not sufficient risk of harm to third parties to keep it illegal. Whatever the logic of the classical liberal position with respect to consenting adults, plural marriage will not be on the legal and political agenda until it has satisfactorily convinced the general public that it does not involve harm to others.

A second question that classical liberals supporting legalization of plural marriage will have to contend with is how the public understands the relevant notion of "equally situated" that is invoked in arguments about equality before the law. Critics of legalizing plural marriage, who may well favor legalizing same-sex marriage, will argue that the applicable notion of equally situated is "wanting to marry one other person." Advocates will insist that the relevant situation is "wanting to enter a voluntary marriage contract." The discussion of "equally situated" earlier in this chapter noted that there is no formulaic way to apply that concept, and this example is evidence for that claim. There is no objective way to decide which notion of "equally situated" is correct. In reality, that question will be decided by the spontaneous order of cultural consensus, just as it has been with so many of the other changes to the laws surrounding marriage. Overturning laws prohibiting interracial marriage and legalizing same-sex marriage, as a large number of states have done, could only happen when enough of the public understood the parties to the illegal marriage to be equally situated to those in legal marriages. It is that perception of a violation of fairness that provides the relevant notion of equally situated.

There was no constituency for same-sex marriage in the 1950s because so few people saw same-sex couples as equally situated with opposite-sex ones (often including the same-sex couples themselves). Only when the underlying culture changed sufficiently to lead enough people to think that same-sex couples were being treated unfairly because they were equally situated could there be a serious movement toward political and legal change. Institutional change has to be able to "stick" and that requires that it is consistent with the underlying culture and its practices.[16] The increased presence of same-sex couples in the lives of ordinary Americans as well as in the media, along with changing cultural views of consensual sexual activity in general, combined to shift people's perceptions of same-sex relationships. That shift made possible the legal and political changes that have taken place in the past two decades with respect to same-sex marriage. That process has not happened yet with plural marriage, though positive media portrayals have increased in the past few years. When the equivalent cultural shift takes place, the ground for legal recognition of such relationships might be sufficiently fertile.[17] At least for now, that time has yet to come.

In response to critics of same-sex marriage who argue that legalizing it will, of necessity, lead to plural marriage, classical liberals can offer three considerations.

First, they can agree that the logic of the classical liberal position on same-sex marriage and consensual behavior among consenting adults in general does suggest a rebuttable presumption in favor of legalizing the practice. They can also argue, however, that the case is not airtight, as we still need to be sure that legalizing plural marriage does not cause a degree or kind of harm that would argue for keeping it illegal. Finally, classical liberals can argue that even if their logic points in the direction of legalization, the underlying cultural change that is necessary for changes in the legal rules of the game to actually stick has not happened yet. When we know more about the question of harm, and when and if that cultural change takes place, then we can seriously entertain the question of plural marriage. In the meantime, as legalization of that practice is not a pressing matter, concerns about a problematic slippery slope should not prevent anyone from considering the merits of same-sex marriage.

## The Separation of Marriage and the State?

The preceding arguments have assumed that the state is playing a central role in defining and sanctioning marriage, and they have then used the issues related to classical liberal concerns with equality before the law to articulate a case for a more inclusive concept of marriage. However, as some libertarians have pointed out, there is an alternative libertarian perspective on marriage and the state: complete separation of the two. Why not get the state completely out of the business of licensing marriages and avoid the controversial issues of who should or should not get such licenses? The argument here is analogous to one libertarian argument for eliminating government-run schools: we would no longer see the same battles over curriculum that arise when there is a "one size fits all" solution being debated. Parents who did or did not want particular kinds of curricula would not be dependent on securing or preventing a political majority in order to get them. Privatization would have the advantage of de-politicizing the cultural debates that surround both education and marriage. Why force those who have strong objections to state-sponsored same-sex marriages to accept that role for government when removing the state's role in the entire process could avoid it? This argument is extremely tempting to libertarians, especially given their broad commitment to as small a government as possible. It also appears to give them the knife needed to cut the Gordian knot of the various culture war issues that arise with the necessarily one-size-fits-all solutions that governments impose.

One of the earliest arguments for privatizing marriage is Boaz (1997). There he distinguishes between two notions of "privatize":

> "Privatizing" marriage can mean two slightly different things. One is to take the state completely out of it. If couples want to cement their relationship with a ceremony or ritual, they are free to do so. Religious institutions are free to sanction such relationships under any rules they choose. A second meaning of "privatizing" marriage is to treat it like any other contract: The state may be called upon to enforce it, but the parties define the terms. When children or large sums of

> money are involved, an enforceable contract spelling out the parties' respective rights and obligations is probably advisable. But the existence and details of such an agreement should be up to the parties.

The first version of privatization is the more radical one, as marriage then becomes only the particular ritual or ceremony that couples (or more?) use to signify that they are married. The state plays no role at all. The less radical second version recognizes the state's role as the *enforcer* of a marriage contract, but takes it out of the process of *defining* what marriage must look like. Later in that article, Boaz (1997) discusses how this might play out in practice:

> Make it a private contract between two individuals. If they wanted to contract for a traditional breadwinner/homemaker setup, with specified rules for property and alimony in the event of divorce, they could do so. Less traditional couples could keep their assets separate and agree to share specified expenses. Those with assets to protect could sign prenuptial agreements that courts would respect. Marriage contracts could be as individually tailored as other contracts are in our diverse capitalist world. For those who wanted a standard one-size-fits-all contract, that would still be easy to obtain. Wal-Mart could sell books of marriage forms next to the standard rental forms. Couples would then be spared the surprise discovery that outsiders had changed their contract without warning. Individual churches, synagogues, and temples could make their own rules about which marriages they would bless.

More recently, Jones (2006) offers a similar argument using the institutional mechanism of "marital corporations" with various married couples as stockholders who all share common values about marriage. Couples wishing to marry "would subscribe to shares of an existing marital corporation, whose charter documents would set forth the terms of the type of marriage to which the subscribing couples agree" (p. 116). He further imagines ways in which the marital corporations could offer terms tailored to particular preferences (e.g., refusing to marry same-sex couples or prohibiting divorce) and could integrate these particular marriage contracts into existing private and government benefit systems. All of this sounds attractive from a libertarian perspective, but there are theoretical and practical problems with the desire to separate marriage and the state that need to be acknowledged.

The important context for seeing these problems is that the definition of marriage matters greatly for many other things that governments do. As Boaz himself notes, there are at least one thousand US federal laws that involve recognizing marital status. So if the US federal government were to recognize whatever contractual arrangements people themselves developed to define their marriages, are libertarians who accept Boaz's or Jones's argument just assuming that governments will do so without politicizing *that* process? This raises the theoretical objection to the version of privatization that is found in both Boaz and Jones. Given the role that public choice considerations of the motivations of politicians play in so much other classical liberal analysis of the state, it would be surprising if libertarians were to miss the point that this proposal would seem to bump the political brawl to another level. Would, for example, religious conservatives stand by and say it is fine for the federal government to accept a contract between two men or two women (or three of anyone) as qualifying as a marriage for the purpose of federal benefits? Would progressives think the government should recognize as legitimate a marriage in which the wife agreed to clear conditions of subservience, even by explicit consent? Are we not just back where we are now, but with the fight over which private contracts should *count* as marriage for the purpose of government benefits and taxes, rather than over how the government *defines* marriage?[18]

The number of ways in which who counts as married matters for the enormous variety of things government does is one reason that government getting out of the marriage business is unlikely to happen any time soon. That is the major practical stumbling block to seeing the separation of marriage and the state as the solution to the ongoing debates over the evolution of marriage. To be clear, the long-run ideal from a libertarian perspective might well be to have the state completely out of the process, as in Boaz's first version of privatization. It is also rhetorically easy for libertarians to proclaim that what they really want is the separation of marriage and the state. The problem is that there has been precious little written to specify exactly what that means *in a world where the state continues to do all the other things it does that depend upon marital status.* As long as governments make marital status a condition for certain benefits or tax treatments, they are unlikely to withdraw from the process of defining who does and does not count as married. The challenge for libertarians who want to make complete separation their political goal is to explain how that will work in the absence of first dismantling all the other things that governments are doing that are intertwined with marital status.[19] The reality is that the marriage-relevant things that governments do are not likely to disappear in the near future.

The danger of making complete privatization the major, or only ideologically acceptable, goal, and thereby treating universal government recognition of same-sex marriage as less important, is that it makes the ideal the enemy of the better. Libertarians can insist on what they see as the more ideologically pure goal of separating marriage and the state, but they do so at the cost of ignoring the injustice of actually existing inequality before the law. That injustice, as argued earlier, matters from the long-run perspective of classical liberalism's commitment to equality before the law. Libertarian support for overturning existing state-level bans on same-sex marriage is a good example of a case where recognizing the gains from a better policy is better than hoping for the longer-run, perhaps larger but far less likely gains of the ideal policy. Full separation may well be much better than equality under the law. However, consideration of the lower likelihood of its happening, plus the discount rate to be applied to possible future gains, would seem to make the current benefits of supporting marriage equality larger than the current benefits of pinning all libertarian hopes on full separation.

Of course supporting marriage equality does not prevent libertarians from *also* making the case for eventual complete separation of marriage and the state. To return to our Social Security example from earlier in the chapter, believing that classical liberalism requires, as a matter of justice, that Social Security payments be made available to all races does not mean libertarians cannot or should not *also* be arguing for the dismantling of Social Security. Yes, more beneficiaries might make that a tougher argument to win, but that is not a reason for ignoring the commitment to equality before the law. So even if libertarians committed to complete separation of marriage and the state think extending existing marriage rights to same-sex couples would make that long-run goal harder, they cannot use that as a sound argument against also supporting marriage equality today.

That said, it is not clear that the premise is correct. It may well be that the expansion of state-granted marriage rights to same-sex couples, and perhaps to groups of more than two down the road, leads to people being willing to more radically rethink the whole nature of marriage and its relationship with the state. That may have the effect of generating more creative thinking about how a more private institution of marriage might emerge in a world where the state continues to do the things it does. At the same time, libertarians might be better off focusing on figuring out how to offer alternatives to the government programs that are deeply entwined with marital status so that those programs can be eliminated. Such alternatives could reduce the costs of separating marriage from the state. For example, doing more to promote a libertarian antipoverty agenda as an alternative to the harmful ways in which the welfare state undermines marriage as an institution would perhaps be a better long-run strategy for separating marriage from the state than focusing on that specific goal right now. Whatever the strategic considerations, there is nothing inconsistent about believing that the best choice in the present is to support marriage equality while maintaining that the ultimate goal is to separate marriage from the state.

## Hayek, Tradition, and the Evolution of Social Institutions

There are, of course, other changes happening with the contemporary institution of marriage. Some of those have been outlined in previous chapters. Marriage in the twenty-first century continues to evolve, just as marriage has for the entirety of its existence. One of the challenges in looking at marriage through the lens of Hayek is that his framework is one that recognizes the power and importance of tradition, while still leaving enough room for institutions to evolve as social and cultural practices change. Traditions, like social institutions as discussed in chapter 2, are for Hayek repositories of distilled collective wisdom. They represent successful social adaptations to the problems that must be solved in any society. For that reason, we overthrow traditions with some peril, which is why Hayek (1978b) has argued that we can never reconstruct human institutions from scratch. At best, we can only criticize existing social arrangements from a vantage point that takes a whole host of other such arrangements as given. That is, each tradition must be individually critically assessed in light of how it fits with other traditions. The important point here is that while Hayek does make a presumption in favor of the power of tradition in general, that presumption is rebuttable if any specific tradition is found not to fit with the rest of a relevant set of traditions. Hayek respects tradition, but he does not revere it.

Given Hayek's respect for tradition, the challenge for Hayekians becomes how fast a correction process of unjust laws should take place, given that institutions have to be rooted in actual human practices and that such institutions have, themselves, often emerged over many generations. How do we balance the claims of justice against the potential confusion that a change in an institution might provoke? Recall chapter 2's discussion of the role that institutions (and thereby traditions) play in coordinating human behavior. Does the ongoing evolution of marriage make it more difficult for people to understand what marriage is and thereby make it more difficult to form more accurate expectations of others' behavior?

The answer will depend on whether one sees same-sex marriage as revolutionary or evolutionary. And that answer may well depend on whether one is focusing on the form of marriage or its functions, a distinction also made in chapter 2. The argument from conservatives that same-sex marriage is revolutionary at least implicitly focuses on the *form* of marriage by arguing that we are so fundamentally changing the institution that it is likely to cause major social confusion and discoordination. The argument in chapter 2 was that the functions of marriage and the family are what really matter and that changing the form that marriage can take need not fundamentally alter what marriage is for, and what it and the family do. The evolution traced in chapters 3 through 5 shows how those functions tend to change slowly and how forms tend to change in response as people have the time to figure out what sorts of arrangements best fulfill those new functions—or at least do not undermine them.

Same-sex marriage is, in this way, much more about a change in form than in function. Because changes in form tend to follow changes in function, they are not as difficult to adjust to. We understand how the new forms fit the already changed functions. In the case of same-sex marriage, we understand that marriage is now mostly about love and emotional commitment, which makes same-sex marriage seem much more evolutionary than revolutionary. By contrast, were we to collectivize child raising for example, that would be a discoordinating break from tradition in a way that same-sex marriage does not seem to be. We understand that raising children is one major function of the family. Collectivizing child raising would eradicate that function and discoordinate our expecations. As this chapter has noted, same-sex marriage is about who is *eligible* to marry, not about the functions marriage performs. The major changes in the functions of marriage and family have already taken place over the past 150 years. The question with respect to same-sex marriage is *who* can be married. The debate over what marriage *does* is largely over and done with, at least for the time being. Thinking in terms of what marriage is for is the more Hayekian question, once we recognize the role of social institutions as problem solvers. The form those institutions take is only relevant to the degree that the form is able to fulfill the functions.

The inclusion of same-sex couples in the institution of marriage does not transform our understanding of marriage in such a fundamental way that it will cause major disruptions, any more than the nationwide legalization of interracial marriage did in 1967. If we think of how traffic lights coordinate the flow of cars as analogous to how traditions and social institutions coordinate human behavior, we can see the dangers of introducing a whole new system if people are not sufficiently ready to change. Roundabouts (traffic circles) have been *gradually* introduced in the United States for this reason. But the actual history of traffic lights provides another example. Garrett Morgan patented the first three-position traffic signal in 1923. Before then, traffic signals were either "stop" or "go," as a look at old movies will demonstrate. The problem was that as cars got faster, the lack of warning that the signal was changing from go to stop caused an increasing number of crashes, leading Morgan to develop the third signal (today, the yellow light) to indicate that the stop signal was about to be deployed.[20] This evolution in the *form* of traffic lights did not change their underlying *function*.

Did the addition of the yellow light fundamentally alter the institution of the traffic light? Did it represent a sharp rejection of tradition? It would seem not. People would have had to make some minor adjustments and learn how long the yellow would last, but there's no historical evidence to indicate any serious problems such as an increase in accidents. The addition of "yellow" to the signaling function of traffic lights gave drivers more information, which enhanced the ability of traffic lights to function as an institution by better aligning the signals with the reality of how people were driving, especially as the number of cars and their speeds both increased. One can view same-sex marriage as doing something similar for the institution of marriage. It brings something in. It widens and improves the institution without undermining its functioning. It does not break with a tradition in a way that undermines expectations, especially in a world where same-sex relationships have become more common and visible. So even if we grant the legitimacy of Hayekian concerns about tradition, same-sex marriage does not appear to threaten the accumulated wisdom embodied in the tradition of marriage, which itself has evolved over human history.

This is consistent with a broader Hayekian view of social change. Historically, Hayek has been championed by many conservatives because of the importance he attaches to tradition. They are not wrong in noting tradition's importance in Hayek's thought. Long-standing institutions are indeed surrogates for all kinds of accumulated wisdom and should be respected accordingly. Those same conservatives, however, frequently neglect the places in Hayek's work where he rejects the idea that we have to revere tradition to the point of stasis. The power of tradition does not mean we can never question it, or that social institutions cannot or should not evolve. Scientific knowledge changes, for example, and that means old traditions can and should be abandoned, especially if they conflict with other important values.

This is the exact point Hayek (1960, p. 451, fn. 18) made over 50 years ago about the criminalization of homosexuality. He suggests that when people had reason to believe (wrongly it turns out) that homosexual behavior could cause harm to others, it was at least understandable why they would wish to criminalize it. But as our scientific understanding has changed, and as treating homosexual acts among consenting adults became increasingly in conflict with the way we treat sexual behavior and other consensual behavior among heterosexual adults, changing the law to reflect that new knowledge and to make it consistent with other laws and values was the right thing to do: "[P]rivate practice among adults, however abhorrent it may be to the majority, is not a proper subject for coercive action for a state whose object is to minimize coercion." This is also consistent with Hayek's evolutionary approach to ethics in general. As Hayek (1989, p. 10) argued in *The Fatal Conceit*, once we understand the role that ethical norms play as evolved responses to specific kinds of social conflicts, there is no possibility of devising a universal, transhistorical ethical system: "Ethics is the last fortress in which human pride must now bow in recognition of its origins." As with much of Hayek's work, both left and right will find this result frustrating, as both often want to impose just that sort of universal ethic, though they disagree about its contents. Hayek's message is that we have to be more patient and recognize the evolutionary nature of social change. For the left this is too slow, and for many on the right it is too fast. That might be good reason to think it is actually just right. Just as evolutionary considerations have come to be taken more seriously in a wide variety of fields, they should have a role to play in our considerations of morality and its relationship to political change.

This is most emphatically not a counsel of despair. Hayek's general stance of intellectual humility, which lies behind so much of his social theory, is at play here too. We cannot design ethical and moral systems, nor can we design social institutions such as the family, any more than we can design an economy or our own minds. Change is possible and necessary, but only within the framework of existing rules, norms, and institutions that have passed that evolutionary test. We cannot reconstruct or redesign, but we can repair the holes and inconsistencies that are the inevitable result of imperfect social evolutionary processes.[21] There are limits to our ability to engage in this process of repair, but that does not mean we should not or cannot do it. There is also no reason to think a Hayekian perspective on social change should not include a strong belief that such repairs should be made as quickly as possible where doing so is feasible.

More generally, the perspective on the family taken in this book is one that has recognized that particular institutions evolve as part of the more general growth that comes with the ongoing process of social evolution and change. I have emphasized the role of economic growth and the changing nature of economic activity as drivers of changes in the family, but ideas matter too, especially the changing nature of our beliefs about human equality over the past few centuries. Like every other evolutionary process, social evolution is a discovery process whose details are beyond our ability to predict. The family has evolved and changed in a whole variety of ways over the course of recorded history, and despite each generation's prediction that the set of changes that *their* generation saw would destroy the institution, it somehow manages to adapt, survive, and even improve. Social institutions are more resilient than we often believe, and the history of the family is an excellent example of that resilience.

The problem we face is not the family collapsing as an institution, but our lack of confidence in the beneficence of social evolutionary processes and the unpredictable changes they bring. In 1960, Hayek included an epilogue in his *The Constitution of Liberty* that he titled "Why I am Not a Conservative." That epilogue offers a number of arguments for Hayek's classical liberalism and explains why it differs from the conservative worldview. One of the most powerful, and most relevant to this book's exploration of the family, is this argument: "The liberal position is based on courage and confidence, on a preparedness to let change run its course even if we cannot predict where it will lead" (Hayek 1960, p. 400). Many conservative commentators who proclaim that the changes in the family over the past generation have put us on the road to disaster ignore the failure of similar predictions throughout history and lack the very confidence that Hayek sees at the core of the classical liberal tradition. By contrast, progressives demonstrate an impatience with the pace of social change and a confidence in their ability to predict which changes are needed. Neither is justified in light of Hayek's arguments.

A Hayekian analysis of the family should lead us to be both humble and optimistic. History teaches us exactly the lesson from the quotation earlier: we have every reason to be confident about the nature of the evolution of the family as long as we allow that change to take place in accordance with people's plans and preferences. Humans are exceptional problem solvers when we are left free to experiment and innovate, as our climb from millennia of abject poverty in the past 250 years demonstrates. There is no reason to believe that the ongoing evolution of the family should make us think differently. What is needed is confidence in where unpredictable change will take us. That confidence remains in short supply in a world still too committed to believing that social order and progress come from design, whether that commitment is the right's attempts to freeze a family that never actually existed, or the left's attempts to rationally reconstruct the family. I hope that this book provides a starting point for further work by classical liberals who want to show that our confidence in the unpredictable results of social evolution, the justification for which Hayek and others have so powerfully articulated with respect to the market economy, applies just as powerfully to the social institution of the family.

# Notes

## 1 Introduction: The Family and Classical Liberalism

1. Jefferson's First Inaugural Address. http://avalon.law.yale.edu/19th_century/jefinau1.asp
2. Notably absent from that list is noninterventionist foreign policy. The events of September 11, 2001, ushered in what appears to be an unfortunate retreat from the noninterventionism that historically characterized classical liberal thought. The very nature of the threat that terrorism poses, in contrast with more traditional military action, has led to much debate among classical liberals as to what constitutes a "defensive" action, or whether pre-emptive strikes of some kind can be justified.
3. One of the more interesting developments of the past few years is the increasing willingness of the Left to support such interventions in personal choices, most frequently under the guise of "public health." For an example of this phenomenon, see Sullum (1998). For more on the differences between conservatives and classical liberals, see Hayek's (1960) postscript to *The Constitution of Liberty*, entitled "Why I am Not a Conservative."
4. For example, see Lehr (1999).
5. Hall (2014, p. 34) writes of Marxist rejection of the family: "The family is not merely dangerous for the practical consequences it has for egalitarianism; it is dangerous primarily as the theoretical bastion of the 'natural' or of 'human nature,' which is the enemy of radical social change."
6. Boettke (1995) very nicely lays out this distinction with respect to Austrian economics.
7. One might point to economic work on the theory of the firm, as firms are neither, themselves, markets nor states. However, as central institutions *of* the market, it is clear why the economics-dominated revival would have paid attention to the firm as an institution.
8. Here it is important to distinguish the classical liberal tradition from conservatism. Obviously, modern conservatism, especially in the United States, has produced a great deal of work on the family.
9. I received the excellent book by Hall (2014) too late to incorporate fully, but I will note that her chapter on "Ayn Rand, Individualism, and the Family" raises

a number of important points about Rand's treatment of the family, paralleling ones I raise in Horwitz (2005b). Readers wondering why I am not treating Rand separately can consult that paper and the Hall book for arguments against Rand's view of the family.

10. See, for example, Beito (2000) and Beito, Gordon, and Tabarrok (2002). Also relevant is the literature on dispute resolution outside of state-provided legal systems, for example, Benson (1990) and Ellickson (1991).
11. Prominent natural rights libertarians would be Ayn Rand, Robert Nozick, Murray Rothbard, and Tibor Machan.
12. Contractarian libertarians of note include James Buchanan and Jan Narveson.
13. Consequentialist libertarians would include Richard Epstein and others strongly influenced by the Chicago School of Economics and Austrian economists such as Friedrich Hayek and Ludwig von Mises. The economist Leland Yeager (2001) offers a particularly sophisticated account of consequentialist classical liberalism. Chris Sciabarra's (2000) *Total Freedom* offers a dialectical take on libertarianism that is in the spirit of the consequentialists. More recently, John Tomasi's (2011) *Free Market Fairness* and the "bleeding heart libertarian" movement have expanded the range of consequentialist arguments.
14. One difference among the consequentialists is the degree to which they think the relevant unit of analysis is individual rights, groups of rights, or whole systems of rights. If consequentialism is at the level of specific rights, then those rights can be added or subtracted if they fail to produce the desired consequences. The Chicago economists might fit into this group. By contrast, people like Hayek or Yeager see rights as interconnected in important ways and believe that we cannot do consequentialist cost-benefit analyses at the level of specific rights.
15. See, for example, Buchanan and Tullock's (1962) classic work. Simmons (2011) offers a very accessible overview of public choice economics.
16. What Marx, for example, objected to about the market was precisely that its order emerged spontaneously rather than as the conscious creation of human beings. As Marx (1906 [1871], p. 92) argues in *Capital*: "The life-process of society, which is based on the process of material production, does not strip off its mystical veil until it is treated as production by freely associated men, and its consciously regulated by them in accordance with a settled plan."
17. Complete citations here would be numerous, but for a comprehensive reference, see Buss (2005) and especially the overview essay by Tooby and Cosmides (2005).
18. I put aside for now the very difficult questions of where the line between "child" and "adult" is and how we should determine where such a line should be. For the point at issue, all that I need to do is stipulate that such a line exists in some form.

## 2 Two Sorts of Worlds at Once

1. Other good examples of tacit knowledge are the skills of a musician or an athlete, where the body moves more quickly than the brain can consciously process. One of the best examples of tacit knowledge is, ironically, the faculty of speech. Speaking in our mother tongue happens without a need to focus consciously on what we are doing. In fact, when we do shift what Polanyi (1958, p. 55) calls our "focal awareness" to the act of speaking, we find ourselves tongue-tied and unable to speak fluently. The same is true of any skilled performance, as is

evidenced by the frequent advice to athletes to stop thinking about what they are doing and just relax and "do it." This also seems related to the concept of "flow" (Csikszentmihalyi 1990).

2. Critics of market economies often focus on the question of "what to produce" without discussing the question of "how to produce it." Figuring out what others want might seems to be not all that difficult, although it is more difficult than it first appears, but figuring out how to produce it using the resources that are least valued in other uses makes the problem extraordinarily complex.
3. A later discussion in this chapter will examine how this notion of limits making learning possible applies to the structure of the human mind as well.
4. See Lon Fuller (1969, p. 139): "There are some outcomes in human relations too absurd to rise to the level of conscious exclusion."
5. On the relationship between coherence and flexibility, see Langlois (1986).
6. See Horwitz (2008a) for more on the family as a spontaneous order.
7. See Horwitz (2001) for more on the links among the Scots, Menger, and Hayek on the concept of spontaneous order.
8. The following paragraphs draw heavily from Horwitz (2005a).
9. Of course such organizations have "rules," but those rules are often processes by which hierarchical decisions are implemented, rather than the abstract rules guiding individual behavior that characterize orders. They are not, as we shall discuss later, "ends-independent," rather they are rules about how to reach the specific ends that the organization is pursuing.
10. To even count as a sentence, the word sequence must obey certain rules, such as having a subject and predicate. Sequences of words that do not obey that rule are not a sentence, although they might be a clause if they at least have some meaning to them. A truly random sequence of words would be neither a clause nor a sentence.
11. This process can be seen in the evolution in the past decade or two of instant messaging or text-message speak, which involves all kinds of abbreviations and acronyms (e.g., LOL for "laughing out loud"), some of which have begun to creep into more general usage. This change in form was driven by the functioning of instant messaging and texting, which put a primacy on speed and, in some cases, had character limits that made abbreviations helpful. In many ways, it is an attempt to make the written word operate with the speed of the spoken word.
12. The literature on Hayek's theory of the mind has exploded over the past decade or two. Rather than an exhaustive list of citations, I will provide just a few here. For my own take on the place of *The Sensory Order* in Hayek's economic and political project, see Horwitz (2000). Caldwell (2004) situates it more broadly in Hayek's methodological project. Several essays in Hayek (1967) offer his later thoughts.
13. The rest of this section draws heavily on Horwitz (2008b).
14. Rather than "re-present" it might be more accurate to say that the model "pre-presents" the current environment.
15. The way in which they describe humans coming into the world with particular learning processes already in place is very similar to Hayek's argument in *The Sensory Order* summarized in the previous section.
16. See the discussion in Tooby and Cosmides (2005, p. 42) and the work cited there.
17. Reading evolutionary psychology from a Hayekian perspective, one is struck by the use of phrases such as "evolution designed this function" or "design features," as the naïve might interpret "design" as implying a "designer." Of course the use

is metaphorical in its attribution of intentionality to the natural processes of selection. In discussing the contributions of evolutionary psychology, this metaphorical use of design needs to be kept in mind.

18. The awarding of the 2002 Nobel Prize in Economics to Vernon Smith and Daniel Kahneman points to the impact of that work.
19. Tooby and Cosmides (2005, p. 23): "These procedures are ecologically rational, providing good solutions when operating in the task environments for which they evolved." Vernon Smith (2003, p. 471), in his Nobel lecture, argues: "Thus, if people in certain contexts make choices that contradict our formal theory of rationality, rather than conclude that they are irrational, some ask why, reexamine maintained hypotheses including all aspects of the experiments—procedures, payoffs, context, instructions, etc.—and inquire as to what new concepts and experimental designs can help us to better understand the behavior. What is the subjects' perception of the problem that they are trying to solve?" Smith then ties this whole approach to understanding our "biological and cultural heritage."
20. The published version of the lecture contains three "head quotes," one from Hume, one from Hayek, and one from Herbert Simon. The quote from Hayek is the "two sorts of worlds at once" passage in *The Fatal Conceit* noted in the introduction and elaborated upon in the last section of this chapter.
21. One of the missing pieces from Smith's analysis, as well as in the criticism by Leeson (2005), is the necessary role of monetary calculation in making possible the movement from personal to impersonal exchange. Explaining how market institutions internalize the benefits from reciprocal behavior, thus creating generalized benefits to exchange, does not necessarily explain how individuals know what to exchange and whether that exchange is likely to be mutually beneficial in *particular circumstances*. For that, access to monetary calculation is required. I address these issues in Horwitz (2008c).
22. The classic example is pregnancy-related nausea. The label "pregnancy/morning sickness" suggests that it is a dysfunctional reaction by female humans. However, if, as experimental evidence suggests, that nausea is a reaction to particular kinds of foods that were, for much of human history, likely to cause damage to the fetus in the first few months, then rather than being a "sickness," it is actually quite an adaptive response. As Bjorklund and Pellegrini (2000, p. 1689) observe: "It is ironic to note that thalidomide, the drug that led to serious deformations of children's limbs when taken early in pregnancy, was sometimes prescribed to alleviate pregnancy sickness." Bringing an evolutionary perspective to these questions can also improve medical practice.
23. For more on the importance of play, see Postrel (1999, Chapter 7), Gottschall (2012, Chapter 2), and Gray (2013).
24. A theory of parenting would be a recommendation about the best *means* to achieve those goals. Taking the insights of evolutionary psychology and Hayekian social theory seriously might be a fruitful way to explore just how children learn and how parents can best teach in the context of the family and the particular goals we will outline.
25. A nice overview of the "two worlds" idea in Hayek can be found in Lea (2007).
26. See also Horwitz (2015) for a discussion of the ways in which the two worlds are more intertwined than Hayek suggests.

## 3 The Family in a World of Poverty

1. Mises (1981 [1922], pp. 76) describes this transition as one from marriage being based on violence to it being based on the idea of contract. See the further discussion in chapter 5.
2. It is true that single parenthood, remarriage, and step-parenthood were part of human history due to the death of one parent or the other (frequently in labor for women and at work for men), but not from divorce. As Stone (1977, pp. 55–56) puts it: "In practice the probability of a durable marriage was low, since it was likely to be broken before very long by the death of the husband or wife. Indeed, it looks very much as if modern divorce is a little more than a functional substitute for death." The complications raised by the sharing of child custody and the economic terms of divorce (spousal death at least involves some form of insurance or inheritance if it was the man who died) have made the modern circumstances distinct from the death-driven family changes of centuries past.
3. Ebeling (1987) remains one of the best, short treatments of the importance of "cooperation in anonymity" as a way to understand the Great Society.
4. Friedman's (2006) *The World Is Flat* offers numerous examples of the ways in which technology has helped flatten the global playing field. His metaphor of the flatter world is a somewhat inelegant and misleading way of making the point that the Law of Association had led us to a globalized division of labor and concurrent degree of cooperation in anonymity.
5. One need only think of the ways in which Ebay had to develop trust-detection processes and signals for it to be successful at facilitating anonymous exchanges in the way it does.
6. Seabright's book offers numerous examples of the ways these trust-promoting institutions emerged and function.
7. This can be seen as the evolutionary-historical backdrop for the proposal floated during the Cold War (attributed to Kenneth Boulding) that some number of US and Soviet military leaders should engage in a cultural exchange of their children each year. The idea was the same as that behind marriage in Paleolithic times, namely, turn strangers into kin, although this would be more honorary kin than real. More narrowly, how much less likely would military leaders have been to push the nuclear button knowing that some number of their children were on the other end?
8. Even as late as the Middle Ages, it could be said that individuals were more the product of kin relationships than the constituent parts. As Flandrin (1979, p. 16) notes about the tenth and eleventh centuries, "[T]he individual was, at that time, less a person in his own right than a member of the *lignage*, in the most concrete sense of the term."
9. Shorter (1975, p. 70) notes this difference and comments that "men had more disposable time [which] permitted at least the possibility of bar-sitting several times a week, although not all men did so." This so-called leisure gap persists to our own time, especially in dual-career families with children (see Hochschild 1989).
10. Shorter (1975, p. 174) points to historical evidence that rising grain prices tracked closely with abandonments, suggesting that the costs of feeding more children were rising faster than any revenue that might come from the higher prices.
11. Although Shorter (1975, p. 177) notes that some poorer women engaged in an interesting form of arbitrage, they "put their own children out at very low rates

in order to take a better-paid nursling from elsewhere." As unpleasant as this is to modern sensibilities, it was yet another way of trying to ensure that women continued to contribute positively to the family's income and got the children cared for.

12. Flandrin (1979, p. 203) reports that the areas of preindustrial France where extended families were more common seemed to have children that were better cared for. His explanation is that "perhaps this was because the extended family offered them better protection than the conjugal family in which . . . the economic functions of the mother prevented her from fulfilling normally her maternal obligations." He also suggests that extended families may have made it more possible for women to nurse their own children, which both reduced their fertility and their own risk of death as well as providing better care for the child, reducing its risk of death.
13. There are plenty of Medieval and Early Modern visual renderings of parents and children, and whole families, that depict love as we would understand it today. As one example, see *An Old Man and His Grandson* (*ca.* 1490) by the Italian Renaissance artist Domenico Ghirlandaio: http://en.wikipedia.org/wiki/An_Old_Man_and_his_Grandson. This piece is widely recognized for its powerful portrayal of familial intimacy. I thank Jessica Skwire Routhier for the pointer to this painting.
14. The song "Do You Love Me?" from *Fiddler on the Roof* captures this nicely when Tevye sings of learning to love each other and Golde responds by describing all she's done for him over the years.
15. See Stevenson and Wolfers (2008) for more on this point.
16. I thank Brian Pitt for calling this passage in Simmel to my attention.
17. As one piece of evidence, consider a *New York Times* article discussing the role that a prospective romantic partner's book preferences (or lack thereof) play in signaling the likely success of the relationship. If one is seen reading a book that the other person does not think much of, the relationship might be over. Conversely, choosing the right book can be an important positive signal. When marital choice is taking place at this level of detailed complementary consumption preferences, we should not be surprised that marriage is taking place later and less frequently and that the reasons for wanting a divorce seem so trivial to older generations. See Donadio (2008).
18. Abelove (1989, p. 129) also speculates that this process turned nonprocreative sex into forms of foreplay.
19. See also Posner (1992, p. 86): "[M]uch of the variance in sexual behavior and customs across cultures and eras is explained by a handful of factors . . . above all, the changing occupational role of women. That changing role is, in turn, a function of infant mortality, the value of children, the technology of contraception, the existence of labor-saving devices in household production . . . and the degree to which well-remunerated work not requiring great physical strength or stamina is available in the economy."
20. Several of the elements of medieval marriage are present in what some observers have called the most realistic portrayal of the Middle Ages ever filmed: *Monty Python and the Holy Grail.* One extended sequence in the film involves the king of Swamp Castle attempting to marry off his reluctant son to an arranged bride. Three elements of the scene are worth noting. First, he offers the son a number of reasons why he should marry her, the last of which, but clearly most important to the king, is that she has "huge tracts of land." Second, the king at one

point inadvertently speaks of "the merger" rather than the marriage. Finally, after a large number of the wedding guests are wounded or killed by an overzealous Sir Lancelot (who is trying to rescue the anguished prince), the king pleads with the survivors to stop "bickering over who killed who" and to get on with the wedding. Taken together, these elements of the scene correspond nicely to the political and economic functions of medieval marriage, as well as taking to a farcical extreme the way in which the completed marriage itself was more important than the happiness of the wedding guests, much less the couple.

21. One need only think of Henry VIII's colorful marital history to see how this power over marriage can play out.
22. Child-swapping of this sort is a long-standing strategy for ensuring that children thrive when economic conditions are challenging. Chapter 5 offers an example of this practice in contemporary times among poor families.
23. Goody (1983, pp. 71–72) comments that adoption's absence in the Hebrew Bible might be the result of levirate marriage being available as a substitute.
24. Goody (1983, p. 81) argues that the enforcement of clerical celibacy was the flip side of these rules because priests who both controlled Church wealth and had children might be tempted to put the needs of their children before the Church and channel wealth in their direction. Celibacy removed the possibility of such kin connections and further served to consolidate the Church's hold over property.
25. Here too the reality of the challenges of the step-family are seen in their frequent appearance in classic literature, especially children's tales.
26. Coontz (2005, p. 108) offers a story from fifteenth-century England that provides details about the community intrusiveness and humiliation required to prove the impotency of a husband, as impotency was another grounds for annulment. In short, a couple was required to be observed in bed by "wise women" who would verify that the husband was unable to perform sexually.
27. One interesting example of a contemporary event that actually really did look like a charivari and was in the context of sexual misbehavior (though in this case the targets were innocent) was the pot banging protests that took place outside the house rented by the Duke University lacrosse players falsely accused of rape in the spring of 2006 (Taylor and Johnson 2007). The organizers of the protests referred to them as a "cacerolazo," claiming it was a tool that women all around the world used to protest sexual assaults. Wikipedia notes that the word is Spanish and that its use in the context of protests originates in 1970s Chile in economic protests by middle- and upper-class women against the Allende government and then later in the Argentine banking crisis of 2001. It makes no reference, and neither do other sources quickly consulted, to it being used in the context of sexual assault. However, the similarity to the charivari is too striking to be coincidental and it seems likely that the protest organizers were blending elements of the Chilean cacerolazo (women banging pots) with the centuries-old charivari's function as an informal community regulator of sexual behavior.

## 4 Capitalism and the Emergence of the Modern Family

1. Space prevents a complete treatment of the issues surrounding the Industrial Revolution, but interested readers can consult the relevant portions of North (1981), Rosenberg and Birdzell (1986), Mokyr (1992), Landes (1998), Simon (2000), and McCloskey (2010).

2. Evidence of this process can be found in paintings of domestic scenes from the eighteenth century where most of the objects in the house were production goods and the largest area of the house was filled with the equipment necessary for putting-out processes. Over the following century, similar domestic scenes more frequently revealed a house full of consumption goods, dominated by a large table or comfortable seating and perhaps kitchen items. Such pictures indicate the shift of the home from a site of production to a site of consumption, which is perhaps the most precise summary of the effects of the Industrial Revolution on the family.
3. Protestant sects were more tolerant of the role of love within the marital relationship prior to the late eighteenth century as Flandrin's (1979, p. 166) discussion of the English Puritans indicates.
4. See MacLeod (1998, p. 20) for such a story about a young girl and his observation that "silence [i.e., pretending not to have seen her parents making love on the kitchen floor] had to substitute for privacy." The thought of that situation brings a shudder to our modern selves, as we imagine being on either side of being caught in flagrante delicto by family members.

   Several years' worth of undergraduates in courses co-taught with a colleague were asked by survey to rank the severity of various parental behaviors that could be viewed as "maltreatment." Students ranked "Parents have sexual intercourse with each other where the child could see them" as more problematic than "Repeatedly fail to keep medical appointments for their child" or "Have never taken their child to the dentist." Overall, they ranked being seen having sex in the middle of a list of 26 possibilities, where they ranked the parent having sex with the child as the most problematic and having a lesbian mother as the least.

   There are two points worth noting about this result. First, in a less sexualized society, and especially one where seeing one's parents, or other household members, having sex was more common, it was likely subjectively less embarrassing to our ancestors than it would be to us, especially where there was little expectation of privacy. Second, it might well be the case that even with the increased privacy of our own time, such situations could become more common as parents (and grandparents!) raised in a more sexual time engage in more frequent sexual activity and take more risks than did previous generations. It could be that we eventually become less horrified by these situations as those same, more sexually open, parents raise children. However, this survey data, which was compiled in the past 10–15 years, suggests otherwise.
5. Even in the early twentieth century, the working poor in London frequently lived in housing with just one or two rooms and multiple people sharing beds. See Pember Reeves (1914). Also see Bryson (2010) for more on the history of the home.
6. See Coontz (1992, p. 128): "[T]he two main goals of social policy [in the antebellum era] were to free the nuclear family from its former entanglements with kin and neighbors and to concentrate previously diffused economic and social responsibilities for children within the nuclear family." Coontz's discussion in that chapter raises a number of interesting issues for classical liberals as she argues that it was the state that effectively created the modern nuclear family through a variety of policies and interventions that gave favored status to this then-new family form. I shall return to her discussion in later chapters.
7. These changes are discussed in more detail in chapter 7.
8. In equilibrium, the wage would be precisely equal to the value of the worker's marginal product (or, even more technically, the present discounted value thereof) as endless competition would push the wage infinitesimally close to that value. In

the real world, where all of these are "best guesses" and where transaction costs are positive and where competition is imperfect, about all that can be said is that employers who keep wages too much lower than the value of the marginal product risk losing their employees and those who pay too much more than that value will experience losses. Markets provide both incentives and signals to avoid paying too much or too little.

9. There is much debate over the degree to which children were net economic assets prior to industrialization. It may well be the case that they were near neutral, or at least that which side of the ledger they netted out to varied by the value of the crops the family was able to produce and sell. However, there are two considerations here. First, the long-run value of children in a society that lacked formal mechanisms for saving for old age has to be factored in. Having a large number of children increased the likelihood of sufficient support in old age. Second, whatever the net value of children was preindustrialization, it was surely less afterward. What matters for economic decision-making is the marginal change, which in this case was surely negative, thus helping to explain the decline in family size.
10. The decline in infant mortality rates that followed in the nineteenth and early twentieth century reduced the number of births per family as parents no longer needed to have as large a number of pregnancies or births to ensure that an adequate number of children survived until adulthood.
11. See also D'Emilio and Freedman (1988, pp. 47–48), who report on the "small minority" of couples practicing some form of contraception during the late eighteenth century in the United States.
12. The rise of telecommuting in our own time is a phenomenon with important implications for a variety of family issues, but it is much more like the putting out system that characterized the transition to wage labor than it is a system in which the household takes on characteristics of a self-contained firm.
13. It is not surprising that the focus of economics began to shift during the nineteenth century from theories of value and theoretical frameworks that were centered on production and the division of its spoils to ones that put consumption and consumer choice as the driving force of value creation in the market. This shift also brought the household into economics as the unit responsible for consumption decisions.
14. See the data and discussion in Cox and Alm (1999).
15. See Clarke (1873, pp. 13–15): "Neither is there any such thing as inferiority or superiority in this matter. Man is not superior to woman, nor woman to man . . . By this it is not intended to say that the sexes are the same. They are different, widely different from each other . . . The loftiest ideal of humanity . . . demands that each shall be perfect in its kind and not hindered in its best work."
16. It is interesting to note how this pattern reverses what we tend to see in more recent decades, where women withdraw from the labor force to care for small children and then return to the labor force when the children are old enough to be in school full time. The modern pattern can be seen as the effect of the high opportunity cost of children working instead of getting an education and the high opportunity cost of women staying at home alone given the wages now available to them. In the nineteenth century, both opportunity costs were substantially lower and at sufficiently low incomes, even a mother's meager wages would be worth the loss of time with her young children.
17. See chapter 5 for additional discussion of these laws.

18. As sexual violence became more commonly depicted in novels by people like Wilkie Collins and Charles Dickens, media outrage over it grew, which was another reflection of growing intolerance of such violence as the practice became rarer. I thank Sarah Skwire for this point.
19. Mintz (2004, p. 136) again: "While the Industrial Revolution did not invent child labor, it did make child labor more visible by removing child and teenage workers from domestic settings." Such domestic settings included cottage industries, putting out, and the family farm.
20. See Hutt (1954, p. 180): "[T]he advantages of the considerable wages which [factory children] brought to their families was not put into the balance; neither was there any attempt to compare them to the poor of other sections of the community." For the urban well-off, their understanding of life on the farm was very much a romanticized version of children frolicking in the meadows, when the reality was otherwise: "We have seen children perishing from sheer hunger in the mud hovel, or in the ditch by the wayside" (William Cook Taylor 1844, pp. 22–23, quoted in Hutt 1954, p. 180). Hutt continues: "Compared to the factory workers, the agricultural laborers lived in abject poverty, and the work to which country children were put was far more exhausting than factory labor." See also Nardinelli (1990, p. 17). Nardinelli also notes that working for wages gave children some leverage against their employers and parents, due to the ability to take alternative offers, which they did not have working on a family farm or in a cottage industry.
21. It is worth asking why it has come to be the conventional wisdom that the laws ended child labor. It likely reflects our evolutionary and intellectual biases that lead us to think we directly control more of the social world than we really can. It is easier, as well as morally more self-satisfying, to believe that we intentionally made something unpleasant go away by taking a stand against it than that underlying processes we do not control were responsible. In addition, it does seem to be a trend that laws against behavior that we find to be morally reprehensible remnants of an unenlightened past tend to get passed when the practices in question have mostly disappeared, making the few examples still in existence all the more reprehensible. This was certainly true of the heightened focus on child labor as the declining need for children's incomes spread downward through the middle class. Even in our own time, cigarette smoking has been the target of increasingly heavy-handed regulation even though smoking rates have been on an ongoing decline for decades, largely independent of laws limiting or prohibiting the activity. It also is easier to legislate against a practice whose economic necessity or desirability has long passed for most people. Finally, we should not forget the role of organized labor in pushing for the end of child labor due to their fear of the competition that lower-wage child workers posed for union labor. The combination of union self-interest and moral reform that drove the prohibitions on child labor will reappear in the next chapter in the context of protective legislation for women. It is also yet another example of the bootleggers and Baptists phenomenon first articulated by Yandle (1983).
22. See also McCloskey (2006, p. 163): "The displacing of land by human capital as the main source of wealth sharply devalued faith, the past, the dead hand, the mortgage, the family line, the ancestors. And it upvalued hope, the future, the children, the individual."
23. Pember Reeves (1914) is an interesting read in this regard, as she documents very carefully, by looking at family budgets, the ways in which most of the objectionable elements of poor families were because they were, after all, poor.

24. Mintz (2004, Chapter 9) provides a useful overview of the Progressive Era's scientific approach to children. The chapter is nicely titled "Children under the Magnifying Glass." Household manuals, including parenting advice, predate this era, for example, the sixteenth-century Italian ones discussed in Bell (2000). What marked the ones at the turn of the twentieth century was the way in which they grabbed the mantle of modern science.
25. The intended audience was women, as fathers made almost no appearance whatsoever in those manuals. The care and feeding of children was clearly relegated to one sphere.
26. The sentimentalization of childhood continues unabated, as in our own time, we see this same tendency in the various calls to protect children from new dangers that prior generations never worried about, including everything from child-proofing a house to fears of child-snatching strangers, including Internet sexual predators. The real probability of any of these fears coming to pass is actually quite small, and many of the worst fears about Internet sexual predation are largely mythical. See Wolak et al. (2008) for a thorough description of the myth and reality of the issue. On the overly protective nature of modern parenting more generally, see Skenazy (2009), which will be a focus of chapter 8.
27. One example of this shielding is the practice of providing "ladies' menus" at restaurants, on which there were no prices. Men, of course, got the ones with the prices on it. In the twentieth century, this was surely a response to both the realities of married life where the man was more likely to be the income earner and spender and dating practices where men were expected to pay. However, it does predate the twentieth century, and the explanation most often given for its use in the nineteenth was that the world of money and commerce was beneath women's dignity and their meal should not be spoiled by having to even think about it. Interestingly, ladies' menus still exist (now often called "blind menus") particularly at clubs and very expensive restaurants, more often outside the United States, and are sometimes requested by the member of the party planning to pay as a way to say to *his or her* guests (who might be parents or in-laws or other family members) that they need not worry about price when ordering. It becomes a sign of generosity on the part of the person picking up the bill, rather than an attempt to shut women out of the world of commerce. This also explains the name change from "ladies' menus" to "blind menus."
28. One could argue that various forms of socialism were the logical endpoint of this extension as one way of capturing the socialist vision was all of humanity seen as one family with resources allocated much like they might be in a household. The phrase "brotherhood of man" can be taken literally. To return to our foundational motif, this is the extension of the morals of the micro-order into the macro-order, which, as Hayek said, would destroy it.

## 5 Gender and Family in the Twentieth Century

1. Interestingly, this was one of the early cases that read the "privileges or immunities" clause of the Fourteenth Amendment very narrowly as was established more clearly in *Slaughter-House Cases* (1873) in the same year. We shall return to some of these constitutional issues in chapter 9.
2. Lemke (2013) argues that one key to the process in the United States was "jurisdictional competition." Increased mobility for women, thanks both to more resources

and reduced transportation costs, enabled them to vote with their feet by moving to those jurisdictions with laws that treated them better. In turn, to the degree areas wished to attract women, they had an incentive to offer women a better deal under the law.

3. In other cases, men used the power of the state to define professional jobs in ways that excluded competition from lower-cost female-dominated substitute occupations. Ehrenreich and English (1973) explore the way in which the American Medical Association "professionalized" the healing arts by a state-authorized cartel that excluded more traditional forms of healing that were dominated by women.
4. In *Muller v. Oregon* (1908), the Supreme Court upheld Oregon's maximum hours law for women, despite the *Lochner v. New York* (1905) decision three years earlier having struck down limits on bakery employees of any sex, on the grounds that women's "physical structure and performance of the maternal functions place her at a disadvantage" that must be compensated for by legislation. For one of the few classical liberal discussions of protective legislation, see the short piece by Taylor (1991).
5. As we will see later in the chapter, a similar story played out during the Rosie the Riveter era of World War II and then into the 1960s as new waves of women entered the workforce, leading to a pent-up demand for cultural and political change that finally broke through in the late 1960s as the modern feminist movement.
6. A fascinating overview of the relationship between contract law and marriage can be found in Temple (1985).
7. There are numerous ways in which current marriage law does not fit into the contract paradigm, as rightly pointed out by Temple (1985) and Morse (2005). It is also not clear that marriage should take the form of a contract with explicit expectations of both parties. Temple and Morse provide contrasting perspectives on that question.
8. Adding to the problems was the poor state of sexual knowledge by both sexes, especially among medical practitioners. And there was a particular ignorance about the female orgasm. The first mechanical vibrators were invented as a labor-saving device for doctors who used to give manual massages to the pelvic areas of women suffering from what was then called "hysteria" but was more likely severe sexual frustration (Coontz 2005, p. 190). It was clear that the "cure" these massages brought about was an orgasm. She also reports on an older man who early in his marriage thought his wife's orgasm was "some sort of fit." D'Emilio and Freedman (1988, p. 181) note that men of this era entered marriage with much more sexual experience than their wives, with prostitution being largely responsible for that difference.
9. On the history of concerns over child sexuality, including contemporary moral panics, see Egan and Hawkes (2010).
10. One of the other more extreme views in the nineteenth century was the argument that women should not be educated at college in the same ways as men, as the workload and environment was said to lead to the omnipresent "hysteria" as well as infertility (Clarke 1873). This view that women's scholarly work was physically damaging, particularly to their fertility, was a hangover from at least the sixteenth century. It may well have been empirically true that the small number of female college graduates at the time had few or no children, but one hardly need invoke infertility when standard economic explanations involving greater human capital, higher wages, and higher opportunity cost of their time can help explain their lower birth rates.

11. Later in this chapter I will return to this point, which is an important factor in explaining the rise of homosexuality as an identity in the twentieth century.
12. Goldin, Katz, and Kuziemko (2006) also note that the male-female college attendance ratio climbed during the 1930s, as the lack of employment opportunities for men during the Great Depression pushed many into college, and the bars on employment for married women (designed to create more jobs for men) made the investment in human capital less valuable. The ratio continued to climb into the 1950s and 1960s, thanks mostly to the GI Bill and the return of male soldiers. The ratio eventually began to fall with in our own time, women being more likely to attend college than men.
13. Coontz (2005, p. 200) comments that contemporary observers of this new use of the car began to refer to the car as "a house of prostitution on wheels."
14. See also D'Emilio and Freedman's (1988, p. 224) discussion of the work of the English sexologist Havelock Ellis, whose turn-of-the-century work had more of an immediate impact, they argue, than Freud's.
15. One of the interesting aspects of the history of sexuality is the way in which new technologies have often first been devoted to sexual purposes. Movies, the home VCR, and the World Wide Web (especially video over the web) all quickly got used for sexual purposes. At one point in the late 1990s, adult websites were one of the few moneymakers on the web, and the technology they used (e.g., webcams and aspects of social networking) got refined and perfected there before spreading to the population as whole.
16. One need only think of the 1920s flappers and their equivalents in Europe, as well as the early appearance of gay and lesbian communities in urban areas, to see the ways in which gender roles were being challenged.
17. This trend toward seeing marriage as a vehicle for personal fulfillment would expand throughout the century, and we will return to this theme in the discussion of the contemporary role of marriage and family in chapter 7.
18. In the technical language of economics, this increased participation was an increase in the supply of labor as opposed to an increase in the quantity of labor supplied.
19. Skwire (2013) discusses the 1924 novel *The Home-Maker*, in which a man is paralyzed in an accident, necessitating that he and his wife reverse roles. They discover that they are both happier with her working and him taking care of the house. He eventually recovers from his paralysis, but the couple decides to conceal that from everyone else so that they can maintain their unorthodox division of labor without the negative repercussions of violating accepted gender roles of the time.
20. In the developed world we take all of these for granted so it is worth noting how much human labor, usually female, was, and in much of the world still is, necessary to ensure that homes had water, food was kept fresh, light was available in the darkness, and human waste was disposed of. Not having to deal with those tasks certainly makes it easier for women to engage in market production. Hans Rosling's video "The Magic Washing Machine" is an incredibly powerful treatment of the liberating effects of affordable household appliances: http://www.ted.com/talks/hans_rosling_and_the_magic_washing_machine.
21. A good piece of anecdotal evidence can be found in the PBS TV series *1900 House*, in which a family in 1999 agrees to live as a similar family would have in 1900, including giving up all of their modern conveniences. One episode includes a look at how they had to do laundry by hand for a family of five and makes the point made earlier that this could take up to three days, which might mean the younger girls staying home from school to help.

22. This was true even of many women who attended college. The old joke about college women looking for their "Mrs." degree was reasonably accurate for many women of this era. Attending college was indeed a path to upward mobility, not by their own efforts but through the opportunity it afforded to meet then marry the right man. This came back to haunt many women, who later found themselves working in ways they never expected to and lacking the skills necessary to command higher wages. This pattern would change in more recent generations.
23. One of the great ironies of those shows was that the women who were playing the stay-at-home moms (such as Barbara Billingsley in *Leave it to Beaver*) were themselves working moms.
24. Coontz's discussion rightly refers to the "long decade" of the 1950s, by which she means 1947 through the early 1960s.
25. One of the more curious developments in the past couple of years has been the nostalgia for the 1950s economy from many progressives. The ironic part of that development is that the progressives who are nostalgic about the *economy* of the 1950s are often the very same ones who have quite rightly criticized conservative nostalgia about the 1950s *family*. I would suggest that the progressive nostalgia for the 1950s economy is as factually challenged as the conservative nostalgia for the 1950s family. See Lindsey (2009).
26. Women's wartime employment was also seen as a patriotic duty on their part, but very clearly a *temporary* one, with the expectation that they would return home at the close of the war. On this set of issues, see May (1988).
27. In her examination of these issues, Stephanie Coontz (1992) rightly raises all of these points and more in arguing that the twentieth-century suburban family was the product of both unique history and specific policies and not some "natural" or "market" outcome. However, she also goes too far in places, including approvingly quoting the philosopher Alan Wolfe claiming that fixed-rate mortgages were not lent "on market principles" and thereby had the effect of "absolving an entire generation from inflation" (as quoted in Coontz 1992, p. 77). Aside from the fact that the later inflation was the product of a government-run central bank, fixed-rate mortgages were hardly "anti-market" in an era when inflation was nearly nonexistent and when the more common problem in American history, both during the Great Depression and the last decades of the nineteenth century, was deflation. To the extent that fixed-rate mortgages combined with the inflation of the 1970s and 1980s artificially reduced the cost of housing, any blame lies squarely on the shoulders of government, including the Federal Reserve, who has responsibility for control over the money supply, and the Johnson and Nixon administrations for the decision to finance the Vietnam War via inflation and closing the gold window, respectively. Coontz's discussion of the savings and loan crisis in that chapter is equally ignorant of the role played by prior regulations in creating the problems she rightly decries, not to mention lacking any analytic framework, such as public choice economics, for understanding why such problematic interventions might have taken place or why government seems unable to police itself.
28. O'Neill (1985) discusses some of these data. The mismatch between women's expected and actual labor force participation in this period is a contributing factor to the gender wage gap not narrowing more quickly, despite high rates of female employment. Because they did not expect to be employed, many young women did not invest in their human capital in ways that would get them higher-paying jobs later on.

29. Coontz (2005, p. 259) reports that in 1976, more than 75 percent of working women said they would continue working even if money was not an issue.
30. The decision in *Eisenstadt* was based on the view that applying the law only to unmarried women or couples was a violation of the Equal Protection clause of the Fourteenth Amendment. It was another step in the process of erasing a number of important legal distinctions between married and unmarried couples. It is also worth noting that this was a time during which a number of states enacted other changes in the legal status of mature minors that also made the Pill available to more females.
31. Parkman (2000) provides perhaps the best, most accessible overview of these issues.
32. Notice that this is still compatible with a decline in the *number* of marriages if people continue to marry later and more people choose not to marry at all. The point in the text is worded carefully so as to reflect the divorce *rate*.
33. The ability to have children outside of legal marriage was certainly hastened along by legal decisions that treated unmarried couples like married ones and that ended the legal category of "illegitimate" for their children. It was also encouraged by more firms offering employment benefits on equal terms to the unmarried and the married.
34. If we imagine a donated egg, a donated sperm, a surrogate mother, and the couple who will raise the child, we have as many as eight adults (assuming each is married) who have had some role in the creation of the child.
35. D'Emilio's 1993 article "Capitalism and Gay Identity" is rightly recognized as making clear these connections in a powerful and comprehensive way. The argument that follows owes much to that paper. D'Emilio, though, is no great friend of capitalism, as he spends the last section of the paper trying to explain why, despite its role in making gay and lesbian identity possible, gays and lesbians should not be cheering capitalism on. One way of viewing my argument to follow is as a response to D'Emilio's hesitance to go where his argument seems to take him.
36. What "laying claim to the concept of family" means remains highly contested in the gay and lesbian community. For some, it is a matter of gays and lesbians gaining entrance to existing institutions of marriage and family (e.g., Sullivan 1995), but for others (e.g., Lehr 1999) such a strategy would too easily marginalize aspects of existing gay and lesbian family structures and miss an opportunity to challenge the more deeply heteronormative aspects of existing institutions as well as reframe other policies in ways that support a broader range of family forms.
37. For a current overview of state-level adoption laws, see the listing available at the Human Rights Campaign website: http://www.hrc.org/state.asp.
38. See also the discussion in Lehr (1999, Chapter 2).
39. Little symbolizes better the broken link between sex and reproduction than homosexual sex. To the extent that heterosexual marriages and families survive without that link, gays and lesbians understandably ask "why not us too, then?"
40. It is also worth pointing out the Libertarian Party was the first US political party to have a gay rights plank in its platform, as far back as the late 1970s.
41. This argument also suggests that even groups that appear to be families by their structure might nonetheless not be doing the things that families should do, which is what is normally meant by a dysfunctional family. Chapter 7 will have more to say about what exactly the functions of the modern family might be.
42. See Horwitz (2015) for a more detailed treatment.

43. Stack (1974, pp. 28–29) also points out the role that child-swapping played in establishing "mutual trust." This fits nicely with Hayek's observation that the Greek word for exchange also meant "to admit into the community" and "to change from an enemy to a friend." Exchange need not be monetary exchange to establish beneficial interdependencies.
44. This splitting of women into functions is also a feature of Margaret Atwood's (1985) dystopian novel *The Handmaid's Tale*. In the world of Gilead, this division of functions is coercively enforced by the state and makes women's, and children's, lives worse off (although it does benefit men in power and a very small number of powerful women). In The Flats, by contrast, these divisions were chosen by the women in question, even if it was a choice conditioned by the need to survive severe poverty, and thereby better served both women's and children's needs.

## 6 Marriage, Divorce, and the Market Process

*This chapter is a revised and extended version of Horwitz and Lewin (2008). I thank Springer for permission to reuse the material and Peter Lewin for his many contributions, over the course of many years, to the chapter.

1. On the theory of the firm, which is most relevant to the concerns of this chapter, see Langlois (1992), Foss (1997), Lewin and Phelan (1999), Sautet (2000), and Lewin (2008).
2. From this perspective, Coase's (1937) problem of accounting for the existence of the firm disappears. It exists because of the potential to add value by specializing. A firm may be one or more persons. So Coase's other problem, accounting for firm boundaries, remains (see generally Demsetz 1997).
3. It is certainly possible in this taxonomy to conceive of firms existing within households as in family agriculture or cottage industries, but this is less relevant to the modern Western institutional setup. At the end of the chapter, I speculate on the possibility that current and future institutional changes affecting the family may in some ways bring it a little closer to the old agricultural family-firm.
4. I assume the existence of a peaceful social environment and, therefore, exclude crime families from this discussion.
5. Family is a subset of household. The argument to follow refers only to households that function like families, no matter their form. A family takes a longer-term perspective than nonfamily households, and there is an indefiniteness to their life as an institution that is not true of other household forms, such as roommates. This longer-run perspective sets up the possibilities of opportunism, lock-in, and related problems.
6. See US Bureau of the Census, http://www.census.gov/acs/www/Downloads/MedAge_revised_final.ppt and Jacobsen (2007, p. 140).
7. The rise in the median age of marriage represents a recovery from the rather abnormally low ages seen in the two decades following World War II, but the decline in the incidence of marriage and the rise in the incidence of divorce are both significant accelerations of what were more slowly moving long-run trends.
8. This emphasis on the beliefs of the producer as driving behavior is characteristic of the Austrian market process approach and its thoroughgoing subjectivism and is particularly appropriate to the analysis of plan failure. The producer is not assumed to be maximizing some objective function, rather he is simply assumed

to be making what he believes are the best choices given the information he has available.

9. Of course divorce was nearly nonexistent for a variety of reasons, but given that there were enormous gains from the marital partnership, even if they were relatively more due to economies of scale in production and consumption than to specialization per se, the more general nature of the relevant human capital helped limit divorce as well.
10. This taxonomy has been anticipated in the literature in various ways (see, e.g., Chiswick and Lehrer 1990, p. 191). The treatment here is, arguably, more extensive yet only scratches the surface. It is ripe for further elaboration and research.
11. Just how important is parents' (particularly the mother's) time, especially in the early years of life, is a matter of some considerable controversy. For the argument in the text it remains sufficient that there is a widespread *perception* that child care is intrinsically mother-time-intensive. The evidence suggests that the best child care, whether parental or market-purchased, takes place in environments where the child-care provider is spending significant, high-quality time with the child. Moreover, the better the parenting at home, the better the child-care outcomes in other settings will be. Put differently, good parenting and high-quality day care are complements, not substitutes.
12. Historically and cross-culturally, this is not the case. In more male-dominated societies, where the husband/father may be presumed to have some "ownership" rights over other family members, he may as a matter of course gain custody regardless of the circumstances surrounding the divorce (Coontz 2005). See also the interesting discussion in Grossbard-Schechtman and Lemennicier (1999), in which different types of marriages are considered. In this regard this chapter echoes theirs in predicting that particular types of marriage law régimes interact with the economic and demographic environment to affect the gains from marriage and the likelihood of divorce.
13. It is important to distinguish between *legal* custody and *physical* custody. Divorced parents may share legal custody (the right to make decisions about and for the child), but the division of physical custody might be anywhere from mom-only to dad-only to equal. For the purposes of analyzing household behavior, it is physical custody that matters. The assumption herein is that even in cases where the parents have joint legal custody, the children spend significantly more time in the physical custody of the mother.
14. These results are also consistent with the view that the increase in labor force participation raised the probability of divorce by increasing the stress in the marriage. Further investigation is needed to determine which direction of causation is most prominent.
15. See Grossbard-Schechtman and Lemennicier (1999), in which the possibility that children may be used as hostages is discussed.
16. See Jacobsen (2007, pp. 117–19), for an overview of the evidence showing the decline in men's hours worked at different age groups, and Cox and Alm (1999, p. 55), for data about the decline in the average length of the work day, week, year, and lifetime.
17. This arrangement's veneer of equality to cover the reality of an unequal distribution of work by gender recalls the way in which the separate spheres doctrine was used to the same effect in the nineteenth century.
18. See Parkman (2000) for an economist's book-length critical analysis of no-fault.

19. As Grossbard-Schechtman and Lemennicier (1999) point out, the calculation of such net worth is inherently problematic. The husband and wife will most likely have quite different estimates, as such estimates are based on different expectations and costs that are subjective in nature.
20. Such analogies can be pushed much further, for example, in fruitfully considering the relationship between spouses to be closely analogous to the relationship between employer and employee as has been done in the definitive work of Grossbard-Schechtman (see, e.g., Grossbard-Schechtman 1993). Work-in-marriage or spousal labor is a crucial determinant of labor supply more generally and, consistent with this chapter, differential patterns of human capital accumulation.
21. One might view the institution of tenure in academia, especially at smaller schools, in precisely this way. Tenure encourages faculty at smaller schools to make the school-specific investments in human capital that are so necessary for colleges to function efficiently (e.g., committee work, getting to know the profile of the student body, creating relationships with administrators or trustees). It is not without some substance that the hiring of tenure-track faculty is sometimes analogized to a marriage.
22. See the discussion and data here: http://marriage.about.com/cs/covenantmarriage/a/covenant_3.htm.
23. This contrasts with the perspective of Grossbard-Schechtman and Lemennicier (1999), who see causation going in the other direction, namely, that the legal environment, including no-fault divorce statutes, have reduced the gains from marriage. No doubt causation goes in both directions. The apparent unpopularity of optional covenant marriages lends credence to the interpretation in the text, but more work on this is required.
24. Some partial evidence for the idea that marriages may just "run their course" comes from data on the number of divorces among people over 60 in Michigan. In 1980, a total of 943 people between 60 and 95 filed for divorce. In 1990, that number was 2,108 and in 1998 it was 2,180, with the largest increases taking place in the over-70 group. See Edgar (2000). These marriages may indeed represent an exhaustion of the gains from marriage. Most of the people interviewed by Edgar, including those consulting counselors and lawyers, offer explanations consistent with the argument in the text.
25. From an Austrian market process perspective, markets are never really in equilibrium. Individuals always have plans that are inconsistent at some level (see Lewin 1997). Such is the nature of rivalrous competitive activity. The concern here is with an increase in the unpredictability of plans. That is, plans always face a certain degree of uncertainty, but with the increase in the rate of social change, the level of uncertainty has risen, perhaps temporarily.
26. Caplan (2011) can be read as making the consumption good argument, and Bailey (2007) offers some evidence that there is a baby boom among wealthier families.

## 7 The Family in a World of Abundance

1. One of the few flaws in Lindsey's (2007) otherwise wonderful book is that he does not stress enough that he is using "abundance" and "scarcity" in a more colloquial way than used by economists. A reader who knows economics has to make a conscious effort to remember how he is using the words.

2. A closer look at these data also indicates that the gap between the poor's ownership of these consumer goods and the rich's has narrowed as well.
3. See Cox and Alm (1999, Chapter 3) for more on both the additional leisure time available to Americans and the explosion of opportunities for filling it.
4. Unfortunately, as chapter 8 will explore, children are now too often seen as akin to another consumption good for parents, or as a path to their own self-actualization as parents.
5. With longer life expectancies, more families are also caring for elderly parents or grandparents who are unable to fully care for themselves. I will not address this as a separate function, but certainly many of the same issues raised by the family's role in child care apply to elder care, varying by the degree of elder care required.
6. Whether particular *forms* of the family are necessary to do so is a question we will address in a bit more detail later.
7. The discussion that follows draws from Horwitz (2005a).
8. This point explains the universality of "peek-a-boo" as a child's game and its importance in child development: it is the easiest way to show that the parent does not disappear if he or she cannot be seen.
9. The importance for children of playing without adults present will be taken up in chapter 8.
10. Though not a focus of this book, this point suggests that policies such as a flat income tax assessed on individuals and something like a basic income guarantee also allocated to individuals would be the least distorting policies with respect to families that existing governments could choose. McCaffery (1999), though not ultimately supportive of a flat tax, provides a fascinating history of the US income tax and its treatment of secondary earners. That treatment has, in turn, had significant effects on the economics of the household given that women have typically been the secondary earners.
11. In chapter 9, this argument will be used in the context in which it was first developed: as a way to avoid comparing the imperfections of the market (or in this case, the family) with an alternative hypothesized ideal government intervention.
12. The argument here is parallel to the distinction between "statistical significance" and "economic significance," with the latter referring to the question of how much the effect *matters* for the particular economic process in question.

## 8 Why Parenting Matters: The Importance of Play, Risk, and Failure for Classical Liberalism

1. Recall the discussion of this same concern in the Progressive Era's manuals for infant care. In our own time, the attempts to parent scientifically are not just about infants.
2. The psychologist Peter Gray (2013) calls this "directive-protective" parenting.
3. Anecdotally, my own experiences working with first-year students on their writing and speaking provide some evidence of this phenomenon. Many children are so used to being praised for everything they do, and never facing real criticism of their work, that when they get critical feedback on their first few papers, they simply do not know how to deal with it. For many, their only reaction is to take it as a personal attack or insult. Even if they can get by that reaction, figuring out how to learn from their mistakes and avoid them in the future is a major challenge. Part of the problem might be that they see grades and other responses from

teachers as indicators of personal merit, rather than as feedback or input into their learning process. As one might say about markets, the real function of profits/losses and grades/responses is as a feedback device for learning, not a judgment of some underlying personal merit. If children do not get to experience real failure and learn from it, why would we expect them to respond to poor grades as if they had, especially if their parents have pushed the notion that grades are about merit? For more, see Hayek (1960, Chapter 6).

4. And seen from a larger historical perspective, childhood has never been less violent and more safe than it is now: "Now that children are safe from being smothered on the day they are born, starved in foundling homes, poisoned by wet nurses, beaten to death by fathers, . . . worked to death in mines and mills, felled by infectious diseases, and beaten up by bullies, experts have racked their brains for ways to eke out infinitesimal increments of safety from a curve of diminishing or even reversing returns" (Pinker 2011, p. 444).
5. See Pinker (2011, p. 446).
6. I have termed this "Helen Lovejoyism," after the wife of Reverend Lovejoy in *The Simpsons*. Helen Lovejoy was known for popping up with "But what about the children!?" every time some new idea or activity with the slightest bit of risk was proposed.
7. Parents in some areas of the United Kingdom have been banned from supervising their own children at public playgrounds for fear they may be pedophiles and go after other people's children (Clark 2009).
8. I explore this possibility in more detail later in the chapter.
9. That is not to say that parenting is irrelevant. Caplan (2011, pp. 86–87) is very careful to say two things: (1) extreme parenting, such as locking your children in a room, will clearly matter; and (2) parenting does matter in the moment, particularly for how your children think of you later in life. What he *is* saying is that parenting does not matter much at all for how successful, measured in a variety of ways, your children will be, though it might matter more for how happy they are, both as children and as adults.
10. Marano (2008, Chapter 8) devotes an entire chapter to how the ways in which we are raising children affects their behavior in college.
11. I put aside the question of economic failure at the individual or household level because I do think there's a coherent classical liberal case for a minimal state-provided safety net at that level. It is an interesting question whether the argument for state provision is the strongest of the possible classical liberal arguments, but I also think that it is not inconsistent with the classical liberal tradition to think that it is.
12. A poll conducted in the fall of 2011 found that 49 percent of Occupy Wall Street protestors in Zuccotti Park in New York City believed the bank bailouts were "necessary." See Schoen (2011).
13. To be clear, her son had been on the subway before and was comfortable in the city, but had never taken the journey by himself.
14. Recall chapter 7's discussion of the role of attachment in creating a model for adult relationships.
15. The results of this 2014 Reason-Rupe Poll can be found at: http://reason.com/poll/2014/08/19/august-2014-reason-rupe-national-survey.
16. Marano (2008, pp. 88–91) raises some similar arguments. Both Marano and Gray provide references to the primary scholarly literature on the developmental role of play.

17. Play need not be games in the sense of things like baseball or basketball but can take all kinds of different forms including fantasy play, language play, social play, and many others. Any activity that is "mentally removed in some way from 'real' or 'serious' life' and in which those involved create a set of rules for engaging in it and maintain the activity by mutual consent can be seen as a form of play" (Gray 2013, p. 140).
18. Gray also notes that the differing context explains why there are more injuries in structured play than free play. In free play, each player must take account of the skill and size of the other players in order to keep the lesser-skilled and smaller ones interested in playing, so better, larger players will ease off on them. The centrality of consent and the ease of exit force players to moderate their behavior in ways that are unnecessary in structured play. Not only is such moderation unnecessary to maintain consent to play, it will be actively discouraged in the competitive environment that characterizes something like Little League versus free play. Gray argues that in free play the means matter more than the ends.
19. This point might contribute to our understanding of the conflicts around sexual consent that have characterized US college campuses in recent years. If many late adolescents have never acquired the skills that are involved in unstructured play, it makes sense that they would find it difficult to engage in the unstructured play that might characterize much sexual interaction. Without the ability to compromise and empathize, or the experience at negotiating rules and having difficult conversations about conflict, it is not surprising that college students might want an external authority (such as college administrators and their judicial processes) to settle conflicts or insist on an explicit set of rules that describes what is okay and what is not. I am thinking here of the sexual contracts or forms of "affirmative consent" that have become in vogue in recent years.

## 9 Knowledge, Incentives, and Parental Rights: A Framework for Classical Liberal Family Policy

1. One issue I will not be addressing is abortion. Doing justice to it would require too much space, and such a contentious discussion would be a distraction from the core concerns of the chapter.
2. I am going to assume throughout this chapter that there is a state and that its primary, if not only, duty is to protect the rights of its citizens against force and fraud by others. Classical liberals with more anarchist leanings might wish to take up the project of thinking through what the principles I develop later might mean in a stateless society. I will say a few words about this question in the conclusion.
3. Mason (2003) offers an analysis of step-families that suggests ways in which parental rights can be unbundled to allow more than two parents to have legal rights to control aspects of a child's upbringing. Her argument is based on the idea of "*de facto* parenthood," which amounts to noting that we might wish to consider giving adults *rights* to control those aspects of the child's life in which they are already *functioning* as a parent, even if the current legal system does not, or cannot, allow them to have such rights. For example, why should not a step-parent who is providing for a child financially and meeting with school teachers be able to sign permission slips and other school-related documents for the child as their legal parent?
4. I thank my colleague Cathy Crosby-Currie for introducing me to the cases mentioned and to participants at a 2009 Liberty Fund colloquium, especially John

Hasnas, for further discussion. My reading of the constitutional history also draws heavily on Barnett (2004). The interested reader should see Root (2014) also.

5. Gilles (1996) has an extended discussion of the relationships among parental rights, education, and constitutional law.
6. That none of these rights are explicitly enumerated in the Constitution is a point to be discussed later.
7. A comprehensive treatment of the *Lochner* case can be found in Bernstein (2011).
8. I hesitate to say "Social Darwinism" here because the set of views commonly associated with "Social Darwinism" bears little resemblance to what Spencer and people like him actually believed. If anything, the real "Social Darwinists" of the era were the progressives who saw in eugenics a scientific path toward "race health" by eliminating the feeble-minded and members of minority groups. See the discussions in Goldberg (2007, Chapter 7) and Leonard (2005). In one of the rich ironies of political and judicial history, it was the very same Justice Holmes who penned one of the most notorious decisions in Supreme Court history in *Buck v. Bell* (1927), in which the Court upheld a Virginia statute compelling the sterilization of the mentally incompetent on eugenic grounds. That decision included his famous phrase "three generations of imbeciles is enough" as well as "It is better for all the world, if instead of waiting to execute degenerate offspring for crime, or to let them starve for their imbecility, society can prevent those who are manifestly unfit from continuing their kind." Holmes is often known today for his attack on the "Social Darwinist" Spencer, but the evidence is much stronger that he was more deserving of that title.
9. I use the word "perception" here quite intentionally. One of the interesting elements of this case is how dangerous the Court perceived the street to be to a girl of nine. It is also worth noting the gender disparity in the law, which as we noted in chapter 5 was typical of this era. Would a court today categorize what the girl was doing as so dangerous? What if it were in a shopping mall? One of the problems with the implied standard created by *Prince* is that the "best interest of the child" is so historically contingent.
10. One is reminded of the *South Park* episode where the parents discover that parents are the people most likely to harm their children and respond by banishing the children to the woods to fend for themselves in the name of protecting them from danger.
11. Root (2014) offers a reading of this history in light of the question of judicial activism versus judicial restraint, and the emergence of more recent calls for principled judicial activism by those who think the Constitution should protect the all of the unenumerated rights recognized in pre–New Deal era jurisprudence, and perhaps more.
12. Gilles (1996, pp. 1011–12) argues that the use of the First Amendment in *Yoder* makes for a better defense of parental rights than the Fourteenth as it relies on enumerated rights, either of the free exercise of religion or, as he would prefer, free speech.
13. See also Root (2014, p. 92).
14. One concern it would not address is the belief among some libertarians that the Bill of Rights should not have been incorporated by the Fourteenth Amendment so as to apply to the states. For those libertarians, the Ninth Amendment approach still centralizes the definition of the relevant rights, rather than relying on a system of "competitive federalism" in which individual states offer alternative protections for rights, allowing for a discovery process of which rights regime people prefer. Although I do not have the room to develop the argument here, I am comfortable

with the Bill of Rights applying to the states, even though I recognize the danger of centralizing judicial determinations of rights in that way.

15. Rothbard adds that the *legal* question of what parents can or cannot do is distinct from the issue of whether parents have a *moral obligation* to care for their children. In Rothbard's political framework, these are separate questions. Questions that he sees as matters of personal morality are not matters of legal enforcement.
16. It is tempting to make a Lockean argument about stewardship rights in children arising from "mixing one's labor" with the child. Aside from the awful pun involved, this might be an interesting direction to explore in the question of how parental rights and their according responsibilities are acquired. On this point, compare Narveson (2002, p. 267):

    In the standard case where the child does have parents and those parents intentionally brought the child into existence, the overwhelming argument for recognizing those parents as having right to the direction and overseeing of those children is the same as the argument for recognizing any producer of a good as the owner of that good: it exists because that person exerted himself to bring the thing into being, and did it for reasons which will be frustrated if it is taken from him.
17. The approach outlined here is consistent with Kuznicki's (2011) defense of the common-law doctrine of the "presumption of legitimacy." He argues: "This doctrine dictates that all children born into a marriage are presumed legitimate, and that the married couple is presumed, though rebuttably, to be the child's parents, with all the attendant parental duties."
18. It is also interesting that many religions have "coming of age" ceremonies where the community recognizes young people as now being responsible for themselves. As part of a traditional Jewish bar or bat mitzvah ceremony, the parents publicly thank God that they no longer have to care for the child.
19. At the risk of being accused of a form of *ad hominem* argument, I cannot help but wonder whether Rothbard's willingness to accept the remorseless logic of his position and not hold parents legally responsible for neglect is related to the fact that he never had children. There are many political arguments that I gladly accept even though they might make me worse off as an individual, but as a parent, I have no doubt that my acting to take stewardship of my children also imposes on me a set of obligations to care for them that should be legally enforceable because I have taken said steps to accept them. There are certainly parents who find Rothbard's argument persuasive, but I am not one of them. Experiencing the helplessness of one's child and watching the developmental process simply makes it impossible to deny both the responsibility that parenthood involves and the ways in which I, as a parent, have accepted that responsibility.
20. Bell's graduated consent framework also includes hypothetical consent and hypothetical unconsent. It would be worth exploring whether these might justify a stronger notion of children's rights. Austin (2007, pp. 67–70) uses a hypothetical consent framework to make the case for strong parental rights on the grounds that the adults that children become would consent to paternalistic treatment and "retroactively legitimize" that paternalism.
21. I leave aside for now the question of where the line is that separates "physical abuse" from mild forms of corporal punishment as this would take us too far afield. I will only note that if one agrees that parental actions that "significantly and intentionally retard" their children's ability to function as an adult later in life are wrong, it is easier to accept very mild forms of corporal punishment that have no lasting

effects and distinguish them from true abuse that leaves permanent scars, whether physical or emotional, that compromise adult functioning.

22. Gilles (1996) applies this type of argument in the context of education.
23. The following draws heavily on Horwitz (2005a).
24. Narveson (2002) recognizes the incentives (or motivation) point but does not include the role of parental knowledge in very explicit ways, other than through his general commitment to pluralism.
25. With respect to their children, parents are the closest analogy to a residual claimant, in that they bear more of the costs and receive more of the benefits of their parenting behavior than anyone other than the child.
26. For a nice overview of all of these issues, see Lopez and Leighton (2012).
27. I have made a very similar argument about private and public responses to natural disasters such as Hurricane Katrina (Horwitz 2009).
28. Compare to this point to Hayek's (1978a, p. 185) famous description of how we should judge market outcomes:

    > Yet we do injustice to the achievement of the market if we judge it, as it were, from above, by comparing it with an ideal standard which we have no way of achieving. If we judge it, as we ought to, from below, that is, if the comparison in this case is made against what we could achieve by any other method—especially against what would be produced if competition were prevented[.]

29. I ignore the most nonsensical and destructive age-related law of all, namely, the 21-year-old drinking age.
30. Elsewhere in Rothbard's (1998) chapter on children and rights, he offers several excellent responses to the judicial and legislative overreach frequently associated with so-called child-savers and the best interest of the child standard. Judicial definitions of neglect are often too low, leading to the violation of parental rights and even greater damage to children who are taken from homes and placed in the state's care. More careful consideration of the comparative institutions perspective and a greater respect for some set of due process rights for children would help swing the balance back to a more appropriate place.
31. A case where parents simply refused modern medicine and did nothing instead might more easily be seen as neglect in an actionable sense, particularly if cost is not an issue.
32. We are already seeing something like this in some divorce cases where one spouse objects to the religious upbringing the other spouse is providing, or perhaps is upset at the other spouse's sexual orientation or behavior. It is an interesting question what power courts should have, if any, in restricting parental behavior in such cases. See Volokh (2006).
33. It might be tempting to use some conception of "hypothetical consent" (see note 20) here to argue that the child would consent to standard medical treatment if he or she could. The dangers of hypothetical consent arguments and the potential slippery slope they create raise serious concerns about giving in to that temptation.
34. See Hayek (1973, Chapter 3) on "Principles vs. Expediency" for more on this point.

## 10 Classical Liberalism and the Contemporary Evolution of Marriage

1. As a result, this chapter will be a broad overview of a number of the important issues at the heart of the same-sex marriage issue, many of which are evolving as

I write. If this were a book exclusively on that issue, a complete treatment would require more depth. My goal in this chapter is to fit the same-sex marriage issue into the analytical framework of the book and of classical liberalism more generally, so I have tried to address a number of aspects of the debate and may not have given them the full treatment that they would get in a book primarily devoted to same-sex marriage.

2. For more on the history of judicial restraint and judicial activism, and how that debate is playing out in contemporary constitutional debates on the political right, see Root (2014).
3. Gerstmann (2004, p. 79) suggests that this was due to the objections of Roosevelt appointee Hugo Black who Warren accommodated by deemphasizing those arguments.
4. The arguments made in chapter 9 about the superiority of a Ninth Amendment approach apply here as well, but are unlikely to make any headway given the history of the right to marry and the equal protection issues at stake.
5. That the logic of the *Lawrence* decision leads in the direction of overturning such bans was recognized clearly, if unhappily, in Justice Scalia's dissent (*Lawrence v. Texas* [2003, pp. 604–605, internal citations omitted]):

   > At the end of its opinion—after having laid waste the foundations of our rational-basis jurisprudence—the Court says that the present case "does not involve whether the government must give formal recognition to any relationship that homosexual persons seek to enter." Do not believe it. More illuminating than this bald, unreasoned disclaimer is the progression of thought displayed by an earlier passage in the Court's opinion, which notes the constitutional protections afforded to "personal decisions relating to *marriage*, procreation, contraception, family relationships, child rearing, and education," and then declares that "[p]ersons in a homosexual relationship may seek autonomy for these purposes, just as heterosexual persons do" (emphasis added). Today's opinion dismantles the structure of constitutional law that has permitted a distinction to be made between heterosexual and homosexual unions, insofar as formal recognition in marriage is concerned. If moral disapprobation of homosexual conduct is "no legitimate state interest" for purposes of proscribing that conduct; and if, as the Court coos (casting aside all pretense of neutrality), "[w]hen sexuality finds overt expression in intimate conduct with another person, the conduct can be but one element in a personal bond that is more enduring"; what justification could there possibly be for denying the benefits of marriage to homosexual couples exercising" [t]he liberty protected by the Constitution"? Surely not the encouragement of procreation, since the sterile and the elderly are allowed to marry.

6. Interested readers should also see Dale (2013) for a different way of making the classical liberal case for equal marriage. Her argument should be read as complementary to the one made here.
7. A representative example of the complexities involved is this story of an Indianapolis bakery that refused service to a gay couple, then faced a great deal of criticism in the media and online, as well as supporters who drove out of their way to buy pastries there as a show of support. The bakery eventually closed, though the owners claimed it was still profitable. The multiple aspects of this case illustrate many of the relevant issues. http://www.indystar.com/story/life/2015/02/27/bakery-refused-cake-gay-couple-closes-doors/24074691/.
8. Of course another solution to this problem is to simply abolish the relevant anti-discrimination laws and allow all private sector actors the freedom of association

and disassociation to serve or not serve whomever they wish. Doing so is consistent with libertarianism, in both its respect for private property and the freedom of association and the recognition that governments still must treat all citizens equally. However, given the weight of the US experience with slavery, that outcome is unlikely any time in the near future, so the real question at the moment is whether a case can be made for exempting religious liberty claims from antidiscrimination laws in the context of same-sex marriage.

9. It remains something of a mystery why those couples denied service have chosen to sue, rather than simply find another provider, as there are many who would happily take the business. As I will note, in a world of modern communications, as much damage can be done to the business through word of mouth as opposed to the law, and much more cheaply.
10. On the polling data, see the May 2014 Gallup poll showing overall support for the legalization of same-sex marriage at 55 percent with 78 percent of respondents between 18 and 29 years old supporting legalization. The results are available at: http://www.gallup.com/poll/169640/sex-marriage-support-reaches-new-high.aspx.
11. Unlike many of the recent changes to marriage that can be seen as providing a liberalization of the institution by offering more options to those who *are* married, same-sex marriage simply expands the eligibility of who can avail themselves of the institution (Eskridge and Spedale 2006, pp. 187–88).
12. The analogy is to immigration. It might be true that brand new immigrants are at the bottom of the US income ladder, but that does not mean they are somehow "worse off." Even the bottom of the US income ladder is an improvement over where most were in their home countries, so this represents improvement if we recognize the appropriate comparison.
13. I leave aside the objections that same-sex marriage will lead to people marrying their pets or similarly ridiculous concerns, as the argument has always been about elements such as the race, and now gender and possibly number, of *consenting adult human beings*. The constitutional and policy questions are "which consenting adults?" and "how many consenting adults?"
14. This is the same basic argument classical liberals might make about *Lawrence v. Texas* (2003) with respect to acts of sodomy.
15. See the discussion in Hall (2014, pp. 91–94).
16. See Boettke (2001, p. 257): "There is simply no way to establish binding rules except through the translation of customary practices into rules of social interaction . . . Constructed, large-scale, attempts at social change which are not rooted in the *de facto* norms of existence of the current order are destined to disrupt social order and retard—rather than promote—social betterment."
17. Several recent TV shows have focused on plural marriage, including HBO's *Big Love*. Showtime's *Polyamory* qualifies in this regard as well. One might also note the increased cultural attention paid to transgendered individuals in both the media and more of the lives of ordinary Americans. Legal changes with respect to this issue might be nearer on the horizon than plural marriage.
18. Jones (2006, pp. 118–19) recognizes this somewhat by arguing that governments could recognize "a range of marital corporations for different purposes." But here too, he seems naïve about the ability of governments to solve these problems without rekindling the same culture wars we see over state provision of marriage licenses.

19. Jones (2006), despite its flaws, offers one attempt at doing so. Kuznicki (2011) is another such attempt coming from a very different perspective. He outlines a conception of civil marriage that enables us to distinguish those aspects of marriage that are negative rights against state interference and those that are welfare rights to specific benefits.
20. See, for example, "Garrett Morgan Patents Three-Position Traffic Signal," at http://www.history.com/this-day-in-history/garrett-morgan-patents-three-position-traffic-signal.
21. This bears a similarity to the Jewish concept of *tikkun olam*, often translated as "repairing the world," and used today as an exhortation to work for social justice. The Mishnah indicates that one source of this concept was the need to make laws consistent so that people could understand correctly whether they have broken the law, or what the legal status of something like a divorce might be. It is explicitly connected with the idea of avoiding social disharmony. One can read Hayek's view of the need to abandon counterproductive traditions as something very similar. See Sacks (1997).

# References


Abelove, Henry. 1989. "Some Speculations on the History of Sexual Intercourse during the Long Eighteenth Century in England," *Genders 6* (Fall): 125–30.

Allen, Douglas. 1998. "No-Fault Divorce in Canada: Its Cause and Effect," *Journal of Economic Behavior and Organizations 37*: 129–49.

Amato, Paul R., Laura Spencer Loomis, and Alan Booth. 1995. "Parental Divorce, Parental Marital Conflict, and Offspring Well-Being during Early Adulthood," *Social Forces 73*: 895–915.

Atwood, Margaret. 1985. *The Handmaid's Tale*, New York: Fawcett Crest.

Austin, Michael W. 2007. *Conceptions of Parenthood: Ethics and the Family*, Aldershot, UK: Ashgate.

Bailey, Ronald. 2007. "Kids as Status Symbols and 'Competitive Birthing,'" *Hit and Run*, August 6, available at: http://reason.com/blog/2007/08/06/kids-as-status-symbols-and-com.

Barnett, Randy. 2004. *Restoring the Lost Constitution: The Presumption of Liberty*, Princeton, NJ: Princeton University Press.

Becker, Gary. 1971. *The Economics of Discrimination*, second edition, Chicago, IL: University of Chicago Press.

———. 1981. *A Treatise on the Family*, Cambridge: Harvard University Press.

Beito, David T. 2000. *From Mutual Aid to the Welfare State*, Chapel Hill: University of North Carolina Press.

Beito, David T., Peter Gordon, and Alex Tabarrok, eds. 2002. *The Voluntary City: Choice, Community, and Civil Society*, Ann Arbor: University of Michigan Press.

Bell, Rudolph M. 2000. *How to Do It: Guides to Good Living for Renaissance Italians*, Chicago, IL: University of Chicago Press.

Bell, Tom W. 2010. "Graduated Consent in Contract and Tort Law: Toward a Theory of Justification," *Case Western Reserve Law Review 61*: 17–84.

Benson, Bruce. 1990. *The Enterprise of Law*, San Francisco, CA: Pacific Research Institute for Public Policy.

Bergstrom, T. C. 1996. "Economics in a Family Way," *Journal of Economic Literature 34*: 1903–34.

Bernstein, David. 2011. *Rehabilitating Lochner: Defending Individual Rights against Progressive Reform*, Chicago, IL: University of Chicago Press.

Bjorklund, David F., and Anthony D. Pellegrini. 2000. "Child Development and Evolutionary Psychology," *Child Development 71*: 1687–708

Boaz, David. 1997. "Privatize Marriage: A Simple Solution to the Gay-Marriage Debate," *Slate*, April 25, available at: http://www.slate.com/articles/briefing/articles/1997/04/privatize_marriage.html.

Boettke, Peter J. 1995. "Why Are There No Austrian Socialists? Ideology, Science, and the Austrian School," *Journal of the History of Economic Thought 17*: 35–56.

———. 2001. "Why Culture Matters: Economics, Politics, and the Imprint of History," in *Calculation and Coordination: Essays on Socialism and Transitional Political Economy*, New York: Routledge: 248–65.

———. 2009. "Why Those Who Value Liberty Should Rejoice: Elinor Ostrom's Nobel Prize," *Foundation for Economic Education*, November 18, available at: http://fee.org/freeman/detail/why-those-who-value-liberty-should-rejoice-elinor-ostroms-nobel-prize.

Boettke, Peter, and Peter Leeson. 2004. "Liberalism, Socialism, and Robust Political Economy," *Journal of Markets & Morality 7*: 99–111.

Boudreaux, Donald J. 2006. "Working for Sears Goods," *Café Hayek*, January 30, available at: http://cafehayek.typepad.com/hayek/2006/01/working_for_sea.html.

Bowlby, John. 1973. "Affectional Bonds: Their Nature and Origin," in Robert Weiss, ed., *Loneliness: The Experience of Emotional and Social Isolation*, Cambridge, MA: MIT Press.

Bryson, Bill. 2010. *At Home: A Short History of Private Life*, New York: Anchor Books.

Buchanan, James M., and Gordon Tullock. 1962. *The Calculus of Consent*, Ann Arbor, MI: University of Michigan Press.

Buss, David M., ed. 2005. *Handbook of Evolutionary Psychology*, Hoboken, NJ: Wiley.

Caldwell, Bruce. 2004. *Hayek's Challenge: An Intellectual Biography of F. A. Hayek*, Chicago, IL: University of Chicago Press.

Caplan, Bryan. 2011. *Selfish Reasons to Have More Kids: Why Being a Great Parent Is Less Work and More Fun than You Think*, New York: Basic Books.

Chiswick, Carmel U., and Evelyn Lehrer. 1990. "On Marriage-Specific Capital: Its Role as a Determinant of Remarriage," *Journal of Population Economics 3*: 193–213.

Chua, Amy. 2011. *Battle Hymn of the the Tiger Mother*, New York: Penguin.

Clark, Laura. 2009. "Parents Banned from Watching Their Children in Playgrounds . . . in Case They are Paedophiles," *Daily Mail* (UK), October 28, available at: http://www.dailymail.co.uk/news/article-1223528/Parents-banned-supervising-children-playgrounds--case-paedophiles.html.

Clarke, Edward H. 1873. *Sex in Education: A Fair Chance for Girls*, Boston: Houghton, Mifflin and Company.

Coase, R. H. 1937. "The Nature of the Firm," *Economica 4*, November: 386–405.

———. 1960. "The Problem of Social Cost," *Journal of Law and Economics 3*, October: 1–44.

Cohen, Lloyd. 1987. "Marriage, Divorce, and Quasi-Rents; or, 'I Gave Him the Best Years of My Life,'" *Journal of Legal Studies 16*: 267–303.

Coontz, Stephanie. 1992. *The Way We Never Were*, New York: Basic Books.

———. 2005. *Marriage, a History: From Obedience to Intimacy or How Love Conquered Marriage*, New York: Viking.

Cox, W. Michael, and Richard Alm. 1999. *Myths of Rich and Poor: Why We're Better Off Than We Think*, New York: Basic Books.

Csikszentmihalyi, Mihaly. 1990. *Flow: The Psychology of Optimal Experience*, New York: Harper and Row.

Dale, Helen. 2013. "The Laws Are Made for People: An Argument for Equal Marriage," *Reason Foundation*, available at: http://reason.org/files/an_argument_for_equal_marriage.pdf.

D'Emilio, John. 1993. "Capitalism and Gay Identity," in Henry Abelove, Michele Aina Barale, and David Halperin, eds., *The Lesbian and Gay Studies Reader*, New York: Routledge.

D'Emilio, John, and Estelle Freedman. 1988. *Intimate Matters: A History of Sexuality in America*, New York: Harper and Row.

Demsetz, Harold. 1969. "Information and Efficiency: Another Viewpoint," *Journal of Law and Economics 12*, April: 1–22.

———. 1997. *The Economics of the Business Firm: Seven Critical Commentaries*, Cambridge: Cambridge University Press.

Donadio, Rachel. 2008. "It's Not You, It's Your Books," *New York Times*, March 30, available at: http://www.nytimes.com/2008/03/30/books/review/Donadio-t.html.

Ebeling, Richard. 1987. "Cooperation in Anonymity," *Critical Review 1*(4): 50–61.

Edgar, J. 2000. "Marriage Plunge Getting Colder," *Detroit Free Press*, May 31.

Egan, R. Danielle, and Gail Hawkes. 2010. *Theorizing the Sexual Child in Modernity*, New York: Palgrave Macmillan.

Ellickson, Robert C. 1991. *Order without Law: How Neighbors Settle Disputes*, Cambridge: Harvard University Press.

Eskridge Jr., William N., and Darren R. Spedale. 2006. *Gay Marriage: For Better or For Worse?* New York: Oxford University Press.

Flandrin, Jean-Louis. 1979. *The Family in Former Times*, Cambridge: Cambridge University Press.

Foss, Nicolai. 1997. "Austrian Insights and the Theory of the Firm," *Advances in Austrian Economics 4*: 175–98.

Friedman, Thomas. 2006. *The World Is Flat*, expanded and updated edition, New York: Farrar, Straus, and Giroux.

Fuller, Lon. 1969. *The Morality of Law*, New Haven, CT: Yale University Press.

Geary, David C., and Mark V. Flinn. 2001. "Evolution of Human Parental Behavior and the Human Family," *Parenting: Science and Practice 1*: 5–61.

Gerstmann, Evan. 2004. *Same-Sex Marriage and the Constitution*, Cambridge: Cambridge University Press.

Gilles, Stephen G. 1996. "On Educating Children: A Parentalist Manifesto," *University of Chicago Law Review 63*: 937–1034.

Goldberg, Jonah. 2007. *Liberal Fascism: The Secret History of the American Left, from Mussolini to the Politics of Meaning*, New York: Doubleday.

Goldin, Claudia. 1991. *Understanding the Gender Gap: An Economic History of American Women*, Oxford: Oxford University Press.

———. 2006. "The Quiet Revolution That Transformed Women's Employment, Education, and Family," *American Economic Review Papers and Proceedings 96*(2): 1–21.

Goldin, Claudia, Lawrence F. Katz, and Ilyana Kuziemko. 2006. "The Homecoming of American College Women: The Reversal of the College Gender Gap," *Journal of Economic Perspectives 20*(4), Fall: 133–56.

Goody, Jack. 1983. *The Development of the Family and Marriage in Europe*, Cambridge: Cambridge University Press.

Gottschall, Jonathan. 2012. *The Storytelling Animal: How Stories Make Us Human*, New York: Houghton Mifflin Harcourt.

Gray, Peter. 2013. *Free to Learn: Why Unleashing the Instinct to Play Will Make Our Children Happier, More Self-Reliant, and Better Students for Life*, New York: Basic Books.

Grossbard-Schechtman, Shoshana. 1993. *On the Economics of Marriage: A Theory of Marriage, Labor, and Divorce*, Boulder, CO: Westview Press.

Grossbard-Schechtman, Shoshana, and Bertrand Lemennicier. 1999. "Marriage Contracts and the Law-and-Economics of Marriage: An Austrian Perspective," *Journal of Socio-Economics 28*: 665–90.

Hadfield, Gillian. 1999. "A Coordination Model of the Sexual Division of Labor," *Journal of Economic Behavior and Organization 40*: 125–53.

Hall, Lauren K. 2014. *Family and the Politics of Moderation*, Waco, TX: Baylor University Press.

Hartup, Willard W. 1989. "Social Relationships and Their Developmental Significance," *American Psychologist 44*(2): 120–26.

Hayek, F. A. 1937. "Economics and Knowledge," in *Individualism and Economic Order*, Chicago, IL: University of Chicago Press, 1948: 33–56.

———. 1945. "The Use of Knowledge in Society," in *Individualism and Economic Order*, Chicago, IL: University of Chicago Press, 1948: 77–91.

———. 1952. *The Sensory Order*, Chicago, IL: University of Chicago Press.

———. 1960. *The Constitution of Liberty*, Chicago, IL: University of Chicago Press.

———. 1967. *Studies in Politics, Philosophy, and Economics*, Chicago, IL: University of Chicago Press.

———. 1973. *Law, Legislation, and Liberty*, vol. 1, Chicago, IL: University of Chicago Press.

———. 1977. *Law, Legislation, and Liberty*, vol. 2, Chicago, IL: University of Chicago Press.

———. 1978a. "Competition as a Discovery Procedure," in *New Studies in Politics, Philosophy, Economics and the History of Ideas*, Chicago, IL: University of Chicago Press: 179–90.

———. 1978b. "The Errors of Constructivism," in *New Studies in Philosophy, Politics, Economics and the History of Ideas*, Chicago, IL: University of Chicago Press: 3–22.

———. 1989. *The Fatal Conceit: The Errors of Socialism*, W. W. Bartley III, ed., Chicago, IL: University of Chicago Press.

Hochschild, Arlie Russell. 1989. *The Second Shift*, New York: Avon.

Hodgson, Geoffrey. 1999. *Economics and Utopia*, New York: Routledge.

Horwitz, Steven. 2000. "From the Sensory Order to the Liberal Order: Hayek's Non-rationalist Liberalism," *Review of Austrian Economics 13*: 23–40.

———. 2001. "From Smith to Menger to Hayek: Liberalism in the Spontaneous Order Tradition," *The Independent Review 6*: 81–97.

———. 2005a. "The Functions of the Family in the Great Society," *Cambridge Journal of Economics 29*: 669–84.

———. 2005b. "Two Worlds at Once: Rand, Hayek, and the Ethics of the Micro and Macro-cosmos," *Journal of Ayn Rand Studies 6*: 375–403.

———. 2008a. "Is the Family a Spontaneous Order?" *Studies in Emergent Order 1*: 163–85, available at: http://docs.sieo.org/SIEO_1_2008_Horwitz.pdf.

———. 2008b. "Analogous Models of Complexity: The Austrian Theory of Capital and Hayek's Theory of Cognition as Adaptive Classifying Systems," in Roger Koppl, ed., *Explorations in Austrian Economics*, volume 11 of *Advances in Austrian Economics*, Bingley, UK: Emerald: 143–66.

———. 2008c. "Monetary Calculation and the Extension of Social Cooperation into Anonymity," *Journal of Private Enterprise 23*(2), Spring: 81–93.

———. 2009. "Wal-Mart to the Rescue: Private Enterprise's Response to Hurricane Katrina," *The Independent Review 13*: 511–28.

———. 2015. "Reciprocity, Calculation, and Non-Market Exchange," in Robert F. Garnett Jr., Paul Lewis, and Lenore T. Ealy, eds., *Commerce and Community: Ecologies of Social Cooperation*, New York: Routledge: 281–302.

Horwitz, Steven, and Peter Lewin. 2008. "Heterogeneous Human Capital, Uncertainty, and the Structure of Plans: A Market Process Approach to Marriage and Divorce," *Review of Austrian Economics 21*: 1–21.

Hutt, W. H. 1954. "The Factory System of the Early Nineteenth Century," in F. A. Hayek, ed., *Capitalism and the Historians*, Chicago, IL: University of Chicago Press: 160–88.

Jacobsen, Joyce P. 2007. *The Economics of Gender*, third edition, New York: Blackwell.

Jefferson, Thomas. 1801. "First Inaugural Address," available at: http://avalon.law.yale.edu/19th_century/jefinau1.asp.

Johnson, William R., and Jonathan Skinner. 1986. "Labor Supply and Marital Separation," *American Economic Review 76*: 455–69.

Jones, Colin P. A. 2006. "A Marriage Proposal: Privatize It," *The Independent Review 11*: 115–19.

Kahneman, Daniel. 2011. *Thinking, Fast and Slow*, New York: Farrar, Straus and Giroux.

Kirzner, Israel M. 1973. *Competition and Entrepreneurship*, Chicago, IL: University of Chicago Press.

Kuznicki, Jason. 2011. "Marriage against the State: Toward a New View of Civil Marriage," *Policy Analysis 671*, Washington, DC: Cato Institute, available at: http://www.cato.org/sites/cato.org/files/pubs/pdf/PA671.pdf.

Lachmann, Ludwig M. 1971. *The Legacy of Max Weber*, Berkeley, CA: The Glendessary Press.

———. 1978 [1956]. *Capital and Its Structure*, Kansas City, MO: Sheed Andrews and McMeel.

Landes, David. 1998. *The Wealth and Poverty of Nations*, New York: Norton.

Langlois, Richard N. 1986. "Coherence and Flexibility: Social Institutions in a World of Radical Uncertainty," in Israel M. Kirzner, ed., *Subjectivism, Intelligibility, and Economic Understanding*, New York: New York University Press: 171–91.

———. 1992. "Transaction-Cost Economics in Real Time," *Industrial and Corporate Change 1*: 99–127.

Lea, Geoffrey. 2007. "A Tale of Two Worlds: The Rules of Personal and Impersonal Exchange," August 6, Library of Economics and Liberty, available at: http://www.econlib.org/library/Columns/y2007/Leatale.html.

Leeson, Peter. 2005. "Social Cooperation and the Apparent Tension between Personal and Impersonal Exchange," *Ama-Gi 7*(1): 1–18.

Lehr, Valerie. 1999. *Queer Family Values: Debunking the Myth of the Nuclear Family*, Philadelphia, PA: Temple University Press.

Lemke, Jayme. 2013. "Jurisdictional Competition and Married Women's Property Rights," working paper available at: http://www.jaymelemke.com/uploads/8/5/1/8/8518983/jurisdictional_competition_and_mwp_rights_12.12.11.pdf.

Leonard, Thomas C. 2005 "Mistaking Eugenics for Social Darwinism: Why Eugenics Is Missing from the History of American Economics," *History of Political Economy 37*, supplement: 200–33.

Levy, David M. 2001. *How the Dismal Science Got Its Name*, Ann Arbor: University of Michigan Press.

Lewin, Peter. 1997. "Hayekian Equilibrium and Change," *Journal of Economic Methodology 4*: 245–66.

———. 1999. *Capital in Disequilibrium*, New York: Routledge.

———. 2008. "The Firm in Disequilibrium: Contributions from the Austrian Tradition," *Explorations in Austrian Economics*, Roger Koppl, ed., volume 11 of *Advances in Austrian Economics*, Bingley, UK: Emerald: 167–92.

Lewin, Peter, and Steven Phelan. 1999. "Firms, Strategies, and Resources: Contributions from Austrian Economics," *Quarterly Journal of Austrian Economics 2*(2): 3–18.

Lindsey, Brink. 2007. *The Age of Abudance*, New York: Collins.

———. 2009. *Paul Krugman's Nostalgianomics: Economic Policies, Social Norms, and Income Inequality*, Washington, DC: Cato Institute.

Lopez, Edward, and Wayne Leighton. 2012. *Madmen, Intellectuals, and Academic Scribblers: The Economic Engine of Political Change*, Stanford, CA: Stanford Economics and Finance.

Lundberg, Shelly, and Robert A. Pollak. 1993. "Separate Spheres Bargaining and the Marriage Market," *Journal of Political Economy 101*: 988–1010.

MacLeod, David I. 1998. *The Age of the Child: Children in America 1890–1920*, New York: Twayne.

Maine, Henry S. 1861. *Ancient Law*, London: John Murray.

Marano, Hara Estroff. 2008. *A Nation of Wimps: The High Cost of Invasive Parenting*, New York: Broadway Books.

Marx, Karl. 1906 [1871]. *Capital v. 1*, New York: Random House Modern Library.

Maslow, Abraham. 1943. "A Theory of Human Motivation," *Psychological Review 50*: 370–96.

Mason, Mary Ann. 1994. *From Father's Property to Children's Rights: The History of Child Custody in the United States*, New York: Columbia University Press.

———. 2003. "The Modern American Stepfamily: Problems and Possibilities," in Mary Ann Mason, Arlene Skolnick, and Stephen D. Sugarman, eds., *All Our Families: New Policies for a New Century*, second edition, New York: Oxford University Press: 95–116.

May, Elaine Tyler. 1988. *Homeward Bound: American Families in the Cold War Era*, New York: Basic Books.

McCaffery, Edward. 1999. *Taxing Women: How the Marriage Penalty Affects Your Taxes*, Chicago, IL: University of Chicago Press.

McCloskey, Deirdre N. 2006. *The Bourgeois Virtues: Ethics for an Age of Commerce*, Chicago, IL: University of Chicago Press.

———. 2010. *Bourgeois Dignity: Why Economics Can't Explain the Modern World*, Chicago, IL: University of Chicago Press.

McElroy, Wendy. 2012. "The Grayness of Children's Rights," *Daily Anarchist*, September 11, available at: http://dailyanarchist.com/2012/09/11/the-grayness-of-childrens-rights/.

McKenzie, Richard, and Gordon Tullock. 1975. *The New World of Economics*, Homewood, IL: Richard Irwin.

Menger, Carl. 1985 [1883]. *Investigations into the Method of the Social Sciences with Special Reference to Economics*, New York: New York University Press.

Mill, John Stuart. 1985 [1859]. *On Liberty*, New York: Penguin Books.

Mintz, Steven. 2004. *Huck's Raft: A History of American Childhood*, Cambridge, MA: Harvard University Press.

Mises, Ludwig von. 1966 [1949]. *Human Action: A Treatise on Economics*, Chicago, IL: Henry Regnery.

———. 1981 [1922]. *Socialism: An Economic and Sociological Analysis*, Indianapolis, IN: Liberty Press.

Mokyr, Joel. 1992. *The Lever of Riches*, Oxford: Oxford University Press.

Morse, Jennifer Roback. 2001. *Love & Economics: Why the Laissez-Faire Family Doesn't Work*, Dallas, TX: Spence.

———. 2005. "Marriage and the Limits of Contract," *Policy Review*, April/May, available at: http://www.hoover.org/research/marriage-and-limits-contract.

Moynihan, Daniel P. 1965. *The Negro Family: The Case for National Action*, US Department of Labor, Office of Policy Planning and Research, available at: http://www.dol.gov/dol/aboutdol/history/webid-meynihan.htm.

Nardinelli, Clark. 1990. *Child Labor in the Industrial Revolution*, Bloomington: Indiana University Press.

Narveson, Jan. 1999. *Moral Matters*, second edition, Peterborough, Canada: Broadview Press.

———. 2002. *Respecting Persons in Theory and Practice*, Lanham, MD: Rowman and Littlefield.

North, Douglass. 1981. *Structure and Change in Economic History*, New York: Norton.

Nozick, Robert. 1974. *Anarchy, State and Utopia*, New York: Basic Books.

Okin, Susan Moller. 1989. *Justice, Gender, and the Family*, New York: Basic Books.

O'Neill, June. 1985. "The Trend in the Male-Female Wage Gap in the United States," *Journal of Labor Economics 3*(1), Part 2, January: S91–S116.

Ostrom, Elinor. 1990. *Governing the Commons: The Evolution of Institutions for Collective Action*, New York: Cambridge University Press.

Ozment, Steven. 1983. *When Fathers Ruled: Family Life in Reformation Europe*, Cambridge: Harvard University Press.

Parkman, Allen M. 1998. "Unilateral Divorce and the Labor-Force Participation Rate of Married Women, Revisited," *American Economic Review 88*: 671–78.

———. 2000. *Good Intentions Gone Awry: No-Fault Divorce and the American Family*, Lanham, MD: Rowman and Littlefield.

Peart, Sandra J., and David M. Levy. 2005. *The "Vanity of the Philosopher": From Equality to Hierarchy in Post-classical Economics*, Ann Arbor: University of Michigan Press.

Peden, Joseph R., and Fred R. Glahe, eds. 1986. *The American Family and the State*, San Francisco, CA: Pacifie Research Institute for Public Policy.

Pember Reeves, Maud. 1914. *Round About a Pound a Week*, second edition, London: G. Bell and Sons.

Pennington, Mark. 2011. *Robust Political Economy: Classical Liberalism and the Future of Public Policy*, Cheltenham, UK: Edward Elgar.

Perrin, Ellen C., Benjamin S. Siegel, and the Committee on Psychosocial Aspects of Child and Family Health. 2013. "Promoting the Well-Being of Children Whose Parents Are Gay or Lesbian," *Pediatrics 2013;131*: e1374–e1383.

Peters, H. Elizabeth. 1992. "Marriage and Divorce: Reply," *American Economic Review 82*: 686–91.

Pinker, Steven. 2011. *The Better Angels of Our Nature: Why Violence Has Declined*, New York: Penguin Books.

Polanyi, Michael. 1958. *Personal Knowledge: Towards a Post-critical Philosophy*, Chicago, IL: University of Chicago Press.

Posner, Richard. 1992. *Sex and Reason*, Chicago, IL: University of Chicago Press.

Postrel, Virginia. 1999. *The Future and Its Enemies: The Growing Conflict over Creativity, Enterprise, and Progress*, New York: The Free Press.

Rauch, Jonathan. 2004. *Gay Marriage: Why It Is Good for Gays, Good for Straights, and Good for America*, New York: Times Books.

Rawls, John. 1971. *A Theory of Justice*, Cambridge: Harvard University Press.

Root, Damon. 2014. *Over-ruled: The Long War for Control of the U.S. Supreme Court*, New York: Palgrave Macmillan.

Rosenberg, Nathan, and L. E. Birdzell. 1986. *How the West Grew Rich*, New York: Basic Books.

Rothbard, Murray N. 1998. *The Ethics of Liberty*, New York: New York University Press.

Rowthorn, Robert. 1999. "Marriage and Trust: Some Lessons from Economics," *Cambridge Journal of Economics 23*: 661–91.

Sacks, Jonathan. 1997. "*Tikkun Olam*; Orthodoxy's Responsibility to Perfect G-d's World," Orthodox Union Advocacy Center, available at: http://advocacy.ou.org/1997/tikkun-olam-orthodoxys-responsibility-to-perfect-g-ds-world/.

Sautet, Frederic. 2000. *An Entrepreneurial Theory of the Firm*, New York and London: Routledge.

Schoen, Douglas. 2011. "Polling the Occupy Wall Street Crowd," *Wall Street Journal*, October 18, available at: http://www.wsj.com/news/articles/SB10001424052970204479504576637082965745362.

Schweber, Silvan. 1977. "The Origin of the *Origin* Revisited," *Journal of the History of Biology 10*: 229–316.

Sciabarra, Chris Matthew. 2000. *Total Freedom: Toward a Dialectical Libertarianism*, University Park, PA: Pennsylvania State University Press.

Seabright, Paul. 2004. *In the Company of Strangers*, Princeton, NJ: Princeton University Press.

Shermer, Michael. 2008. *The Mind of the Market: How Biology and Psychology Shape Our Economic Lives*, New York: Henry Holt.

Shorter, Edward. 1975. *The Making of the Modern Family*, New York: Basic Books.

Simmel, Georg. 1978 [1907]. *The Philosophy of Money*, Boston: Routledge & Kegan Paul.

Simmons, Randy T. 2011. *Beyond Politics: The Roots of Government Failure*, Oakland, CA: The Independent Institute.

Simon, Julian. 2000. *The Great Breakthrough and Its Cause*, Ann Arbor: University of Michigan Press.

Skenazy, Lenore. 2009. *Free-Range Kids: Giving Our Children the Freedom We Had without Going Nuts with Worry*, San Francisco, CA: Josey-Bass.

Skwire, Sarah. 2013. "A Traditional Marriage," *Foundation for Economic Education*, April 5, available at: http://fee.org/freeman/detail/a-traditional-marriage.

Smith, Adam. 1976 [1776]. *An Inquiry into the Nature and Causes of the Wealth of Nations*, ed. by Edwin Cannan (1904 edn.), Chicago, IL: University of Chicago Press.

Smith, George H. 1991. "Children's Rights in Political Philosophy," in *Atheism, Ayn Rand, and Other Heresies*, Buffalo, NY: Prometheus Books: 269–294.

Smith, Vernon. 1998. "The Two Faces of Adam Smith," *Southern Economic Journal 65*: 1–10.

———. 2003. "Constructivist and Ecological Rationality in Economics," *American Economic Review 93*: 465–508.

Stack, Carol B. 1974. *All Our Kin: Strategies for Survival in a Black Community*, New York: Harper and Row.

Stevenson, Betsey, and Justin Wolfers. 2006. "Bargaining in the Shadow of the Law: Divorce Laws and Family Distress," *The Quarterly Journal of Economics 121*: 267–88.

———. 2008. "Marriage and the Market," *Cato Unbound: Can Marriage Survive?*, available at: http://www.cato-unbound.org/2008/01/18/betsey-stevenson-justin-wolfers/marriage-market.

Stone, Lawrence. 1977. *The Family, Sex and Marriage in England 1500–1800*, New York: Harper and Row.

Sullivan, Andrew. 1995. *Virtually Normal: An Arugument about Homosexuality*, New York: Alfred A. Knopf.

Sullum, Jacob. 1998. *For Your Own Good: The Anti-smoking Crusade and the Tyranny of Public Health*, New York: The Free Press.

Taylor, Joan Kennedy. 1991. "Protective Labor Legislation," in Wendy McElroy, ed., *Freedom, Feminism, and the State*, second edition, New York: Holmes and Meier: 187–92.

Taylor, Stuart, and K. C. Johnson. 2007. *Until Proven Innocent*, New York: Thomas Dunne Books.

Temple, Gregg. 1985. "Freedom of Contract and Intimate Relationships," *Harvard Journal of Law and Public Policy 8*: 121–53.

Tomasi, John. 2011. *Free Market Fairness*, Princeton, NJ: Princeton University Press.

Tooby, John, and Leda Cosmides. 2005. "Conceptual Foundations of Evolutionary Psychology," in David M. Buss, ed., *Handbook of Evolutionary Psychology*, Hoboken, NJ: Wiley: 5–67.

US Census Bureau. 2007. "Survey of Income and Program Participation (SIPP), 2004 Panel, Wave 2 Topical Module," available at: http://www.census.gov/population/socdemo/marital-hist/2004/Table2.2004.xls, accessed February 27, 2015.

Volokh, Eugene. 2006. "Parent-Child Speech and Child Custody Speech Restrictions," *New York University Law Review 81*: 631–733.

Weston, Kath. 1991. *Families We Choose*, New York: Columbia University Press.

Wittman, Donald. 2005. "The Internal Organization of the Family: Economic Analysis and Psychological Advice," *Kyklos 58*: 121–44.

Wolak, Janis, David Finkelhor, Kimberly J. Mitchell, and Michele L. Ybarra. 2008. "Online 'Predators' and Their Victims: Myths, Realities, and Implications for Prevention and Treatment," *American Psychologist 63*(2): 111–28.

Yandle, Bruce. 1983. "Bootleggers and Baptists: The Eudcation of a Regulatory Economist," *Regulation 7*(3), May/June: 12–16.

Yeager, Leland. 2001. *Ethics as Social Science: The Moral Philosophy of Social Cooperation*, Cheltenham, UK: Edward Elgar.

Yu, Tianyi, Gregory S. Pettit, Jennifer E. Lansford, Kenneth A. Dodge, and John E. Bates. 2010. "The Interactive Effects of Marital Conflict and Divorce on Parent-Adult Children's Relationships," *Journal of Marriage and Family 72*: 282–92

## Supreme Court Cases

Slaughter-House Cases, 83 U.S. 36 (1873)
Bradwell v. Illinois 83 U.S. 130 (1873)
Lochner v. New York 198 U.S. 45 (1905)
Muller v. Oregon 208 U.S. 412 (1908)
Meyer v. Nebraska, 262 U.S. 390 (1923)
Pierce v. Society of Sisters of the Holy Names of Jesus and Mary, 268 U.S. 510 (1925)
Buck v. Bell, 274 U.S. 200 (1927)
West Coast Hotel Co. v. Parrish, 300 U.S. 379 (1937)
United States v. Carolene Products Company, 304 U.S. 144 (1938)
Prince v. Massachusetts, 321 U.S. 158 (1944)
Griswold v. Connecticut 381 U.S. 479 (1965)

Loving v. Virginia 388 U.S. 1 (1967)
Eisenstadt v. Baird 405 U.S. 438 (1972)
Wisconsin v. Yoder, 406 U.S. 205 (1972)
Roe v. Wade 410 U.S. 113 (1973)
Zablocki v. Redhail 434 U.S. 374 (1978)
Turner v. Safley 482 U.S. 78 (1987)
Planned Parenthood of Southeastern Pennsylvania v. Casey, 505 U.S. 833 (1992)
Washington v. Glucksberg, 521 U.S. 702 (1997)
Troxel v. Granville, 530 U.S. 57 (2000)
Lawrence v. Texas 539 U.S. 558 (2003)
Obergefell v. Hodges 576 U.S. ___ (2015)

# Index

CPSIA information can be obtained at www.ICGtesting.com
Printed in the USA
LVOW04*1431080915

453260LV00010BA/237/P

9 781137 448224